Blueprints Visual Scripting for Unreal Engine

Third Edition

Unleash the true power of Blueprints to create impressive games and applications in UE5

Marcos Romero

Brenden Sewell

BIRMINGHAM—MUMBAI

Blueprints Visual Scripting for Unreal Engine 5
Third Edition

Copyright © 2022 Packt Publishing

Publishing Product Manager: Rohit Rajkumar

Senior Editor: Aamir Ahmed

Content Development Editor: Feza Shaikh

Technical Editor: Simran Udasi

Copy Editor: Safis Editing

Project Coordinator: Rashika Ba

Proofreader: Safis Editing

Indexer: Rekha Nair

Production Designer: Shyam Sundar Korumilli

Marketing Coordinator: Teny Thomas

First published: July 2015

Second edition: August 2019

Third edition: April 2022

Production reference: 1290422

Published by Packt Publishing Ltd.

Livery Place

35 Livery Street

Birmingham

B3 2PB, UK.

ISBN 978-1-80181-158-3

`www.packt.com`

Contributors

About the authors

Marcos Romero is the author of the Romero Blueprints blog, which is one of the main references on the internet to learn about Blueprints. Epic Games invited Marcos to the Unreal Engine 4 closed beta program to experiment and collaborate with the evolution of the tools. He was also one of the first recipients of Unreal Dev Grants for Education. Marcos is a well-known figure in the Unreal community and, for Epic Games, he wrote the official *Blueprints Compendium* and *Blueprints Instructors' Guide*.

I would like to thank Luis Cataldi and Tom Shannon from Epic Games for sharing and recommending my Blueprint materials to developers around the world.

I'd also like to thank Elinaldo Azevedo, Filipe Mendes, and Ingrid Mendes, for their dedication to Beljogos, which is a local game development group that I founded in the city of Belém, northern Brazil.

Brenden Sewell is a creative director with a decade of experience leading teams in the development of compelling interactive experiences that entertain, teach, and inspire. Prior to joining E-Line, he explored the intersection of educational practice and industry game development, culminating in his work as the principal game designer at the Center for Games and Impact. There, he specialized in the development of immersive games for STEM education and teachers' professional development. Since joining the E-Line team, he has led developments from concept, prototyping, and production, to release on a variety of projects ranging from a brain-training first-person shooter to a construction sandbox exploring the future of digital fabrication.

About the reviewer

Agne Skripkaite is an Unreal Engine software engineer. Coming from a strong background in physics (with a Bachelor's of Science in Physics from the University of Edinburgh), Agne likes to focus on the *why* of things and the overarching structure of code in games. In the past, they have worked on Unreal Engine VR applications – both room-scale and seated games, becoming an experienced user comfort and motion sickness mitigation specialist for these contexts. This is the fifth Packt Publishing book on Unreal Engine that Agne has reviewed as a technical editor.

Table of Contents

3

Object-Oriented Programming and the Gameplay Framework

4

Understanding Blueprint Communication

Part 2: Developing a Game

5

Object Interaction with Blueprints

6
Enhancing Player Abilities

7
Creating Screen UI Elements

8
Creating Constraints and Gameplay Objectives

Part 3: Enhancing the Game

9
Building Smart Enemies with Artificial Intelligence

10
Upgrading the AI Enemies

11
Game States and Applying the Finishing Touches

Preface

Unreal Engine's Blueprint visual scripting system enables designers to script their games as well as programmers to create base elements that can be extended by designers. With this book, you'll explore all the features of the Blueprint Editor, along with expert tips, shortcuts, and best practices.

The book guides you through using variables, macros, and functions, and helps you learn about **object-oriented programming (OOP)**. You'll discover the Gameplay Framework and advance to learning how Blueprint Communication allows one Blueprint to access information from another Blueprint. Later chapters will focus on building a fully functional game step by step. You'll start with a basic **first-person shooter (FPS)** template, and each chapter will build on the prototype to create an increasingly complex and robust game experience. You'll then progress from creating basic shooting mechanics to more complex systems, such as user interface elements and intelligent enemy behavior. The book demonstrates how to use arrays, maps, enums, and vector operations and introduces the elements needed for VR game development. In the final chapters, you'll learn how to implement procedural generation and create a product configurator.

By the end of this book, you'll have learned how to build a fully functional game and have the skills required to develop an entertaining experience for your audience.

Who this book is for

This book is for anyone interested in developing games or applications with Unreal Engine 5. Whether you are brand new to game development or have just not had any exposure to Unreal Engine 5's Blueprint Visual Scripting system, this is a great place to start learning about how to build complex game mechanics quickly and easily without writing any text code. No programming experience is required!

What this book covers

Chapter 1, Exploring the Blueprint Editor, covers the Blueprint Editor and all the panels that are integrated into it. We will explore the **Components** tab, the **My Blueprint** tab, the **Details** tab, and the **Viewport** and **Event Graph** tabs. Then, we will go through what components are and how to add them to a Blueprint.

Chapter 2, Programming with Blueprints, explains programming concepts that are used in Blueprints. We will learn about how to use variables, operators, events, actions, macros, and functions.

Chapter 3, Object-Oriented Programming and the Gameplay Framework, teaches OOP concepts and explores the Gameplay Framework.

Chapter 4, Understanding Blueprint Communication, explores different types of Blueprint Communication, which allows one Blueprint to access the information of another Blueprint.

Chapter 5, Object Interaction with Blueprints, covers how to bring new objects to a level to help build the world in which the game will be set. We will move on to manipulating materials on objects, first through the object editor, and then by triggering during runtime via Blueprints.

Chapter 6, Enhancing Player Abilities, teaches you how to use Blueprints to generate new objects during gameplay, and how to link actions in Blueprints to player control inputs. You'll also learn about how to create Blueprints that allow objects to react to collisions with our generated projectiles.

Chapter 7, Creating Screen UI Elements, demonstrates setting up a **graphical user interface (GUI)** that will track the player's health, stamina, ammo, and current objective. Here, you will learn how to set up a basic user interface using Unreal's GUI Editor and how to use Blueprints to link the interface to the gameplay values.

Chapter 8, Creating Constraints and Gameplay Objectives, covers how to constrain the player's abilities, define the gameplay objectives for a level, and track those objectives. We'll walk through setting up collectible ammo packs that will refill the ammo of the player's gun, as well as utilizing the level Blueprint to define a win condition for our game.

Chapter 9, Building Smart Enemies with Artificial Intelligence, is a crucial chapter that covers how to create an enemy zombie AI that will pursue the player around the level. We'll walk through setting up a navigation mesh on our level and see how to use Blueprints to get enemies to traverse between patrol points.

Chapter 10, Upgrading the AI Enemies, teaches us how to create a compelling experience by modifying the zombie AI to have states in order to give the zombies a little more intelligence. In this chapter, we'll set up the patrol, searching, and attack states for the zombies by using visual and auditory detection. Additionally, we'll explore how to make new enemies appear gradually as the game is playing.

Chapter 11, Game States and Applying the Finishing Touches, adds the finishing touches that are required to make our game a complete experience before we finalize our game for release. In this chapter, we'll create rounds that will make the game increasingly difficult, game saves so that the player can save their progress and return, and player death to make the game's challenge meaningful.

Chapter 12, Building and Publishing, covers how to optimize graphics settings to get our game performing and looking its best, and how to set up project information for distribution. Then, we'll learn about how to create shareable builds of the game for various platforms.

Chapter 13, Data Structures and Flow Control, explains what data structures are and how they can be used to organize data in Blueprints. We'll learn about the concept of containers and how to use arrays, sets, and maps to group multiple elements. This chapter shows other ways to organize data using enumerations, structures, and data tables. In this chapter, we'll also see how to control the flow of execution of a Blueprint by using various types of flow control nodes.

Chapter 14, Math and Trace Nodes, covers some math concepts that are required for 3D games. We will learn the difference between world and local coordinates and how to use them when working with components. This chapter shows us how to use vectors to represent the position, direction, velocity, and distance. The concept of traces is explained and various types of traces are presented. We'll also see how to use traces to test collisions in the game.

Chapter 15, Blueprints Tips, contains several tips to increase the quality of Blueprints. We will learn about how to use various editor shortcuts that speed up our work. This chapter demonstrates some Blueprint best practices that will help you decide where and what types of implementation should be undertaken. Finally, we'll learn about more useful Blueprint miscellaneous nodes.

Chapter 16, Introduction to VR Development, explains some VR concepts and explores the VR template. This chapter explores the functionalities of the VRPawn Blueprint of the VR template and explains how to create objects that can be grabbed by the player using motion controllers. We will learn about the Blueprint functions used to implement teleportation and how to use the interface for Blueprint communication. We will also see how the menu works in the VR template.

Chapter 17, Animation Blueprints, presents the main elements of the Unreal Engine animation system, including Skeleton, Skeletal Mesh, Animation Sequences, and Blend Spaces. It shows how to script an Animation Blueprint using the Event Graph and the Anim Graph. It explains how state machines are used in an animation and how to create new states for an animation.

Chapter 18, Creating Blueprint Libraries and Components, shows how to create Blueprint Macro and Function Libraries with common functionalities that can be used throughout the project. It explains in more detail the concept of components. We will also learn how to create Actor components with encapsulated behavior and Scene components with location-based behavior.

Chapter 19, Procedural Generation, shows several ways to generate level content automatically. You can use the construction script of a Blueprint to script procedural generation and use the Spline tool to define a path that will be used as a reference to position the instances. Also, you can create an Editor Utility Blueprint to manipulate assets and actors in edit mode.

Chapter 20, Creating a Product Configurator Using the Variant Manager, explains how to create a product configurator, which is a type of application used in industry to attract consumers to a specific product. You will learn how to use the Variant Manager panel and variant sets to define a product configurator. The Product Configurator template is an excellent resource for studying various Blueprint concepts in practice. We will analyze the BP_Configurator Blueprint, which dynamically creates the user interface using UMG widget Blueprints with the variant sets.

Appendix, Quiz answers, contains the answers to all the quiz questions, chapter-wise.

To get the most out of this book

Although some basic knowledge of the Windows OS or macOS is required, experience in programming or Unreal Engine 5 is not necessary.

This book is focused on Unreal Engine 5, which means you only need a copy of Unreal Engine to get started. Unreal Engine 5 can be downloaded for free from https://www.unrealengine.com/ and comes with everything you need to follow along with this book.

Download the example code files

The code bundle for the book is also hosted on GitHub at `https://github.com/PacktPublishing/-Blueprints-Visual-Scripting-for-Unreal-Engine-5`. If there's an update to the code, it will be updated on the existing GitHub repository.

We also have other code bundles from our rich catalog of books and videos available at `https://github.com/PacktPublishing/`. Check them out!

Download the color images

We also provide a PDF file that has color images of the screenshots and diagrams used in this book. You can download it here: `https://static.packt-cdn.com/downloads/9781801811583_ColorImages.pdf`.

Conventions used

There are a number of text conventions used throughout this book.

`Code in text`: Indicates code words in the text, database table names, folder names, filenames, file extensions, pathnames, dummy URLs, user input, and Twitter handles. Here is an example: "In the Level Editor, select the instance of `BP_EnemyCharacter` that we placed on the level."

Bold: Indicates a new term, an important word, or words that you see on screen. For instance, words in menus or dialog boxes appear in **bold**. Here is an example: "Change **Parameter Name** to **Metallic**, and then click and drag the output pin from our **Metallic** node to the **Metallic** input pin of the **Material definition** node."

> **Tips or Important Notes**
> Appear like this.

Get in touch

Feedback from our readers is always welcome.

General feedback: If you have questions about any aspect of this book, email us at `customercare@packtpub.com` and mention the book title in the subject of your message.

Errata: Although we have taken every care to ensure the accuracy of our content, mistakes do happen. If you have found a mistake in this book, we would be grateful if you would report this to us. Please visit `www.packtpub.com/support/errata` and fill in the form.

Piracy: If you come across any illegal copies of our works in any form on the internet, we would be grateful if you would provide us with the location address or website name. Please contact us at `copyright@packt.com` with a link to the material.

If you are interested in becoming an author: If there is a topic that you have expertise in and you are interested in either writing or contributing to a book, please visit `authors.packtpub.com`.

Share Your Thoughts

Once you've read *Blueprints Visual Scripting for Unreal Engine 5*, we'd love to hear your thoughts! Scan the QR code below to go straight to the Amazon review page for this book and share your feedback.

https://packt.link/r/180181158X

Your review is important to us and the tech community and will help us make sure we're delivering excellent quality content.

Part 1: Blueprint Fundamentals

This part will explore the basic building blocks of Blueprints. You will gain a solid understanding of how Blueprints work and will be able to start creating your own games.

This part comprises the following chapters:

- *Chapter 1, Exploring the Blueprint Editor*
- *Chapter 2, Programming with Blueprints*
- *Chapter 3, Object-Oriented Programming and the Gameplay Framework*
- *Chapter 4, Understanding Blueprint Communication*

1
Exploring the Blueprint Editor

Welcome to the amazing world of game development with Unreal Engine 5. In this book, we will learn how to develop games in Unreal Engine using the Blueprints Visual Scripting language, which was created by Epic Games for Unreal Engine.

The first step that is needed before we can learn about Blueprints is to prepare our development environment. Unreal Engine is free to download. We will learn how to install Unreal Engine 5 and create a new project. After that, we will learn about some of the basic concepts of Blueprints and explore each panel of the Blueprint Editor.

In this chapter, we will cover the following topics:

- Installing Unreal Engine
- Creating new projects and using templates
- Blueprints Visual Scripting
- The Blueprint Class Editor interface
- Adding Components to a Blueprint

Installing Unreal Engine

To use Unreal Engine, you must first install the Epic Games Launcher:

1. Access the website at `https://www.unrealengine.com`.

2. Register and download the Epic Games Launcher.

3. Install and start the launcher.

4. Click the **Unreal Engine** tab on the left-hand side.

5. Click on the **Library** tab that appears at the top of the screen.

6. Click the + button next to **ENGINE VERSIONS** to add a version of Unreal Engine to the launcher. You can use the newest version available.

7. Click the **Install** button. The launcher will start downloading the files needed for installation and may take a long time to complete.

8. Click the **Launch** button to start an already installed version. It is possible to have multiple versions of Unreal Engine installed on the same machine – you simply set one of them as the current version. The **Launch** button at the top right of the launcher will start the current version.

Figure 1.1 – Launching Unreal Engine

The Blueprint Visual Scripting system is already a well established and stable technology. This book uses version 5.0.0, but the examples created in this book should work without problems in later versions.

Creating new projects and using templates

After starting up Unreal Engine Editor, the **Unreal Project Browser** will appear. The **Recent Projects** box on the top left is used to open existing projects and the other boxes on the left are categories of templates used to create a new project. The following screenshot shows the templates of the **Games** category.

Figure 1.2 – Templates under the Games category

Templates are basic containers with some key files and a level that provide a basic starting point for different types of projects. They are useful for rapid prototyping or to learn the basic mechanics of a specific type of project. The use of templates is optional. All templates can be simply recreated in the blank template. The following are descriptions of each template in the **Games** category:

- **First Person**: For games with a first-person perspective. This template features a player character represented by a pair of arms equipped with a gun that fires a simple sphere projectile. The character can be moved around the level using a keyboard, controller, or virtual joystick on a touch device.

- **Handheld AR**: For augmented reality applications for Android and iOS devices. This template features runtime logic for toggling AR mode on and off, along with some example code for hit detection and light estimation handling.

- **Third Person**: Contains a playable character with a camera that follows it. The camera is positioned behind and slightly above the character. The character has walking, running, and jumping animations and can be moved around the level using a keyboard, controller, or virtual joystick on a touch device.

- **Top Down**: Contains a character controlled by a mouse with a camera at a great distance above it. The player's character is controlled using a mouse or touchscreen to click on the required destination and uses the navigation system to avoid obstacles when moving to destinations. This top-down view is often used in action role-playing games.

- **Virtual Reality**: Contains the essential features for virtual reality games. This template features teleport locomotion, grabbable objects, interactive objects, and a VR spectator camera. The template has a level where the player can move around and contains objects that can be grabbed and interacted with.

- **Vehicle**: Contains a regular vehicle and a complex vehicle with suspension. The level of this template contains a simple track and obstacles.

At the bottom right of the **Unreal Project Browser**, there are the **Project Defaults** with project configuration options available for the selected template. In the examples of this book, we will use the values selected on the screenshot. These options can be modified later in the project, and they are as follows:

- **Blueprint/C++**: There are templates made with **Blueprint** or the **C++** programming language. In this book, we will only use **Blueprint** templates. A project in Unreal Engine 5 can be developed using **Blueprint**, **C++**, or a combination of both. You can add **C++** code to **Blueprint** projects and **Blueprint** to **C++** projects.

- **Target Platform**: **Desktop** or **Mobile**. Use **Desktop** if you are developing your project for use on computers or game consoles. Choose **Mobile** if your project will be viewed on a mobile device. In this book, we will use the **Desktop** option.

- **Quality Preset**: **Scalable** or **Maximum**. These options affect the project's performance. The **Scalable** option disables some complex features, and the **Maximum** option enables all the features available in the target platform. In this book, we will use the **Scalable** option.

- **Starter Content**: If this checkbox is marked, the project will include **Starter Content**. **Starter Content** is a content pack with simple meshes, materials, and particle effects. The examples in this book assume that **Starter Content** is being used.

- **Raytracing**: If this checkbox is marked, the project will use real-time raytracing, which is a performance-intensive feature. The examples in this book will not use raytracing.

Select the **Third Person** template, choose a **location** folder, and fill in the **Name** field for the project. Select the **Project Defaults** mentioned in the previous list and then click the **Create** button. After the project loads, the Unreal Engine Level Editor will be displayed, as shown in the following screenshot:

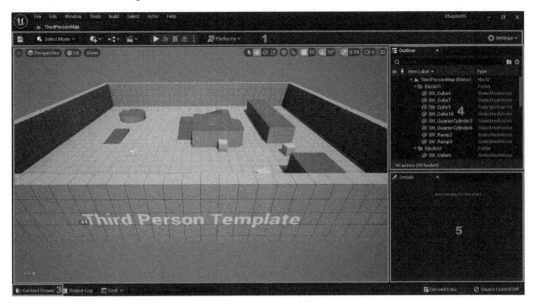

Figure 1.3 – The Unreal Engine Level Editor

These are the key panels of the Level Editor:

1. **Toolbar**: Located at the top of the Level Editor. It contains buttons with commonly used operations. The toolbar buttons are separated into four groups. The first group from the left provides quick access to features such as saving your work and adding various objects and code to the project. The second group of buttons are used to change the editing mode of the Level Editor. The third group lets you play the current level and provides various platform-specific options. The final **Settings** button all the way on the right provides easy access to project settings.

2. **Viewport**: Located at the center of the Level Editor. It shows the Level that is being created. You can use the **Viewport** panel to move around the Level and add objects on the Level. When holding down the right mouse button, move the mouse to rotate the camera and use the WASD keys to move around.

3. **Content Browser**: This can be accessed by clicking on the **Content Drawer** button located at the bottom-left corner of the Level Editor. It is used to manage the assets of the project. An asset is a piece of content in an Unreal Engine project. For example, **Materials**, **Static Meshes**, and **Blueprints** are all assets. If you drag an asset from the **Content Browser** and drop it into the Level, the Editor creates a copy of the asset to place in the Level.

4. **Outliner**: Located to the right of the Level Editor. It lists the objects that are in the Level.

5. **Details**: Located to the right of the Level Editor, below **Outliner**. It shows the editable properties of an object that is selected in the **Viewport**.

Now that we have an overview of the Unreal Engine Level Editor, let's focus on the Blueprints Visual Scripting.

Blueprints Visual Scripting

The first question you should be asking is: what is a Blueprint?

The word *Blueprint* has more than one meaning in Unreal Engine. First, it is the name of a visual scripting language created by Epic Games for Unreal Engine. Second, it can refer to a new type of game object created using the Blueprint language.

There are two main types of Blueprints: **Level Blueprint** and **Blueprint Class**. Each Level of the game has its own **Level Blueprint** and it is not possible to create a separate **Level Blueprint**. On the other hand, **Blueprint Class** is used to create interactive objects for the game and can be reused in any Level.

Opening the Level Blueprint Editor

To open the **Level Blueprint** Editor, click on the **Blueprints** button located in the leftmost group of buttons in the toolbar of the Unreal Editor. Then, select the **Open Level Blueprint** option from the dropdown, as shown in the following screenshot:

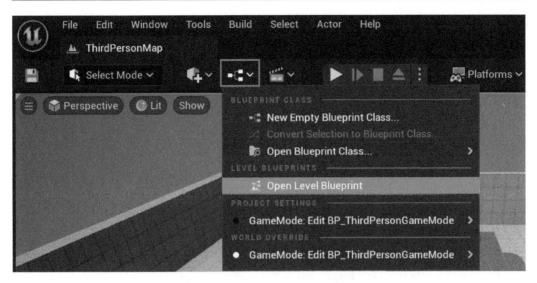

Figure 1.4 – Opening a Level Blueprint

The Editor will open the **Level Blueprint** of the current Level. The **Level Blueprint** Editor is simpler than the **Blueprint Class** Editor because it has only the **My Blueprint** panel, the **Details** panel, and the **Event Graph** Editor. The following screenshot shows the **Level Blueprint** Editor:

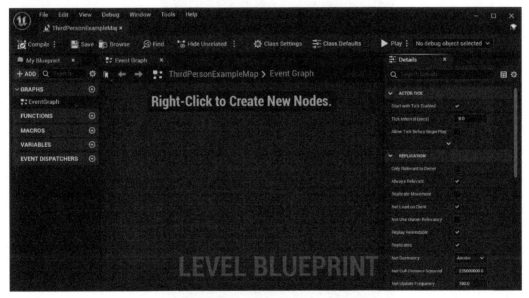

Figure 1.5 – The Level Blueprint Editor

For now, we will not do anything with the **Level Blueprint**. We opened it to get our first glance at the interface. Close the **Level Blueprint** Editor to return to the **Level Editor** window. Now, we will create a **Blueprint Class** to open the **Blueprint Class** Editor and see all the panels available.

Creating a Blueprint Class

There are three ways to create a Blueprint Class:

1. Click the same **Blueprints** button in the toolbar that we used to open the **Level Blueprint**. Then, click the **New Empty Blueprint Class** button in the dropdown.

2. Click the **Content Drawer** button to open the **Content Browser**, then click the **Add** button and select **Blueprint Class** under the **Create Basic Asset** category.

3. Right-click anywhere on an empty space in the **Content Browser** and select **Blueprint Class** from the menu that appears.

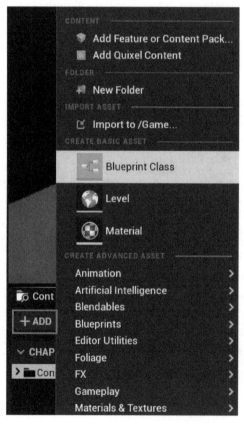

Figure 1.6 – Creating a Blueprint Class

On the next window, you must choose the parent class of the new Blueprint. For now, think of the parent class as the Blueprint type. The window shows the most **Common** classes, but if you need to choose another parent class, then just expand the **All Classes** option. When you choose the parent class, this window will close, and a new Blueprint asset will appear in the **Content Browser** to be renamed. You can click the **Cancel** button because we are just familiarizing ourselves with the process.

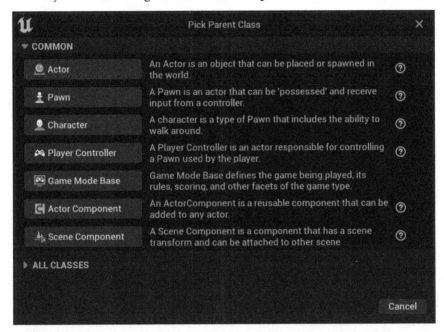

Figure 1.7 – Blueprint Parent Class

Now that we've learned how to open the current Level Blueprint and how to create a Blueprint Class, we will explore the panels of the Blueprint Class Editor. You can open the Blueprint Class Editor by right-clicking on a Blueprint asset in the **Content Browser** and selecting **Edit**, or by double-clicking on a Blueprint asset.

The Blueprint Class Editor interface

The Blueprint Class Editor contains several panels. Each panel is used to edit one aspect of a Blueprint. The Blueprint Class Editor is usually simply called the Blueprint Editor. The main panels of the Blueprint Editor are listed as follows:

1. **Toolbar**
2. **Components**
3. **My Blueprint**

4. **Details**

5. **Viewport**

6. **Event Graph**

These panels can be found in the next screenshot. We will use the **BP_ThirdPersonCharacter** Blueprint of the **Third Person** template as an example. It is located in the `ThirdPerson/Blueprints` folder. Double-click the **BP_ThirdPersonCharacter** Blueprint to open the Blueprint Class Editor.

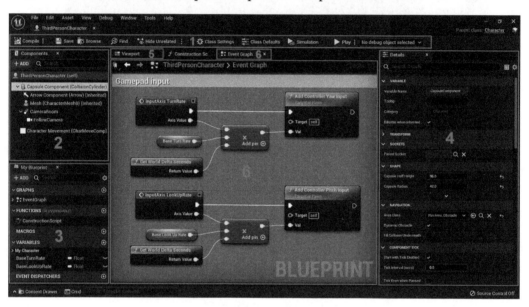

Figure 1.8 – Blueprint Editor panels

The Toolbar panel

The **Toolbar** panel is located at the top of the Blueprint Class Editor and contains some essential buttons for editing Blueprints:

Figure 1.9 – Toolbar panel

The buttons are described as follows:

- **Compile**: Converts the Blueprint script into a lower-level format that can be executed. That means a Blueprint must be compiled before running the game or the changes made will not be reflected. Click this button to compile the current Blueprint. A green check icon will appear if there is no error.

- **Save**: Saves all changes made to the current Blueprint.

- **Browse**: Shows the current **Blueprint Class** in the **Content Browser**.

- **Find**: Searches within a Blueprint.

- **Hide Unrelated**: When active, it hides the nodes unrelated to the selected nodes.

- **Class Settings**: Allows editing of the settings for the class in the **Details** panel. The **Class Settings** options contain properties such as **Description**, **Category**, and **Parent Class**.

- **Class Defaults**: Allows editing of the **Class Defaults** in the **Details** panel. **Class Defaults** are the initial values of the Blueprint variables.

- **Simulation**: Allows the execution of the Blueprint inside the Blueprint Editor.

- **Play**: Allows you to play the current Level.

- **Debug Object**: This dropdown allows the selection of an object to debug. If none is selected, it will debug any object created with the current Blueprint Class.

The Components panel

The **Components** panel shows all the Components that are part of the current Blueprint.

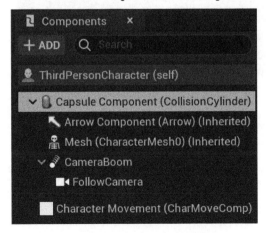

Figure 1.10 – Components panel

Components are ready-to-use objects that can be added to Blueprints. To do this, click on the **Add** button of the **Components** panel. A Blueprint can be created with various features just by using Components.

The properties of a selected Component can be edited on the **Details** panel and the visual representation of some Components can be seen on the **Viewport** panel.

Static Meshes, lights, sounds, box collisions, particle systems, and cameras are examples of Components found in the **Components** panel.

The My Blueprint panel

My Blueprint is a panel where we can create **Variables**, **Macros**, **Functions**, and **Graphs** for the Blueprint:

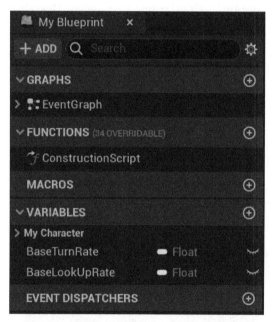

Figure 1.11 – My Blueprint panel

New elements can be added by clicking on the **Add** button at the top of the panel, or the + button next to each category.

The properties of a selected element can be edited in the **Details** panel.

The Details panel

The **Details** panel allows you to edit the properties of a selected element of a Blueprint. The selected element can be a **Component**, **Variable**, **Macro**, or **Function** element. The properties shown in the **Details** panel are organized into categories.

The next screenshot shows the properties of a **CapsuleComponent**. There is a **Search** box at the top of the panel that can be used to filter the properties.

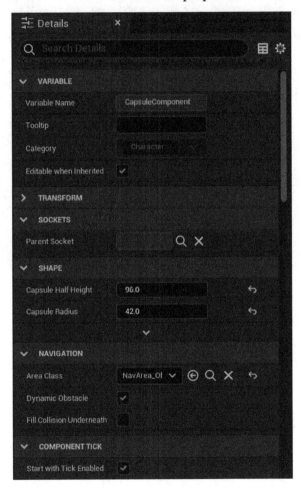

Figure 1.12 – Details panel

The Viewport panel

The **Viewport** panel shows the visual representation of a Blueprint and its Components. The **Viewport** panel has controls similar to the Level Editor, which you can use to manipulate the location, rotation, and scale of the Components.

The following screenshot shows the **Viewport** panel. There is a **SkeletalMesh** Component that represents the player, a **Camera** Component that defines the view of the player, and a **Capsule** Component used for collision detection.

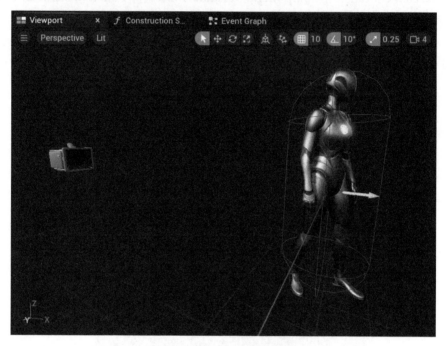

Figure 1.13 – Viewport panel

The Event Graph panel

It is in the **Event Graph** panel that we are going to program the behavior of a Blueprint. The **Event Graph** contains **Events** and **Actions** that are represented by nodes and connected by wires.

An Event is represented by a red node and is triggered by gameplay Events. A Blueprint can have several Actions that will be performed in response to an Event. The next screenshot shows two Events: **InputAxis TurnRate** and **InputAxis LookUpRate**:

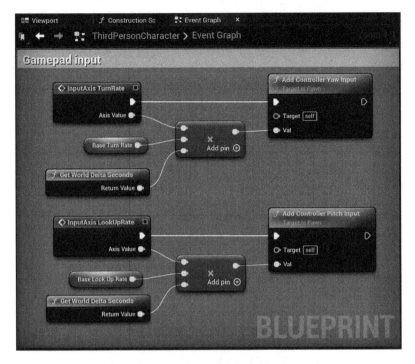

Figure 1.14 – Event Graph panel

You can move around the Event Graph by right-clicking and dragging it to see the other Events.

The other nodes are Actions representing functions, operators, and variables. We will learn about these elements in *Chapter 2, Programming with Blueprints.*

After this overview of the Blueprint Editor panels, we are now able to create our first Blueprint. Close the Blueprint Class Editor and navigate back to the Level Editor.

Adding Components to a Blueprint

Now, let's create our first Blueprint. It will be a very simple Blueprint that will only contain **Components**. For now, we will not use **Events** or **Actions**:

1. Click the **Content Drawer** button to open the **Content Browser**, then click the **Add** button and select **Blueprint Class**.

2. On the next screen, choose **Actor** as the parent class.

3. Rename the Blueprint we just created to BP_RotatingChair. Blueprints cannot have spaces in their name and there is a convention of starting Blueprint names with BP_.

4.   Double-click this Blueprint to open the Blueprint Editor.

5.   On the **Components** panel, click the **Add** button and select **Static Mesh**, as shown in the following screenshot. This **Static Mesh** will visually represent this Blueprint.

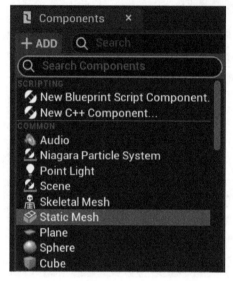

Figure 1.15 – Adding a Static Mesh Component

6.   On the **Details** panel, there is a property named **Static Mesh**, which has a dropdown input. Click on the dropdown and select the **Static Mesh** property named **SM_Chair**. This **Static Mesh** is part of the starter content. The following screenshot shows the selected **SM_Chair**:

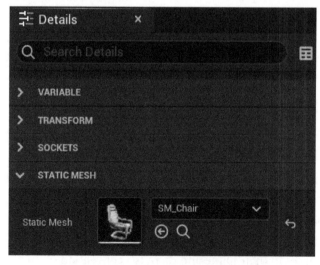

Figure 1.16 – Selecting a Static Mesh asset

7. Let's add another Component. Click the **Add** button of the **Components** panel and type `rotating movement` in the **Search** box.

8. Click on the **Rotating Movement** Component to add it. By default, this Component will rotate the Blueprint around the *z* axis, so we don't need to change its properties.

9. Click the **Compile** button and save the Blueprint.

10. On the Level Editor, drag the **BP_RotatingChair** Blueprint from the **Content Browser** and drop it somewhere in the Level.

11. Press the **Play** button of the Level Editor to see the rotating chair. You can use the *WASD* keys to move the character and the mouse to rotate the camera. You can exit the Level being played by pressing the *Esc* key. The next screenshot shows the example in execution:

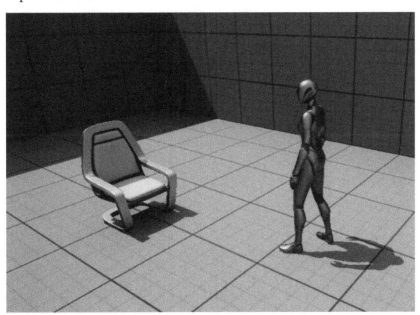

Figure 1.17 – The rotating chair

Summary

In this chapter, we learned how to install Unreal Engine and create new projects using the available templates. We learned that there are two main types of Blueprints: **Level Blueprint** and **Blueprint Class**.

Then, we explored the different types of panels that are part of the Blueprint Editor. Our familiarization with these panels will help when developing with Blueprints. Finally, we also created a simple Blueprint using only **Components**.

In the next chapter, we will learn how to program the behavior of Blueprints using **Events** and **Actions**.

Quiz

1. You can have multiple versions of Unreal Engine installed on your computer.

    a. True

    b. False

2. The Level Blueprint Editor has more panels than the Blueprint Class editor.

    a. True

    b. False

3. Which type of Blueprint is appropriate for creating objects that can be reused in any Level?

    a. Level Blueprint

    b. Blueprint Class

4. Which panel in the Blueprint Editor is where Events and Actions can be added?

    a. Components panel

    b. Event Graph panel

    c. My Blueprint panel

    d. Details panel

5. Which panel in the Blueprint Editor shows the variables and functions of the current Blueprint?

    a. Details panel

    b. Components panel

    c. My Blueprint panel

    d. Event Graph panel

2
Programming with Blueprints

This chapter presents the basic programming concepts used in Blueprints. Programming is essentially a way of writing instructions that will be understood and executed by a computer. Most programming languages are text-based, but Blueprint presents a different form of visual programming by using a node-based interface.

Some programming languages are known as scripting languages when they exist in a special environment or when they have a well-defined purpose. For example, Blueprints is the visual scripting language of Unreal Engine.

In this chapter, we will cover the following topics:

- Storing values in variables
- Defining the behavior of a Blueprint with events and actions
- Creating expressions with operators
- Organizing the script with macros and functions

Storing values in variables

A variable is a programming concept. It consists of an identifier that points to a memory location where a value can be stored. For example, a character in a game may have variables to store the value of its health, its speed, and the quantity of ammunition.

A Blueprint can have many variables of various types. The variables of a Blueprint are listed on the **My Blueprint** panel. Clicking the + button in the **VARIABLES** category creates a variable:

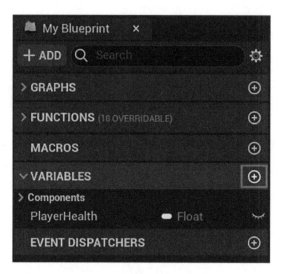

Figure 2.1 – Creating a variable

The **type** of a variable defines the content that a variable can store. Blueprint is a strongly typed language. This means that you must define the variable type when creating the variable, and this type cannot be modified during program execution.

When you create a variable, its attributes are displayed in the **Details** panel. The first attribute of a variable is its name, and the second attribute is its type. The various types are as follows:

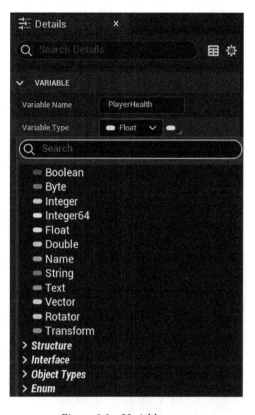

Figure 2.2 – Variable types

Each type is represented by a color. These are the types of variables:

- **Boolean**: Can only hold values of true or false.

- **Byte**: This is an 8-bit number. It can store integer values between 0 and 255.

- **Integer**: This is a 32-bit number. It can store integer values between −2,147,483,648 and 2,147,483,647.

- **Integer64**: This is a 64-bit number. It can store integer values between −9,223,372,036,854,775,808 and 9,223,372,036,854,775,807.

- **Float**: This is a 32-bit floating-point number. It can store number values with fractional parts and has a precision of seven decimal digits.

- **Double**: This is a 64-bit floating-point number. It can store number values with fractional parts and has a precision of 16 decimal digits.

- **Name**: Piece of text used as an object identifier.

- **String**: Can store a group of alphanumeric characters.

- **Text**: This type is used for text that will be localized, meaning it allows for easier implementation of translation into different languages.

- **Vector**: Contains the **X, Y**, and **Z** float values, which represent a 3D vector.

- **Rotator**: Contains the **X (Roll), Y (Pitch)**, and **Z (Yaw)** float values, which represent a rotation in 3D space.

- **Transform**: Can store location, rotation, and scale.

There are also other types of variables related to **Structure**, **Interface**, **Object Types**, and **Enum**. We will learn about these types in the upcoming chapters.

The following screenshot shows the **Details** panel with the attributes that can be modified in **VARIABLE**:

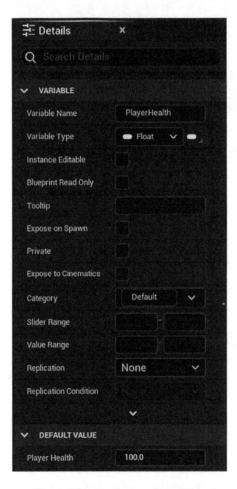

Figure 2.3 – Attributes of a variable

These attributes can be individually described as follows:

- **Variable Name**: This is the identifier of the variable.

- **Variable Type**: This specifies the type of values that can be stored in this variable.

- **Instance Editable**: When this box is checked, each copy of this Blueprint placed in the level can store a different value in this variable. Otherwise, the same initial value is shared by all copies, called **instances**.

- **Blueprint Read Only**: If checked, the variable cannot be changed by Blueprint nodes.

- **Tooltip**: This contains information shown when the cursor hovers over the variable.

- **Expose on Spawn**: If checked, the variable can be set when spawning the Blueprint.

- **Private**: If checked, child Blueprints cannot modify it.

- **Expose to Cinematics**: If checked, this variable will be exposed to **Sequencer**.

- **Category**: This can be used to organize all variables in the Blueprint.

- **Slider Range**: This sets the minimum and maximum values that will be used by a **User Interface** (**UI**) slider to modify this variable.

- **Value Range**: This sets the minimum and maximum values allowed for this variable.

- **Replication** and **Replication Condition**: They are used in networked games.

- **DEFAULT VALUE**: This contains the initial value of the variable. The Blueprint must be compiled before you can set the default value.

Variables are used to represent the current state of a Blueprint, but the behavior is defined by events and actions, which will be discussed in the following section.

Defining the behavior of a Blueprint with events and actions

Most of the time, we will use Blueprints to create new Actors. In Unreal Engine, Actors are game objects that can be added to a level.

Unreal Engine informs the state of a game for an Actor using events. We define how an Actor responds to an event by using actions. Both events and actions are represented by nodes in the **Event Graph** panel.

Events

To add events to a Blueprint, use the **Event Graph** panel. Right-click the **Event Graph** panel to open **Context Menu**, which has a list of available events and actions. If you need more space in the **Event Graph** panel, you can right-click and drag to move it to an empty area of **Event Graph**. **Context Menu** has a **Search** bar that can be used to filter the list of nodes. There is also the **Context Sensitive** checkbox that filters the possible actions based on the node selected. The following screenshot shows **Context Menu** and some of the events available:

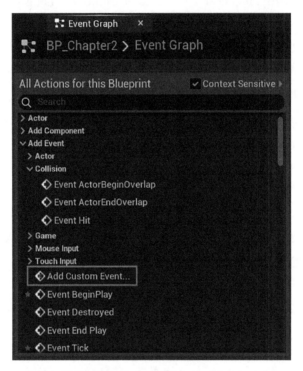

Figure 2.4 – Events in Context Menu

You can add several events in the **Event Graph** panel, but you can add each event only once. In addition to the events provided by Unreal Engine, you can create your own events by clicking on **Add Custom Event…**. The next screenshot shows a **Custom Event** node and its **Details** panel where you can rename the custom event and add input parameters. We will learn about parameters later in this chapter, in the *Creating macros* topic:

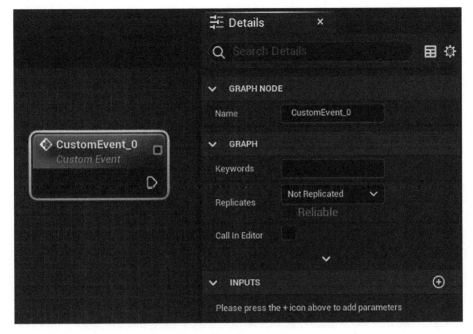

Figure 2.5 – Creating a custom event

These are some of the events that are available:

- **Collision Events**: These are executed when two Actors collide or overlap.

- **Input events**: These are triggered by input devices, such as the keyboard, mouse, touch screen, and gamepads.

- **Event BeginPlay**: This is executed either when the game is started for Actors already present on the Level Editor, or immediately after the Actor is spawned if that happens during runtime.

- **Event End Play**: This is executed when the Actor is about to be removed during runtime.

- **Event Tick**: This is called every frame of the game. For example, if a game runs at 60 frames per second, this event will be called 60 times in a second.

We will now learn how to create actions that connect to events.

Actions

When an event is triggered, we use actions to define how a Blueprint will react to this event. You can use actions to get or set values in the Blueprint variables or call functions that modify the state of a Blueprint.

The following screenshot shows the **Event BeginPlay** event of a Blueprint. In this example, the Blueprint has a string variable named **Bot Name**:

1. The SET action assigns the **Archon** value to the **Bot Name** variable.

2. The next action, **Print String**, displays the value that is received on the **In String** pin on the screen. These values that are passed to the functions are known as parameters.

3. The **In String** pin is connected to a GET node of the **Bot Name** variable that returns the value of the **Bot Name** variable and passes it to the **Print String** function:

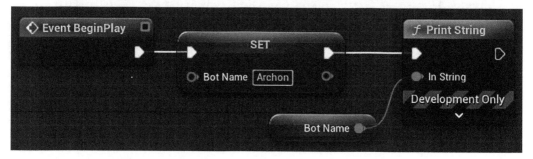

Figure 2.6 – Event BeginPlay with some actions

4. To add the GET and SET Actions of a variable to Event Graph, simply drag the variable from the **My Blueprint** panel and drop it in **Event Graph** to show the GET and SET options.

Other functions such as **Print String** are added from **Context Menu** that appears when you right-click on the **Event Graph** panel. The **GET** and **SET** actions can also be searched in **Context Menu**.

The white lines that connect the actions are also known as the execution path.

The execution path

The white pins of nodes are called **execution pins**. The other colored pins are the **data pins**. The execution of the nodes of a Blueprint starts with a red event node, and then follows the white wire from left to right until it reaches the last node.

There are some nodes that control the flow of execution of the Blueprint. These nodes determine the execution path based on conditions. For example, the **Branch** node has two output execution pins named **True** and **False**. The execution pin that will be triggered depends on the Boolean value of the **Condition** input parameter. The following screenshot shows an example of the **Branch** node:

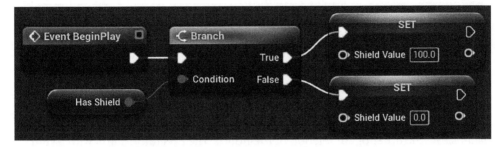

Figure 2.7 – Branch node with two execution paths

In this example, when **Event BeginPlay** fires, the **Branch** node evaluates the value of the **Has Shield** Boolean variable. If the value is **True**, then the **True** pin will be executed and will set the value to 100.0 in the **Shield Value** variable. If it is **False**, the value 0.0 will be set in the **Shield Value** variable.

We saw how to modify the value of a variable using an action. The next step is to learn how to create expressions with variables.

Creating expressions with operators

Operators are used to create expressions using variables and values. These operators are found in **Context Menu** within the **Utilities | Operators** category.

The main types of operators are arithmetic, relational, and logical.

Arithmetic operators

The arithmetic operators (+, -, x, and /) can be used to create mathematical expressions in Blueprints. The following screenshot shows the equivalent nodes in Blueprints. These operators receive two input values on the left and give the operation result on the right. The arithmetic operators can have more than two input parameters; just click on the **Add pin** button on the node to add another input parameter. The input values can be obtained from a data wire or entered directly in the node:

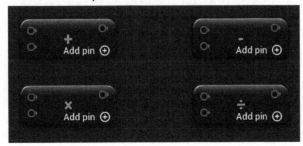

Figure 2.8 – Arithmetic operation nodes

> **Note**
>
> The * symbol is the multiplication operator in programming languages. Blueprints also recognize * as the multiplication operator but use the letter X as the label of the multiplication node. You need to use the * symbol or write the word multiply when searching for multiplication nodes in the **Context Menu**.

The following screenshot shows a simple arithmetic expression. The numbers on the screenshot show the order of completion of the nodes. The execution starts with **Event BeginPlay**. The **SET** node assigns a new value to the **Magic Points** variable, but this value must be obtained using the data wire that is connected to the output of a multiplication node, which will need to get the value of the **Willpower** variable using another data wire to multiply by 20.0:

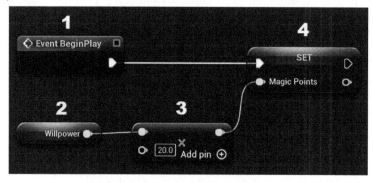

Figure 2.9 – Multiply operation

Relational operators

Relational operators perform a comparison between two values and return a Boolean value (**True** or **False**) as a result of the comparison. The following screenshot shows the relational operators in Blueprints:

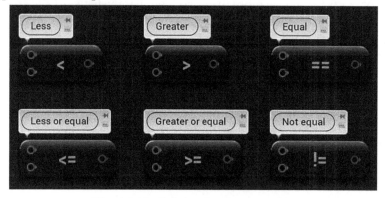

Figure 2.10 – Relational operation nodes

The following screenshot shows an example with a relational operator, assuming these actions are performed when a game object receives damage. A **Branch** node is used to test whether the **Health** variable value is less than or equal to 0.0. If it returns **True**, then this game object will be destroyed. If it returns **False**, nothing will happen since there are no actions connected to the **False** branch of execution.

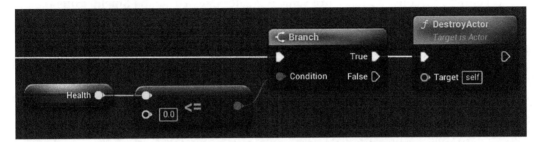

Figure 2.11 – Testing a condition with a relational operator

Logical operators

Logical operators perform an operation between Boolean values and return a Boolean value (**True** or **False**) as a result of the operation. The following screenshot shows the logical operators in Blueprints:

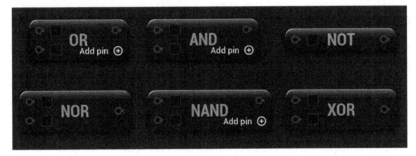

Figure 2.12 – Logical operation nodes

These are the descriptions of these operators:

- **OR**: Returns a value of **True** if any of the input values are **True**.

- **AND**: Returns a value of **True** if and only if all input values are **True**.

- **NOT**: Receives only one input value, and the result will be the opposite value.

- **NOR**: This is a combination of **NOT** and **OR** operators. It returns a value of **True** if both inputs are **False**, otherwise, the return value is **False**.

- **NAND**: This is a combination of **NOT** and **AND** operators. It returns a value of **False** if both inputs are **True**, otherwise, the return value is **True**.

- **XOR**: This operator is called **exclusive OR**. It returns a value of **True** if the two inputs are different (one is **True** and the other is **False**). If the two inputs are the same, the return value is **False**.

The following screenshot shows an example of using the **AND** operator. The **Print String** node will only be executed if the **Health** value is greater than 70.0 and **Shield Value** is greater than 50.0:

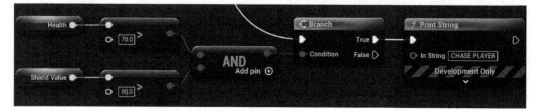

Figure 2.13 – Testing a condition with an AND operator

We already know how to use actions and operators; the next step is learning how to organize them in macros and functions.

Organizing the script with macros and functions

When we are creating Blueprint scripts, sometimes, a group of actions is used in more than one place in Blueprint. These actions can be converted into macros or functions, simplifying the initial script because this group of actions will be replaced by only one node. Also, if you need to change something in this group of actions, this change will only be implemented in the macro or function rather than having to search every location where this group of actions was used. This is a good programming practice to use as it simplifies code and debugging.

Creating macros

To create macros, use the **My Blueprint** panel and click the + button in the **MACROS** category. The following screenshot shows the **My Blueprint** panel with a macro named SetupNewWave:

Figure 2.14 – Creating a macro

When a macro is created, a new tab is opened in the same place as the **Event Graph**. This tab looks like the **Event Graph** but contains only the nodes relevant to the macro. You will add the macro actions in this tab. You can close the **Macro** tab, and to open it again, double-click the macro name on the **My Blueprint** panel. You can click the **Event Graph** tab to return to **Event Graph**:

Figure 2.15 – The macro tab

The attributes of a macro are displayed in the **Details** panel. In this panel, you can define input and output parameters. Input parameters are values passed to macros/functions. Output parameters are values returned from macros/functions. The following screenshot shows the **Details** panel of the SetupNewWave macro with two input parameters and one output parameter. In macros, the white execution pins are defined as input/output parameters of type **Exec**, so you can add as many as you like. In the following example, we create an input execution pin named **In** and an output execution pin named **Out**:

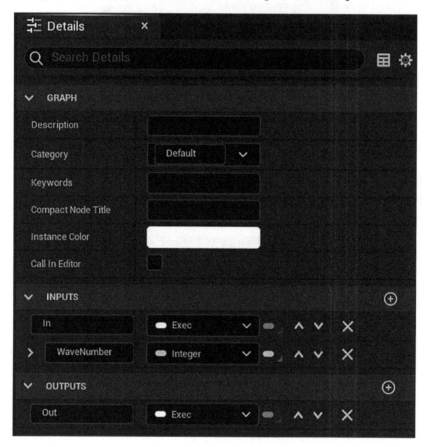

Figure 2.16 – Attributes of a macro

The following screenshot shows the contents of the `SetupNewWave` macro. The idea of this macro is to set some variables for the next wave of enemies in a game. It receives the current **Wave Number** as an input parameter, stores this value in the **Current Wave** variable, and determines the number of enemies by multiplying the current **Wave Number** by 5:

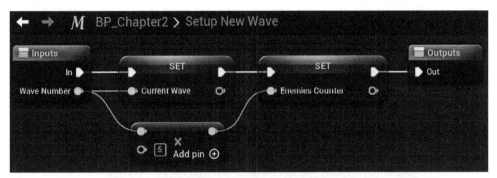

Figure 2.17 – Macro example

To add the macro to **Event Graph**, drag the name of the macro from the **My Blueprint** panel and drop it in **Event Graph**, or look for it in **Context Menu**. When the macro is executed, the actions that are in it will be executed. The following screenshot shows the `SetupNewWave` macro being called in **Event BeginPlay** with a value of 1 in the **Wave Number** input parameter.

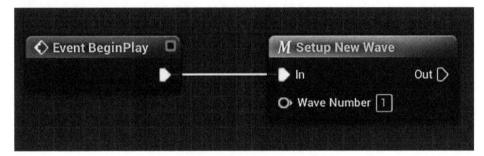

Figure 2.18 – Calling a macro

Creating functions

One of the advantages of functions is that a function created in one Blueprint can be called from another Blueprint. To create functions, use the **My Blueprint** panel and click the + button in the **FUNCTIONS** category. The following screenshot shows the **My Blueprint** panel with a function named `CalculateWaveBonus`:

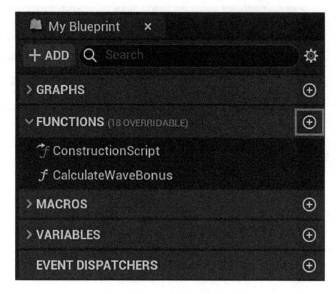

Figure 2.19 – Creating a function

As with macros, the attributes of the function are displayed in the **Details** panel, where input and output parameters can be defined. The following screenshot shows the **Details** panel of the `CalculateWaveBonus` Function, with two input parameters and one output parameter:

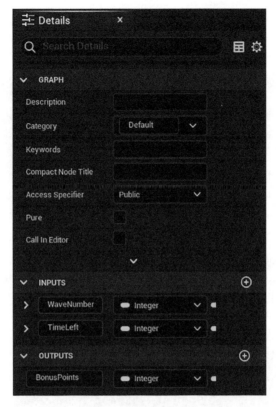

Figure 2.20 – Attributes of a function

When creating a function, we can define whether it will be **Pure**. To do this, check the **Pure** attribute shown in the previous screenshot. A **Pure** function has no execution pins; therefore, it can be used in expressions. **Pure** functions should not modify the variables of their Blueprint, so they are mostly used as **get-type** functions, which are functions that just return a value. The following screenshot shows the visual difference between a standard function and a **Pure** function:

Figure 2.21 – Standard and Pure functions

The following screenshot shows the contents of the CalculateWaveBonus function. This function calculates the bonus points of a wave based on **Wave Number** and **Time Left**. The value found is returned via the **Bonus Points** output parameter:

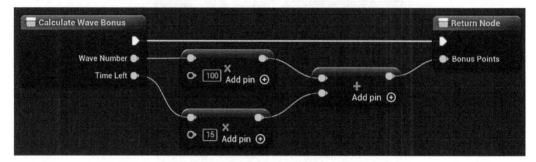

Figure 2.22 – Function example

The following screenshot is of the node that represents the CalculateWaveBonus function. It can be added to the **Event Graph** panel from **Context Menu** by right-clicking **Event Graph** or by dragging the function name from the **My Blueprint** panel and dropping it in **Event Graph**:

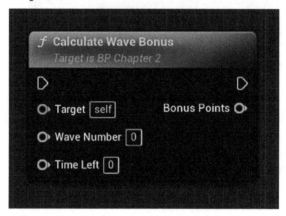

Figure 2.23 – Function node

Step-by-step example

Let's create a function step by step and execute it to see it in practice. The function name is `CalculatePower`. It receives the player's level as an input parameter and returns their power value using the following expression:

`PowerValue = (PlayerLevel x 7) + 25`

1. Click on the **Content Drawer** button to open the **Content Browser**, then click the **Add** button and select **Blueprint Class**.

2. On the next screen, choose **Actor** as the parent class.

3. Rename the Blueprint created to `FunctionExample`.

4. Double-click this Blueprint to open the **Blueprint Editor**.

5. In the **My Blueprint** panel, click the + button in the **Functions** category to create a function. Change the name of the function to `CalculatePower`.

6. Use the **Details** panel of this function to create an input parameter named `PlayerLevel` of **Integer** type and an output parameter named `PowerValue` of **Integer** type.

7. On the tab created for the **CalculatePower** function, create the expression seen in the following screenshot. You can add the nodes of operators by right-clicking on the graph to open **Context Menu** and search for add and multiply. To connect the nodes, click on one of the pins, drag the mouse and drop it on the other pin. Don't forget to insert the values 7 and 25 in the operator nodes. Compile the Blueprint.

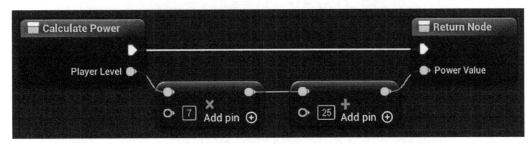

Figure 2.24 – CalculatePower function

8. In the Event Graph, there is an Event BeginPlay node grayed out as it has no actions connected. The Event BeginPlay node will light up when you connect any node to it. Create the nodes seen in the next screenshot. Insert the value 3 in the **Player Level** parameter of the **Calculate Power** node. These nodes will calculate the PowerValue using the value 3 for Player Level.

9. Click on the arrow of the **Print String** node to see more input parameters.

10. Click on the color square to the right of the **Text Color** parameter. This will open a **Color Picker** panel. Click any red color on the color wheel and click the **OK** button to close the **Color Picker** panel.

11. Change the **Duration** parameter to 10.0.

12. Connect the **PowerValue** pin to the **B** pin of the **Append** node to automatically create a conversion node from integer to string. In the **A** parameter, type POWER: with a trailing space after :.

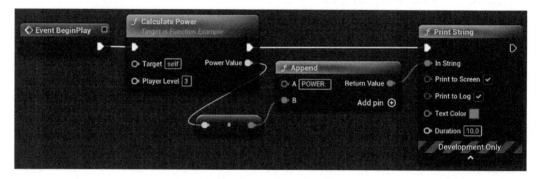

Figure 2.25 – Event BeginPlay

13. Compile and save the Blueprint. In the Level Editor, drag and drop the **FunctionExample Blueprint** into the level.

14. Play the level to see the PowerValue printed on the screen.

Figure 2.26 – The result of the CalculatePower function

Macros versus functions versus events

Sometimes, it is not clear when to create a macro, a function, or a custom event, since they have several characteristics in common. The following table shows a comparison between them to help you to choose the most appropriate for your requirements:

	Macros	Functions	Events
Input parameters	Yes	Yes	Yes
Output parameters	Yes	Yes	No
Multiple execution paths (input/output)	Yes	No	No
Callable by another Blueprint	No	Yes	Yes
Latent actions (for example, delay)	Yes	No	Yes
Timeline nodes	No	No	Yes

Summary

In this chapter, we learned how to store values in the variables of a Blueprint and how to use actions to define the response of a Blueprint to an event. After that, we saw how to create expressions with operators and organize our script with macros and functions. These are the key elements needed to define how a Blueprint should act within a game.

In the next chapter, we'll learn about the Gameplay Framework, which is a group of classes with common functionality used in game development.

Quiz

1. What type of variable can only hold values of true or false?

    a. Double

    b. Text

    c. Boolean

    d. Byte

2. Which of the following events is not a collision event?

    a. Hit

    b. Tick

    c. ActorBeginOverlap

    d. ActorEndOverlap

3. The Branch node can be used to create different execution paths.

    a. True

    b. False

4. Which of the following logical operators returns a value of true only if all input values are true?

    a. NOT

    b. OR

    c. AND

5. Which of the following cannot be called by another Blueprint?

    a. Macros

    b. Functions

    c. Custom events

3
Object-Oriented Programming and the Gameplay Framework

Blueprints are based on the principles of **object-oriented programming** (**OOP**). One of the goals of OOP is to bring programming concepts closer to the real world.

The Unreal Engine Gameplay Framework encompasses all the core systems required for a video game, such as game rules, player input and controls, cameras, and user interfaces.

In this chapter, we will learn about the following topics:

- Getting familiar with OOP concepts
- Managing Actors
- Exploring the Gameplay Framework classes

Getting familiar with OOP

Let's learn about some elementary concepts of OOP, such as classes, instances, and inheritance. These concepts will help you learn about various elements of Blueprints Visual Scripting.

Classes

In OOP, a class is a template for creating objects and providing the initial values for state (variables or attributes) and implementations of behavior (events or functions).

Many real-world objects can be thought of in the same way, even if they are unique. As a very simple example, we can think of a person class. In this class, we can have attributes such as name and height, and actions such as move and eat. Using the person class, we can create several objects of this class. Each object represents a person with different values for their name and height attributes.

When we create a Blueprint, we are creating a new class that can be used to create objects in the levels of a game. As the following screenshot shows, the option that appears when creating a new Blueprint asset is **Blueprint Class**:

Figure 3.1 – Creating a Blueprint Class

Encapsulation is another important concept. It allows us to hide the complexity of a class when it is viewed from the point of view of another class. The variables and functions of a Blueprint class can be **private**, which means that they can only be accessed and modified in the Blueprint Class where they were created. The **public** variables and functions are those that can be accessed by other Blueprint Classes.

Instances

An object created from a class is also known as an **instance** of that class. Each time you drag a Blueprint Class from **Content Browser** and drop it into the Level, you create a new instance of this Blueprint Class.

All instances are created with the same default values for their variables as were defined in the Blueprint Class. However, if a variable is marked as **Instance Editable**, the variable's value can be changed in the Level for each of the instances without affecting the values held by the other instances.

For example, imagine that a Blueprint was created to represent a character type in a game. The following screenshot shows that three instances of this Blueprint Class were added to the Level:

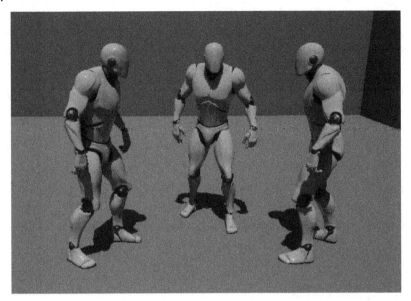

Figure 3.2 – Instances of a Blueprint Class

Inheritance

In OOP, classes can inherit variables and functions from other classes. When we are creating a Blueprint, the first thing we must do is choose the parent class of this Blueprint. A Blueprint Class can only have one parent class but can have several child classes. The parent class is also known as the **superclass**, while the child class is known as the **subclass**.

As an example of using inheritance, imagine that we are creating several Blueprints that represent different types of weapons in a game. We can create a base Blueprint Class called Weapon with everything that is common to all weapons in the game. Then, we can create the Blueprints that represent each of the weapons using the Weapon class as the parent class. The following diagram shows the hierarchy between these classes:

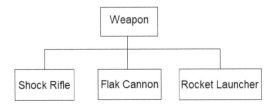

Figure 3.3 – Class hierarchy

One advantage of inheritance is that we can create a function in the parent class and override it in the child classes with different implementations. For example, there can be a function named `Fire` in the `Weapon` parent class. The child classes inherit the `Fire` function, so the `Shock Rifle` class overrides the `Fire` function with a version that fires an energy beam, and the `Rocket Launcher` class overrides the `Fire` function to launch rockets. At runtime, if we have a reference to the `Weapon` class and call the `Fire` function, the instance class will be identified to run its version of the `Fire` function.

Inheritance is also used to define the class type of a class since it accumulates all the types of its parent class. For example, we can say that an instance of the `Shock Rifle` class is of the `Shock Rifle` type and of the `Weapon` type. Because of this, if we have a function with a `Weapon` input parameter, it can receive instances of the `Weapon` class or any instances of its child classes.

These elementary concepts of OOP will help us understand the Gameplay Framework. Unreal Engine has some essential classes that are used in the development of games. These classes are parts of the Gameplay Framework. The main class of the Gameplay Framework is **Actor**.

Managing Actors

The Actor class contains all the functionality an object needs to exist in a Level. Therefore, the Actor class is the parent class for all objects that can be placed or spawned in a Level. In other words, any object that can be placed or spawned in a Level is a subclass of the Actor class. Most of the Blueprints that we'll create will be based on the Actor class itself or its child classes. Therefore, the features we will look at in this section will be useful for these Blueprints.

Referencing Actors

Variable types such as integer, float, and Boolean are known as primitive types because they only store simple values of the specified type. When working with objects or Actors, we use a type of variable known as an **object reference**. References in Blueprints allow different objects to talk to each other. We will explore this communication in greater detail in *Chapter 4, Understanding Blueprint Communication*.

For example, the following diagram represents instances of two Blueprint Classes in memory. The instance of the `BP_Barrel` Blueprint Class has an integer variable named `Hit Counter`, with a current value of 2. The other variable, named `BP_Fire`, is an object reference, which is referencing an instance of **Blueprint Effect Fire**. We can access the public variables and functions of another Blueprint using an object reference variable:

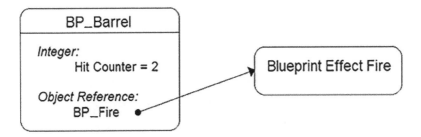

Figure 3.4 – Object reference

In a Blueprint, we can create variables that reference other objects/Actors. Let's create a step-by-step functional example to see this concept in action:

1. Create a project based on the First Person template with the starter content.

2. Click on the **Content Drawer** button to open **Content Browser**, then click the **Add** button and select **Blueprint Class**.

3. On the next screen, choose **Actor** as the parent class.

4. Name the Blueprint BP_Barrel and double-click it to open the Blueprint Editor.

5. Click the **Add** button in the **Components** panel and choose the **Static Mesh** Component. In the **Details** panel, choose the **Shape_Cylinder** Static Mesh:

Figure 3.5 – Setting the static mesh

6.   In the **My Blueprint** panel, create a variable named `BP_Fire`. In the **Details** panel, click on the drop-down menu of the **Variable Type** parameter. The **Object Types** category lists the classes that are available in Unreal Engine and the Blueprints Classes that we created in the project. Search for `fire` and hover over **Blueprint Effect Fire** to display a submenu and then choose **Object Reference**:

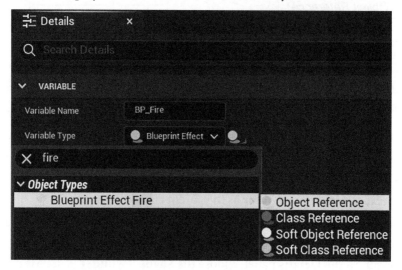

Figure 3.6 – Creating an Object Reference

7.   The default value of an **Object Reference** variable is **None** (also known as null), which means that the variable is not referencing any instances. We can assign an instance to this variable in the Level Editor. To do this, check the **Instance Editable** attribute of the variable so that it is accessible in the Level Editor.

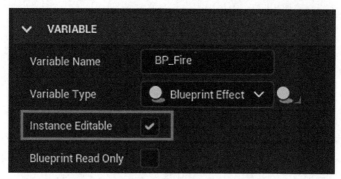

Figure 3.7 – Making the variable editable in the instances placed in the Level

8.   Drag the `BP_Fire` variable from the **My Blueprint** panel and drop it into **Event Graph**. Choose the **Get BP_Fire** option to create a node. Drag from the blue pin of the **BP_Fire** node and drop in the graph to open **Context Menu**. Search for `hidden` and choose the **Set Hidden in Game (P_Fire)** function:

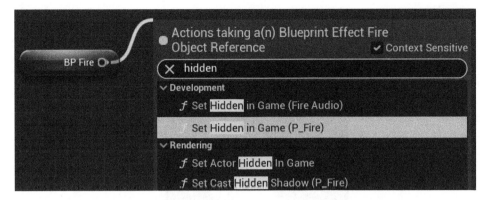

Figure 3.8 – Searching for a function in Context Menu

9. Right-click **Event Graph** and add **Event Hit**. Connect the **Event Hit** node to the **Set Hidden in Game (P_Fire)** node. The **New Hidden** parameter must be unchecked. These actions will unhide the particle system component of the instance referenced by BP_Fire when an instance of the BP_Barrel Blueprint is hit:

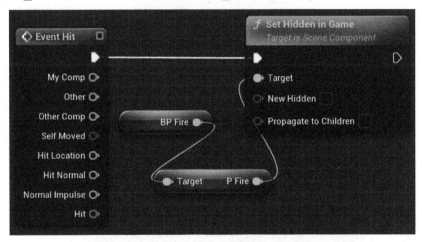

Figure 3.9 – Actions of the Event Hit

10. Compile the Blueprint and return to the Level Editor. Drag the BP_Barrel Blueprint from **Content Browser** and drop it into the Level.

11. In **Content Browser**, go to the `Content | StarterContent | Blueprints` folder, drag `Blueprint_Effect_Fire`, and drop it on top of the `BP_Barrel` Blueprint that was added to the Level:

Figure 3.10 – BP_Barrel and Blueprint_Effect_Fire

12. In the **Details** panel of the `Blueprint_Effect_Fire` instance, select the **P_Fire** component, search for `hidden`, and check the **Hidden In Game** attribute:

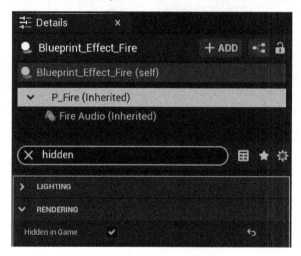

Figure 3.11 – Hiding the particle system of Blueprint_Effect_Fire

13. In the **Details** panel of the `BP_Barrel` instance, click on the drop-down menu of the `BP_Fire` variable to list the Actors of the Level that are instances of `Blueprint_Effect_Fire`. Select the instance that we dropped on top of `BP_Barrel` to assign its instance to the `BP_Fire` variable.

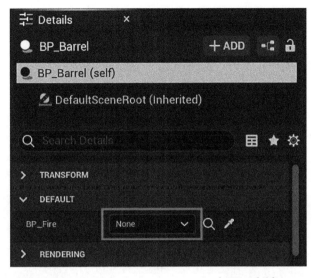

Figure 3.12 – Assigning an instance in the Level Editor

14. Click the **Play** button of the Level Editor to test the Level. Look in the direction of the BP_Barrel instance we placed on the Level. The Blueprint_Effect_Fire instance is hidden. Shoot the BP_Barrel instance using the left mouse button. When the BP_Barrel instance is hit, the Blueprint_Effect_Fire instance will appear.

Spawning and destroying Actors

There is a function called **Spawn Actor from Class** that creates an Actor instance. To add this function to **Event Graph**, right-click the **Event Graph** panel to open **Context Menu**, write spawn in the search box to filter the results, and click the function name.

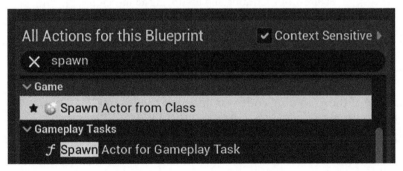

Figure 3.13 – The Spawn Actor from Class function in Context Menu

This function receives the class of the Actor and the Transformation that will be applied as input parameters. The Transformation defines the location, rotation, and scale that will be used by the new Actor. Another input parameter, called **Collision Handling Override**, defines how to handle the collision at the time of creation. A reference to the new instance is available in the **Return Value** output parameter and can be stored in a variable.

To remove an Actor instance from the Level, use the **DestroyActor** function. The **Target** input parameter indicates which instance will be removed. The following screenshot shows an example of using the **Spawn Actor from Class** and **DestroyActor** functions.

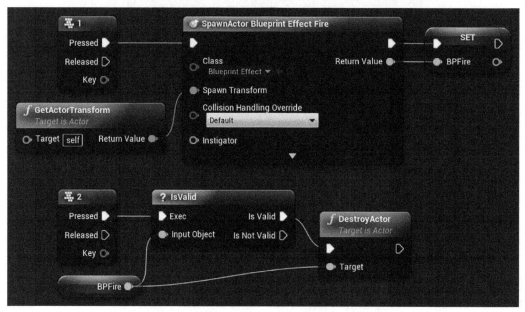

Figure 3.14 – Creating and destroying an instance

- To add the *1* key Input Event, right-click on the Event Graph and type 1 in the search box. The *1* key Input Event can be found in **Input > Keyboard Events**.

- Pressing the *1* key creates an instance of **Blueprint Effect Fire** using the same Transformation of the Blueprint instance that contains this script. For example, if the preceding code was added to the Event Graph of the ThirdPersonCharacter (found in the Third Person Template in Content | ThirdPersonBP | Blueprints), then once the game is launched, pressing *1* on the keyboard will create a fire effect at the current location of the player character.

- The reference to the new **Blueprint Effect Fire** instance is stored in the BPFire variable. If you didn't have the variable to store the instance, you could easily promote the return value of the **SpawnActor** function to a variable, which then automatically gives it the right variable type. To do this, drag from the **Return Value** pin and drop on the Event Graph to open **Context Menu** and select **Promote to variable**:

Figure 3.15 – Promoting the Return Value to variable

- When you press the *2* key, a test is done using the **Is Valid** Macro to check whether the BPFire variable is referencing a valid instance. This check is necessary to avoid calling a function using a null reference. If the value of BPFire is **None**, then it is not valid. If it is valid, then it calls the **DestroyActor** function that receives the BPFire variable as the **Target** input parameter and destroys the **Blueprint Effect Fire** instance that was previously created.

- Just a note, pressing the *2* key will only delete the last **Blueprint Effect Fire** instance created. If you create more than one fire instance before delete, the others will remain in the Level because the BPFire variable is overridden when a **Blueprint Effect Fire** instance is created.

Construction Script

One of the panels in the Blueprint Editor is called **Construction Script** and is shown in the following screenshot. **Construction Script** is a special function that all Actor Blueprints perform when the Blueprint is first added to the Level, when a change is made to its properties in the Level Editor, or when an instance of this Blueprint is spawned at runtime:

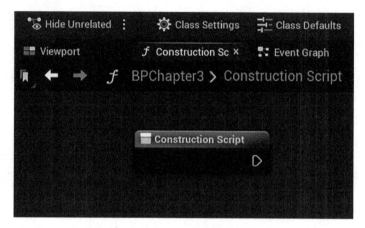

Figure 3.16 – Construction Script panel

Construction Script is very useful for creating flexible Blueprints that allow the Level Designer to configure some features of an instance of these Blueprints within the Level Editor.

As an example, let's create a Blueprint with an **Instance Editable Static Mesh** so we can choose a different Static Mesh for each instance of the Blueprint that is on the Level:

1. Create or use an existing project that has the starter content.

2. Click the **Add** button in **Content Browser** and choose the **Blueprint Class** option.

3. On the next screen, choose **Actor** as the parent class.

4. Name the Blueprint `BPConstruction` and double-click it to open the Blueprint Editor.

5. Click the **Add** button in the **Components** panel and choose the **Static Mesh** Component. Rename the Component `StaticMeshComp`, as shown in the following screenshot:

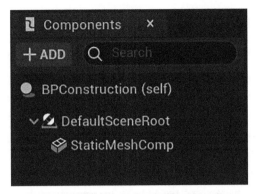

Figure 3.17 – Adding the Static Mesh Component

6. In the **My Blueprint** panel, create a new variable named **SM_Mesh**. In the **Details** panel, click the **Variable Type** drop-down menu and search for Static Mesh. Hover over **Static Mesh** to display a submenu and then choose **Object Reference**. Check the **Instance Editable** attribute, as shown in the following screenshot:

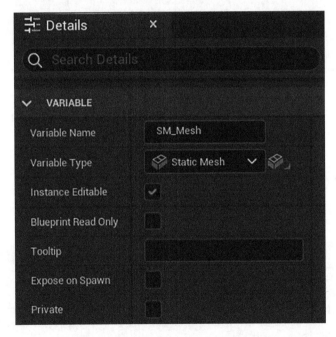

Figure 3.18 – Details of the SM_Mesh variable

> **Important Note**
> **Object Reference** variables can also refer to instances that are created at runtime.

7. Press the **Compile** button on the toolbar. Let's define an initial Static Mesh for the
    SM_Mesh variable at the bottom of the **Details** panel. Click the drop-down menu of
    the **Default** value attribute and choose the **SM_TableRound** Static Mesh.

8. Click the **Construction Script** panel. Drag the StaticMeshComp Component
    from the **Components** panel and drop it into the **Construction Script** graph to
    create a node.

9. Click on the blue pin of the StaticMeshComp node, then drag and drop in the
    graph to open **Context Menu**. Search for set static mesh and choose the
    function with this name, as shown in the following screenshot:

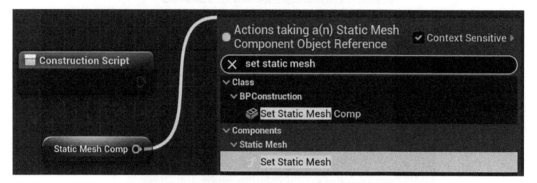

Figure 3.19 – Selecting a function in Context Menu

10. Drag the **SM_Mesh** variable from the **My Blueprint** panel, drop it into the
    Construction Script graph, and choose the **Get SM_Mesh** option in the menu
    that appears. Connect the **SM_Mesh** node pin to the **New Mesh** pin of the **Set
    Static Mesh** function. **Construction Script** should look similar to the following
    screenshot. When **Construction Script** executes the **Set Static Mesh** function, it
    gets the Static Mesh from the **SM_Mesh** variable and sets it on the **Static Mesh
    Comp** Component:

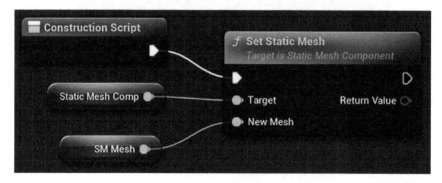

Figure 3.20 – Construction Script Actions

11. Compile the Blueprint. In the Level Editor, drag BPConstruction from **Content Browser** and drop it into the Level to create an instance. Drag and drop the BPConstruction again to create one more instance. Select one of the instances on the Level and, in the **Details** panel of the Level Editor, check that the **SM_Mesh** variable is visible and editable, as shown in the following screenshot:

Figure 3.21 – BPConstruction instance details

12. Click the drop-down menu of the **SM_Mesh** variable and choose another Static Mesh, such as **SM_Couch**. The Construction Script will immediately execute and change the Static Mesh of the instance that was selected. The following screenshot shows two instances of the BPConstruction class. The instance on the left of the screenshot is using the default Static Mesh, but the instance on the right had its Static Mesh modified to **SM_Couch**:

Figure 3.22 – Two instances of BPConstruction

The Actor class is the main class of the Gameplay Framework, but there are other classes for different purposes we need to know.

Exploring the other Gameplay Framework classes

One of the first steps when creating a new Blueprint is choosing the parent class that will be used as a template. The following screenshot shows the panel that is displayed for choosing the parent class. The classes that are displayed on the buttons are known as **Common Classes** and are part of the Gameplay Framework. To use another class as the parent class, expand the **All Classes** category and search for your desired class:

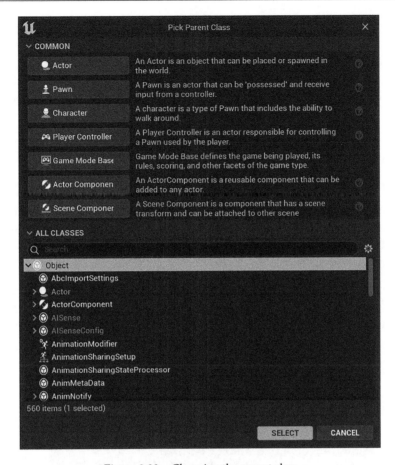

Figure 3.23 – Choosing the parent class

The following diagram shows the hierarchy of **Common Classes**. In Unreal Engine, there is a parent class called **Object**. Classes inherit the characteristics of the class above it, which is their parent class. Based on the inheritance concept of OOP, we can state that an instance of the **Character** class is of type **Character**, type **Pawn**, and type **Actor**:

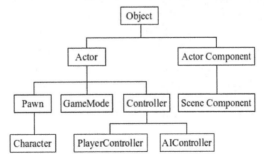

Figure 3.24 – Hierarchy of Common Classes

By analyzing this hierarchy, we can see that the **Actor Component** and **Scene Component** classes are not Actors. These classes are used to create Components that can be added to Actors. Two examples of Components are `Static Mesh Component` and `Rotating Movement Component`, which we used in previous examples. We will cover the creation of Components in *Chapter 18, Creating Blueprint Libraries and Components*.

Let's take a closer look at some of the **Common Classes**.

Pawn

Pawn is a child class of **Actor**. A **Pawn** is an **Actor** that can be possessed by a **Controller** in the game. The **Controller** class represents a player or an **artificial intelligence** (**AI**). Conceptually, an instance of the **Pawn** class is the physical body of the game character, whereas an instance of the **Controller** class possessing it is a kind of brain of the character, allowing it to move in the Level and perform other actions.

Create a Blueprint based on the **Pawn** class and click the **Class Defaults** button to display it on the **Details** panel. The parameters that are inherited from the **Pawn** class are shown in the following screenshot:

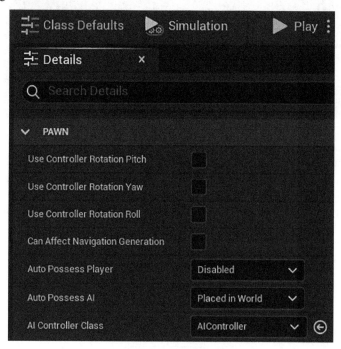

Figure 3.25 – Pawn Class defaults

Some parameters show that the **Pawn** class can use the rotation values of the **Controller** class that is possessing it. Others parameters indicate how the **Pawn** class must be possessed by the **Controller** class.

The two main child classes of **Pawn** are **Character** and **WheeledVehicle**.

Character

The **Character** class is a child class of the **Pawn** class; therefore, an instance of the **Character** class can also be possessed by an instance of a **Controller** class. This class was created to represent characters that can walk, run, jump, swim, and fly.

A Blueprint based on the **Character** class would inherit the following character-specific Components:

- **CapsuleComponent**: This is used for collision testing.

- **ArrowComponent**: This indicates the current direction of the character.

- **Mesh**: This Component is a Skeletal Mesh that visually represents the character. The animation of the **Mesh** Component is controlled by an animation Blueprint.

- **CharacterMovement**: This Component is used to define various types of character movements, such as walking, running, jumping, swimming, and flying.

These Components are shown in the following screenshot:

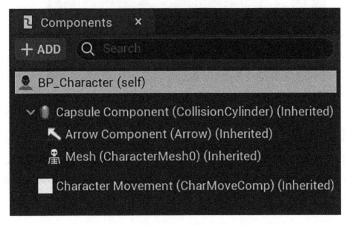

Figure 3.26 – Character Class Components

The **CharacterMovement** Component handles movement as well as replication and prediction in multiplayer games. It contains a lot of parameters that define various types of movements for the character:

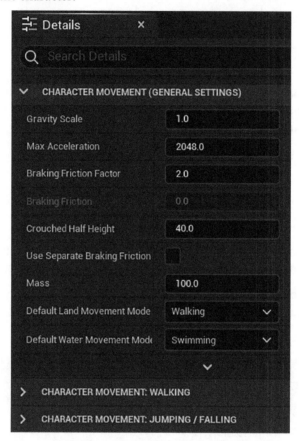

Figure 3.27 – Character Movement variables

PlayerController

The **Controller** class has two main child classes: **PlayerController** and **AIController**. The **PlayerController** class is used by human players, while the **AIController** class uses AI to control the **Pawn**.

Instances of **Pawn** and **Character** classes can only receive input events if an instance of **PlayerController** is possessing them. Input Events can be placed in the Event Graph of either the **PlayerController** or the **Pawn**. The advantage of putting the input Events in **PlayerController** is that these Events become independent of the **Pawn**, making it easier to change a **Pawn** class that is being possessed by the **Controller** class. Whichever way you choose, keep it consistent in your project.

The following screenshot shows how to change a **Pawn** possessed by **PlayerController** in-game and shows the use of the **Possess** function. In this example, there are two characters in the Level that can be controlled by the player by pressing the *1* or *2* keys. Only the **Character** instance currently being possessed receives the **PlayerController** commands:

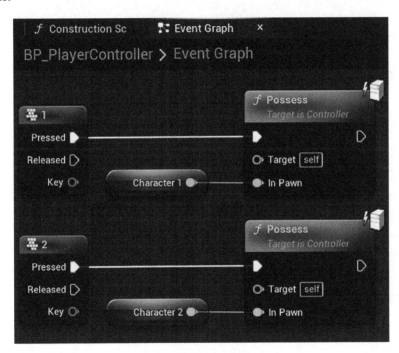

Figure 3.28 – Possessing a Pawn

Game Mode Base

Game Mode Base is the parent class for creating **Game Mode**. A **Game Mode** class is used to define the rules of the game and specifies the default classes used for the creation of **Pawn**, **PlayerController**, **GameStateBase**, **HUD**, and other classes. To change these classes in **Game Mode**, click the **Class Defaults** button to display them on the **Details** panel, as shown in the following screenshot:

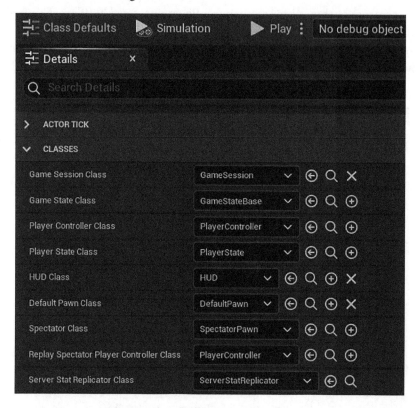

Figure 3.29 – Game Mode Class defaults

To specify the default **Game Mode** class of a project in the Level Editor, click **Edit | Project Settings....** Then, in the **Project** category, select the **Maps & Modes** option. Choose **Game Mode** in the **Default GameMode** property's dropdown, as shown in the following screenshot. In the **Selected GameMode** category, you can override some of the classes that are used by **Default GameMode**:

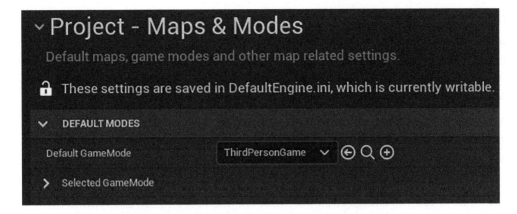

Figure 3.30 – Specifying the Game Mode of a project

Each Level can have a different **Game Mode**. The **Game Mode** of a Level overrides **Default GameMode** of the project. To specify **Game Mode** of a Level, click the **Settings** button in the Level Editor and choose the **World Settings** option. Choose **Game Mode** in the **GameMode Override** property's dropdown, as shown in the following screenshot:

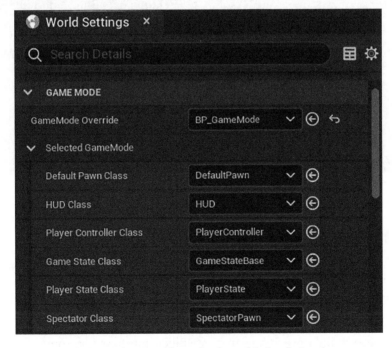

Figure 3.31 – Specifying the Game Mode of a Level

Game Instance

Game Instance is not one of **Common Classes**, but it is important to know about the existence of this class. The **Game Instance** class and its data persist between Levels because an instance of the **Game Instance** class is created at the beginning of the game and is only removed when the game is closed.

All Actors and other objects in a Level are destroyed and respawned each time a Level is loaded. So, the **Game Instance** class is an option to use if you need to preserve some variable values in the Level transition.

To assign the **Game Instance** class for use in your game, modify the project's settings by going to **Edit | Project Settings | Maps & Modes** on the Level Editor, as shown in the following screenshot:

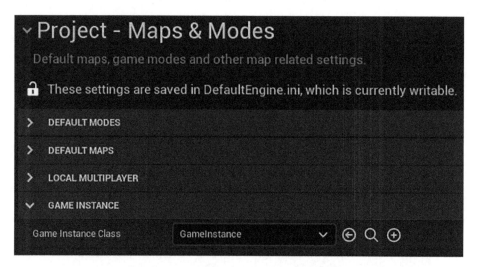

Figure 3.32 – Specifying the Game Instance Class

Summary

In this chapter, we learned about some of the principles of OOP that aid our understanding of how Blueprints work. We learned how the Actor class is the parent class that's used for objects that can be placed or spawned into a Level.

We also saw that the Gameplay Framework contains classes that are used to represent certain game elements and learned how to create Blueprints based on some of the **Common Classes**.

Our next step is to learn how our Blueprints can communicate with each other, which we will cover in the next chapter.

Quiz

1. What is the name of the function used to create an Actor instance?

    a. **Create Actor**

    b. **Spawn Actor from Class**

    c. **Generate Actor instance**

2. The Construction Script runs when the Level begins to play.

    a. True

    b. False

3. The Character class is a subclass of the Actor class.

    a. True

    b. False

4. An instance of the Pawn class represents the brain, and an instance of the Controller class represents the physical body.

    a. True

    b. False

5. Which of the following classes should be used to define the rules of the game?

    a. Game Instance

    b. Game Session

    c. Game Mode

    d. Game State

4
Understanding Blueprint Communication

This chapter presents **Blueprint Communication**, which allows one Blueprint to access information from, and call the functions and events of, another Blueprint. In this chapter, we will explain **Direct Blueprint Communication** and show you how to reference Actors on a Level Blueprint. The concept of casting is explained in depth because it is an essential part of Blueprint Communication. We are also going to learn about **Event Dispatchers**, which enable communication between Blueprint classes and the Level Blueprint, as well as how to bind Events.

For each of these topics, we will do step-by-step examples to facilitate our understanding of the concepts and practice the creation of Blueprint scripts.

The following topics will be covered in this chapter:

- Direct Blueprint Communication
- Casting in Blueprints
- Level Blueprint Communication
- Event Dispatchers
- Binding Events

Direct Blueprint Communication

Direct Blueprint Communication is a simple method of communication between Blueprints/Actors. It is used by creating an object reference variable that stores a reference to another Actor/Blueprint. Then, we can call Actions using this object reference variable as the **Target** input parameter of these Actions.

As an example, let's create a Blueprint called `BP_LightSwitch`. The `BP_LightSwitch` Blueprint has an object reference variable of the **Point Light** type that references a **Point Light** placed in the Level. When the player overlaps the `BP_LightSwitch` Blueprint on the Level, it toggles the visibility of the **Point Light**.

To create the Blueprint, follow these steps:

1. Open any existing project that you created that contains **starter content** or create one if you want.

2. Click on the **Content Drawer** button to open **Content Browser**, then click the **Add** button and select **Blueprint Class**.

3. On the next screen, choose **Actor** as the parent class.

4. Name the Blueprint `BP_LightSwitch` and double-click it to open the Blueprint Editor.

5. Click the **Add** button in the **Components** panel and choose the **Static Mesh** Component. In the **Details** panel, choose the **SM_CornerFrame** Static Mesh, as shown in the following screenshot. This Static Mesh is a simple visual representation of our light switch. Also, change **Collision Presets** to **OverlapAllDynamic** so that Static Mesh will not block the player's movement:

Figure 4.1 – Choosing the Static Mesh

6.   In the **My Blueprint** panel, create a new variable named `Light`:

Figure 4.2 – Creating a variable

7. In the **Details** panel, click the **Variable Type** drop-down menu and search for Point Light. Hover over **Point Light** to display a submenu and then choose **Object Reference**. Check the **Instance Editable** attribute, as shown in the following screenshot:

Figure 4.3 – Creating a variable of type Point Light

8. Drag the Light variable from the **My Blueprint** panel and drop it into the **Event Graph**.

9. Choose the **Get Light** option to create a node. Drag from the blue pin of the **Light** node and drop in the graph to open **Context Menu**. Make sure **Context Sensitive** is checked to show the **Actions** that can be used with a **Point Light** object reference.

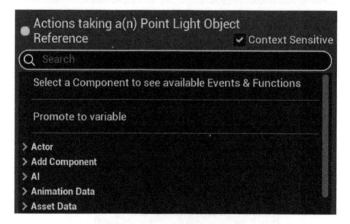

Figure 4.4 – Context Menu

10. Search for `toggle` and choose the function named **Toggle Visibility (PointLightComponent)**, as shown in the following screenshot:

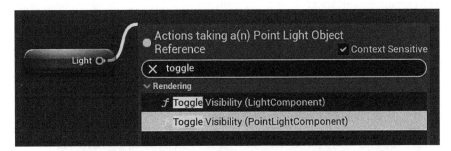

Figure 4.5 – Adding the function Toggle Visibility

11. Right-click **Event Graph** and add **Event ActorBeginOverlap**. Drag from the blue pin of the `Light` node, drop it in the graph to open **Context Menu**, and add the **Is Valid** macro, which is the one with the white question mark. This macro is used to test whether the `Light` variable is referencing an instance. Connect the nodes, as shown in the following screenshot. **Compile** this Blueprint:

Figure 4.6 – Actions of Event ActorBeginOverlap

> **Important Note**
>
> Always use the **Is Valid** macro before executing a function using an object reference variable. The variable can be invalid for several reasons. Executing a function using an invalid variable will cause an error at runtime.

12. In the Level Editor, click the **Create** button located on the toolbar. Hover over **Lights** to display a submenu and drag **Point Light** and drop it somewhere in the Level to create an instance:

Figure 4.7 – Creating a Point Light

13. In the **Details** panel, click on the name of the **Point Light** instance and change the name to Lamp. Set the **Mobility** attribute to **Movable** to be able to change the light properties at runtime.

Figure 4.8 – Details panel of the Point Light instance

14. Drag the `BP_LightSwitch` Blueprint class from **Content Browser** and drop it in the Level in a place near the **Point Light** instance that we added to the Level. The next screenshot shows the **Details** panel of `BP_LightSwitch`. The `Light` variable appears in the **Details** panel because we checked the **Instance Editable** attribute. Click the drop-down menu of the `Light` variable to show all **Point Light** instances that are in the Level and select the **Point Light** instance that we renamed to `Lamp` in the preceding step. Essentially, this is Direct Blueprint Communication. `BP_LightSwitch` has an object reference to another Actor/Blueprint and can call its Actions:

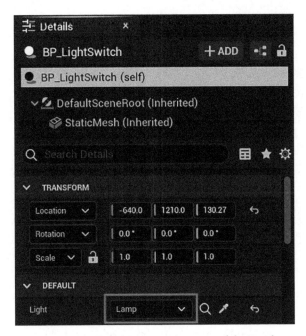

Figure 4.9 – Referencing an instance of the Level

15. Click the **Play** button to see the BP_LightSwitch Blueprint in action. Every time your character overlaps the instance of BP_LightSwitch, it toggles the visibility of the selected **Point Light**. The following screenshot shows an example using the **Third Person** template. The **Point Light** variable is on the wall, and the BP_LightSwitch Blueprint is on the floor:

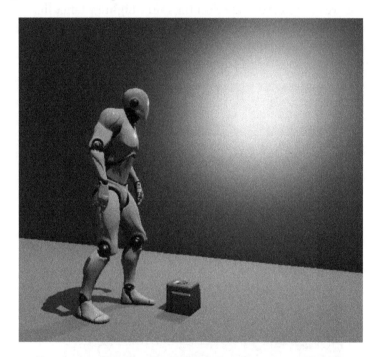

Figure 4.10 – Touching the BP_LightSwitch to turn on the light

In this section, we learned how to create a variable that refers to an instance of another Blueprint. But sometimes we need to access attributes of the subclass of the instance being referenced. In this case, we need to **cast** the reference.

Casting in Blueprints

There is a node named **Cast To** that tries to convert reference variable types to new specified types. To understand casting, it is necessary to remember the concept of inheritance between classes, which we covered in *Chapter 3, Actors and the Gameplay Framework*.

The following diagram represents a Blueprint called BP_GameModeWithScore. **Game Mode Base** is the parent class of this Blueprint. Based on the inheritance concept, we can use a variable of the **Game Mode Base** object reference type to reference an instance of BP_GameModeWithScore. However, this variable is unable to access the variables and functions of a **subclass** like those defined in the BP_GameModeWithScore Blueprint, because a **Game Mode Base** reference only knows the variables and functions that are defined in the **Game Mode Base** class:

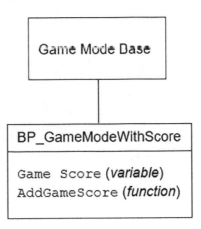

Figure 4.11 – BP_GameModeWithScore inherits from Game Mode Base

Therefore, if we have a **Game Mode Base** object reference, we can try to cast this reference using the Cast To BP_GameModeWithScore function. If the instance is of the BP_GameModeWithScore type, then **Cast To** will succeed and return a BP_GameModeWithScore object reference that we can use to access the variables and functions of BP_GameModeWithScore.

Another use of the **Cast To** node is to safely test whether an object reference is of a desired type and this step-by-step example will illustrate both use cases:

1. Create or use an existing project, based on the Third Person template, with the starter content.

2. Click the **Add** button in **Content Browser** and choose the **Blueprint Class** option.

3. On the next screen, choose **Game Mode Base** as the parent class.

4. Name the Blueprint BP_GameModeWithScore and double-click it to open the Blueprint Editor.

5. In the **My Blueprint** panel, create a variable named GameScore of type integer and create a function named AddGameScore:

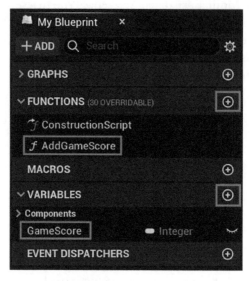

Figure 4.12 – Creating a variable and a function

6. In the **Details** panel of the AddGameScore function, add an **Input Parameter** named Score of type integer. This function is used to add points to the GameScore variable:

Figure 4.13 – Adding an input parameter

7. In the graph of the function, add the **Actions** shown in the following screenshot. To add the **GET** and **SET** nodes of the **Game Score** variable, simply drag the variable, drop it into the graph, and choose either **GET** or **SET**. The **Print String** function is used to display the current value of the **Game Score** variable on the screen:

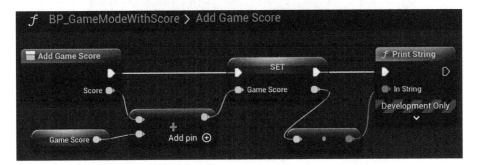

Figure 4.14 – The Actions of the Add Game Score function

Important Note

The node that is between **SET** and **Print String** is a converter. To create it, simply connect the **SET** output parameter to the **In String** input parameter of **Print String**. Because the parameters are of different types, the converter is created automatically.

---

8. Compile and save the BP_GameModeWithScore Blueprint. The next step is to set the Level to use BP_GameModeWithScore as **Game Mode**.

9. In the Level Editor, click the **Settings** button located on the right of the toolbar and choose **World Settings**:

Figure 4.15 – Accessing the World Settings

10. In the **GameMode Override** attribute, click the drop-down menu and choose BP_GameModeWithScore, as shown in the following screenshot:

Figure 4.16 – Changing the Game Mode used by the Level

11. Create a Blueprint and use **Actor** as the parent class. Name it as BP_Collectable and open it in the Blueprint Editor.

12. Click the **Add** button in the **Components** panel and choose the **Static Mesh** Component. In the **Details** panel, choose the **SM_Statue** Static Mesh and in **Materials**, go to **Element 0** and choose **M_Metal_Gold**. Also, change **Collision Presets** to **OverlapAllDynamic**, as shown in the following screenshot:

Figure 4.17 – Setting up the Static Mesh

13. Right-click **Event Graph** and add **Event ActorBeginOverlap**. **Other Actor** is the instance that overlaps the `BP_Collectable` Blueprint. Drag from the blue pin of **Other Actor** and drop in the graph to open **Context Menu**.

14. Choose the **Cast To ThirdPersonCharacter** action, as shown in the following screenshot. **ThirdPersonCharacter** is the Blueprint that represents the player in the Third Person template. We are using the **Cast To** action to test whether the instance referenced by **Other Actor** is the player:

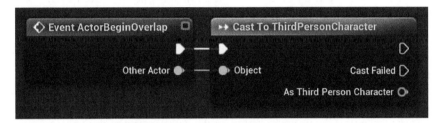

Figure 4.18 – Casting the Other Actor reference

15. Right-click **Event Graph** and add the **Get Game Mode** function. Drag from the blue pin of **Return Value** and drop it in the graph to open **Context Menu**. Choose the **Cast To BP_GameModeWithScore** action.

16. Drag from the blue pin of **As BP Game Mode With Score**, drop it in the graph, and choose the **Add Game Score** action in the **Context Menu**. Type 50 in the **Score** input parameter.

17. Right-click **Event Graph** and add the **DestroyActor** function. Connect the white pins of the nodes. The content of **Event ActorBeginOverlap** is shown in the following screenshot:

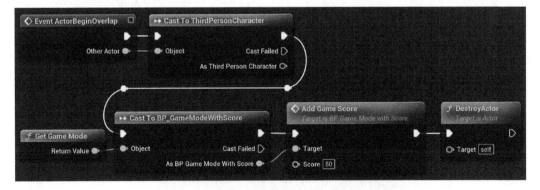

Figure 4.19 – Actions of Event ActorBeginOverlap

> **Important Note**
>
> The **Get Game Mode** function returns a reference to **Game Mode** used by the current Level. But the type of the return value is **Game Mode Base**. By using a variable of this type, we were unable to access the **Add Game Score** function. Therefore, it was necessary to use **Cast To BP_GameModeWithScore**.

18. Compile `BP_Collectable`. In the Level Editor, drag and drop some instances of `BP_Collectable` in the Level. Click the **Play** button to test the Level. Use your character to collect the statues and see your current score printed on the screen.

> **Important Note**
>
> The two white connection pins that appear in the previous screenshot are called **reroute nodes**. They can be added from **Context Menu** and are used to aid in the organization of the Blueprint.

This practical example shows two common ways of using the **Cast To** node. One way is to test whether an instance is of a specific type. The other way is to have access to variables and functions of a subclass. Now that we know how to use **Cast To**, let's learn how to add references and events of Actors in the Level Blueprint.

Level Blueprint Communication

Unreal Engine has a special type of Blueprint called **Level Blueprint**. Each Level of the game has a default Level Blueprint. They are useful for creating Events and Actions that only happen at the current level. To access the Level Blueprint, click the **Blueprints** button at the toolbar of the Level Editor and choose the **Open Level Blueprint** option, as shown in the following screenshot:

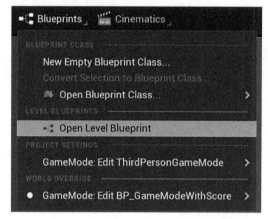

Figure 4.20 – Opening Level Blueprint

In the Level Blueprint, we can easily create references to Actors that are on the Level. To see this in practice, let's create an example where **Box Trigger** is added to the Level. When an Actor overlaps the trigger, **Blueprint_Effect_Sparks** is activated, producing the effect of a spark:

1. Create or use an existing project based on the Third Person template with the starter content.

2. In the Level Editor, click the **Create** button located on the toolbar. In the **Basic** category, there is a **Box Trigger**, as shown in the following screenshot. Drag the **Box Trigger** and drop it somewhere in the Level:

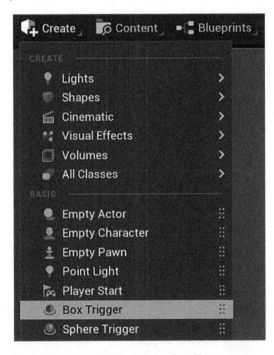

Figure 4.21 – Creating a Box Trigger

3. Resize and place the **Box Trigger** in a location in the Level through which the player must pass. The following screenshot shows an example. The **Box Trigger** is hidden in the game:

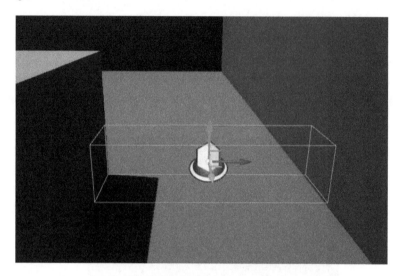

Figure 4.22 – Resizing and placing the Box Trigger

4. Confirm that the **Box Trigger** is selected and open the Level Blueprint by clicking the **Blueprints** button at the toolbar of the Level Editor and choosing **Open Level Blueprint**.

5. Right-click **Event Graph** and add the Event labeled **Add On Actor Begin Overlap** that is within the **Add Event for Trigger Box 1** category, as shown in the following screenshot:

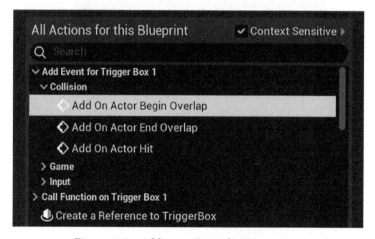

Figure 4.23 – Adding an Event for Trigger Box

6. Return to the Level Editor. In **Content Browser**, go to `Content |
    StarterContent | Blueprints` and open **Blueprint_Effect_Sparks**.

7. On the **Components** tab, select the **Sparks** Component and in the **Details** tab,
    search for the `auto activate` attribute and uncheck it, as shown in the following
    screenshot. We did this so that the **Sparks** starts inactive so we can activate it at
    runtime. Compile **Blueprint_Effect_Sparks**:

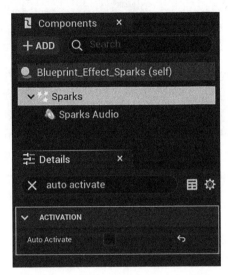

Figure 4.24 – Disabling Auto Activate of the Sparks component

8. In the Level Editor, drag **Blueprint_Effect_Sparks** from **Content Browser** and drop
    it in the Level near the **Box Trigger** to create an instance.

9. Confirm that **Blueprint_Effect_Sparks** is selected and open the Level Blueprint.
    Right-click on **Event Graph** and select **Create a Reference to Blueprint_Effects_
    Sparks**, as shown in the following screenshot:

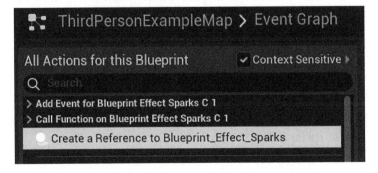

Figure 4.25 – Creating a reference to Blueprint_Effect_Sparks

10. Drag from the **Blueprint_Effect_Sparks** blue pin of the node and drop it in the graph to open **Context Menu**. Search for `activate` and choose **Activate (Sparks)**. Connect the white pin of the **OnActorBeginOverlap (TriggerBox)** event to the white pin of the **Activate** function, as shown in the following screenshot:

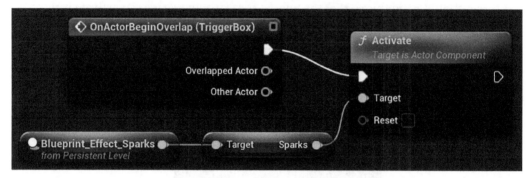

Figure 4.26 – Activating Sparks when overlapping the TriggerBox

11. Compile the Level Blueprint and click the **Play** button of the Level Editor to test the Level. Move your character to the location of the **Box Trigger** to activate the sparks.

In this example, we saw how to add references and events of Actors in the Level Blueprint. This is the essence of **Level Blueprint Communication**. There is another form of communication between Blueprints and Level Blueprint called **Event Dispatchers**.

Event Dispatchers

An Event Dispatcher allows a Blueprint to inform other Blueprints when an Event happens. The Level Blueprint and other Blueprint classes can listen to this Event, and they may have different Actions that run when the Event is triggered.

We create Event Dispatchers in the **My Blueprint** panel. As an example, let's create a Blueprint named BP_Platform. When an Actor overlaps the BP_Platform Blueprint, it calls an Event Dispatcher called PlatformPressed. The Level Blueprint is listening for the PlatformPressed Event and spawns an explosion when this Event is triggered:

1. Create or use an existing project based on the Third Person template with the starter content.

2. Create a Blueprint and use **Actor** as the parent class. Name it BP_Platform and open it in the Blueprint Editor.

3. Click the **Add** button in the **Components** panel and choose the **Static Mesh** Component. In the **Details** panel, choose the **Shape_Cylinder** Static Mesh and change the **Z** value of the **Scale** attribute to 0.1. Also, change **Collision Presets** to **OverlapAllDynamic**, as shown in the following screenshot:

Figure 4.27 – Setting up the Static Mesh

4. Compile the Blueprint. In the **My Blueprint** panel, create an **Event Dispatcher** and name it `PlatformPressed`. An Event Dispatcher can have input parameters. Let's create one to send a reference of the `BP_Platform` instance that was overlapped. In the **Details** panel, create a new parameter in the **Inputs** category, name it `BP_Platform`, and set it as a `BP Platform` type object reference, as shown in the following screenshot:

Figure 4.28 – Creating an input parameter

5. Right-click **Event Graph** and add **Event ActorBeginOverlap**. Drag the `PlatformPressed` Event Dispatcher and drop it in **Event Graph**. Choose **Call** in the submenu. Right-click **Event Graph**, search for `self`, and select the **Get a reference to self** action. The **Self** Action returns a reference of the current instance. Connect the Actions, as shown in the following screenshot:

Figure 4.29 – Calling the Platform Pressed Event Dispatcher

6. Compile the Blueprint. In the Level Editor, drag `BP_Platform` from **Content Browser** and drop it in the Level to create an instance.

7. Make sure the BP_Platform instance is selected and click the **Blueprint** button at the toolbar of the Level Editor and choose **Open Level Blueprint**. Right-click **Event Graph** and select **Add Platform Pressed**, as shown in the following screenshot:

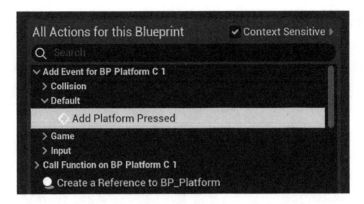

Figure 4.30 – Adding Platform Pressed in the Level Blueprint

8. Right-click **Event Graph**, search for spawn actor, and select **Spawn Actor from Class**. Click the drop-down menu in the **Class** parameter and select **Blueprint Effect Explosion**. Drag from the blue pin of the **PlatformPressed (BP_Platform)** Event, drop it in the graph to open **Context Menu**, and choose the **GetActorTransform** Action. Connect the nodes, as shown in the following screenshot:

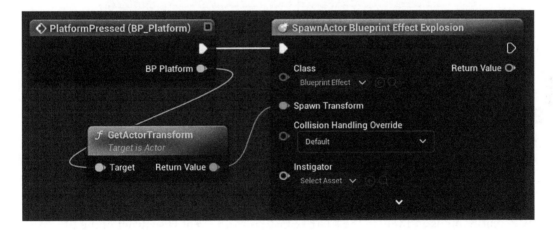

Figure 4.31 – Spawning an instance of Blueprint Effect Explosion

9. Compile the Level Blueprint and click the **Play** button of the Level Editor to test the Level. Move your character to the location where `BP_Platform` is. When your character overlaps it, the Level Blueprint will spawn an explosion at the same place:

Figure 4.32 – Touching the BP_Platform to spawn an explosion

We saw how the Level Blueprint can listen to an Event Dispatcher, but we can also make a Blueprint listen to an Event Dispatcher of another Blueprint by binding events.

Binding Events

There is a **Bind Event** node that binds one Event to another Event or to an Event Dispatcher, which can be in another Blueprint. When an Event is called, all the other Events that are bound to it are also called.

As an example, let's create a child Blueprint Class of **Blueprint_Effect_Sparks**. This new Blueprint binds an Event to the `PlatformPressed` Event Dispatcher of the `BP_Platform` Blueprint that we created in the previous example:

1. Open the project used in the example of Event Dispatcher.
2. Create a Blueprint, expand the **All Classes** menu, and search for **Blueprint_Effect_Sparks**, which we'll use as the parent class. Name it `BP_Platform_Sparks` and open it in the Blueprint Editor.

3. On the **Components** tab, select the **Sparks** Component and in the **Details** tab, search for the `auto activate` attribute and uncheck it if it is checked. This should already be unchecked since we changed it in **Blueprint_Effect_Sparks**.

4. In the **My Blueprint** panel, create a variable named BP_Platform of the BP_Platform type object reference. Check the **Instance Editable** attribute in the **Details** panel:

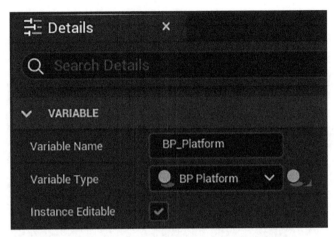

Figure 4.33 – Creating a variable of type BP_Platform

5. Right-click **Event Graph** and add **Event BeginPlay**. Drag the BP_Platform variable from the **My Blueprint** panel and drop it in **Event Graph**. Choose the **GET** option to create a node.

6. Drag from the blue pin of the **BP Platform** node and drop it in the graph to open **Context Menu**. Add the **Is Valid** macro to test whether the **BP Platform** variable is referencing an instance. Connect the white pin of the **Event BeginPlay** to the **Exec** pin of the **Is Valid** macro.

7. Drag again from the blue pin of the **BP Platform** node and add the **Bind Event to PlatformPressed** action. Connect the **Is Valid** pin to the white pin of the **Bind Event** node:

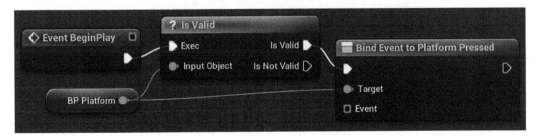

Figure 4.34 – Action to Bind Event to Platform Pressed

8. Drag from the red pin of the **Bind Event** node, drop it in the graph, and choose **Add Custom Event**.

9. Drag the **Sparks** Component from the **Components** panel and drop it in the graph. Drag from the blue pin of the **Sparks** node, drop it in the graph, and choose **Activate**.

10. Connect the nodes, as shown in the following screenshot, and compile `BP_Platform_Sparks`:

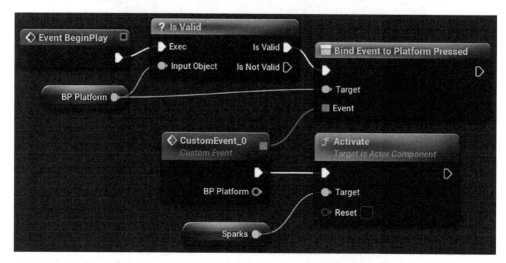

Figure 4.35 – The Custom Event bound to Platform Pressed

11. Add an instance of `BP_Platform_Sparks` near the instance of `BP_Platform` that is already on the Level. On the **Details** panel of the Level Editor, click the drop-down menu of the `BP_Platform` variable and select one instance.

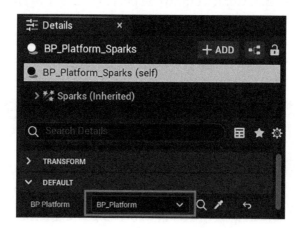

Figure 4.36 – Referencing an instance of the Level

12. Click the **Play** button of the Level Editor to test the Level. Move your character to the location of `BP_Platform`. When your character overlaps it, the `PlatformPressed` Event Dispatcher is triggered, and the Custom Event of `BP_Platform_Sparks` is executed, activating the sparks:

Figure 4.37 – Touching the BP_Platform to activate the sparks

Summary

This was a practical chapter. We created step-by-step examples for each type of Blueprint Communication. We learned about how a Blueprint can reference another Blueprint using Direct Blueprint Communication and how to reference Actors on the Level Blueprint. We saw how to use casting to access variables and functions of a child class, and how to test whether an instance reference is of a certain class.

We learned about how to use an Event Dispatcher to inform us when an Event happens, and how to respond to this Event Dispatcher in the Level Blueprint. We also saw that we could bind an Event of another Blueprint to an Event Dispatcher.

This chapter concludes *Section 1*. We have now learned about the Blueprint fundamentals necessary to start scripting games and applications in Unreal Engine 5.

In *Section 2*, we will start to build a first-person shooter from scratch with step-by-step tutorials. In the next chapter, we will create the project, add objects to the Level, manipulate the Materials of the objects, and add movement.

Quiz

1. It is possible to call functions of another Blueprint using an object reference variable.

    a. True

    b. False

2. The Cast To node is used to convert an object reference to a reference of any other Blueprint Class.

    a. True

    b. False

3. In the Level Blueprint, it is possible to create references to Actors that are in the Level.

    a. True

    b. False

4. The Level Blueprint cannot listen to an Event Dispatcher of a Blueprint class.

    a. True

    b. False

5. The Bind Event node can be used to bind an Event of a Blueprint to an Event Dispatcher of another Blueprint.

    a. True

    b. False

Part 2: Developing a Game

In this part, you will start to build a first-person shooter from scratch with the help of step-by-step tutorials. Blueprints will be used to develop the gameplay mechanics and user interface.

This part comprises the following chapters:

5
Object Interaction with Blueprints

When setting out to develop a game, one of the first steps toward exploring your idea is to build a prototype. Fortunately, Unreal Engine 5 and Blueprints make it easier than ever to quickly get the essential gameplay functionality working so that you can start testing your ideas sooner. We will begin by prototyping simple gameplay mechanics using some default assets and a couple of Blueprints.

In this chapter, we will cover the following topics:

- Creating a new project and a Level
- Placing objects in a Level
- Changing an object's Material through Blueprints
- Moving objects in the world with Blueprints

By the end of this chapter, we will have learned how to create a Blueprint target that changes its Material when it is hit and moves back and forth between two points regularly. Each instance of the Blueprint target in the Level can be set to different speeds, directions, and times to change direction.

Creating the project and the first Level

In this section, we will start by creating a project using one of the Unreal Engine templates. We will then explore the template to see what gameplay elements it provides.

Our game will be a first-person shooter. So, let's create a project using the **First Person** template, which is in the **Games** category:

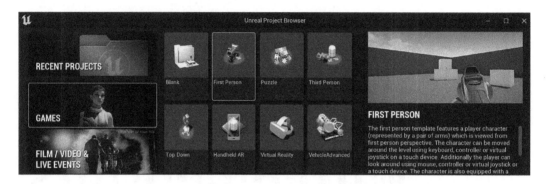

Figure 5.1 – Choosing the First Person template

Below the game templates, you can see a folder path field used to designate where you would like to store your project. You can use the default folder or choose one you prefer. The next screenshot shows the project defaults you should use in this project. These **PROJECT DEFAULTS** options were explained in *Chapter 1, Exploring the Blueprint Editor*. There is also a **Project Name** field to input the name by which your project will be known. I named the project UE5BpBook, as shown in this screenshot:

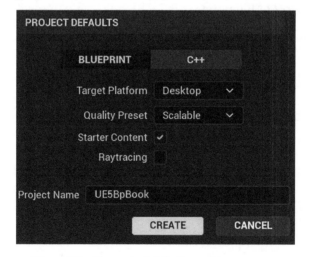

Figure 5.2 – The project defaults used in our game

Now that we have a template selected and the project settings set up the way we like, we can create the project. To do so, follow these steps:

1. Click on the blue **Create** button. After the engine is done with initializing the assets and setting up your project, the Unreal Editor will open the Level Editor.

2. Press the **Play** button to try the default gameplay that is built into the **First Person** template. You must click on the viewport for the game to start reacting to input.

   You can move the player character using the *W*, *A*, *S*, and *D* keys and look around by moving the mouse. You can fire projectiles using the left mouse button. The projectile will affect some physics objects in the Level. Try shooting at the white boxes scattered around the Level and observe them moving.

3. In Play mode, the **Play** button will be replaced with a **Pause** button, a **Stop** button, and an **Eject** button. You can press *Shift + F1* to access the mouse cursor and click the **Pause** button to temporarily halt the play session, which can be useful when you want to explore the properties of an interaction or Actor that you have just encountered during gameplay.

Clicking the **Stop** button ends the play session and takes you back to editing mode. Clicking the **Eject** button detaches the camera from the player, allowing you to move freely through the Level. Go ahead and try playing the game before we continue.

Adding objects to our Level

Now, we want to start adding our own objects to the Level. Our goal is to create a simple target Actor that changes color when shot with the included gun and projectile. We can create a simple Actor by following these steps:

1. In the Level Editor, click the **Create** button located on the toolbar. Hover over **Shapes** to display a submenu and drag **Cylinder** and drop it somewhere in the Level to create an instance:

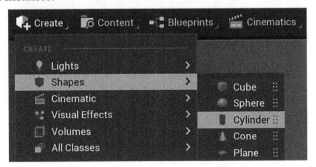

Figure 5.3 – Adding a Cylinder shape to the Level

This creates a new **Cylinder** Actor and places it in our Level. You can reposition the Cylinder as you wish by dragging and dropping it. You should see the Actor in the Viewport as well as in the **World Outliner** panel, where it is named **Cylinder** by default:

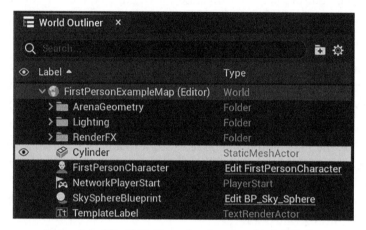

Figure 5.4 – World Outliner showing the added Cylinder

2. In the **Details** panel, change the name of the **Cylinder** instance to CylinderTarget, as shown here:

Figure 5.5 – The Details panel of the Cylinder shape

We've added an Actor to the Level that will be used as a target; we're now going to learn how to create a Material to apply to the Actor.

Exploring Materials

Earlier, we set ourselves the goal of changing the color of the Cylinder when it is hit by a projectile. To do so, we need to change the Actor's **Material**. A Material is an asset that can be added to an Actor's mesh to create its look. You can think of a Material as a coat of paint applied on top of an Actor's mesh or shape. Since an Actor's Material determines its color, one method for changing the color of an Actor is to replace its Material with one of a different color. To do this, let's first create a Material of our own. It will make an Actor appear red.

Creating Materials

Follow these steps to create a Material:

1. Click the **Content Drawer** button to open the content browser, and then click the FirstPersonBP folder to access it. Click the **Add** button, select **New Folder**, and name it Materials. This step is not necessary, but it is good practice to keep the project file hierarchy tidy.

2. Navigate to the newly created folder, right-click in an empty space in the content browser, and select **Material** to create a Material asset. Name it M_TargetRed:

Figure 5.6 – Creating a Material asset

Material properties and nodes

Now, let's open the Material Editor and learn how to use nodes that modify the Material.

These are the steps to define the look of our simple Material:

1. Double-click on M_TargetRed to open a new Editor window for editing the Material, like this:

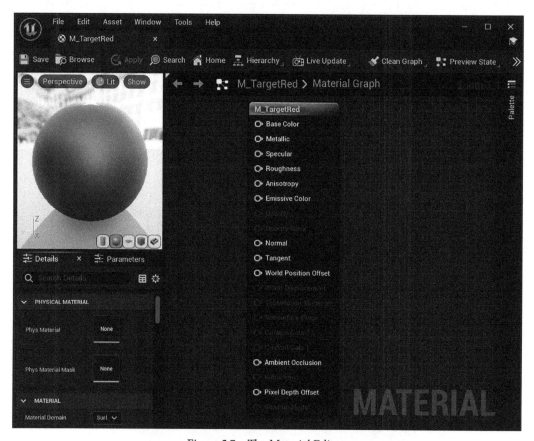

Figure 5.7 – The Material Editor

You are now looking at the Material Editor, which shares many features and conventions with Blueprints. The center of this screen is called the **graph**, and this is where we place all the nodes that define the logic of our Materials. The node you see in the center of the graph, labeled with the name of the Material, is called the **result node** of the Material. This node, as seen in the previous screenshot, has a series of input pins that other Material nodes can attach to define this Material's properties.

2. To give the Material a color, we need to create a node that provides information about the color to the input labeled **Base Color** on this node. To do so, right-click in an empty space near the node. A popup with a search box and a long list of expandable options appears:

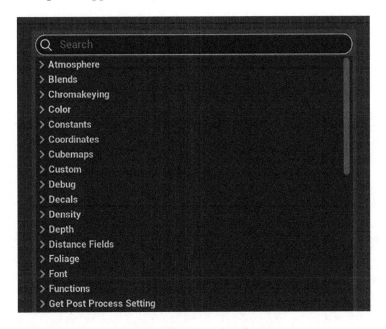

Figure 5.8 – The Material nodes menu

This shows all the available Material node options that we can add to this Material. The search box is context-sensitive, so if you start typing the first few letters of a valid node name, you will see the list below the search field shrink to include only those nodes that include those letters in their names. The node we are looking for is called **VectorParameter**, so we start typing this name in the search box and click on the **VectorParameter** result to add that node to our graph:

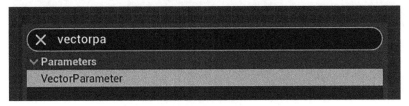

Figure 5.9 – Adding a VectorParameter node

3. Rename the added node `Color`. A vector parameter in the Material Editor allows us to define a color, which we can then attach to the **Base Color** input on the tall Material definition node.

4. We first need to give the node a color selection. Double-click on the black square in the middle of the node to open **Color Picker**. We want to give our target a bright red color when it is hit, so either drag the center point in the color wheel to the red section of the wheel or fill in the RGB or hex values manually. When you have selected the shade of red you want to use, click on **OK**. You will notice that the black box in your vector parameter node has now turned red:

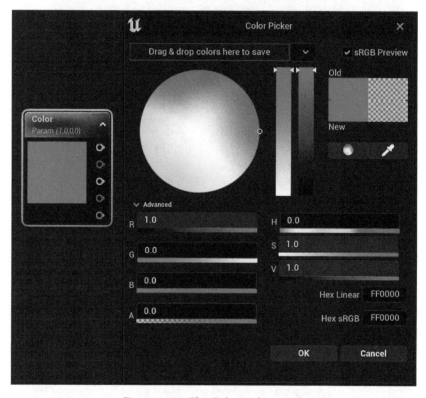

Figure 5.10 – The Color Picker panel

The final step is to link our color vector parameter node to the base Material node. In the same way as with Blueprints, you can connect two nodes by clicking and dragging from one node's output pin to another. Input pins are located on the left side of a node, while output pins are always located on the right side. For our Material, we need to click and drag a wire from the top output pin of the **Color** node to the **Base Color** input pin of the Material node, as shown in the following screenshot:

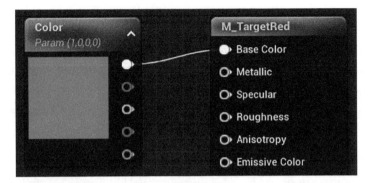

Figure 5.11 – Setting the base color of the Material

We can define a simple Material using the **Base Color** input pin. We'll now see how to use other input pins of the Material node.

Adding substance to our Material

We can optionally add some polish to our Material by taking advantage of some of the other input pins on the Material definition node. 3D objects look unrealistic with flat single-color Materials applied, but we can add additional reflectiveness and depth by setting a value for the Materials' **Metallic** and **Roughness** inputs. To do so, follow these steps:

1. Right-click in an empty grid space and type scalarpa into the search box. The node we are looking for is called **ScalarParameter**:

Figure 5.12 – Adding a ScalarParameter node

2. Once you have a **ScalarParameter** node, select it and go to the **Details** panel. **ScalarParameter** takes a single float value. Set **Default Value** to 0.1, as we want any additional effects on our Material to be subtle.

3. Change **Parameter Name** to **Metallic**, then click and drag the output pin from our **Metallic** node to the **Metallic** input pin of the Material definition node.

4. Let's make an additional connection to the **Roughness** parameter, so right-click on the **Metallic** node we just created and select **Duplicate**. This generates a copy of that node without the wire connection.

5. Select this duplicate **Metallic** node and then change the **Parameter Name** field in the **Details** panel to **Roughness**. Let's keep the same default value of 0.1 for this node.

6. Click and drag the output pin from the **Roughness** node to the **Roughness** input pin of the Material definition node.

The result of our Material should look like this:

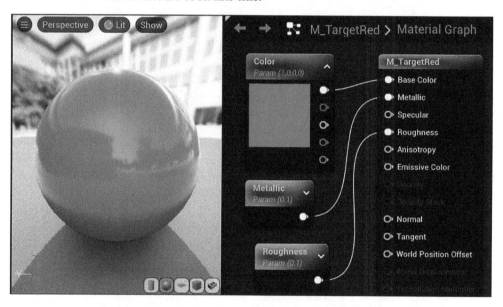

Figure 5.13 – The result of the M_TargetRed Material

We have now made a shiny red Material that ensures our targets stand out when they are hit. Click on the **Save** button at the top-left corner of the Editor to save the asset. Close the Material Editor to return to the Level Editor.

We have learned how to use the Material Editor to create a simple Material using the **Base Color**, **Metallic**, and **Roughness** input pins. In the next section, we will see how to change the Material of an Actor during runtime.

Creating the target Blueprint

We now have a Cylinder in the world, as well as the Material we want to apply to the Cylinder when it is shot. The final piece of the interaction is the game logic that evaluates that the Cylinder has been hit, and then changes the Material on the Cylinder to our new red Material. To create this behavior, we must convert our Cylinder into a Blueprint. To do so, follow these steps:

1. Make sure you have the `CylinderTarget` object selected in the Level. In the **Details** panel, click on the icon on the right of the **Add** button:

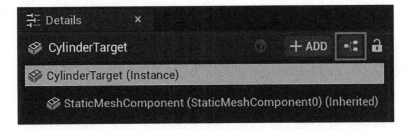

Figure 5.14 – Creating a Blueprint from an Actor in the Level

2. You will then see a window with the title of **Create Blueprint From Selection**. Rename the Blueprint BP_CylinderTarget. In the **Path** field, select the /Game/FirstPersonBP/Blueprints folder. In **Creation Method**, use the **New Subclass** option. The **StaticMeshActor** parent class is already selected because it is the parent class of the **Cylinder** Actor. Click the **Select** button to create the Blueprint:

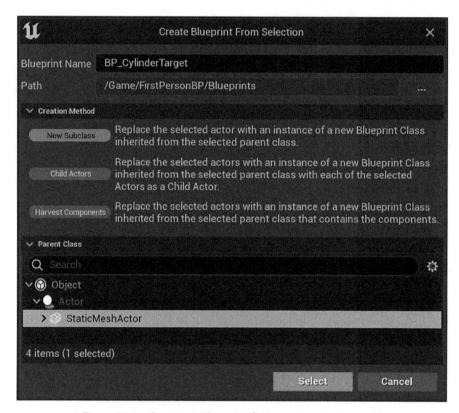

Figure 5.15 – Creating a Blueprint from an Actor in the Level

The Blueprint Editor opens with BP_CylinderTarget in the **Viewport** tab. You can see that the Blueprint already has a Static Mesh component with a Cylinder mesh assigned to it.

We will explore the use of components in *Chapter 6, Enhancing Player Abilities*; for now, we want to create a simple Blueprint that will react to a hit. To do so, click on the **Event Graph** tab.

Detecting a hit

To create a hit detection mechanism, follow these steps:

1. To create our hit detection event, right-click in an empty space of the EventGraph and type `hit` in the search box. The **Event Hit** node is what we are looking for, so select it when it appears in the search results. **Event Hit** is triggered every time another Actor hits the Actor controlled by this Blueprint:

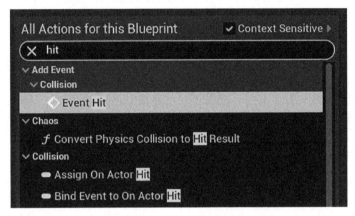

Figure 5.16 – Adding Event Hit

Now that we have the **Event Hit** node, we need to find an Action that will enable us to change the Material of an Actor.

2. Click and drag a wire from the white execution pin of the **Event Hit** node to an empty space to open the context menu. Type `set material` in the search box. The node we want to select is called **Set Material (StaticMeshComponent)**:

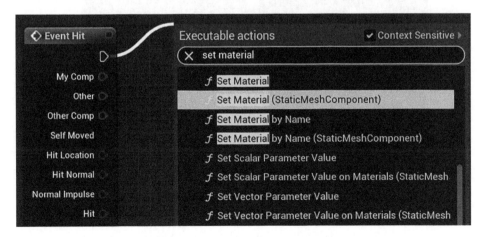

Figure 5.17 – Adding the Set Material node (StaticMeshComponent)

> **Important Information**
>
> If you cannot find the node you are searching for in the **Context Sensitive** search, try unchecking **Context Sensitive** to find it from the complete list of node options. Even if the node is not found in the **Context Sensitive** search, there is still a possibility that the node can be used in conjunction with the node you are attempting to attach it to.

We've added the **Set Material** node, but now we need to adjust its input parameters.

Swapping a Material

Once you have placed the **Set Material** node, note that it is already connected via its input execution pin to the **Event Hit** node's output execution pin. This Blueprint now fires the **Set Material** Action whenever the Blueprint's Actor hits another Actor. However, we haven't yet set up the Material that will be used when the **Set Material** Action is called. Without setting the Material, the Action will fire but won't produce any observable effect on the Cylinder target:

1. To set the Material that will be used, click on the drop-down field labeled **Select Asset** underneath **Material**, which is inside the **Set Material** node. In the asset finder window that appears, type red in the search box to find the **M_TargetRed** Material that we created earlier. Clicking on this asset attaches it to the **Material** field inside the **Set Material** node:

Figure 5.18 – Selecting the M_TargetRed Material

2.   We have now done everything we need with this Blueprint to turn the target Cylinder red. **Compile** and **Save** the Blueprint.

Now that we have set up a basic gameplay interaction, it is wise to test the game to ensure that everything is happening the way we want it to. You can click on the **Play** button of the Blueprint Editor to test the game. Try both shooting and running into the BP_CylinderTarget Actor you created:

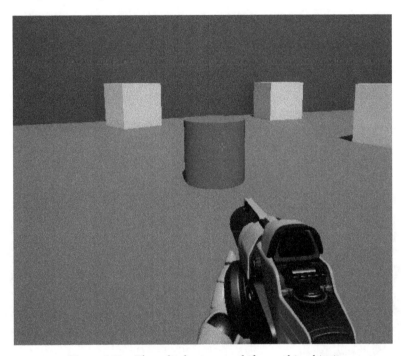

Figure 5.19 – The cylinder turns red if something hits it

In the next section, we will look at how to improve the BP_CylinderTarget Blueprint.

Improving the Blueprint

When we run the game, we see that the Cylinder target changes colors upon being hit by a projectile fired from the player's gun. This is the beginning of a framework of gameplay that can be used to get enemies to respond to the player's Actions. However, you might also have noticed that the target Cylinder changes color, even when the player runs into it directly. Remember that we wanted the Cylinder target to turn red only when hit by a player projectile and not due to any other object colliding with it. Unforeseen results such as these are common whenever scripting is involved, and the best way to avoid them is to check your work by playing the game as often as possible when you are constructing it.

To fix our Blueprint so that the Cylinder target only changes color in response to a player projectile, return to the **BP_CylinderTarget** tab and look at the **Event Hit** node again.

The remaining output pins on the **Event Hit** node are variables that store data about the event that can be passed to other nodes. The color of the pins represents the type of data variable they pass. Blue pins pass objects, such as Actors, whereas red pins contain a Boolean (`true` or `false`) variable.

The blue output pin, labeled **Other**, contains a reference to the other Actor that hit the Cylinder target. This is useful for us to ensure that the Cylinder target changes color only when hit by a projectile fired from the player, rather than changing color because of any other Actors that might bump into it.

Let's do a change to ensure that we are only triggering the Cylinder target in response to a player projectile hit. Drag the **Event Hit** node to the left to make room for another node, and then click and drag a wire from the **Other** output pin to an empty space. In the context menu, type `projectile`. You should see some results that look like the following screenshot. The node we are looking for is called **Cast To FirstPersonProjectile**:

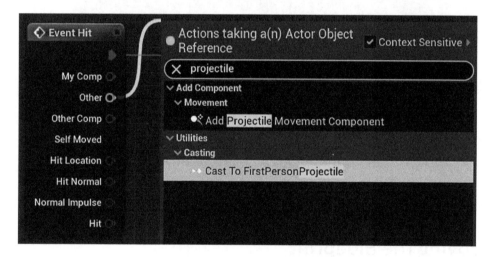

Figure 5.20 – Adding the Cast To node

`FirstPersonProjectile` is a Blueprint included in Unreal Engine 5's **First Person** template, which controls the behavior of the projectiles that are fired from your gun. The `Cast` node is used to ensure that the Action attached to the execution pin of this node occurs only if the Actor hitting the Cylinder target is an instance of `FirstPersonProjectile`.

When the node appears, you should already see a blue wire between the **Other** output pin of the **Event Hit** node and the **Object** pin of the casting node. Connect the white execution pin of **Event Hit** to the execution pin of the **Cast To FirstPersonProjectile** node, and connect the output execution pin of the **Cast To FirstPersonProjectile** node to the execution pin of the **Set Material** node:

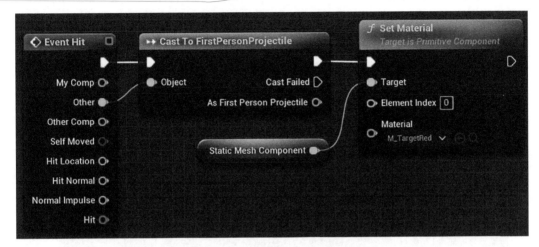

Figure 5.21 – The Event Hit Actions

Now, compile, save, and click on the **Play** button to test the game again. This time, you should notice that the Cylinder target retains its default color when you walk up and touch it, but if you move away and shoot it, it turns red.

We learned how to use the **Cast To FirstPersonProjectile** node to ensure that some Actions will only be performed if the instance interacting with the Blueprint is of a specific class. In the next section, we will make our Cylinder target move in the Level.

Adding movement

Now that we have a target that responds to the player shooting, we can add some sort of challenge to start making our project feel like a game. A simple way to do this is to add some movement to our target. To accomplish this, we first must declare that our target Actor is an object that is intended to move, and then we need to set up logic within the Blueprint that manages how it moves. Our goal is to make the target Cylinder move back and forth across our Level.

Changing the Actor's Mobility and Collision settings

To allow our target to move, we first must change its **Mobility** setting to **Moveable**. This allows an Actor to be manipulated while playing the game. To do this, follow these steps:

> **Important Information**
>
> By default, basic Actors that are placed in the world are set to **Static**. Static means that an object cannot move or be manipulated during gameplay. Static objects are significantly less resource-intensive to render, and this should be our default choice for non-interactive objects so that we can maximize frame rates.

1. Open `BP_CylinderTarget` again. On the **Components** panel, select **Static Mesh Component**. On the **Details** panel, switch the **Mobility** toggle, located underneath the **TRANSFORM** properties, from **Static** to **Movable**:

Figure 5.22 – Changing Mobility to Movable

Because we want to target this object with our gun, we also need to ensure that the target is capable of being collided with so that our bullets don't pass through it.

2. In the **Details** panel, find the category called **COLLISION** and look for **Collision Presets** in the drop-down menu. There are many other options in this drop-down, and by choosing the **Custom** option, you can even set the object's **Collision** interaction with different object types individually. For our purpose, we just need to ensure that this drop-down menu is set to **BlockAllDynamic**:

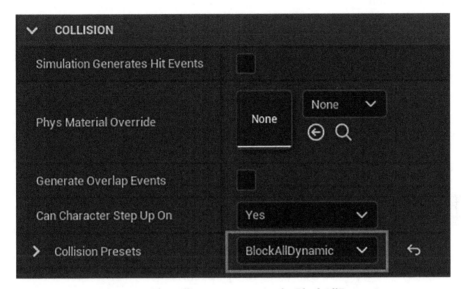

Figure 5.23 – The collision presets must be BlockAllDynamic

Breaking down our goal

Now that we have made our target moveable, we are ready to set up Actions that tell the Cylinder how to move. To move the Cylinder, we need four pieces of data:

- Where is the Cylinder currently located?
- What direction it is supposed to move in?
- How fast it should move?
- When should it switch between directions?

We will get the current location by using a function that returns the coordinates of the Cylinder in the world. The speed, direction, and time to change direction are the values we are providing to the Blueprint, but some calculations are necessary to turn those values into information that the Blueprint can use to move the object.

Follow these steps:

1. In the **My Blueprint** panel, create a variable named `Speed`. This variable will hold a number that represents the speed of movement of `BP_CylinderTarget`. In the **Details** panel, change **Variable Type** to **Float** and check the **Instance Editable** attribute:

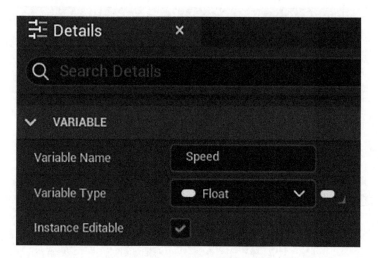

Figure 5.24 – The Speed variable

2. Compile the Blueprint to be able to set the default value. Set **DEFAULT VALUE** to `200.0`:

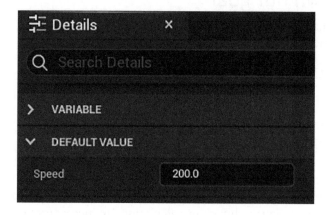

Figure 5.25 – The default value of the Speed variable

3. In the **My Blueprint** panel, create another **Float** variable named `TimeToChange`. Check the **Instance Editable** attribute. Compile the Blueprint and set **DEFAULT VALUE** to 5.0. This means the Cylinder will change direction after 5 seconds:

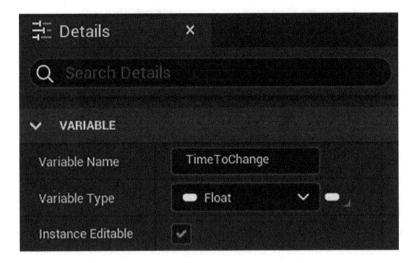

Figure 5.26 – The TimeToChange variable

4. In the **My Blueprint** panel, create another variable named `Direction`. In the **Details** panel, change **Variable Type** to **Vector** and check the **Instance Editable** attribute:

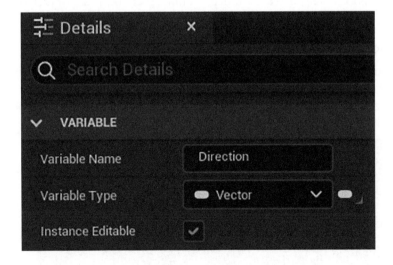

Figure 5.27 – The Direction variable of the Vector type

5. A vector contains the *X*, *Y*, and *Z* float values. Compile the Blueprint and set **DEFAULT VALUE** to 1.0 for the *Y* axis. This means it will follow the *Y* axis in the positive direction:

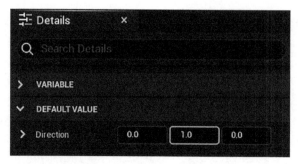

Figure 5.28 – The default value of the Direction vector

Readying direction for calculations

Now, let's explore the steps necessary to get the information we need to provide a movement instruction. It might look intimidating at first, but we will break down each section and see how each node fits into the larger goal.

The first calculation we need to perform is to take our vector value for direction and normalize it. Normalizing is a common procedure in vector math that ensures that the vector is converted to a length of 1 unit, which makes it compatible with the rest of our calculations. Fortunately, there is a Blueprint node that takes care of this for us:

1. Drag the Direction variable from the **My Blueprint** panel and drop it into the EventGraph. Choose the **Get Direction** option to create a node.

2. Drag from the output pin of the **Direction** node and drop in the graph to open the context menu. Search for normalize and select the **Normalize** node underneath the category labeled **vector**. This connects our **Direction** variable to a node that automatically does the normalizing calculation for us:

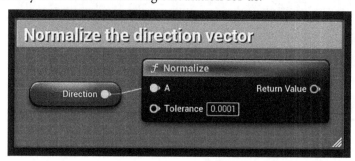

Figure 5.29 – Normalizing a vector

> **Important Information**
>
> It is good practice to leave comments on the sets of Blueprints as you create them. Comments can help describe what a particular set of Blueprints is intended to accomplish, which can be helpful if you are returning to a Blueprint after some time and need to make sense of your prior work. To leave a comment on a Blueprint, click and drag a selection box around the nodes you want to create a comment around so that you can select them. Then, right-click on one of the selected nodes and select the bottom option, **Create Comment from Selection**.

Getting relative speed using delta time

Delta time is the time difference between the previous frame that was drawn and the current frame. Delta time is used because the time taken between the frames of the gameplay can differ. By multiplying our speed value by delta time, we can ensure that the speed at which our object moves is the same, regardless of the game's frame rate:

1. Drag the **Speed** variable from the **My Blueprint** panel and drop it into the EventGraph. Choose the **Get Speed** option to create a node.

2. Right-click in an empty space of the EventGraph to open the context menu and search for delta. Select the **Get World Delta Seconds** option.

3. Drag from the output pin of the **Speed** node and drop it into an empty space. Type an asterisk (*) in the search field (*Shift + 8* on most computers) and select the **Multiply** node:

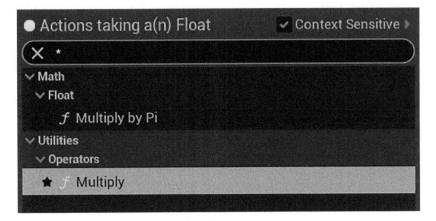

Figure 5.30 – Adding the Multiply node

4. Drag from the output pin of the **Get World Delta Seconds** node and drop in the other input pin of the **Multiply** node to multiply the two values, like this:

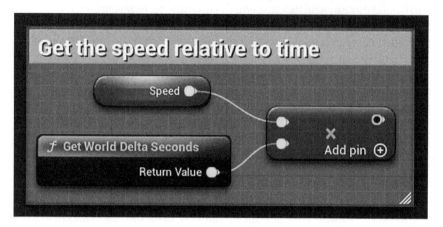

Figure 5.31 – Multiplying speed with delta seconds

Updating location

Now that we have a normalized vector direction and a speed value relative to time, we need to multiply these two values and add them to the current location:

1. Drag from the output pin of the **Normalize** node and drop it into an empty space. Type an asterisk (*) in the search field and select the **Multiply** node.

2. The previous step created a **Vector x Vector** node, but we need to multiply the vector with a float. So, right-click on the second input pin, hover over **Convert Pin...**, and select **Float**:

Figure 5.32 – Converting a multiply input pin

3. Connect the output pin of the **Float x Float** node to the **Float** input pin that we converted, as shown in the following screenshot:

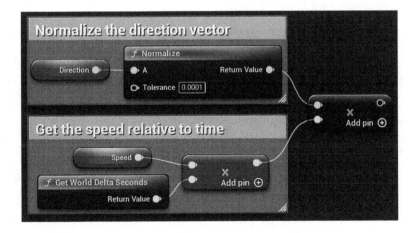

Figure 5.33 – Multiplying a vector with a float

4. We will use **Event Tick** to update the location of the Cylinder. Right-click in an empty space of the EventGraph to open the context menu and search for `tick`. Select the **Event Tick** option.

5. To move the Actor, we will use the **AddActorWorldOffset** node. This node has an input parameter named **Delta Location**, which is a vector representing the change of location of the Actor. Right-click to open the context menu, search, and add the **AddActorWorldOffset** node. Connect **Event Tick** to the **AddActorWorldOffset** node:

Figure 5.34 – Using Event Tick to update location

6. Connect the output pin of the **Vector x Float** node to the **Delta Location** input pin. Completed, **Event Tick** looks like this:

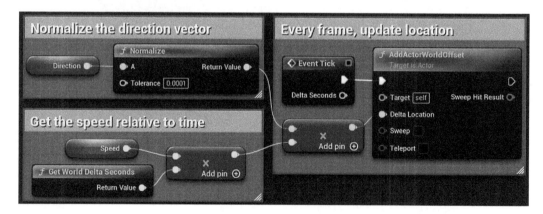

Figure 5.35 – All Actions of Event Tick

In this section, we learned how to use a normalized vector, delta time, and speed to move our Cylinder target. Compile the Blueprint, save, and play the game now. Note that the Cylinder target moves according to the defined speed and direction as soon as the game begins. However, since we don't have any instructions that cause the target to stop moving, it will proceed in the same direction for as long as the game runs, even moving through objects and out of the Level we created. To avoid this problem, in the next section, we will make the Cylinder target change its direction periodically.

Changing direction

In this section, we will implement the logic to change the target's direction periodically. This will result in a target that moves back and forth between two points regularly, much like a shooting gallery target:

1. Right-click in an empty space of the EventGraph to open the context menu and search for custom event. Select the **Add Custom Event** option. Rename the event ChangeDirection:

Figure 5.36 – Creating a custom event

2. We are going to invert the **Direction** vector by multiplying it by -1:

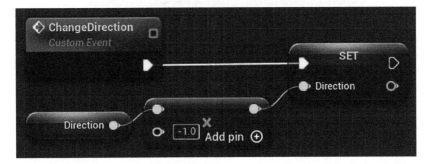

Figure 5.37 – Invert the direction of a vector by multiplying it by -1

3. Drag the **Direction** variable from the **My Blueprint** panel and drop it into the EventGraph. Choose the **Get Direction** option to create a node.

4. Drag from the output pin of the **Direction** node and drop it into an empty space. Type an asterisk (*) in the search field and select the **Multiply** node.

5. The previous step created a **Vector x Vector** node, but we need to multiply the vector with a float. So, right-click on the second input pin, hover over **Convert Pin...**, and select **Float**. Insert -1 in the **Float** parameter.

6. Drag the Direction variable from the **My Blueprint** panel and drop it into the EventGraph. Now, choose the **Set Direction** option to create a node. Connect the **Set Direction** node to the output pin of the **Multiply** node and the **ChangeDirection** event. This completes the **ChangeDirection** event.

7. We will use a **timer** to run the **ChangeDirection** event periodically. Right-click in an empty space of the EventGraph to open the context menu and search for timer event. Select the **Set Timer by Event** option. Check the **Looping** parameter:

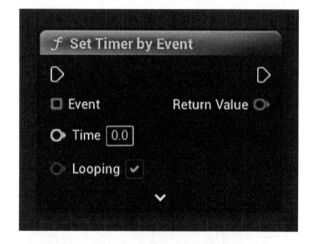

Figure 5.38 – Adding the Set Timer by Event node

8. Right-click to open the context menu and add **Event BeginPlay**. Drag the
    TimeToChange variable from the **My Blueprint** panel and choose the **Get
    TimeToChange** option. Connect the nodes as shown in the following screenshot:

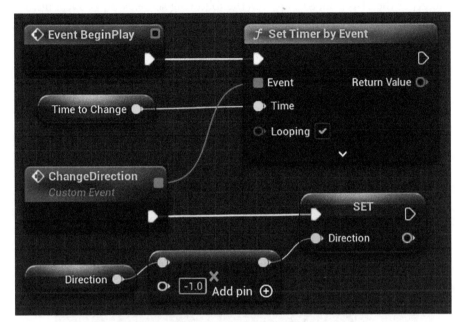

Figure 5.39 – The timer will run the ChangeDirection Event periodically

9. Compile and save the Blueprint.

Testing moving targets

Now that we have updated our Blueprint, we can test to ensure that the
BP_CylinderTarget instance moves as expected. First, we must place the
BP_CylinderTarget instance in a position that allows it to move along the y axis
without bumping into other objects. The coordinates I used were 220 on the x axis,
-600 on the y axis, and 220 on the z axis.

Note that these values only work relative to the default layout of the **First Person** template map. If you have adjusted your Level, then you can adjust the location of the Cylinder in your Level or change the values of the instance editable variables, such as the speed, the time to change, or the direction, as shown in the following screenshot, and test until you find a good patrol spot. Click on **Play**. If the Blueprint is functioning correctly, then you will see the Cylinder move back and forth between two points at a steady rate:

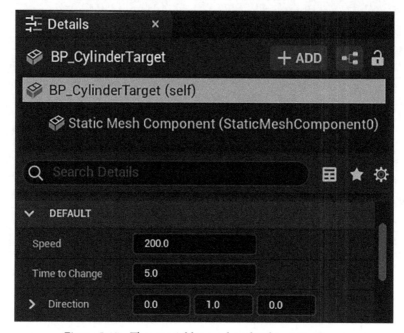

Figure 5.40 – These variables can be edited in an instance

You can add other BP_CylinderTarget instances and try other directions, such as following the *x* axis or up and down (the *z* axis).

Summary

In this chapter, we created a project and an initial Level using a first-person shooter template. We then set up a target object that reacts to the player's gunfire by changing its appearance. Finally, we set up a Blueprint that allows us to rapidly create moving targets. The skills we have learned about here will serve as a strong foundation for building more complex interactive behavior in later chapters, or even entire games of your own making.

You may wish to spend some additional time modifying your prototype to include a more appealing layout or feature faster moving targets. As we continue building our game experience, remember that you always can linger on a section and experiment with your own functionality or customization. One of the greatest benefits of a Blueprint's visual scripting is the speed at which you can test new ideas, and each additional skill that you learn will unlock exponentially more possibilities for game experiences that you can explore and prototype.

In the next chapter, we will be looking more closely at the player controller that comes with the **First Person** template. We will extend the existing Blueprint that governs player movement and shoot with a gun that is tweaked to our liking, producing more interesting visual impacts and sound effects.

Quiz

1. It is not possible to change the Material of a mesh using Blueprint script.

    a. True

    b. False

2. You can create a Blueprint class using an Actor that is in the Level.

    a. True

    b. False

3. The resulting vector of the `Normalize` function is a vector with a length equal to 1.

    a. True

    b. False

4. The amount of time a timer waits to execute an event is called delta time.

    a. True

    b. False

5. `Event Tick` is executed every frame.

    a. True

    b. False

6
Enhancing Player Abilities

In this chapter, we will expand on the core shooting interaction that we created in *Chapter 5*, *Object Interaction with Blueprints*, by making modifications to the player character Blueprint. The player character Blueprint that comes with the **First Person** template initially looks complex, especially when compared to the relatively simple Cylinder target Blueprint that we have already created from scratch. We will be looking into this Blueprint and breaking it down to see how each of its sections contributes to the player's experience and allows them to control their character and shoot a gun.

It would be quick and easy to just use an existing asset that works, without spending time learning how it accomplishes its functionality. However, we want to ensure that we can repair problems as they arise, as well as extend the functionality of the player controls to fit our needs better. For this reason, it is always advisable to take some time to investigate and learn about any external assets you might bring into a project that you are building.

By the end of this chapter, we want to succeed in modifying the player character, so that we can add the ability to sprint, zoom the view, and destroy the objects we shoot with enjoyable explosions and sound effects. Along the way to achieving these goals, we will be covering the following topics:

- Player inputs and controls
- **Field of View** (FOV)
- Timelines and branching logic
- Adding sounds and particle effects to an object interaction

Adding the running functionality

We'll begin our exploration of the `FirstPersonCharacter` Blueprint by adding simple functionality that will give our players more tactical options for moving around in the Level. Now, the player is limited to moving at a single speed. We will adjust the Blueprint to increase the movement speed of the **Character Movement** Component when the player presses the *Left Shift* key, but first let's learn about the Actions that are present in the **Event Graph** of `FirstPersonCharacter`.

Breaking down the character movement

Let's begin by opening the `FirstPersonCharacter` Blueprint. In **Content Browser**, access the `Content | FirstPersonBP | Blueprints` folder and double-click on the `FirstPersonCharacter` Blueprint. You will open the **Event Graph** and see a large series of Blueprint nodes. You can look around the **Event Graph** by right-clicking on the graph and dragging it. The first group of nodes we will look at is bounded by the **Event Graph** comment labeled **Stick input**, as shown here:

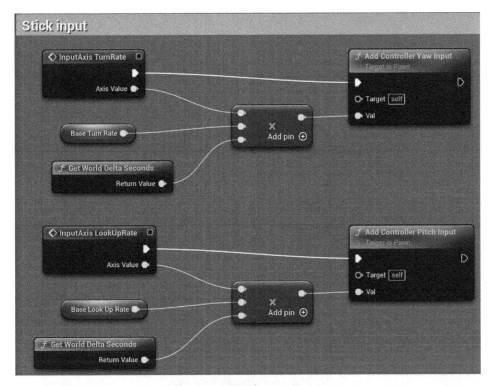

Figure 6.1 – Stick input Events

The red Event nodes are triggered at every frame and pass the **Axis Values** of **TurnRate** and **LookUpRate** from a controller input. These values are usually mapped to the left/right and up/down axis triggers of an analog stick. Note that there are only two axis triggers. Detecting a look down or a turn left Event is covered by these very nodes and is represented as a negative number in the **Axis Value** that is passed.

Then, the values from the two axis triggers are each multiplied by a variable, representing the base rate at which the player is intended to be able to turn around or look up or down. The values are also multiplied by the world delta seconds to normalize against varying frame rates, despite the triggers being called every frame. The value resulting from multiplying all the three inputs is then passed to the **Add Controller Pitch Input** and **Add Controller Yaw Input** functions. These are the functions that add translations between the controller input and the effect on the player camera.

Below the **Stick input** group of Blueprint nodes, there is another comment block, called **Mouse input**, and it looks quite like the **Stick input** group:

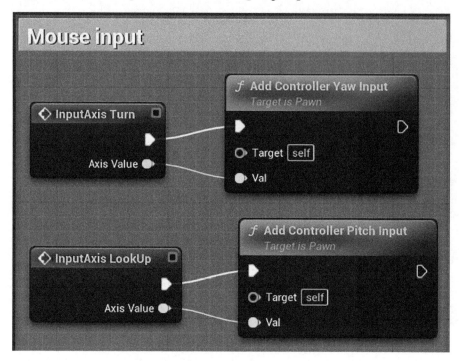

Figure 6.2 – Mouse input Events

Mouse input converts input from mouse movements (as opposed to controller axis sticks) into data, and then passes those values directly to the corresponding camera yaw and pitch input functions, without needing the same kind of calculations that are necessary for analog input.

Now, let's look at the group of nodes that manage player movement, as shown in this screenshot:

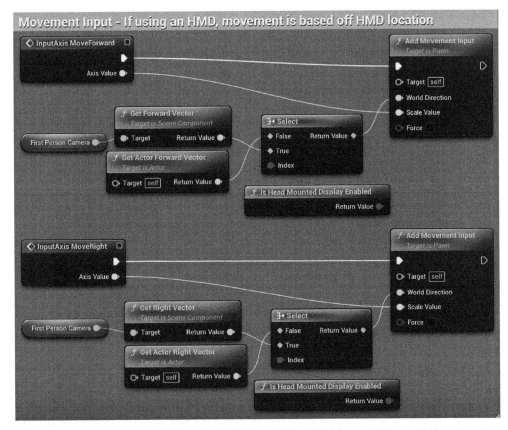

Figure 6.3 – Movement input Events

The **Select** nodes test whether the player is using a **virtual reality head-mounted display** (**VR HMD**). If a VR HMD is enabled, then the vectors used are from **FirstPerson Camera**; if it isn't, then the vectors used are from the Actor root Component.

Functionally, the other nodes are set up similarly to the **Stick input** and **Mouse input** groups. The axis value is taken from the forward and right movement axis inputs on a controller or keyboard. Again, these nodes represent backward and left movements as well, in the form of negative values for the **Axis Value** outputs. The significant difference in movement translation is that we require the direction that the Actor is going to be moved in, so that the degree of movement can be applied in the correct direction. The direction is pulled from the **Get Actor Vector** nodes (both forward and right) and attached to the **World Direction** input of the **Add Movement Input** nodes.

The last movement-related group of nodes to look at is the node group contained within the comment block labeled **Jump**. This group is simply made up of a trigger node that detects the pressing and releasing of the key mapped to jumping and applies the Jump function from when the button is pressed until it is released.

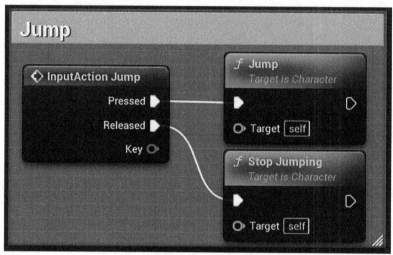

Figure 6.4 – Jump input Event

We saw the **Actions** of the FirstPersonCharacter that control the character movement. We will learn now how to map a keypress to an Action.

Customizing control inputs

We have seen how the **First Person** template has mapped certain player input Actions, such as moving forward or jumping, to Blueprint nodes in order to produce the behavior for the Actions. To create new kinds of behavior, we will have to map new physical control inputs to additional player Actions. To do that, follow these steps:

1. To change the input settings for your game, click on the **Settings** button on the far right of the toolbar, and select the **Project Settings** option:

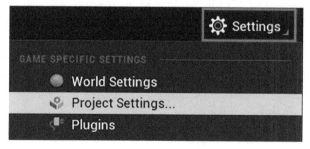

Figure 6.5 – Accessing the Project Settings

2. On the left side of the window that appears, look for the **Engine** category and select the **Input** option.

3. Inside the **Engine** category, in the **Input Settings** menu, you will see two sections under the **Bindings** category called **Action Mappings** and **Axis Mappings**. Click on the > symbol on the left of each section to show the existing mappings.

   Action Mappings are keypress and mouse click Events that trigger player Actions. **Axis Mappings** map player movements and Events that have a range, such as the *W* key and *S* key both affecting the **Move Forward** Action, but on different ends of the range. Both our **Sprint** and **Zoom** functions are simple Actions that are either active or inactive, so we will add them as **Action Mappings**:

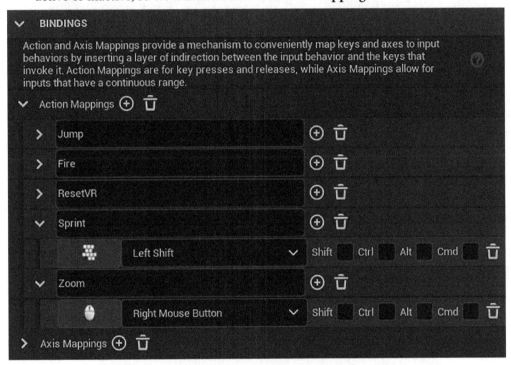

Figure 6.6 – Creating Action Mappings

4. Click on the + sign next to **Action Mappings** twice to add two new **Action Mappings**.

5. Name the first Action `Sprint` and select the **Left Shift** key from the drop-down menu to map that key to your **Sprint** Event. Name the second Action `Zoom` and map it to **Right Mouse Button**.

The changes are saved when you close the window.

Adding a Sprint ability

Now that we have a basic understanding of how the movement input nodes take the controller input and apply it to our in-game character, we'll extend that functionality with a **Sprint** ability. We'll set up a new series of nodes within the `FirstPersonCharacter` Blueprint. They will look like this:

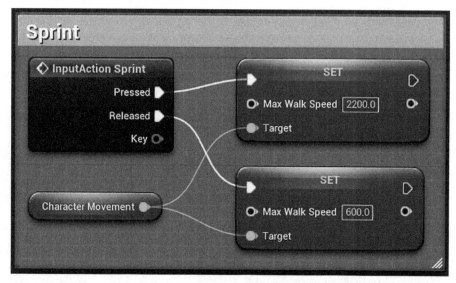

Figure 6.7 – Implementing the Sprint ability

First, we will need to add the Event that will activate our **Sprint** Action. Recall that we previously mapped the **Sprint** Action to the *Left Shift* key. To add the Event, follow these steps:

1. Right-click on the empty grid space to the left of the other movement functions and search for `Sprint`. Select the **Sprint** Event to place the node.

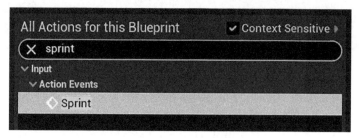

Figure 6.8 – Adding the Input Action Sprint event

2. Look at the **Components** panel of the Blueprint Editor and select **Character Movement (CharMoveComp) (Inherited)**. The **Details** panel will change to show a long series of variables related to movement, as seen in the following screenshot:

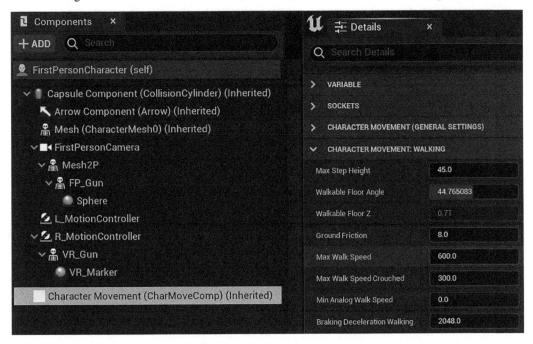

Figure 6.9 – Character Movement variables

In this list of variables, you can find **Max Walk Speed** in the **Walking** category. This is the value that determines the maximum speed at which the player can move, and it should be the target of our **Sprint** function. However, changing the value in the **Details** panel from the default of 600 would modify the player's movement speed consistently, regardless of whether **Left Shift** was being pressed or not. Instead, we want to pull this value out of the **Character Movement** Component and into our Blueprint's **Event Graph**.

3. To do so, click on the **Character Movement** Component in the **Components** panel and drag it onto **Event Graph**, near our **InputAction Sprint** Event. This will produce a **Character Movement** node, as seen in this screenshot:

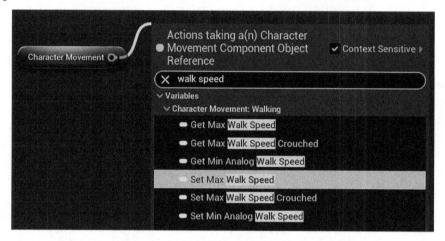

Figure 6.10 – Character Movement node

4. Click and drag the output pin from the **Character Movement** node to empty grid space and type walk speed. Select the **Set Max Walk Speed** option. It will connect the **Character Movement** node to the new node, setting the maximum walk speed value.

5. Connect the **Pressed** output execution pin from the **InputAction Sprint** trigger to the input execution pin of the **Set Max Walk Speed** node, to enable you to press **Left Shift** to modify the maximum movement speed.

6. Finally, change the **Max Walk Speed** value within the node from 0.0 to 2200, to provide a nice boost of speed over the default of 600.

    We also need to ensure that the player slows down again once the *Shift* key is released.

7. To do so, drag the output pin from the **Character Movement** node again, and then search for and select another **Set Max Walk Speed** node to place it on **Event Graph**. This time, connect the **Released** output execution pin of the **InputAction Sprint** node to the input execution pin of the new node. Then, change the **Max Walk Speed** value from 0.0 to the default of 600. To keep up with our good commenting practice, click and make a selection box around all four nodes, right-click on one of the selected nodes, and select **Create Comment from Selection**, then label the group of nodes as Sprint.

8. Now compile, save, and press **Play** to test your work. You should notice a significant boost in speed if you press down the *Left Shift* key.

We learned how to map a keypress to an Action and modify the max speed of the character to simulate a sprint ability. Our next step is to add an ability to the player that allows them to get a closer view of a target.

Animating a zoomed view

A core element of modern first-person shooters is a variable **field of view** (**FOV**) in the form of a player's ability to look down the scope of a gun to get a closer view of a target. This is a significant contributor to the feeling of accuracy and control that modern shooters provide. Let's add a simple form of this functionality to our prototype. To do that, follow these steps:

1. In an empty section of the grid next to your **Mouse input** nodes, right-click, search for zoom, and add a **Zoom** Event node.

2. We want to modify the FOV value that is contained within the **First Person Camera** Component, so go to the **Components** panel and drag **First Person Camera** out onto **Event Graph**.

3. Drag the output pin of **First Person Camera** node into empty grid space, search for the **Set Field Of View** node, and place it. Lowering the FOV gives the effect of zooming into a narrower area in the center of the screen. Since the Default FOV value is set to 90, for our zoom, let's set the FOV in the set node to 45, like this:

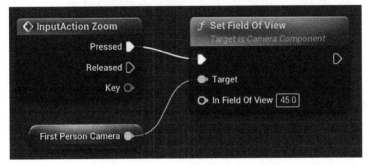

Figure 6.11 – Changing the Field of View

4. Click and drag the output execution pin from the **InputAction Zoom** node to the input execution pin of the **Set Field Of View** node. Compile, save, and click on **Play**.

You will notice that when you are playing the game and press the right mouse button, the FOV will snap to a narrow, zoomed-in view. Any instance where the main camera snaps from one position to another can be jarring for a player, so we will have to modify this behavior further. Also, the FOV does not reverse when the key is released. We will solve both problems using a timeline.

Using a timeline to smooth transitions

To change the FOV smoothly, we will need to create an animation that shows a gradual change in the Actor over time. To do so, return to the **Event Graph** instance of the `FirstPersonCharacter` Blueprint and follow these steps:

1. Press *Alt* and click on the **Pressed** output execution pin of the **InputAction Zoom** node to break the connection.

2. Drag a new wire out from **Pressed** to empty grid space. Search for and select **Add Timeline** to add a timeline node:

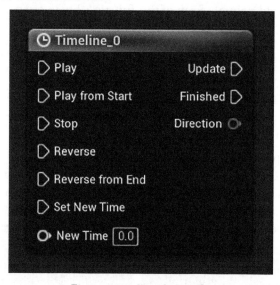

Figure 6.12 – Timeline node

> **Important Note**
>
> There are different ways of accomplishing animations in Unreal Engine 5. Timelines are perfect for simple value changes, such as the rotation of a door. For more complex, character-based, or cinematic animations, you would want to look into **Sequencer**, which is the engine's built-in animation system. **Sequencer** and complex animations are out of the scope of this book, but there are many dedicated learning resources available for using **Sequencer**. I recommend starting with the Unreal documentation, which is available at `https://docs.unrealengine.com/en-us/Engine/Sequencer`.

3. A timeline will allow us to change a value (such as the FOV on a camera) over a designated amount of time. To change the value within the timeline, double-click on the **Timeline_0** node.

This will open up the **Timeline Editor**. You will see four buttons in the top-left corner of the **Editor**. Each of these will add a different kind of value that can be changed over the course of the timeline. Because FOV is represented by a numerical value, we will want to click on the button with the **f** label (**Add Float Track**). Doing so will add a track to the timeline and prompt you to name this track.

4. Let's label this as **Field of View**. We will now have to edit the values over different time intervals, as shown here:

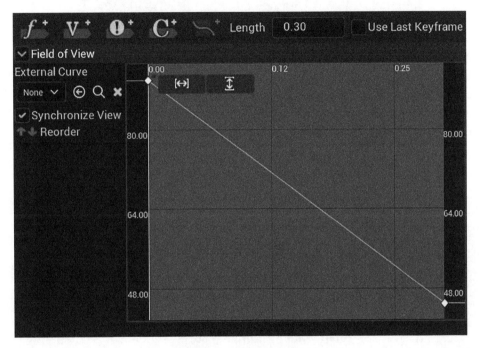

Figure 6.13 – Timeline Editor

5. To accomplish this, hold down *Shift* and click on a point that is close to the **0.0** point on the graph. You will see the **Time** and **Value** fields appear in the top-left part of the graph as shown in *Figure 6.14*.

    These allow precision tuning of our timeline. Ensure that the time is set to exactly 0.0 and set the value to 90, our default FOV. If the point disappears from the view, you can use the two small buttons in the top-left of the graph to zoom into the graph so that the point becomes visible. These buttons are inside the red rectangle in *Figure 6.14*.

6. We want the zoom animation to be quick, so at the top of the **Timeline Editor**, find the field next to **Length** and change to value to 0.3 to limit the range of the animation to 0.3 seconds.

7. Now, press *Shift* and click at the end of the light gray area on the right of the graph. Adjust the fields to 0.3 for **Time** and 45 for **Value**:

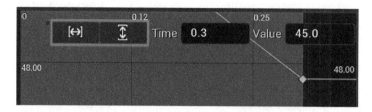

Figure 6.14 – Time and value of the second point

Notice how the line that represents the value gradually slopes down from 90 degrees to 45 degrees. This means that when this animation is called, the player's FOV will smoothly transition from being zoomed out to being zoomed in, rather than a jarring switch between the two values. This is the advantage of using timelines over changing the values directly with a set value Blueprint.

8. Now, return to **Event Graph**. We want to connect our timeline to our set FOV operation, just like what is shown in this screenshot:

Figure 6.15 – Using the timeline to modify the FOV

9. You will notice that the **Timeline_0** node now has a new output pin called **Field Of View**. Connect this pin to the **In Field Of View** input pin of the **Set Field of View** node. Now, connect the **Update** output execution pin from the **Timeline_0** node to the **Set Field of View** node.

    This sets up the functions so that every time the FOV value is updated, it passes the new value to the **Set Field Of View** function. Because of our timeline setup, many values between 90 and 45 will be passed to set, enabling a gradual transition between the two extremes over 0.3 seconds.

10. Finally, we want the zooming to end when the right mouse button is released. To do this, drag the **Released** pin from the **InputAction Zoom** node to the **Reverse** pin of the **Timeline** node.

    This will cause the timeline animation to play in reverse order when the right mouse button is released, ensuring that we have a smooth transition back to our normal camera view. Also, remember to apply a comment to the node group so that you remember what this functionality does if you revisit it later.

11. Now, compile, save, and play to test the transition in and out of your zoom view by holding down the right mouse button.

These steps complete our implementation to animate a zoomed view. Now, let's make some adjustments to the `FirstPersonProjectile` Blueprint.

Increasing the projectile's speed

Now that we have given the player character a new gameplay option to navigate the world, our focus will be back on the shooting mechanics. Right now, the shots fired from the gun on the controller are spheres that slowly arc through the air. We want to better approximate the fast-moving bullets that we are used to from traditional shooters.

To change the properties of **Projectile**, we need to open the Blueprint called
`FirstPersonProjectile`, which is in the `Content | FirstPersonBP |
Blueprints` folder. Once opened, look at the **Components** panel and click on
Projectile. This is a projectile movement Component that has been added in the
`FirstPersonProjectile` Blueprint to define how the sphere will travel once it is
created in the world:

1. In the **Details** panel, you will see that **Projectile** has a lot of variables that describe
    its movement. We are interested in only a few of these at this time:

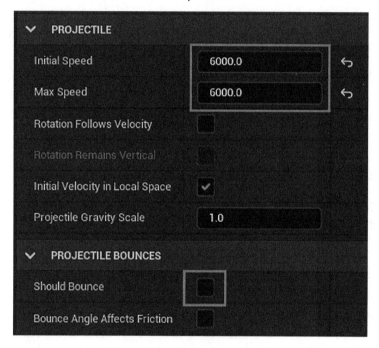

Figure 6.16 – Projectile variables

First, find the **Initial Speed** and **Max Speed** fields, which are currently set to 3000. **Initial
Speed** determines how fast the projectile travels when it is first created at the tip of our
gun, and **Max Speed** determines how fast it can go if an additional force is applied to it
after creation. If we had a rocket, we might wish to apply acceleration to the rocket after it
is launched to signify the thruster engaging. However, since we are representing a bullet
coming from a gun, it makes more sense to make its initial speed the fastest that the
bullet will ever travel at. Adjust both **Initial Speed** and **Max Speed** to twice their original
value: 6000.

Let's change the **Projectile Gravity Scale** from 1.0 to 0.1. That way, the bullet appears
very light and thus not affected by gravity much.

Additionally, you might have noticed that the current projectile bounces off walls and objects as if it were a rubber ball. However, we want to mimic a harder and more forcefully impacting projectile. To remove the bouncing, look for the **Projectile Bounces** section in the **Details** panel and uncheck the box next to **Should Bounce**. The other values dictate the way in which the projectile bounces only if **Should Bounce** is checked, so there is no need to adjust them.

One last change to make in **Event Graph** is to connect the **False** pin of the **Branch** node to the **DestroyActor** function so that the projectile is always `Destroyed` when it collides with anything:

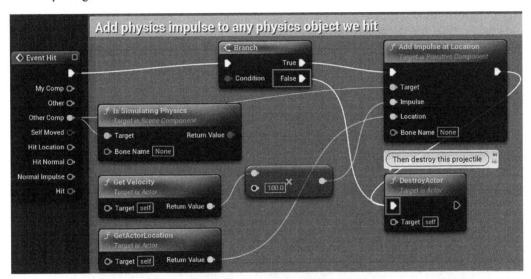

Figure 6.17 – Projectile Event Graph

Now, compile, save, and click on **Play**. You will find that shooting the gun results in a much further-reaching projectile and that the projectile does not bounce off the walls anymore.

We modified the projectile's speed and unchecked the bouncing property to make the projectile behaves like a bullet. The next Blueprint we will modify is the `BP_CylinderTarget` to simulate an explosion when it is destroyed.

Adding sound and particle effects

Now that we have the player moving and shooting to our liking, let's turn our attention to the enemy targets. Shooting one of the target Cylinders currently results in it changing its color to red. However, there is nothing that the player can currently do to destroy a target outright.

We can add more dynamics to our enemy interaction by producing Blueprint logic that destroys the target if it is shot more than once, while also increasing the reward for the player by producing a satisfying sound and visual effect once the target is destroyed.

Changing target states with branches

Since we want to generate effects that will be triggered by changes in the state applied to our target Cylinder, we must ensure that this logic is contained within our `BP_CylinderTarget` Blueprint, which is in the `Content | FirstPersonBP | Blueprints` folder. Open the Blueprint and look at the node group connected to **Event Hit**. Right now, when our projectile hits the Cylinder object, these nodes tell it to swap to a red material. To add the ability to change how the Cylinder behaves when it is shot more than once, we will need to add a check to our Blueprints to see if the Cylinder has already been hit, and then trigger a different result depending on its state.

We will use a **Branch** node to help us handle this scenario:

Figure 6.18 – Using the Branch node to check if the Cylinder has already been hit

The **Branch** node takes a Boolean variable as an input. Since Boolean values can only be either **True** or False, the **Branch** node can produce only two outcomes. These two outcomes can be executed by linking additional nodes to the two output execution pins, representing the **True** path and the **False** path.

The first step of creating **Branch** is to determine what will be represented by your Boolean, and what will cause the conditional value to change from **False** to **True**. In our case, we want to create a **Primed** variable to show that the target has been hit and that it could be destroyed with a second hit. Let's go ahead and create a **Primed** Boolean variable:

1. In the **My Blueprint** panel, click on the + button of the **Variables** category to add a new variable. Set **Variable Type** to **Boolean** and give the name `Primed` to the new variable.

2. Compile and save the Blueprint. Because we do not want our targets to be in a **Primed** state before they have been hit for the first time, we will leave the default value of our variable as **False** (represented by an unchecked box).

3. Now that you have a **Primed** Boolean variable, drag it from the **My Blueprint** panel to **Event Graph**, and select the **Get** option that appears in the submenu when you drop the variable on Event Graph..

4. Click and drag a wire from the output pin of the new **Primed** node to empty grid space on **Event Graph**. Search for and add the **Branch** node.

5. Finally, we can add **Branch** to our **Event Hit** Blueprint group. Break the connection between the **Cast To FirstPersonProjectile** and **Set Material** nodes by holding down the *Alt* key and clicking on one of the execution pins.

6. Drag the **Set Material** node out of the way for a moment, and then connect the output execution pin of the **Cast To** node to the input execution pin of the **Branch** node. This Blueprint will now call the **Branch** evaluation every time the target Cylinder is hit by a projectile.

Now that we have our **Branch** node set up, we need to provide the target Cylinder with instructions on what to do in each state. Namely, what should happen when it is first hit (the **Primed** variable is **False**) and what should happen when it is hit a second time (the **Primed** variable is **True**).

Let's handle when the target is hit for the first time. In this case, we must change **Material** to **TargetRed**. Additionally, we will also have to set our **Primed** Boolean variable to **True**. This way, when the target is hit again, the **Branch** node will route the behavior to the **True** execution pin. The **False** execution sequence of nodes will look like this:

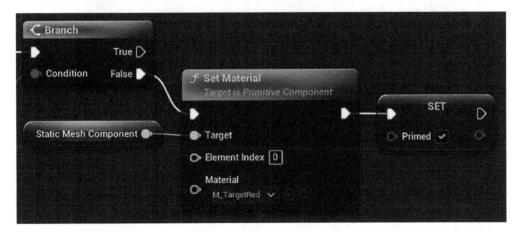

Figure 6.19 – Changing to a red material when hit for the first time

7. Drag the **Set Material** node you moved aside before to the right of the **Branch** node, and then connect the **False** output execution pin of the **Branch** node to the **Set Material** node's input execution pin.

8. Now, drag the **Primed** variable from the **My Blueprint** panel to **Event Graph**, and select the **SET** option. Connect this node to the **Set Material** node's output execution pin and click on the checkbox next to **Primed** within the **SET** node. This will ensure that the next time **Target** is hit, **Branch** evaluates to **True**.

We defined the actions of the **False** path of the **Branch** node. The next step is to define the sequence of actions that will be triggered from the **True** path of the **Branch** node.

Triggering sound effects, explosions, and destruction

There are three things we wanted to accomplish when destroying a target. These were hearing an explosion, seeing an explosion, and removing the target object from the game world. We'll start with the often undervalued, but always critical, element of satisfying game experiences: sound.

The most basic interaction we can design with sound is to play a .wav sound file at a location in the game world once, and this will work perfectly for our purpose. Drag a wire from the **True** execution node of the **Branch** node to empty grid space, and search for the **Play Sound at Location** node:

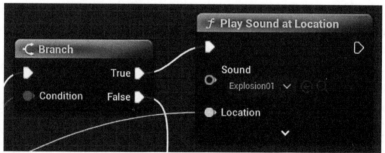

Figure 6.20 – Playing an explosion sound

Play Sound at Location is a simple node that takes a **Sound** file input and a **Location** input, and then—as you might have guessed—plays the sound at that location. There are several sound files included in the **Starter Content** we brought into this project, and you can see the list of these by clicking on the drop-down menu underneath the **Sound** input. Find and select **Explosion01** to set an explosion **Sound** effect.

Now that we have set **Sound**, we need to determine where the sound will play. We can use a process like the one we used to set the FOV by taking the Static Mesh Component of the Cylinder target, extracting its location value, and then linking that location vector directly to our **Sound** node. However, the **Event Hit** trigger will make this process easier on us.

One of the many output pins on the **Event Hit** node is called **Hit Location**. This pin contains the location in the space where the two objects evaluated by **Event Hit** collide with one another. The location of our projectile hitting the target is a perfectly reasonable place to generate the explosion effect, so go ahead and drag a wire from **Hit Location** on the **Event Hit** node to the **Location** input pin on **Play Sound at Location**.

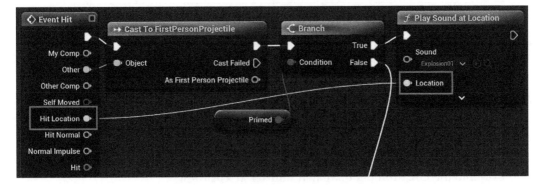

Figure 6.21 – Using the Hit Location

Compile, save, and play to test the Blueprint. Shooting one of the moving targets once will cause it to turn red. Every hit after that should produce an explosion sound effect.

Now that we have set up the sound of our explosion, let's add the visual effect and destroy the Cylinder, following these steps:

1. Drag a wire from the output execution node of **Play Sound at Location** to empty grid space. Search for and select the **Spawn Emitter at Location** node.

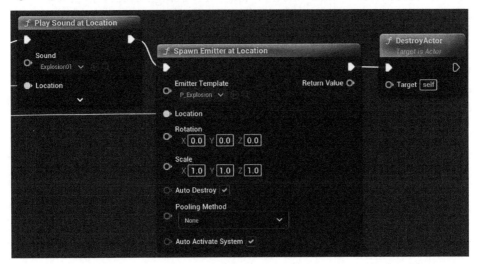

Figure 6.22 – Spawning particle effects

> **Important Note**
>
> An emitter is an object that will produce particle effects in a particular location. Particle effects are collections of small objects that combine to create the visual effect of objects that are fluid, gaseous, or otherwise intangible, such as waterfall impacts, explosions, or light beams.

The **Spawn Emitter at Location** node looks similar to the **Sound** node we are attaching it to, but with more input parameters and the **Auto Destroy** toggle.

2. In the drop-down menu beneath **Emitter Template**, find and select the **P_Explosion** effect. This is another asset that came packed with the Starter Content we pulled into our project and will produce a satisfying-looking explosion wherever its emitter is attached.

3. Since we want the explosion to be generated in the same location as the sound of the explosion, we will click and drag the same **Hit Location** pin of the **Event Hit** node over into the **Location** pin of **Spawn Emitter at Location**.

    The explosion is a 3D effect that looks the same from all angles, so we can leave the **Rotation** input alone. The toggle for **Auto Destroy** determines whether the emitter can be triggered more than once. We will destroy the Actor that contains this emitter once this particle effect is created, so we can leave the toggle box checked.

4. Finally, we want to remove the target Cylinder from the game world after the sound and visual explosion effects are played. Drag the output execution pin from the **Spawn Emitter at Location** node and drop it into empty grid space. Search for and add the **DestroyActor** node. This node takes only a single **Target** input with a default value of **self**, which is a reference to the current instance.

5. Extend the comment box around the entire **Event Hit** sequence of nodes and update the text to describe what the new sequence accomplishes. I chose `When hit, turn red and set to primed. If already primed, destroy self`. The result of this chain of nodes should look like the following screenshot:

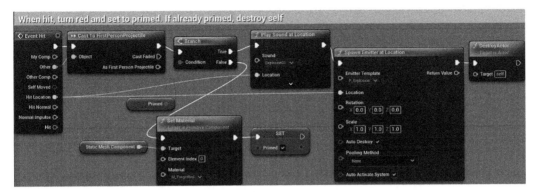

Figure 6.23 – Event Hit actions

Once you have left a useful comment around the Blueprint nodes, compile, save, and click on **Play** to test the new interactions. You should see and hear the Cylinders explode once they have been shot twice by the player's gun.

We saw how to use the **Branch** node to decide the execution flow based on the **Primed** variable that represents the current state of the Cylinder. We also learned how to use Blueprint nodes to play sound and spawn particle effects.

Summary

We've now started going down the path of making our game feel satisfying to the player. We have added sound and visual effects, a player character that has most of the capabilities we would expect from a modern shooter, and targets that react to the player's interactions. The skills we have covered in the first chapters have been combined to start creating increasingly complex and interesting behavior.

In this chapter, we created some customized player controls to allow sprinting and zooming in with our gun. In the process, we explored how the movement controller translates information from a player's inputs into the game experience. We also opened the door to creating simple animations using timelines. Then, we added more feedback to the player's interaction with the environment by attaching an explosion effect and sound to the enemy targets, as well as adding another requirement for them to be hit by two projectiles.

In the next chapter, we will explore adding a UI to our game that provides the player with feedback on their state relative to the world.

Quiz

1. Action and Axis mappings are represented by red Event nodes in the Event Graph.

    a. True

    b. False

2. **Set Field Of View** is a function of the **Character Movement** Component.

    a. True

    b. False

3. A Timeline node can be used to create simple animations.

    a. True

    b. False

4. You can add Particle Effects in runtime using the **Spawn Emitter at Location** function.

    a. True

    b. False

5. The function named **Play Sound** plays a sound at a given location.

    a. True

    b. False

7
Creating Screen UI Elements

At the core of any gaming experience is the method game designers use to communicate the goals and rules of the game to the player. One method of doing this, which is common across all forms of games, is using a **Graphical User Interface (GUI)** to display and broadcast important information to the player. In this chapter, we will set up a GUI that will track the player's health and stamina, and we will set up counters that display the targets eliminated and the ammo of the player. You will learn how to set up a basic **User Interface (UI)** using Unreal's GUI Editor and how to use Blueprints to tie that interface to gameplay values. We will create UI elements using the **Unreal Motion Graphics (UMG) UI Designer**.

In the process, we will cover the following topics:

- Creating simple UI meters with the UMG
- Connecting UI values to player variables
- Tracking the ammo and eliminated targets

By the end of the chapter, you will know how to use the UMG Editor to create progress bars that display the status of health and stamina and also know how to display the number of targets eliminated and the ammo of the player.

Creating simple UI meters with UMG

In this section, we will learn how to use the UMG Editor to create the UI elements that we will use in our game and how to position them on the screen.

The UMG Editor is a visual UI authoring tool. We can use the UMG Editor to create menus and a **Heads-Up Display (HUD)**. A HUD is a transparent display that provides information without requiring the user to look away from the main view. It was initially developed for military aviation. The acronym HUD has become common in games because the information is displayed on the game screen. We want to show meters on the HUD with the amounts of health and stamina the player currently possesses. These meters that appear on the HUD are known as **UI meters**.

The health and stamina UI meters will look like this:

Figure 7.1 – The Health and stamina UI meters

The number of targets eliminated and the ammo of the player will be displayed using text:

Figure 7.2 – Targets eliminated and ammo counters

To create a HUD that will display the UI meters for health and stamina, we will first need to create variables within the player character that can track these values. We will also create the variables that will count the targets eliminated and the ammo of the player.

Follow these steps to create the variables:

1. In the Content Browser, access the `/Content/FirstPersonBP/Blueprints` folder and double-click on the `FirstPersonCharacter` Blueprint.

2. Find the **Variables** category of the **My Blueprint** panel in the Blueprint Editor. Click on the + sign to add a variable, name it `PlayerHealth`, and change **Variable Type** to **Float**.

3. Follow the same steps again to create a second **Float** variable called `PlayerStamina`.

4. Next, create a third variable, but this time, select **Integer** as **Variable Type** and name it `PlayerCurrentAmmo`.

5. Finally, create a second **Integer** variable and name it `TargetsEliminated`. The list of variables should look like this:

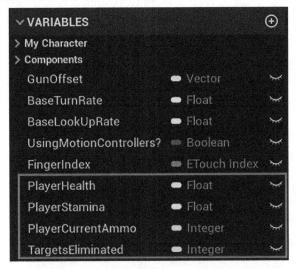

Figure 7.3 – The FirstPersonCharacter variables

6. Compile the `FirstPersonCharacter` Blueprint. Select the **PlayerCurrentAmmo** variable, and in the **Details** panel, set **DEFAULT VALUE** to `30`:

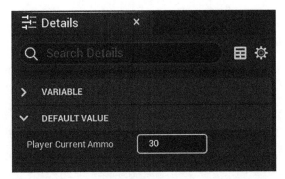

Figure 7.4 – Setting the default value of a variable

7. Set **DEFAULT VALUE** of **PlayerHealth** and **PlayerStamina** to `1.0`. This value is used with the UI meters that will display the degree of fullness between `0.0` and `1.0`. **DEFAULT VALUE** of **TargetsEliminated** was automatically set to `0.0` when we compiled and that is the appropriate value, so there is no need to adjust it.

8. Compile, save, and close the Blueprint Editor.

Now, we will learn how to draw shapes that represent UI meters.

Drawing shapes with Widget Blueprints

The UMG Editor uses a specialized type of Blueprint called a **Widget Blueprint**. Since the **First Person** template has no UI elements by default, we should create a new folder to store our GUI work. Follow these steps to create a folder and a Widget Blueprint:

1. In the Content Browser, access the `/Content/FirstPersonBP/` folder. Right-click in an empty space next to the list of folders and select the **New Folder** option. Name the folder `UI`:

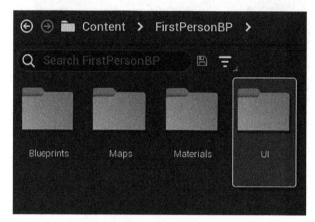

Figure 7.5 – Creating the UI folder

2. Open the **UI** folder you just made, and then right-click in the empty folder space. Go to **User Interface | Widget Blueprint** and name the resulting Blueprint `HUD`:

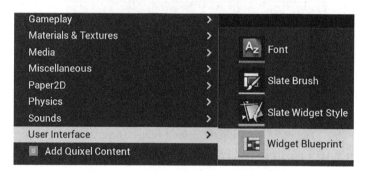

Figure 7.6 – Creating a Widget Blueprint

3. Double-click on this Blueprint to open the UMG Editor. We will use this tool to define how our UI is going to look on the screen.

4. In the UMG Editor, find the panel labeled **Palette**. Inside it, open the category named **PANEL**. You will see a series of containers listed that can organize the UI information:

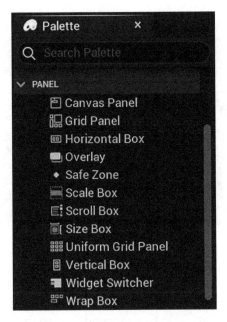

Figure 7.7 – The UMG Editor panel widgets

5. Select and drag **Horizontal Box** out of the **Palette** panel onto the **Hierarchy** panel, releasing it on top of the **Canvas Panel** object. Click **Horizontal Box** under the **Canvas Panel** to select it. In the **Details** panel at the right side of the Editor, change the name of **Horizontal Box** to `Player Stats`:

Figure 7.8 – Changing the name of the horizontal box

6. You should now see the **Player Stats** horizontal box nested underneath the **Canvas Panel** object in the **Hierarchy** panel. Our goal is to create two labeled **Player Stats** bars using a combination of vertical boxes, text, and progress bars. The setup will look like this:

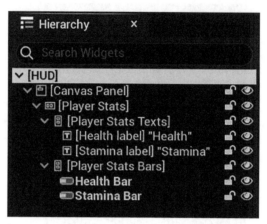

Figure 7.9 – The Player Stats hierarchy

7. Two vertical boxes will contain the text and progress bars of health and stamina. Look again at the **Panel** category within the **Palette** panel, then drag the **Vertical Box** object onto the **Player Stats** horizontal box in **Hierarchy**, and change its name to `Player Stats Texts`. Do this a second time so that the two vertical boxes are aligned underneath **Player Stats**. Change the name of the second **Vertical Box** object to `Player Stats Bars`.

8. Now, look under the **Common** category of the **Palette** panel to find the textboxes and progress bars we need to create the UI. Drag two **Text** objects onto **Player Stats Texts** and two **Progress Bar** objects onto **Player Stats Bars**, as shown in *Figure 7.9*. We already have the UI elements that will be used to display **Player Stats** in our HUD. The next step is to adjust their appearance and positions on the screen.

Customizing the meter's appearance

Now, we need to adjust the UI elements and organize them on the screen. The large rectangular outline in the **Graph** view represents the boundaries of the screen that the player will see, which is called the **canvas**. This is the **Canvas Panel** object that is at the top level of **Hierarchy**. Elements positioned toward the top-left corner of the canvas will appear at the top-left corner of the in-game screen:

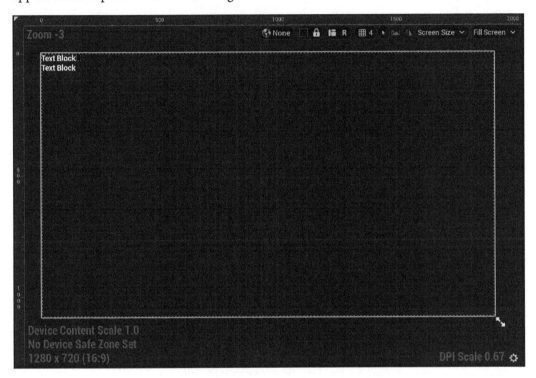

Figure 7.10 – The canvas panel

These are the next steps to set up the health and stamina UI elements:

1. Select **Player Stats** from **Hierarchy** and look at the central graph panel. You will see some size controls that allow you to manipulate the size of the selected objects using the mouse. We will set the position and size of the **Player Stats** horizontal box in the **Details** panel. Set **Position X** to 50.0, **Position Y** to 30.0, **Size X** to 500.0, and **Size Y** to 80.0:

Figure 7.11 – Player Stats' size and position

2. In the **Hierarchy** panel, select the first progress bar underneath **Player Stats Bars**. In the **Details** panel, change the name to Health Bar. Then, in the **Size** toggle under the **SLOT** category, click on the **Fill** button to adjust the vertical height of the bar:

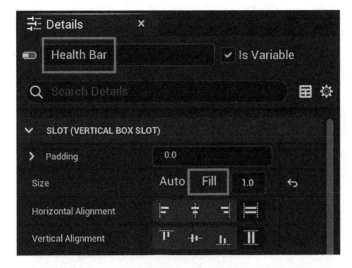

Figure 7.12 – Setting the size of the Health bar to Fill

3. Find **Fill Color and Opacity** under the **APPEARANCE** category, click on the colored rectangle to open **Color Picker**, and select any red color:

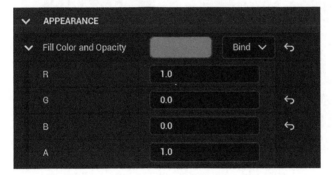

Figure 7.13 – Setting the color of the Health bar

4. Now, let's repeat the same steps for the player's stamina. In the **Hierarchy** panel, click on the second progress bar. In the **Details** panel, change the name to Stamina Bar and click on the **Fill** button. In **Fill Color and Opacity**, select any green color.

5. In the **Hierarchy** panel, click on the **Player Stats Bars** vertical box, and in the **Details** panel, click on the **Fill** button to scale the horizontal size of both the bars.

6. We have our meters looking as we want them to, so now, let's adjust the text labels. Click on the first text object underneath **Player Stats Text** in the **Hierarchy** panel. In the **Details** panel, change the name to Health label.

7. Click on the **Right Align Horizontally** button next to **Horizontal Alignment** to position the text against the bar. Change the **Text** field under the **CONTENT** category to Health. If you wish to change the font size or style, then you can adjust it from the **Font** drop-down menu and fields underneath the **APPEARANCE** category:

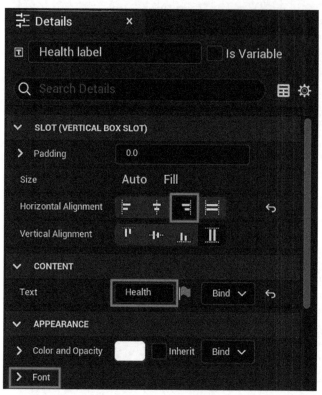

Figure 7.14 – Setting the color of the Health bar

8. Let's repeat the same steps for the stamina label. In the **Hierarchy** panel, click on the second text object.

9. In the **Details** panel, change the name to Stamina label and click on the **Right Align Horizontally** button next to **Horizontal Alignment**. Change the **Text** field of this one to Stamina and adjust the font size and style if you want.

The final bit of adjustment to make is to anchor the UI meters to a side of the screen. Since screen sizes and ratios can vary, we want to ensure that our UI elements remain in the same relative position on the screen. **Anchors** are used to define a widget's desired position on a canvas, regardless of the screen size.

10. To establish an anchor for our meters, select the **Player Stats** top-level object, and in the **Details** panel, click on the **Anchors** dropdown. Select the first option that appears, which shows a gray rectangle at the top-left corner of the screen:

Figure 7.15 – Setting the anchor of Player Stats

This will anchor our meters at the top-left corner, ensuring that they will always appear in that corner regardless of the resolution or ratio.

For now, you can experiment with the progress bars by changing the **Percent** property in the **PROGRESS** category. The range of **Percent** values is 0.0 (empty) to 1.0 (full):

Figure 7.16 – Percent determines the fill position of the progress bar

The following screenshot shows the progress bars with **Percent** set to `1.0`:

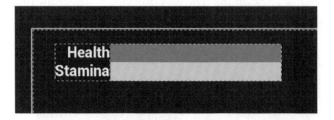

Figure 7.17 – The final appearance of the progress bars

That concludes the customization of the health and stamina UI elements. The next step is to create some UI text elements to display the ammo and targets eliminated counters.

Creating ammo and targets eliminated counters

The ammo and targets eliminated counter displays will work in a similar way to our player statistics meters, except that we want to represent their values through text rather than a continuous meter. The hierarchy of the new UI elements will look like this:

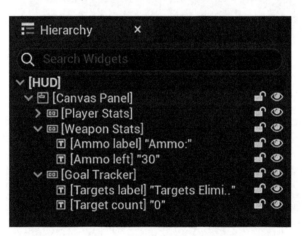

Figure 7.18 – The Weapon Stats and Goal Tracker hierarchy

Player Stats has been minimized, so we can focus on the **Weapon Stats** and **Goal Tracker** elements.

Follow these steps to create these UI elements:

1. Select and drag **Horizontal Box** out of the **Palette** panel onto the **Hierarchy** panel, releasing it on top of the **Canvas Panel** object. In the **Details** panel, change the name of **Horizontal Box** to `Weapon Stats`.

2. We will place the **Weapon Stats** horizontal box at the top-right corner of the screen. In the **Details** panel, click on the **Anchors** dropdown and select the third option. Set **Position X** to -200.0, **Position Y** to 30.0, **Size X** to 160.0, and **Size Y** to 40.0:

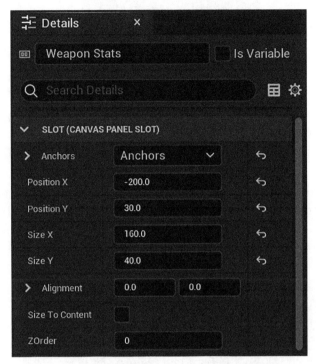

Figure 7.19 – Weapon Stats' size and position

3. Drag a **Text** object onto **Weapon Stats**. In the **Details** panel, change the name to Ammo label. Change the **Text** field under the **CONTENT** category to Ammo: (including the colon).

4. Drag another **Text** object onto **Weapon Stats**. In the **Details** panel, change the name to Ammo left. The value of this element is going to change as ammo is used, but we can give it a default value to visualize on the UMG Editor. Since we have set the default of our ammo variable on the player Blueprint as 30, go ahead and change the **Text** value of **Ammo left** to 30 as well.

5. Select **Weapon Stats** in the **Hierarchy** panel. The icon that looks like a flower is the **Anchor Medallion**, which represents the anchor position of the selected element on the canvas panel:

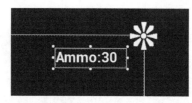

Figure 7.20 – Weapon Stats' Anchor Medallion

6. We will repeat these steps for the goal tracker. Select and drag **Horizontal Box** out of the **Palette** panel onto the **Hierarchy** panel, releasing it on top of the **Canvas Panel** object. In the **Details** panel, change the name of **Horizontal Box** to `Goal Tracker`.

7. We will place the **Goal Tracker** horizontal box at the top-center of the screen. In the **Details** panel, click on the **Anchors** dropdown and select the second option. Set **Position X** to -100.0 and **Position Y** to 50.0. Check the **Size To Content** property so that we don't need to change the values of **Size X** and **Size Y**. The size of this horizontal box will automatically adjust based on the size of its child elements:

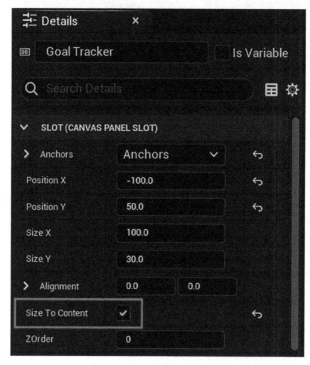

Figure 7.21 – Goal Tracker uses the Size To Content property

8. Drag a **Text** object onto **Goal Tracker**. In the **Details** panel, change the name to `Targets label`. Change the **Text** field under the **CONTENT** category to `Targets Eliminated:` (including the colon).

9. We will increase the font size used by the **Text** objects of **Goal Tracker** to stand out on screen. In the **APPEARANCE** category, change the **Font** size to `32`:

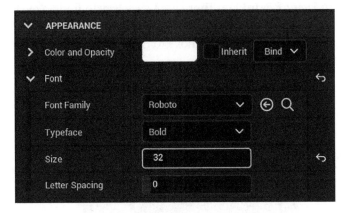

Figure 7.22 – Changing the font size

10. Drag another **Text** object onto **Goal Tracker**. In the **Details** panel, change the name to `Target count`. Change the **Text** field under the **CONTENT** category to `0` and set the **Font** size to `32`. **Goal Tracker** will look like this:

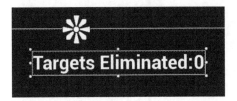

Figure 7.23 – Goal Tracker anchored at the top-center

11. Compile, save, and close the **HUD** Widget Blueprint.

With the UI elements aligned the way we want, we now need to ensure that the game will actually know how to display the HUD. To do this, we need to revisit the Character Blueprint.

Displaying the HUD

To display the HUD in the game, follow these steps:

1. In the Content Browser, access the `/Content/FirstPersonBP/Blueprints` folder and double-click on the `FirstPersonCharacter` Blueprint.

2. We will modify **Event BeginPlay**. There is an easy way to find an event in the EventGraph. Find the **Graphs** category of the **My Blueprint** panel and double-click on **Event BeginPlay**. The Editor will move to the position in the EventGraph where **Event BeginPlay** is already placed:

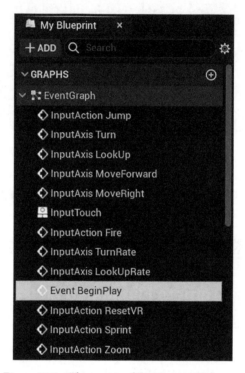

Figure 7.24 – The events of FirstPersonCharacter

3. Delete the previous nodes that were connected to **Event BeginPlay** because they deal with the case of playing the game in VR, and we will not use VR in this example game.

> **Important Information**
>
> In most cases, **Event BeginPlay** will call the subsequent Actions as soon as the game is started. If the Blueprint instance isn't present when the game starts, then instead, it will trigger as soon as the instance is spawned. Since the `FirstPersonCharacter` player instance is present as soon as the game begins, attaching the displaying logic to this event will create the HUD immediately.

4. Drag a wire from the output execution pin of **Event BeginPlay** and add a **Create Widget** node. Within the node, you will see a drop-down menu labeled **Class**. This is our opportunity to use the Widget Blueprint we created. Recall that we named our Widget Blueprint **HUD**. If you click the drop-down menu, then you will see the **HUD** option. Select it to have the player Character Blueprint generate the UI elements you created. The following screenshot shows the **Create HUD Widget** node associated with our HUD Widget Blueprint:

Figure 7.25 – Creating an instance based on the HUD Widget Blueprint

5. Although we now have a Widget generated when the game starts, there is a final step required to get the Widget containing our UI elements to appear on the screen. Drag the **Return Value** output pin into empty grid space and add an **Add to Viewport** node.

6. Create a comment around the three nodes. Label the comment Draw HUD on Screen. The nodes should appear as follows:

Figure 7.26 – The Add to Viewport node shows the Widget Blueprint on screen

7. Now, compile, save, and click on **Play** to test the game.

We've learned how to create text elements and progress bars in the UMG Editor. We've also learned how to use containers, such as horizontal and vertical boxes, to organize UI elements on screen.

When playing the game, you should see the two meters representing the player's health and stamina, as well as numerical counters for ammo and eliminated targets. But as you shoot from your gun, you may notice one very important problem – none of the UI values change! We will address this missing component in the next section.

Connecting UI values to player variables

To allow our UI elements to pull data from our player variables, we need to revisit the HUD Widget Blueprint. To get our UI to update with player data, we will create a **binding**. Bindings give us the ability to tie variables or functions of a Blueprint to a Widget. Whenever the variable or function is updated, that change is reflected in the Widget automatically.

So, instead of manually updating both the player's health stats and our Widget every time the player takes damage (so that the health meter display changes), we can bind the meter to the PlayerHealth player variable. Then, only one value will need to be updated.

Creating bindings for health and stamina

To create the bindings of the `PlayerHealth` and `PlayerStamina` variables with the progress bars' UI, follow these steps:

1. In the Content Browser, access the `/Content/FirstPersonBP/UI` folder and double-click on the **HUD** Widget Blueprint.

2. In the **HUD** UMG Editor, find the **Hierarchy** panel and click on the **Health Bar** object nested underneath the **Player Stats Bars** object.

3. With **Health Bar** now selected, locate the **Percent** field in the **Progress** category of the **Details** panel. Click on the **Bind** button next to **Percent** and select **Create Binding**, as shown in the following screenshot:

Figure 7.27 – Creating binding for the Health bar

4. The UMG Editor will switch from the **Designer** view to the **Graph** view. A new function has been created, allowing us to script a connection between the meter and the `PlayerHealth` variable. Right-click on any empty graph space and add a **Get Player Character** node.

5. Drag a wire from the **Return Value** output pin of the new node to empty space and add the **Cast To FirstPersonCharacter** node.

6. Break the execution pin connection between the **Get Health Bar Percent 0** and **Return Node** nodes, and instead, connect **Get Health Bar Percent 0** to our casting node, as shown here:

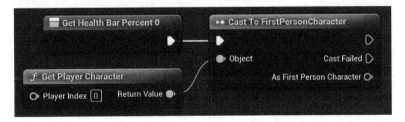

Figure 7.28 – Getting a reference to the FirstPersonCharacter instance

7. Next, drag a wire from the **As First Person Character** output pin to empty grid space, and add a **Get Player Health** node. Finally, connect the **Cast To FirstPersonCharacter** node execution pin to **Return Node**, as shown in the following screenshot:

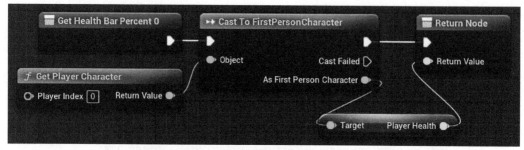

Figure 7.29 – The value of the Player Health variable will be used as the percent of Health Bar

8. That's all we need to do to connect **Player Health** to the **Health Bar** UI. We need to follow the same operation for the player's stamina. Click on the button at the top-right of the screen labeled **Designer** to return to the **Canvas** view:

Figure 7.30 – Buttons to change the UMG Editor mode

9. Select **Stamina Bar** in the **Hierarchy** panel. By following the steps outlined previously for **Health Bar**, create a binding that connects the **Player Stamina** variable to the meter:

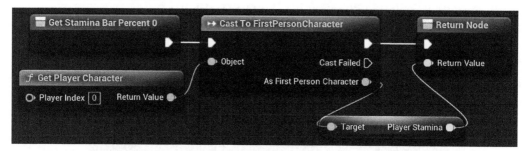

Figure 7.31 – The value of the Player Stamina variable will be used as the percent of Stamina Bar

10. Compile and save your work.

The next step is to hook up our bindings for the ammo and goal counters.

Making text bindings for the ammo and targets eliminated counters

The ammo and targets eliminated counters will be represented by texts on the HUD. Follow these steps to bind the counters:

1. Click on the **Designer** button to return to the canvas interface once more. This time, we want to select the **Ammo left** text object in **Hierarchy**, which can be found under **Weapon Stats**.

2. In the **Details** panel, find the **Bind** button next to the **Text** field and create a new binding, as shown here:

Figure 7.32 – Creating a binding for Ammo left

3. We will follow the same pattern for this binding as we did for health and stamina. In the **Get Ammoleft Text 0** graph view that appears, create a **Get Player Character** node, cast it using the **Cast To FirstPersonCharacter** node, and then drag from the **As First Person Character** pin to add a **Get Player Current Ammo** node.

4. Finally, attach both the cast node and the **Player Current Ammo** node to **Return Node**. You will notice that when you attach the **Player Current Ammo** output pin to the **Return Value** input pin, a new **ToText (integer)** node will be created and linked automatically. This is because Unreal Engine knows that for you to display a numerical value as text on the screen, it first needs to convert the number into a text format that the Widget knows how to display. The conversion node will be hooked up already, so there is no need to make further modifications. The following screenshot shows the nodes that are used in the binding:

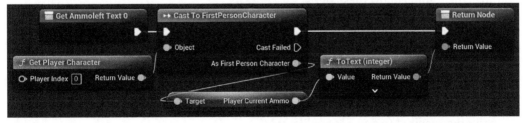

Figure 7.33 – The value of the Player Current Ammo variable will be used as the Text of Ammo left

5. The final binding to create is for the target count. Return to the **Designer** view and select the **Target Count** object in **Hierarchy** under **Goal Tracker**. Click on the **Bind** button next to the **Text** field in the **Details** panel. By following the preceding steps, create the Blueprint nodes that grabs the player character, casts it to the **Cast To FirstPersonCharacter** node, and connects the **Targets Eliminated** variable to the casting and return nodes. As with the ammo count, a **To Text (integer)** node for conversion will be automatically generated and connected for you. The result should look like this:

Figure 7.34 – The value of Targets Eliminated variable will be used as the text of the Target count

We've now successfully bound all our UI elements to player variables. Now is a good time to compile and save our work. Because of our bindings, the UI will now do its job of responding to events that occur within our game. However, we still need to create the events that will trigger changes in the variables we have connected. In the next section, we will modify the player variables based on Actions that the player takes while playing.

Tracking the ammo and targets eliminated

To get our UI to respond to the player interacting with the environment, we need to modify the player and target Blueprints. Let's start with the ammo counter to decrease when the player fires a shot from their gun.

Reducing the ammo counter

We need to modify the player fire logic so that the ammo counter is decreased when the player fires their gun. Follow these steps:

1. In the Content Browser, access the `/Content/FirstPersonBP/Blueprints` folder and double-click on the `FirstPersonCharacter` Blueprint.

2. Find the large series of Blueprint nodes contained within the **Spawn projectile** comment block. We want to ensure that the counter tracking the player's current ammo count reduces by one each time the player fires a shot. The Blueprint scripting required to do so looks like this:

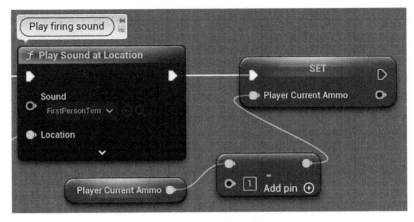

Figure 7.35 – Decreasing Player Current Ammo

3. Find the final node in the chain, **Play Sound at Location**. Drag a wire from the output execution pin of this node to empty grid space and add a **SET Player Current Ammo** node.

4. Drag a wire from the **Player Current Ammo** input pin to empty space and create a **Subtract** node.

5. Drag a wire from the top input pin of the **Subtract** node and add a **GET Player Current Ammo** node.

6. In the bottom field of the **Subtract** node, enter a value of 1. This sequence translates to the following: *after playing the firing sound, set the player's current ammo count to the existing ammo count minus one.*

7. Compile, save, and press **Play** to see your ammo counter decrease every time you fire a shot from your gun. Note that we are not preventing the player from shooting when they are out of ammo, and the ammo counter will continue to register negative numbers. We will fix it in *Chapter 8, Creating Constraints and Gameplay Objectives.*

Important Note

The **SET Player Current Ammo** node and the subtract node of the previous screenshot can be replaced by the **Decrement Int** node, which subtracts 1 from the input variable and sets a new value in it. There is also the **Increment Int** node, which adds 1 to the input variable.

Increasing the targets eliminated counter

Now, we want to increase our targets eliminated counter by 1 every time a target Cylinder is destroyed. These are the steps:

1. In the Content Browser, access the `/Content/FirstPersonBP/Blueprints` folder and double-click on the `BP_CylinderTarget` Blueprint.

2. We will add our new nodes close to the end of **Event Hit**, after all the nodes except **DestroyActor**. There must not be other nodes after a **DestroyActor** node whose **Target** is **self** because this node removes the current instance from the Level.

3. Break the link between the **Spawn Emitter at Location** and **DestroyActor** nodes, and then move **DestroyActor** to the right to make room for the new Blueprint nodes.

4. The goal is to create a series of nodes that will access the **Targets Eliminated** variable from the player character and increase it by one, before going on to destroy the Actor. The result will look like this:

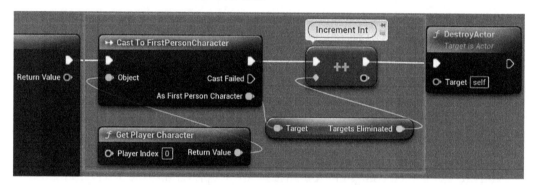

Figure 7.36 – Increasing Targets Eliminated

5. Right-click on any empty graph space and add a **Get Player Character** node.

6. Drag a wire from the **Return Value** output pin of the **Get Player Character** node and add the **Cast To FirstPersonCharacter** node.

7. Drag a wire from the **As First Person Character** pin and add a **GET Targets Eliminated** node.

8. Drag a wire from the output of **Targets Eliminated** and add the **Increment Int** node, which will add 1 to the **Targets Eliminated** variable.

9. Finally, connect the execution pins of the **Cast To FirstPersonCharacter**, **Increment Int**, and **DestroyActor** nodes, ensuring that **DestroyActor** is the final node in the chain.

10. Compile, save, and play the game to see the **Targets Eliminated** counter on the screen increase every time you destroy a Cylinder target:

Figure 7.37 – Destroying the Cylinder target to increase the Targets Eliminated counter

Now, the ammo and targets eliminated counters are being modified by events that occur within our game, and the updated values are displayed immediately in the HUD. The script to modify the health and stamina meters will be implemented in the next chapters.

Summary

In this chapter, we enhanced the player experience by adding a HUD that tracks the player's interaction with the environment. In doing so, we developed another conduit through which we can communicate information to the player of our game. We now have the skeletal structure of a first-person shooter, including guns that shoot, targets that explode, and a UI that exposes the state of the world to the player. We have already come a long way from the initial test scene, which featured minimal player interaction.

In the next chapter, we will begin transitioning from building the foundation of our game structure to constructing the design of our game. The core of any game is made up of the rules that the player must follow to create a fun experience. While the game, in its current form, features some basic rules that define how the targets react to being shot, the overall experience lacks a goal for the player to achieve. We will rectify this by establishing a `win` condition for the player, as well as providing additional constraints that make the experience holistic and consistent.

Quiz

1. What is the name of the specialized type of Blueprint used to create a UI?

    a. UMG Blueprint

    b. Widget Blueprint

2. The `Percent` property determines the fill position of a progress bar.

    a. True

    b. False

3. The *X* and *Y* values of an element's position in a canvas are always relative to the top-left corner of the screen.

    a. True

    b. False

4. We can bind a property of a Widget to a function to retrieve the updated value of a variable.

    a. True

    b. False

5. To create an instance of a Widget Blueprint and show it on the screen, you need to use the `Create Widget` and `Add to Viewport` nodes.

    a. True

    b. False

8
Creating Constraints and Gameplay Objectives

In this chapter, we'll define a ruleset for our game, which will guide the player through the gameplay experience. We want to give the player the ability to start the game and immediately identify what they must do to win the game. In its most basic form, a game could be defined by the win condition and the steps the player can take to reach that win condition. Ideally, we want to ensure that each step the player takes toward that goal is fun.

We'll begin by applying some constraints to the player to increase the level of difficulty. A game without a challenge quickly becomes boring, and we want to ensure that every mechanic in our game provides the player with an interesting choice or challenge. We'll then set up a goal for the player to achieve, along with the necessary adjustments to our enemy targets to make that goal challenging to reach.

In this process, we'll work to accomplish the following:

- Reducing stamina while the player is sprinting and regenerating it when the player is not sprinting
- Preventing the player's gun from firing if they run out of ammo
- Creating ammo pickups that allow the player to regain ammo
- Defining a win condition based on the number of targets eliminated
- Creating a menu that allows the player to replay or quit the game upon winning

By the end of the chapter, we will have a game with constraints and goals that make the gameplay more interesting. We will learn how to create collectible objects and how to create a menu system.

Constraining player actions

One important consideration to make when adding enhanced capabilities for the player is the impact that they have on both the challenge and feel of the game experience. Recall that we added the ability for the player to sprint in *Chapter 6, Enhancing Player Abilities*, by holding down the *Shift* key. As it currently stands, holding down the *Shift* key while moving provides a significant increase in the speed at which the player can move. Without constraints applied to this ability, such as an enforced waiting period between uses, there would be nothing discouraging the player from always holding down the *Shift* key as they move.

This goes against the goal we set out to accomplish by adding a sprint functionality, which was to provide more options to the player. If an option is so attractive that the player feels compelled to always utilize it, then it doesn't increase the number of interesting choices available to the player. From the player's perspective, the result would be the same if we just increased the base speed of the player to the sprint speed.

We can rectify this, and other issues currently faced by our game prototype, by adding constraints that limit a player's abilities, to increase decision making.

Draining and regenerating stamina

To add a constraint to the sprinting ability of the player, we'll need to return to the player character Blueprint where we originally defined the ability. We need to create some variables that will keep track of whether the player is sprinting, how much stamina sprinting should cost, and the stamina recharge rate. We are going to create a custom event to drain the player's stamina at a consistent rate while they are sprinting and to recharge the stamina when they are not sprinting. Also, we will create other variables and macros to organize the script.

These are the variables that we will create:

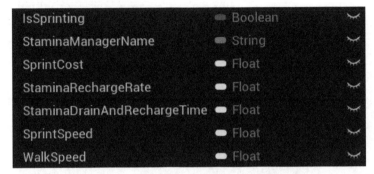

Figure 8.1 – Variables used in the stamina system

These are the macros that we will create to organize the stamina system:

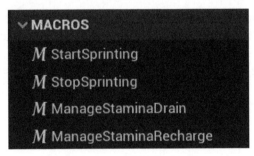

Figure 8.2 – Macros used in the stamina system

Creating the variables

Follow these steps to create the variables needed for the new stamina system:

1. In **Content Browser**, access the /Content/FirstPersonBP/Blueprints
   folder and double-click on the FirstPersonCharacter Blueprint.

2. In the **VARIABLES** category of the **My Blueprint** panel, click the + button to add
   a variable. In the **Details** panel, name the variable IsSprinting and change
   Variable Type to **Boolean**:

Figure 8.3 – The IsSprinting Boolean variable

3. Create another variable in the **My Blueprint** panel. In the **Details** panel, name the
   variable StaminaManagerName and change **Variable Type** to **String**. Compile
   the Blueprint and set **DEFAULT VALUE** to ManageStamina. This variable
   stores the name of the stamina custom event, and we will use it when starting and
   stopping the timer. We are creating this variable to avoid bugs due to spelling errors
   that could occur if the name was always typed in manually:

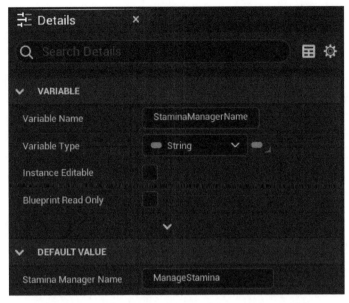

Figure 8.4 – The StaminaManagerName string variable

4. Now we will start to create the **Float** variables. In the **VARIABLES** category of the **My Blueprint** panel, click the **+** button to add a variable. In the **Details** panel, name the variable `SprintCost` and change **Variable Type** to **Float**. Compile the Blueprint and set **DEFAULT VALUE** to `0.05`:

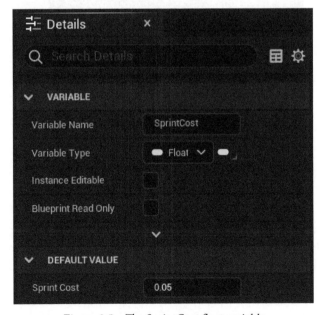

Figure 8.5 – The SprintCost float variable

5. Follow the same steps again to create a second **Float** variable called `StaminaRechargeRate`. Compile the Blueprint and set **DEFAULT VALUE** to `0.01`.

6. Create another **Float** variable called `StaminaDrainAndRechargeTime`. Compile the Blueprint and set **DEFAULT VALUE** to `0.2`.

7. Create another **Float** variable called `SprintSpeed`. Compile the Blueprint and set **DEFAULT VALUE** to `2200`.

8. Create another **Float** variable called `WalkSpeed`. Compile the Blueprint and set **DEFAULT VALUE** to `600`. We created the `SprintSpeed` and `WalkSpeed` variables so that we can modify the speed values in one place instead of looking in the script for the various places where these values are used.

Creating the StopSprinting macro

Now, let's create the first macro. We will start with the simplest of the macros: `StopSprinting`.

These are the steps to create the macro:

1. In the **My Blueprint** panel, click the + button in the **MACROS** category to create a macro. Change the name of the macro to `StopSprinting`:

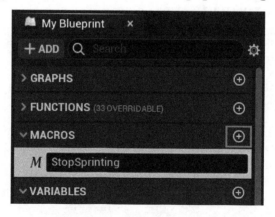

Figure 8.6 – Creating a macro

2. By default, macros don't have execution pins. We need to add them as parameters. Use the **Details** panel of the macro to create an input parameter named `In` of the **Exec** type and an output parameter named `Out` of the **Exec** type:

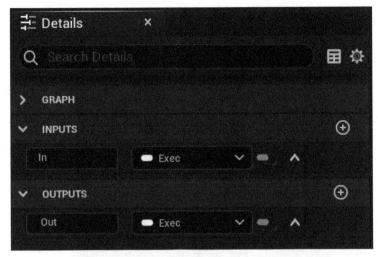

Figure 8.7 – Adding the execution pins in a macro

3. On the tab created for the **StopSprinting** macro, add the nodes seen in the following screenshot. All it does is set **Is Sprinting** to `false` and **Max Walk Speed** back to the value stored in the **Walk Speed** variable:

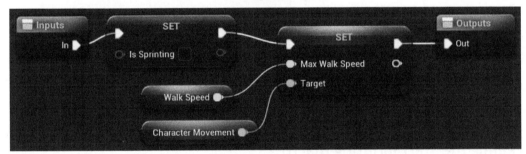

Figure 8.8 – The StopSprinting macro

4. Drag a wire from the **In** pin of the **Inputs** node and add a **SET Is Sprinting** node. Leave the **Is Sprinting** input parameter unchecked.

5. Click on the **Character Movement** component in the **Components** panel and drag it onto **Event Graph**:

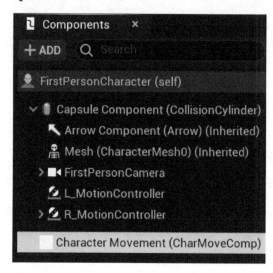

Figure 8.9 – Drag the Character Movement component to Event Graph

6. Drag a wire from the output pin of the **Character Movement** node and add the **SET Max Walk Speed** node.

7. Drag a wire from the input pin of **SET Max Walk Speed** and add a **GET Walk Speed** node.

8. Connect the white execution pins of the **SET Is Sprinting**, **SET Max Walk Speed**, and **Outputs** nodes. Compile the Blueprint.

Creating the StartSprinting macro

The StartSprinting macro contains the actions that set up the sprinting.

Follow these steps to create the macro:

1. In the **My Blueprint** panel, click the + button in the **MACROS** category. Change the name of the macro to StartSprinting.

2. In the **Details** panel of the macro, create an input parameter named In of the **Exec** type and an output parameter named Out of the **Exec** type as shown in *Figure 8.7*.

3. On the tab created for the **StartSprinting** macro, add the nodes seen in the
    following screenshot. The first half of the **StartSprinting** macro is almost the same
    as **StopSprinting**, just with appropriate values. The **Branch** node checks whether
    we already have the **Stamina Manager** timer going. If we have, the macro is done
    and we can exit. If the timer does not exist yet, we set it:

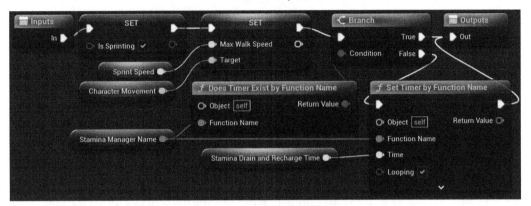

Figure 8.10 – The StartSprinting macro

4. Drag a wire from the **In** pin of the **Inputs** node and add a **SET Is Sprinting** node.
    Check the **Is Sprinting** input parameter.

5. Click on the **Character Movement** component in the **Components** panel and drag
    it onto **Event Graph**.

6. Drag a wire from the output pin of the **Character Movement** node and add the **SET
    Max Walk Speed** node.

7. Drag a wire from the input pin of the **SET Max Walk Speed** node and add a **GET
    Sprint Speed** node.

8. Connect the white execution pins of the **SET Is Sprinting** and **SET Max Walk
    Speed** nodes.

9. Drag a wire from the white output pin of the **SET Max Walk Speed** node and add
    a **Branch** node.

10. Drag a wire from the **True** output pin of the **Branch** node and connect it to the
    Out pin of the **Outputs** node.

11. Drag a wire from the **Condition** input pin of the **Branch** node and add a **Does
    Timer Exist by Function Name** node.

12. Drag a wire from the **Function Name** pin of the **Does Timer Exist by Function Name** node and add a **GET Stamina Manager Name** node.

13. Drag a wire from the **False** output pin of the **Branch** node and add a **Set Timer by Function Name** node. Connect the white output pin of the **Set Timer by Function Name** node to the **Out** pin of the **Outputs** node.

14. Drag a wire from **GET Stamina Manager Name** and connect it to the **Function Name** pin of the **Set Timer by Function Name** node.

15. Drag a wire from the **Time** pin of the **Set Timer by Function Name** node and add a **GET Stamina Drain and Recharge Time** node.

16. Check the **Looping** input parameter of the **Set Timer by Function Name** node. Since the value of the **Stamina Drain and Recharge Time** variable is 0.2, this timer will call the function/event five times a second. Compile the Blueprint.

Creating the ManageStaminaDrain macro

The ManageStaminaDrain macro drains **Player Stamina** and checks for conditions that stop the sprinting.

These are the steps to create the macro:

1. In the **My Blueprint** panel, click the + button in the **MACROS** category to create another macro. Change the name of the macro to ManageStaminaDrain.

2. In the **Details** panel of the macro, create an input parameter named In of the **Exec** type and an output parameter named Out of the **Exec** type as shown in *Figure 8.7*.

3. On the tab created for the **ManageStaminaDrain** macro, add the nodes seen in the following screenshot. There are two conditions for the player to keep sprinting and draining stamina: the player needs to be moving and **Player Stamina** must be greater than zero.

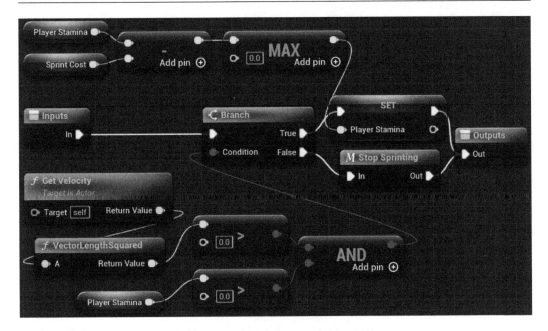

Figure 8.11 – The ManageStaminaDrain macro

4. Drag a wire from the **In** pin of the **Inputs** node and add a **Branch** node.

5. Drag a wire from the **Condition** input pin of the **Branch** node and add an **AND** Boolean node.

6. Drag a wire from the top input pin of the **AND** node and add a **Greater** node.

7. Right-click on the empty space of **Event Graph** and add a **Get Velocity** node.

8. Drag a wire from the **Return Value** pin of the **Get Velocity** node and add a **VectorLengthSquared** node. If the return value of the **VectorLengthSquared** node is greater than zero, then the player is moving. As in our case, we only want to know if the velocity is greater than zero, we use **VectorLengthSquared** instead of **VectorLength** to avoid a square root.

9. Drag a wire from the **Return Value** pin of the **VectorLengthSquared** node and connect it to the top input pin of the **Greater** node.

10. Drag a wire from the bottom input pin of the **AND** node and add a **Greater** node.

11. Drag a wire from the top input pin of the **Greater** node and add a **GET Player Stamina** node.

12. Drag a wire from the **True** output pin of the **Branch** node and add a **SET Player Stamina** node. Connect the white output pin of the **SET Player Stamina** node to the **Out** pin of the **Outputs** node.

13. Drag a wire from the input pin of **SET Player Stamina** and add a **Max (float)** node. This node returns the highest value of the input parameters. We use this node to ensure that **Player Stamina** will never be less than 0.0.

14. Drag a wire from the top input pin of the **Max (float)** node and create a **Subtract** node.

15. Drag a wire from the top input pin of the **Subtract** node and add a **GET Player Stamina** node.

16. Drag a wire from the bottom input pin of the **Subtract** node and add a **GET Sprint Cost** node.

17. Drag a wire from the **False** output pin of the **Branch** node and add the **Stop Sprinting** macro node. Connect the white output pin of the **Stop Sprinting** node to the **Out** pin of the **Outputs** node.

Creating the ManageStaminaRecharge macro

The `ManageStaminaRecharge` macro recharges **Player Stamina** until it is full.

Follow these steps to create the macro:

1. In the **My Blueprint** panel, click the + button in the **MACROS** category to create another macro. Change the name of the macro to `ManageStaminaRecharge`.

2. In the **Details** panel of the macro, create an input parameter named `In` of the **Exec** type and an output parameter named `Out` of the **Exec** type as shown in *Figure 8.7*.

3. On the tab created for the **ManageStaminaRecharge** macro, add the nodes seen in the following screenshot. If **Player Stamina** is full (nearly equal to 1.0), we clear the timer for **Stamina Manager**. If **Player Stamina** isn't full, we increment it.

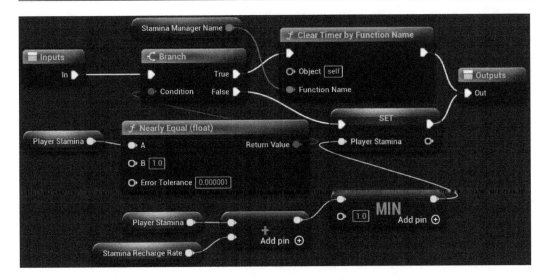

Figure 8.12 – The ManageStaminaRecharge macro

4. Drag a wire from the **In** pin of the **Inputs** node and add a **Branch** node.

5. Drag a wire from the **Condition** input pin of the **Branch** node and add a **Nearly Equal (float)** node. Enter the value 1.0 in the **B** input parameter of the **Nearly Equal (float)** node. We are using the **Nearly Equal (float)** node because it has an **Error Tolerance** property that is needed to compare values with floating-point precision.

6. Drag a wire from the **A** input parameter of the **Nearly Equal (float)** node and add a **GET Player Stamina** node.

7. Drag a wire from the **True** output pin of the **Branch** node and add a **Clear Timer by Function Name** node.

8. Drag a wire from the **Function Name** parameter of **Clear Timer by Function Name** and add a **GET Stamina Manager Name** node.

9. Connect the white output pin of **Clear Timer by Function Name** to the **Out** pin of the **Outputs** node.

10. Drag a wire from the **False** output pin of the **Branch** node and add a **SET Player Stamina** node. Connect the white output pin of **SET Player Stamina** to the **Out** pin of the **Outputs** node.

11. Drag a wire from the input pin of **SET Player Stamina** and add a **Min (float)** node. Enter the value 1.0 in the second input parameter of the **Min (float)** node. This node returns the lowest value of the input parameters. We use this node to ensure that **Player Stamina** will never be greater than 1.0.

12. Drag a wire from the top input pin of the **Min (float)** node and create an **Add** node.

13. Drag a wire from the top input pin of the **Add** node and add a **GET Player Stamina** node.

14. Drag a wire from the bottom input pin of the **Add** node and add a **GET Stamina Recharge Rate** node.

Updating the InputAction Sprint event

We need to modify the **InputAction Sprint** event to use the new stamina system.

Follow these steps:

1. Look in the **GRAPHS** category of the **My Blueprint** panel and double-click on **InputAction Sprint**. The editor will move to the position in **Event Graph** where **InputAction Sprint** is already placed:

Figure 8.13 – Finding the InputAction Sprint event

2. Delete the previous nodes that were connected to **InputAction Sprint**. We will add the nodes seen in the following screenshot. When the *Shift* key is pressed, the game checks whether there is enough stamina to begin sprinting, that is, whether the current **PlayerStamina** amount is greater than or equal to **SprintCost**. If the player has enough stamina to start sprinting, the **Start Sprinting** macro is called. When the *Shift* key is released, the **Stop Sprinting** macro is called.

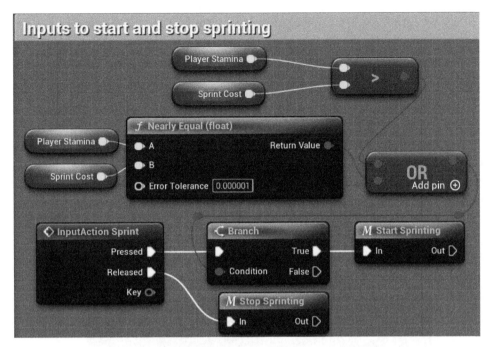

Figure 8.14 – The new version of the InputAction Sprint event

3. Drag a wire from the **Pressed** output pin of the **InputAction Sprint** node and add a **Branch** node.

4. Drag a wire from the **Condition** input pin of the **Branch** node and add an **OR** Boolean node.

5. Drag a wire from the top input pin of the **OR** node and add a **Greater** node. We cannot use the **Greater Equal** node because we need to use the **Nearly Equal (float)** node to verify that the two **Float** variables are equal.

6. Drag a wire from the top input pin of the **Greater** node and add a **GET Player Stamina** node.

7. Drag a wire from the bottom input pin of the **Greater** node and add a **GET Sprint Cost** node.

8. Drag a wire from the bottom input pin of the **OR** node and add a **Nearly Equal (float)** node.

1. Drag a wire from the **A** input pin of the **Nearly Equal (float)** node and add a **GET Player Stamina** node.

2. Drag a wire from the **B** input pin of the **Nearly Equal (float)** node and add a **GET Sprint Cost** node.

3. Drag a wire from the **True** output pin of the **Branch** node and add the **Start Sprinting** macro node.

4. Drag a wire from the **Released** output pin of the **InputAction Sprint** node and add the **Stop Sprinting** macro node.

5. Change the label of the comment box to Inputs to start and stop sprinting.

Creating the ManageStamina custom event

We will now create the custom ManageStamina event, which checks whether the player is sprinting and calls the appropriate macro to drain or recharge the stamina.

These are the steps to create the custom event:

1. Right-click on the empty space of **Event Graph**. Search for custom event and select **Add Custom Event…**. Rename the custom event to ManageStamina.

Figure 8.15 – Adding a custom event

2. Add the nodes shown in the following screenshot. This checks whether the player is sprinting and calls the appropriate macro:

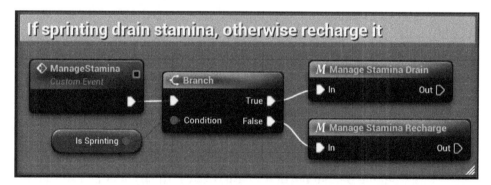

Figure 8.16 – The ManageStamina custom event

Compile, save, and test the game. As you sprint around the level, you should see your stamina meter running out if you're holding the left *Shift* key, and the stamina recharging when it's not held down and the player is walking or at rest.

We've completed the actions needed to manage stamina and sprinting, and our next step is to implement a constraint related to the player's ammunition.

Preventing firing actions when out of ammo

For the next constraint that we'll place on the player's abilities, we need to restrict the player from firing their gun when they reach an ammo count of 0. We will add a **Branch** node right after the **InputAction Fire** event:

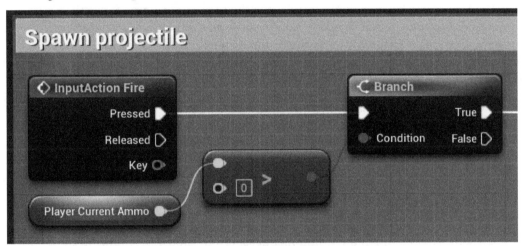

Figure 8.17 – Testing whether a player has ammo

To do that, follow these steps:

1. In the **GRAPHS** category of the **My Blueprint** panel, double-click on the **InputAction Fire** event to move to the position in **Event Graph** where **InputAction Fire** is already placed.

2. Drag from the **Pressed** pin of **InputAction Fire** and drop on an empty space to open **Context Menu**. Add a **Branch** node. The **Branch** node will automatically connect to **InputAction Fire** and to the next node in the chain.

3. Drag a wire from the **Condition** input pin of the **Branch** node to empty space and add a **Greater** node.

4. Drag a wire from the top input pin of the **Greater** node and add a **GET Player Current Ammo** node. Leave the bottom input field of the **Greater** node at its default value of 0.

Now, compile, save, and test your game. You should find that the gun no longer fires when the ammo counter reaches 0.

We have completed the player constraints, and now we need a new Blueprint to provide ammo for the player.

Creating collectible objects

Restricting the player from firing their gun when they run out of ammo forces the player to be considerate of the accuracy of the shots they attempt within the game. However, limiting ammo would be unduly punishing without a way of acquiring more. We don't want ammo to naturally recharge like our stamina meter. Instead, we'll create a collectible ammo pickup to allow the player to regain ammo by exploring and traversing the level.

To create the **BP_AmmoPickup** Blueprint, follow these steps:

1. In the **Content Browser**, access the /Content/FirstPersonBP /Blueprints folder. Click the **Add** button and select **Blueprint Class**.

2. On the next screen, choose **Actor** as the parent class.

3. Name the Blueprint BP_AmmoPickup and double-click it to open the Blueprint Editor.

4. Click the **Add** button in the **Components** panel and choose the **Static Mesh** component. In the **Details** panel, choose the **Shape_Pipe** Static Mesh and in **MATERIALS**, go to **Element 0** and choose **M_Door**. Change the **X**, **Y**, and **Z** values of the **Scale** attribute to 0.5, as shown in the following screenshot:

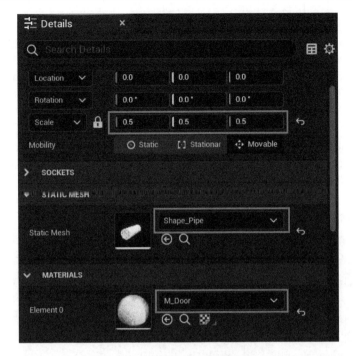

Figure 8.18 – Setting up the Static Mesh

5.   Change **Collision Presets** of **Static Mesh** to **OverlapAllDynamic**:

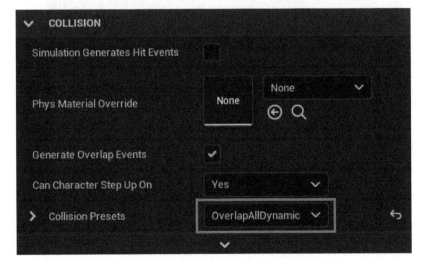

Figure 8.19 – Setting Collision Presets

> **Important Note**
>
> While prototyping a game, it is most often useful to take advantage of readily available assets rather than taking the time to create each asset from scratch. This allows you to focus your time and effort on determining what mechanics will result in the best play experience rather than spending time creating art assets that might later be discarded if the mechanic is removed from the design.

6. We will create the `AmmoPickupCount` variable to store the amount of ammo the player will receive when collecting an ammo pickup. In the **VARIABLES** category of the **My Blueprint** panel, click on the + button to add a variable. In the **Details** panel, name it `AmmoPickupCount`, change **Variable Type** to **Integer**, and check the **Instance Editable** property:

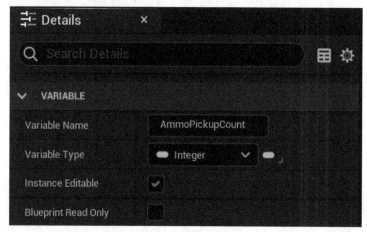

Figure 8.20 – The AmmoPickupCount variable

7. Compile the Blueprint, and then set the **AmmoPickupCount Default Value** to 15.

8. We will use **Event ActorBeginOverlap** of **BP_AmmoPickup** to check whether it is the player (**FirstPersonCharacter**) who is overlapping the instance of **BP_AmmoPickup** and to increase the **Player Current Ammo** value. These are the nodes that we will use:

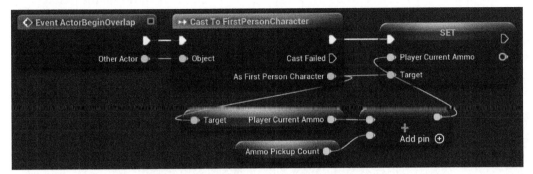

Figure 8.21 – Increasing the player's ammo

9. Right-click on the empty space of **Event Graph** and add **Event ActorBeginOverlap**.

10. Drag a wire from the **Other Actor** output pin of the **Event ActorBeginOverlap** node and add the **Cast To FirstPersonCharacter** node.

11. Drag a wire from the **As First Person Character** pin and add a **SET Player Current Ammo** node.

12. Drag another wire from the **As First Person Character** pin and add a **GET Player Current Ammo** node.

13. Drag a wire from the **GET Player Current Ammo** output pin to empty space and create an **Add** node.

14. Drag a wire from the bottom input pin of the **Add** node and add a **GET Ammo Pickup Count** node.

15. Connect the output pin of the **Add** node to the input pin of the **SET Player Current Ammo** node.

16. The previous steps complete the nodes shown in *Figure 8.21*. Next, let's play a sound and destroy the instance when the collectible is picked up, as shown in the following screenshot:

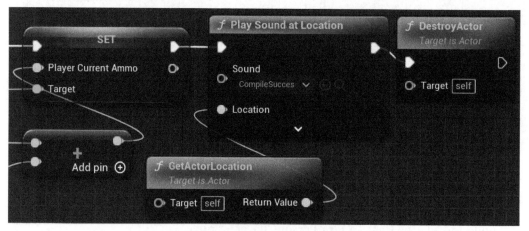

Figure 8.22 – Playing a sound and destroying the instance

17. Drag a wire from the white output pin of the **SET Player Current Ammo** node to empty space and add a **Play Sound at Location** node.

18. For our prototype, we will use a sound wave from **Engine Content**. Click on the **Sound** dropdown, then click on the gear icon to access the **VIEW** options. Check the **Show Engine Content** option and select the **CompileSucess** sound wave from the list:

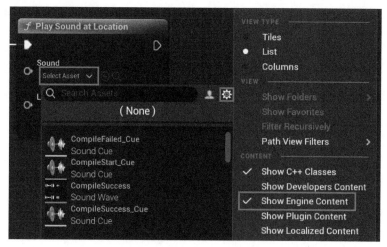

Figure 8.23 – Show Engine Content in the asset list

19. Drag a wire from the **Location** input pin to empty space and add a **GetActorLocation** node.

20. Drag a wire from the white output pin of the **Play Sound at Location** node to empty space and add a **DestroyActor** node to ensure that each collectible can only be grabbed once.

21. Compile and save the **BP_AmmoPickup** Blueprint.

22. Now, return to the level editor and drag the **BP_AmmoPickup** Blueprint from the **Content Browser** into the level to create an instance. Add more instances in different locations around the Level to seed the area with ammo pickups. Save the level and click **Play** to test the game. You should see your ammo counter increase every time you step onto one of the ammo pickups.

Figure 8.24 – Collect the ammo pickup to increase your ammo counter

We've learned how to create a Blueprint for a pickup that modifies the player's status when it is collected. One of the final steps we need to carry out to establish a full game loop is to create a condition for the player to win. We will look at that next.

Setting a gameplay win condition

We will modify our **HUD** Blueprint and player character Blueprint to account for a target goal that the player must strive to achieve. We will display the target goal in the HUD next to the target count, so the player can easily see how many targets need to be destroyed to reach their goal.

We will also create another Widget Blueprint representing a win menu screen that will be shown to the player when they reach their goal. Finally, we will implement the logic needed to check whether the player has won and to show the win menu screen.

Displaying a target goal in the HUD

First, we need to create a variable in the **FirstPersonCharacter** Blueprint that will establish how many targets we are asking the player to destroy to win the game. Then, we need to display this information to the player in the **HUD** Blueprint.

Follow these steps to display the target goal:

1. In the **Content Browser**, access the `/Content/FirstPersonBP/Blueprints` folder and double-click on the **FirstPersonCharacter** Blueprint.

2. In the **VARIABLES** category of the **My Blueprint** panel, click on the + sign to add a variable, name it `TargetGoal`, and change **Variable Type** to **Integer**.

3. Compile the `FirstPersonCharacter` Blueprint and set **Default Value** to 2 for now:

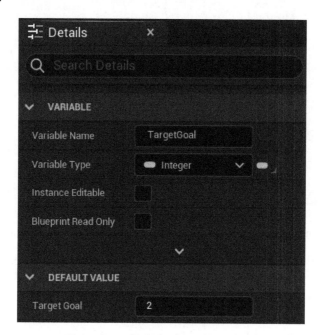

Figure 8.25 – The TargetGoal integer variable

4. Compile, save, and close the Blueprint Editor.

5. In the **Content Browser**, access the `/Content/FirstPersonBP/UI` folder and double-click on the **HUD** Blueprint to open the UMG editor. We will add two **Text** objects to **Goal Tracker** as shown in the following screenshot:

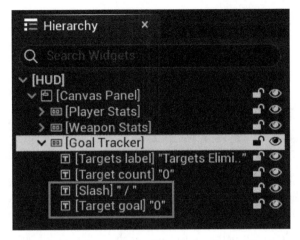

Figure 8.26 – The HUD Goal Tracker with new elements

6. In the **Designer** view, drag a **Text** object from the **Palette** panel onto the **Goal Tracker** object in the **Hierarchy** panel.

7. In the **Details** panel, change the name to Slash. Change the **Text** field under the **Content** category to / (including the spaces before and after the slash) and set the font size to 32.

8. Drag another **Text** object onto **Goal Tracker**. In the **Details** panel, change the name to Target goal. Change the **Text** field under the **Content** category to 0 and set the font size to 32. The new **Goal Tracker** will look like this:

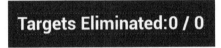

Figure 8.27 – The Goal Tracker shows the target count and target goal

9. Now we need to bind the Target goal of the HUD to the TargetGoal variable of the **FirstPersonCharacter** Blueprint. In the **Details** panel, find the **Bind** button next to the **Text** field and create a new binding, as shown here:

Figure 8.28 – Creating a binding for Target goal

10. We will follow the same pattern for this binding as we did in the other HUD bindings we created in *Chapter 7, Creating Screen UI Elements*. Add a **Get Player Character** node, cast it using the **Cast To FirstPersonCharacter** node, and then drag from the **As First Person Character** pin to add a **Get Target Goal** node. Finally, attach both the **Cast To** node and the **Target Goal** node to **Return Node**:

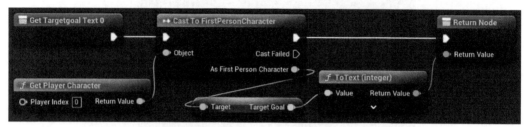

Figure 8.29 – The value of the Target Goal variable will be shown on the HUD

11. Compile, save, and play the game.

You should see that the target counter increments as targets are destroyed. The **Target Goal** shown on the right of the target counter does not change. Now, we need to ensure that the player gets feedback when they reach their target goal.

Creating a win menu screen

To give the player feedback once they have won the game, we are going to create a **WinMenu** screen that will appear upon destroying the required number of targets. To create this **WinMenu**, we are going to need another Blueprint widget, like the one we created for the HU:

1. In the **Content Browser**, access the `/Content/FirstPersonBP/UI` folder and then right-click in the empty folder space. Go to **User Interface | Widget Blueprint** and name the resulting Blueprint `WinMenu`:

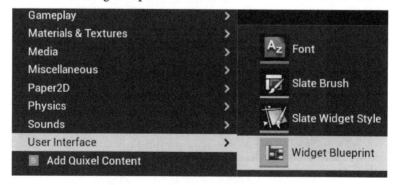

Figure 8.30 – Creating a Widget Blueprint

2. Double-click on this Blueprint to open the UMG Editor. We are going to set up three elements for this menu screen. The first will be a simple text object that broadcasts You Win! to the player. The other two elements will be buttons that allow the player to restart the game or quit it:

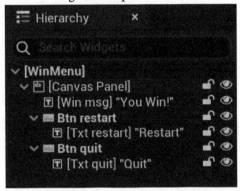

Figure 8.31 – The elements of the WinMenu Widget Blueprint

3. Drag a **Text** object from the **Palette** panel onto the **CanvasPanel** object in the **Hierarchy** panel. In the **Details** panel, change the name to Win msg, click on the **Anchors** dropdown, and select the option with the anchor in the center of the screen:

Figure 8.32 – The anchor of this object is in the center of the screen

4. Set **Position X** to `-190.0` and **Position Y** to `-250.0`. Check the **Size To Content** property, so we don't need to adjust the values of **Size X** and **Size Y**:

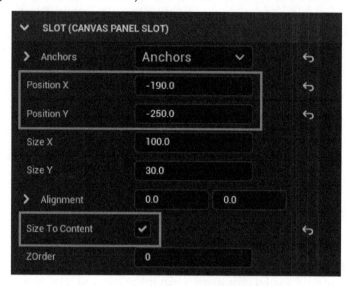

Figure 8.33 – The position of an object is relative to its anchor

5. Change the **Text** field under the **CONTENT** category to `You Win!`. In the **APPEARANCE** category, set the font size to `72`, and in **Color and Opacity**, click on the colored rectangle to open the color picker and select any green color:

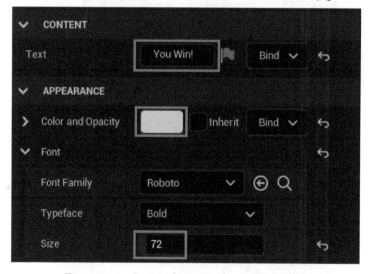

Figure 8.34 – Setting the text, color, and font size

6. Drag a **Button** object from the **Palette** panel onto the **CanvasPanel** object in the **Hierarchy** panel. In the **Details** panel, change the name to Btn restart, click on the **Anchors** dropdown and select the option with the anchor in the center of the screen.

7. Set **Position X** to -180.0, **Position Y** to -50.0, **Size X** to 360.0, and **Size Y** to 100.0:

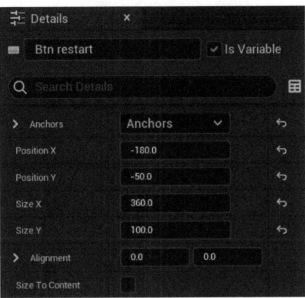

Figure 8.35 – Setting the position and size of the button

8. Drag a **Text** object from the **Palette** panel onto the **Btn restart** object in the **Hierarchy** panel. In the **Details** panel, set the name to Txt restart, change the **Text** field under the **Content** category to Restart, and set the font size to 48.

9. Drag another **Button** object from the **Palette** panel onto the **CanvasPanel** object in the **Hierarchy** panel. In the **Details** panel, change the name to Btn quit, click on the **Anchors** dropdown and select the option with the anchor in the center of the screen.

10. Set **Position X** to -180.0, **Position Y** to 150.0, **Size X** to 360.0, and **Size Y** to 100.0.

11. Drag a **Text** object from the **Palette** panel onto the **Btn quit** object in the **Hierarchy** panel. In the **Details** panel, set the name to Txt quit, change the **Text** field under the **Content** category to Quit, and set the font size to 48.

The **WinMenu** Widget Blueprint should look like this in the UMG Editor:

Figure 8.36 – The WinMenu elements

12. Now, we need to add actions that will execute when the **Restart** button is pressed. Click on the **Btn restart** object, scroll down to the bottom of the **Details** panel, and click on the + button next to the **On Clicked** event. This will add an event that triggers when the button is clicked:

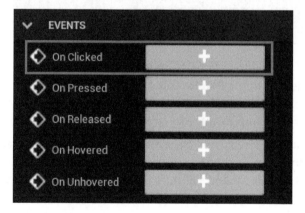

Figure 8.37 – Adding a button event

13. You will be taken to the **Graph** view, where an **On Clicked (Btnrestart)** node will appear. Drag from the output pin of **On Clicked (Btnrestart)** onto **Graph** and add an **Open Level (by Object Reference)** node. In the **Level** parameter, select the level we are using, which is **FirstPersonExampleMap**. This node will reload the level when the player clicks on the button, resetting all aspects of the level, including targets, ammo collectibles, and the player.

14. Drag from the output pin of **Open Level (by Object Reference)** onto **Graph** and add a **Remove from Parent** node. This node removes the **WinMenu** widget from the view. We want the menu to go away once the level is reset:

Figure 8.38 – The actions of the Restart button

15. We will do similar steps for the **Quit** button. Return to the **Designer** view and click on the **Btn quit** object, scroll down to the bottom of the **Details** panel, and click on the + button next to the **On Clicked** event to add an event.

16. You will be taken to the **Graph** view, where an **On Clicked (Btnquit)** node will appear. Drag from the output pin of **On Clicked (Btnquit)** onto **Graph** and add a **Quit Game** node so that the player can shut down the game by clicking the **Quit** button:

Figure 8.39 – The action of the Quit button

17. Compile, save, and close the UMG editor.

Now that our **WinMenu** has been created, we need to tell the game when to show it to the player.

Displaying the WinMenu

As we did with the **HUD** Widget Blueprint, we will display the **WinMenu** from within the **FirstPersonCharacter** Blueprint. We will create a custom event named **End Game** that will be called when the game ends.

Follow these steps:

1. In the **Content Browser**, access the /Content/FirstPersonBP/Blueprints folder and double-click on the FirstPersonCharacter Blueprint.

2. Right-click on the Event Graph and add a custom event. Rename it End Game:

Figure 8.40 – Adding a custom event

3. Drag a wire from the output execution pin of **End Game**, add a **Set Game Paused** node, and check the **Paused** checkbox. This node will pause the game while the player chooses an option in the **WinMenu**:

Figure 8.41 – Pausing the game

4. Right-click on **Event Graph** and add a **Get Player Controller** node. Drag from the **Return Value** output pin and add a **SET Show Mouse Cursor** node. Check the checkbox next to **Show Mouse Cursor** and attach this node to the output execution pin of **Set Game Paused**. This will enable the player to regain control over the mouse cursor after the game is paused:

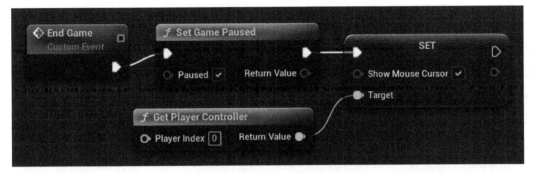

Figure 8.42 – Showing the mouse cursor

5. Drag a wire from the output execution pin of the **SET Show Mouse Cursor** node and add a **Create Widget** node. In the **Class** parameter, select **Win Menu**.

6. Drag the **Return Value** output pin of the **Create Widget** node and add an **Add to Viewport** node:

Figure 8.43 – Creating and displaying the WinMenu

7. Create a comment around the nodes of the **End Game** event. Label the comment **End Game: Shows Win Menu**. Compile and save the Blueprint.

The final step is to determine the conditions that will result in the **End Game** custom event being triggered.

Triggering a win

We want the **End Game** event to happen once the player has destroyed enough cylinder targets to meet the target goal. We will create a custom event named **CheckGoal** in the **FirstPersonCharacter** Blueprint that will be called by **BP_CylinderTarget** each time a target is destroyed.

These are the actions of the **CheckGoal** custom event that we will create:

Figure 8.44 – Checking whether the goal was achieved

To do that, follow these steps:

1. Right-click on the Event Graph of the **FirstPersonCharacter** Blueprint and add a custom event. Rename it `CheckGoal`.

2. Drag a wire from the white output pin of the **CheckGoal** node to empty grid space and add a **Branch** node.

3. Drag a wire from the **Condition** input pin of the **Branch** node to empty space and add a **Greater Equal** node.

4. Drag a wire from the top input pin of the **Greater Equal** node and add a **GET Targets Eliminated** node.

5. Drag a wire from the bottom input pin of the **Greater Equal** node and add a **GET Target Goal** node.

6. Drag a wire from the **True** output pin of the **Branch** node and add a **Delay** node. Enter 1.0 in the **Duration** parameter. This node is used to wait 1 second before showing the **WinMenu**.

7. Drag a wire from the **Completed** output pin of the **Delay** node and add the **End Game** node. This node will call the **End Game** custom event that we created to show the **WinMenu**.

8. Compile, save, and close the Blueprint Editor.

Now, we will modify **BP_CylinderTarget** to call the **CheckGoal** event each time a target is destroyed:

1. In the **Content Browser**, access the /Content/FirstPersonBP/Blueprints folder and double-click on the BP_CylinderTarget Blueprint.

2. Move **Event Graph** to the end of the **Event Hit** actions. Drag the **DestroyActor** node to the right to make room for another node.

3. Drag a wire from the **As First Person Character** output pin of the **Cast To** node and add the **Check Goal** node. Connect the white output pin of the **++** node to the white input pin of the **Check Goal** node and connect the output pin of the **Check Goal** node to the white input pin of the **DestroyActor** node:

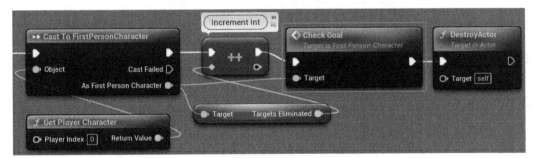

Figure 8.45 – Calling the Check Goal event

4. Compile, save, and play the game. If all Blueprints are set up correctly, then you should see the game pause and the **WinMenu** appears as soon as you destroy a second target. Clicking on the **Restart** button will reload the level and clicking **Quit** will close the session:

Figure 8.46 – Showing the WinMenu in the game

We've created a target goal for the player and created a **WinMenu** Widget Blueprint that is displayed when the player achieves the goal. The **WinMenu** gives feedback and some options for the player to choose from when they finish the game.

Summary

In this chapter, we have enhanced the play experience by adding constraints to the player's abilities and established a goal for the player to achieve. In the process, you have learned how to use timers to repeat actions, how to create collectible objects in the game world, and how to create a menu system.

This chapter concludes *Part 2*. The elements that make up the foundation of a video game experience are present in the game that we've built. If you desire, make a copy of the project, increase the target goal, and spend some time customizing the level layout to create a properly challenging game experience that is uniquely yours.

In *Part 3*, we'll begin tackling a more advanced subject of Blueprint scripting and game development: **artificial intelligence (AI)**. We will also add new features to the game and see how to build and publish the game.

In the next chapter, we will replace our cylinder targets with smart enemies that can patrol between points and pursue the player around the level.

Quiz

1. You should avoid using macros because they make scripts disorganized.

   a. True

   b. False

2. You can use timers as an alternative to the Event Tick because you can set a low repetition rate for actions.

   a. True

   b. False

3. In our example game, we can define different amounts of ammunition in each instance of BP_AmmoPickup on a level because the AmmoPickupCount variable is checked as **Instance Editable**.

   a. True

   b. False

4. You can have only one Widget Blueprint added to the Viewport at the same time.

   a. True

   b. False

5. A Widget Blueprint can have buttons that trigger events when clicked.

   a. True

   b. False

Part 3: Enhancing the Game

In this part, you will learn the basic **Artificial Intelligence (AI)** techniques required to create a smart enemy using Behavior Trees and Navigation Meshes. Additionally, new features will be added to the game in order to make it more interesting. We will also demonstrate how to build and publish a game.

This part includes the following chapters:

- *Chapter 9, Building Smart Enemies with Artificial Intelligence*
- *Chapter 10, Upgrading the AI Enemies*
- *Chapter 11, Game States and Applying the Finishing Touches*
- *Chapter 12, Building and Publishing*

9
Building Smart Enemies with Artificial Intelligence

In this chapter, we'll add another challenge to our gameplay by making enemies that pose a threat to our player. To do so, we'll leave behind our target cylinders in favor of enemies that have AI behavior. We want to set up enemies that have the potential to pose a threat to the player and can analyze the world around them to make decisions. To accomplish this, we are going to learn about Unreal Engine's built-in tools for handling AI behavior and how those tools interact with our Blueprint scripting. In the process, we will cover these topics:

- Setting up the enemy actor to navigate

- Creating navigation behavior

- Making the AI chase the player

By the end of the chapter, we will be able to create a Behavior Tree that handles enemy navigation in the level and make them chase the player when they are in their line of sight.

Setting up the enemy actor to navigate

Until now, our targets have been represented by basic cylinder geometry. This worked well for prototyping a non-responsive target that is only present as an aiming challenge for the player. However, an enemy that will move around and present a threat to the player will need a recognizable appearance that will at least indicate its direction of travel to the player. Fortunately for us, Epic has created a freely available asset package for Unreal Engine that we can use to add a humanoid model to our game – one that is suitable for our new enemy type.

In the following sections, we will learn how to import an asset package from the Marketplace, expand the play area, use a navigation mesh, and create the AI assets used by the enemies.

Importing from the Marketplace

First, we'll step out of the Unreal Engine Editor and focus on the Epic Games Launcher.

Follow these steps to import a free asset package from the Marketplace:

1. Open **Epic Games Launcher** and click on the **Unreal Engine** section on the left side of the window.

2. Click on the **Marketplace** tab at the top and search for `animation starter pack`.

3. Click on the **Add to Cart** button of **Animation Starter Pack**:

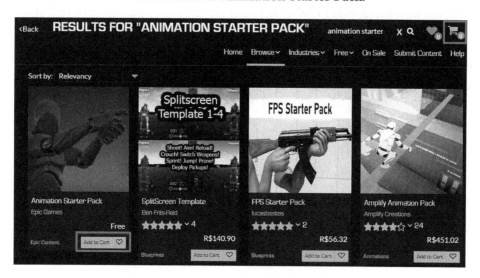

Figure 9.1 – The Unreal Engine Marketplace

4. Click on the **Shopping Cart** icon located at the top right.

5. Click on the **Check Out** button in the **Shopping Cart** panel.

6. When the panel closes, click on the image of **Animation Starter Pack** to open the asset page.

7. Click on the **Add to project** button and select the project you have been using to build your game. A folder called `AnimStarterPack` will be added to the `Content` folder of your project.

Animation Starter Pack has the assets that we need to represent the enemy. Now, we need more space in the play area for the player and the enemies.

Expanding the play area

To provide an interesting environment for our intelligent enemies to chase the player, we need to make some changes to the default first-person example map layout. The existing layout, while being serviceable for shooting targets, is too cramped for a player to be able to avoid an enemy that is chasing them.

To quickly add a little bit of variety to the gameplay, we will expand the play area to be twice as wide as it was earlier. We will also create an elevated area that is accessible by ramps to both the player and the enemies. The following screenshot shows the new level layout:

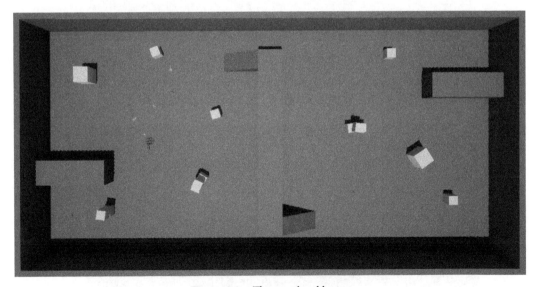

Figure 9.2 – The new level layout

Follow these steps to modify the level layout:

1. Open the project in the Unreal Editor.

2. Remove the **First Person Template** label. Also, remove all the instances of **BP_CylinderTarget** from the level. You can select them by clicking on the instances in the Viewport or finding them in the World Outliner.

3. Click on **Floor** to select it. Hold the *Alt* key and click and drag the *Y*-axis arrow to make a copy of **Floor**. Move the **Floor** copy on the *Y* axis until the play area is twice as wide:

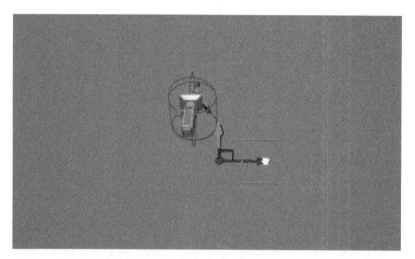

Figure 9.3 – Hold the Alt key and click and drag to duplicate the Floor mesh

4. We need to scale up **LightmassImportanceVolume** and **PostProcessVolume** to cover the new play area. These volumes are used for lighting and effects:

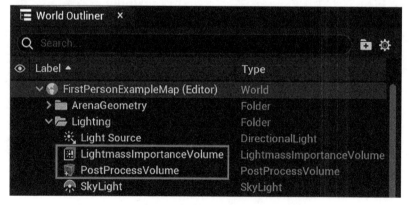

Figure 9.4 – These volumes must cover the play area

Setting up the enemy actor to navigate   223

5. In the **World Outliner** panel, click on **LightmassImportanceVolume**. Then, in the **Details** panel, click on the **Lock** icon of the **Scale** property to unlock it and set the *Y*-axis (green) value of **Scale** to 2.0.

6. Next, in the Level Editor, move **LightmassImportanceVolume** on the *Y* axis until it covers the play area:

Figure 9.5 – Increasing the Y scale of LightmassImportanceVolume

7. In the **World Outliner** panel, click on **PostProcessVolume**, and then, in the **Details** panel, set the *Y*-axis (green) value of **Scale** to 44.0. Once that is done, go to the Level Editor and move **PostProcessVolume** on the *Y* axis until it covers the play area:

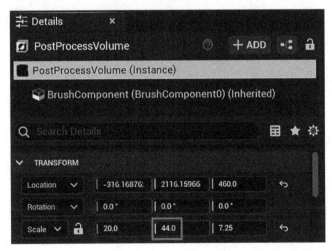

Figure 9.6 – Increasing the Y scale of PostProcessVolume

8. In the Level Editor, click the wall named **Wall3**, which is in the middle of the play area. In the **Details** panel, set the *Y*-axis (green) value of **Location** to 5945.0.

9. Next, click the wall named **Wall1**. Hold the *Alt* key and click and drag the *Y* arrow to make a copy of the wall. In the **Details** panel, set the *Y*-axis (green) value of **Location** to 4000.0.

10. Then, click the wall named **Wall2**. Hold the *Alt* key and click and drag the *Y* arrow to make a copy of the wall. In the **Details** panel, set the *Y*-axis (green) value of **Location** to 4000.0. The following screenshot shows how the play area is looking now:

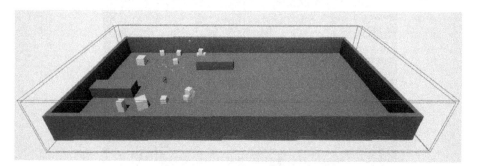

Figure 9.7 – The play area is twice as wide now

11. Click the piece of wall named **BigWall2**. Hold the *Alt* key and click and drag the *Y* arrow to make a copy of the wall. In the **Details** panel, set the *Y*-axis (green) value of **Location** to 5295.0:

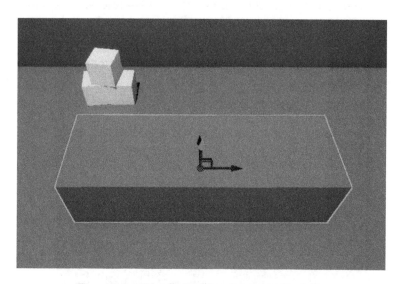

Figure 9.8 – Copy BigWall2 and move to the right

12. We will transform **BigWall2** to create a larger wall in the center of the play area. Click **BigWall2** to select it. In the **Details** panel, set **Location** to $X = -280$, $Y = 2000$, and $Z = 322$ and **Scale** to $X = 30$, $Y = 4$, and $Z = 3$:

Figure 9.9 – Modifying the BigWall2 transform

13. Now, we will add a ramp to access an elevated area. In the content browser, access the `Content/StarterContent/Shapes` folder. Drag the **Shape_Wedge_B** asset and drop it in the level. In the **Details** panel, set **Location** to $X = -1630$, $Y = 2500$, and $Z = 170$, **Rotation** to $X = 0$, $Y = 0$, and $Z = 90$, and **Scale** to $X = 6$, $Y = 3$, and $Z = 3$:

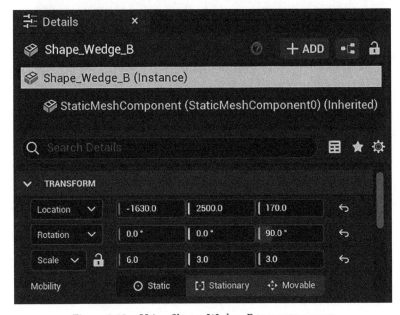

Figure 9.10 – Using Shape_Wedge_B to create a ramp

14. Under **MATERIALS**, change **Element 0** from **Shape_Wedge_B** to the gray **CubeMaterial** material:

Figure 9.11 – Changing the Shape_Wedge_B material

15. We will create another ramp to access the elevated area. Click the **Shape_Wedge_B** instance that is in the level. Hold the *Alt* key and click and drag the *X* arrow to make a copy of the ramp. In the **Details** panel, set **Location** to $X = 1070$, $Y = 1500$, and $Z = 170$ and **Rotation** to $X = 0$, $Y = 0$, and $Z = -90$:

Figure 9.12 – Changing the location and rotation of the second ramp

Our elevated area should look like this:

Figure 9.13 – The elevated area can be accessed by ramps

16. Grab some of the white boxes that are on one side of the level and distribute them on the other side.

17. Add more instances of **BP_AmmoPickup** on the level.

We have created a level layout with more space for action between the player and enemies. Now, we will create a NavMesh that is necessary for enemies to move through the level.

Making the level traversable with a NavMesh asset

To create AI behavior that allows our enemies to traverse the level, we need to create a map of the environment that the AI will know how to read and navigate with. This map is created with an asset known as a **NavMesh**, which is an abbreviation for **Navigation Mesh**.

Follow these steps to create a NavMesh for our play area:

1. In the Level Editor, click the **Create** button located on the toolbar. Hover over
    Volumes to display a submenu and click on **Nav Mesh Bounds Volume**:

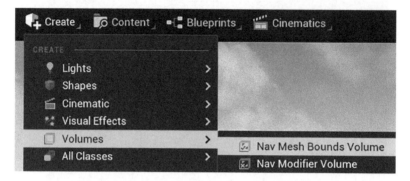

Figure 9.14 – Adding a NavMesh to the level

2. Now, we need to move and scale up the **Nav Mesh Bounds Volume** object until the
    entire walkable space of our level is contained within it. In the **Details** panel, set
    Location to $X = -316$, $Y = 2116$, and $Z = 460$ and **Scale** to $X = 20$, $Y = 44$, and
    $Z = 7$:

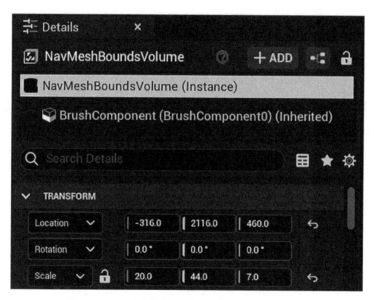

Figure 9.15 – Modifying the NavMesh transform

3. Press the *P* key on your keyboard to see whether the NavMesh is placed correctly. If
    so, you'll see a green mesh on top of your floors, as seen in the following screenshot:

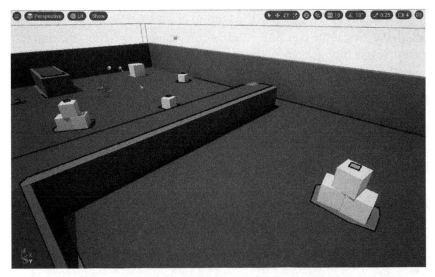

Figure 9.16 – Press the P key to toggle the NavMesh visibility on and off

With our play area and NavMesh now set up, we can return our focus to creating the enemy and its AI.

Creating the AI assets

We need to create assets of four types that will work together to manage the behavior of our enemy:

- **Character**: A blueprint class that represents the enemy character in the level.

- **AI Controller**: A blueprint class that serves as a connection between the character and the Behavior Tree. It routes the information and actions that are generated within the Behavior Tree to the character, which will enact those actions.

- **Behavior Tree**: A Behavior Tree is the source of the decision-making logic that will instruct our enemy on what conditions should cause it to perform which actions.

- **Blackboard**: A Blackboard is a container for all the data used in the decision-making that is shared between the AI controller and the Behavior Tree.

These are the steps to create the four assets:

1. In the content browser, access the /Content/FirstPersonBP/ folder. Right-click in the empty space next to the list of folders and select the **New Folder** option. Name the new folder Enemy.

2. Open the Enemy folder you created, and then right-click in the empty folder space and select **Blueprint Class**.

3. Open the **ALL CLASSES** group at the bottom of the popup and type `ASP_` into the search bar. Select the `Ue4ASP_Character` class to create a new character Blueprint. This is the base character class from **Animation Starter Pack** that we added to the project at the beginning of the chapter:

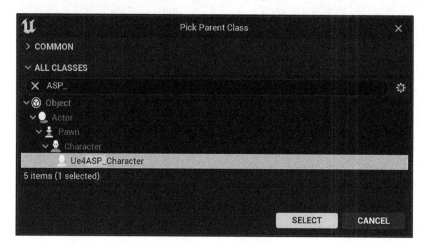

Figure 9.17 – Selecting the parent class of the EnemyCharacter Blueprint

4. Rename the Blueprint `BP_EnemyCharacter`.

5. Now, we will create the **AIController** child class. Right-click in the empty space of the `Enemy` folder and select **Blueprint Class**.

6. Open the **All Classes** group at the bottom of the popup and type `AIController` into the search bar. Select the **AIController** class and name the resulting Blueprint `BP_EnemyController`.

7. To create the **Behavior Tree** asset, right-click in the empty space of the `Enemy` folder, hover over **Artificial Intelligence** to display a submenu, and select **Behavior Tree**:

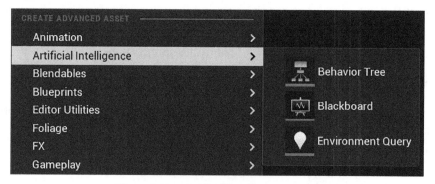

Figure 9.18 – Artificial Intelligence assets

8. Rename the **Behavior Tree** asset BT_EnemyBehavior.

9. Finally, to create the **Blackboard** asset, right-click in the empty space of the Enemy folder, hover over **Artificial Intelligence** to display a submenu, and select **Blackboard**. Name it BB_EnemyBlackboard.

10. The following screenshot shows the assets of the Enemy folder:

Figure 9.19 – The Enemy folder assets

These are the assets that we will use to implement the AI of the enemy character. Next, we need to make some modifications to the BP_EnemyCharacter Blueprint.

Setting up the BP_EnemyCharacter Blueprint

As we created BP_EnemyCharacter as a Ue4ASP_Character child class, it inherited information about the desired mesh, texture, and animations from the character created for the animation pack we imported. Some of this information we want to keep, such as the mesh and animations. However, we need to ensure that BP_EnemyCharacter knows how to be controlled by the right AI Controller. We will also change the material of BP_EnemyCharacter and hide the capsule component that is being shown in the game.

> **Note**
>
> When you open a Blueprint that does not have any scripts, a simple editor is displayed to edit the default values only. You need to click on the **Open Full Blueprint Editor** link at the top to see the usual layout.

Follow these steps to make the adjustments:

1. Open the BP_EnemyCharacter Blueprint.

2. Click the **Class Defaults** button located on the toolbar:

Figure 9.20 – Accessing Class Defaults

3. In the **Details** panel, find the **PAWN** category. The last element of this category is a drop-down list for **AI Controller Class**. Change the selection of this drop-down list to our new **BP_EnemyController** class:

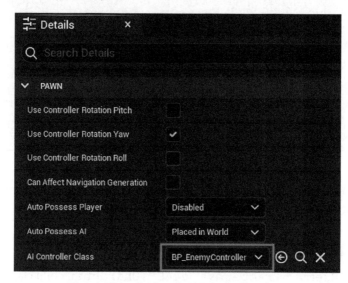

Figure 9.21 – Setting the AI Controller class

4. In the **Components** panel, click on **Mesh (CharacterMesh0) (Inherited)**. Then, in the **Details** panel, find the **MATERIALS** category and change **Element 0** of **MATERIALS** to the **M_TargetRed** material we created:

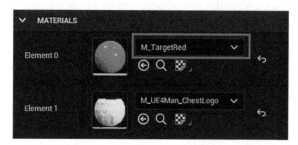

Figure 9.22 – Changing the mesh material

5. In the **Components** panel, click on **CapsuleComponent (CollisionCylinder) (Inherited)**. In the **Details** panel, change **Collision Presets** to **BlockAllDynamic**, and in the **RENDERING** category, check the **Hidden in Game** property:

Figure 9.23 – Hiding CapsuleComponent

6. Compile the blueprint and drag the BP_EnemyCharacter blueprint onto the level to create an instance of the enemy in our play area.

In this section, we learned how to import assets from the Marketplace. We expanded the level and made it traversable using a NavMesh. We created the AI assets, and now we are ready to implement the navigation behavior of the enemy.

Creating navigation behavior

The first goal for our enemy will be to get it to navigate between points that we create on the map. To accomplish this, we'll need to create points on the map that the enemy will navigate to, and then we need to set up the behavior that will cause the enemy to move to each of the points in a cycle.

Setting up patrol points

Let's start by creating the path we want the AI to patrol. We will use a **Sphere Trigger** to represent a patrol point, since it generates overlap events and is hidden in the game. We need at least two patrol points on the level, since each instance of BP_EnemyCharacter can navigate between two patrol points.

Follow these steps to create the patrol points:

1. In the Level Editor, click the **Create** button located on the toolbar, and then click on **Sphere Trigger**. Place the Sphere Trigger anywhere on the floor:

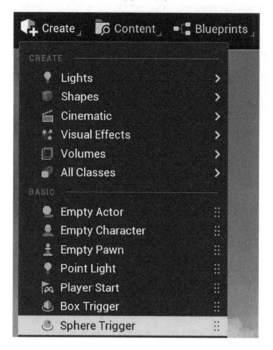

Figure 9.24 – Creating a Sphere Trigger

2. In the **Details** panel, rename the Sphere Trigger `PatrolPoint1`.

3. Create another Sphere Trigger and name it `PatrolPoint2`. Place it far away from the first patrol point so that movement between the two points is noticeable.

With our patrol points established, we can move on to building the intelligence of our enemy.

Creating the Blackboard keys

A Blackboard stores information using keys and values. `BB_EnemyBlackboard` will have two keys, one for storing the current patrol point and another to store a reference to the player character. This information will be referenced by the Behavior Tree.

These are the steps to create the keys:

1. Open `BB_EnemyBlackboard` from the content browser.

2. Click on **New Key** and select **Object** as **Key Type**.

3. Name this new key `CurrentPatrolPoint`.

4. Click on the expansion arrow next to **Key Type** and change **Base Class** to **Actor** with the dropdown:

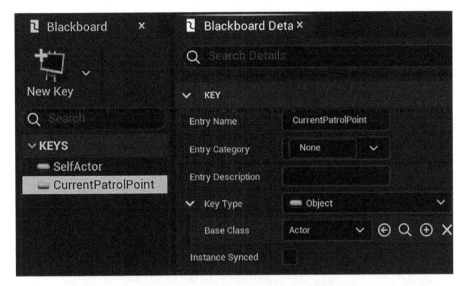

Figure 9.25 – Creating the CurrentPatrolPoint key

5. Now, let's create the key for the player character. Click on **New Key** and select **Object** as **Key Type**.

6. Name this new key `PlayerCharacter`. Click on the expansion arrow next to **Key Type** and change **Base Class** to **Character**:

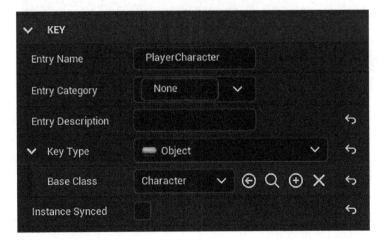

Figure 9.26 – Creating the PlayerCharacter key

Now, we need to set the value of the **CurrentPatrolPoint** key within **Blackboard** to the actual patrol point in the level. We can do this from the BP_EnemyCharacter Blueprint.

Creating the variables in BP_EnemyCharacter

We will create variables in BP_EnemyCharacter to store the patrol points and the key names of the Blackboard.

Follow these steps to create the variables:

1. Open the BP_EnemyCharacter Blueprint.

2. In the **Variables** category of the **My Blueprint** panel, click the + button to add a variable and name it PatrolPoint1.

3. In the **Details** panel, click the **Variable Type** drop-down menu and search for Actor. Hover over **Actor** to display a submenu, and then choose **Object Reference**. Check the **Instance Editable** attribute:

Figure 9.27 – Creating a variable that references an Actor instance

4. Follow the same steps to create a second **Actor** variable called PatrolPoint2.

5. Create another **Actor** variable called CurrentPatrolPoint. This time, leave the **Instance Editable** attribute unchecked.

6. These are the variables we created. The open eye icon means that the variable is **Instance Editable**, so the references of **PatrolPoint1** and **PatrolPoint2** variables will be set in the Level Editor:

Figure 9.28 – The patrol point variables

7. Create another variable in the **My Blueprint** panel. In the **Details** panel, name the variable `PatrolPointKeyName` and change **Variable Type** to **Name**. Compile the Blueprint and set **DEFAULT VALUE** to `CurrentPatrolPoint`:

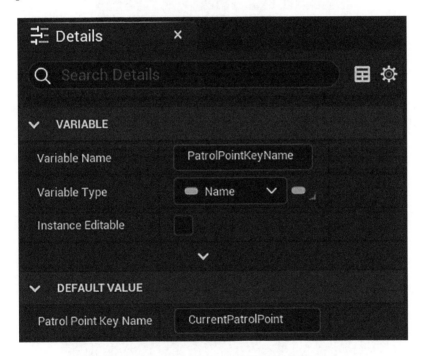

Figure 9.29 – This variable stores a Blackboard key name

Now, we can update the values on `BB_EnemyBlackboard` using these variables.

Updating the current patrol point key

We will create a macro to update the **CurrentPatrolPoint** key of `BB_EnemyBlackboard` because it will be used in multiple places.

These are the steps to create the macro:

1. In the **My Blueprint** panel, click the + button in the **MACROS** category to create a macro. Change the name of the macro to `UpdatePatrolPointBB`:

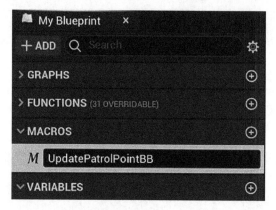

Figure 9.30 – Creating a macro

2. In the **Details** panel of the macro, create an input parameter named `In` and an output parameter named `Out` both of the **Exec** type:

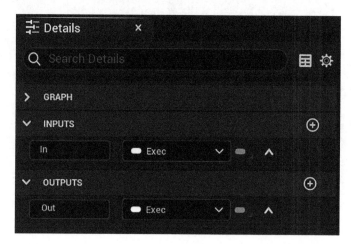

Figure 9.31 – Adding the execution pins in a macro

3. On the tab created for the **UpdatePatrolPointBB** macro, add the nodes seen in the following screenshot:

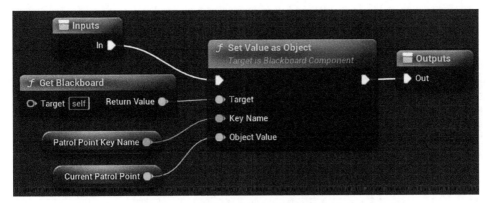

Figure 9.32 – The UpdatePatrolPointBB macro

4. Right-click on the graph and add a **Get Blackboard** node. This is a utility function that searches for the Blackboard being used by the AI controller.

5. Drag a wire from the **Return Value** pin of **Get Blackboard** and add a **Set Value as Object** node.

6. Drag a wire from the **Key Name** pin of the **Set Value as Object** node and add a **GET Patrol Point Key Name** node.

7. Drag a wire from the **Object Value** pin of the **Set Value as Object** node and add a **GET Current Patrol Point** node.

8. Connect the white execution pins of the **Inputs**, **Set Value as Object**, and **Outputs** nodes. Compile the Blueprint.

Next, we need to check when a BP_EnemyCharacter instance overlaps with a patrol point to update the **CurrentPatrolPoint** key of BB_EnemyBlackboard.

Overlapping a patrol point

We will use **Event ActorBeginOverlap** to verify when an instance of BP_EnemyCharacter reaches one of its two patrol points, and then we swap the patrol point that the instance is moving toward. Every time we update the **CurrentPatrolPoint** variable, we need to call the **UpdatePatrolPointBB** macro.

In **Event BeginPlay**, we will set an initial patrol point to **CurrentPatrolPoint** and call the **UpdatePatrolPointBB** macro.

Follow these steps to create the events:

1. In the EventGraph of BP_EnemyCharacter, drag a wire from the white execution pin of **Event BeginPlay** and add a **SET Current Patrol Point** node.

2. Drag a wire from the input pin of **SET Current Patrol Point** and add a **GET Patrol Point 1** node.

3.   Drag a wire from the white output pin of the **SET Current Patrol Point** node and add the **UpdatePatrolPointBB** macro node:

Figure 9.33 – Setting an initial patrol point

4.   Now, let's create the **Event ActorBeginOverlap** event, which swaps the patrol points. The event first checks whether the enemy overlaps with **Patrol Point 1**. If it is true, then the event sets **Patrol Point 2** as **Current Patrol Point**. If it is false, then the event checks whether the enemy overlaps with **Patrol Point 2**. In this case, the event sets **Patrol Point 1** as **Current Patrol Point**:

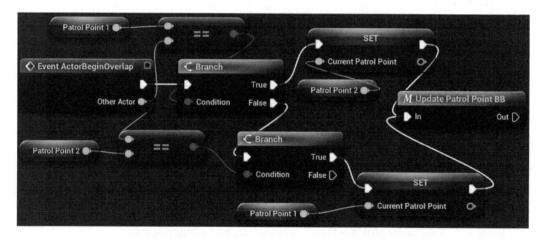

Figure 9.34 – Swapping the patrol points

5.   The nodes of *steps 5–8* are to check whether the enemy overlaps with **Patrol Point 1**. Drag a wire from the white execution pin of the **Event ActorBeginOverlap** node and add a **Branch** node.

6.   Drag a wire from the **Condition** input pin of the **Branch** node and add an **Equal** node.

7.   Drag a wire from the top input pin of the **Equal** node and add a **GET Patrol Point 1** node.

8.   Connect the bottom input pin of the **Equal** node to the **Other Actor** output pin of the **Event ActorBeginOverlap** node.

9. The nodes of *steps 9–11* set **Patrol Point 2** as **Current Patrol Point**. Drag a wire from the **True** output pin of the **Branch** node and add a **SET Current Patrol Point** node.

10. Drag a wire from the input pin of the **SET Current Patrol Point** node and add a **GET Patrol Point 2** node.

11. Drag a wire from the white output pin of the **SET Current Patrol Point** node and add the **UpdatePatrolPointBB** macro node.

12. The nodes of *steps 12–15* are to check whether the enemy overlaps with **Patrol Point 2**. Drag a wire from the **False** output pin of the **Branch** node and add another **Branch** node.

13. Drag a wire from the **Condition** input pin of the second **Branch** node and add an **Equal** node.

14. Connect the top input pin of the **Equal** node to the **Other Actor** output pin of the **Event ActorBeginOverlap** node.

15. Drag a wire from the bottom input pin of the **Equal** node and add a **GET Patrol Point 2** node.

16. The nodes of *steps 16–18* set **Patrol Point 1** as **Current Patrol Point**. Drag a wire from the **True** output pin of the second **Branch** node and add a **SET Current Patrol Point** node.

17. Drag a wire from the input pin of the new **SET Current Patrol Point** node and add a **GET Patrol Point 1** node.

18. Connect the white output pin of the **SET Current Patrol Point** node to the input pin of the **UpdatePatrolPointBB** node.

19. Compile and save the Blueprint.

These are the actions needed in the BP_EnemyCharacter Blueprint to handle the patrol points. The next step is to modify the BP_EnemyController Blueprint to run the Behavior Tree.

Running the Behavior Tree in the AI Controller

The AIController class has a function named **Run Behavior Tree**. It receives a Behavior Tree asset as a parameter. We created the BP_EnemyController Blueprint using AIController as the parent class to run our BT_EnemyBehavior Behavior Tree.

These are the steps to run the Behavior Tree:

1. Open the BP_EnemyController Blueprint.

2. In the EventGraph, drag a wire from the white execution pin of **Event BeginPlay** and add a **Run Behavior Tree** node.

3.   Set the **BTAsset** input parameter to **BT_EnemyBehavior**:

Figure 9.35 – Running the Behavior Tree

4.   Compile and save the Blueprint.

We have completed the necessary actions in the Blueprints to navigate the patrol points. We can now move on to the heart of the AI – the Behavior Tree.

Teaching our AI to walk with the Behavior Tree

Behavior Tree is a tool used to model the behavior of characters. It has control flow nodes and task nodes.

The two primary control flow nodes you will utilize are **Selector** and **Sequence**. A **Selector** node runs each of the nodes connected underneath it – called its **children** – from left to right, but it succeeds and stops running as soon as one child successfully runs. Thus, if a **Selector** node has three children, then the only way the third child node will run is if the first two children failed to execute because the conditions attached to them were false. A **Sequence** node is just the opposite. It also runs all the children in a sequence from left to right, but the **Sequence** node only succeeds if all the children succeed. The first child to fail causes the whole sequence to fail, ending the execution and aborting the sequence.

Follow these steps to create our first Behavior Tree:

1.   In the content browser, double-click the BT_EnemyBehavior asset to open the Behavior Tree Editor.

2.   In the **Details** panel, click the **BEHAVIORTREE** category and select **BB_EnemyBlackboard** as **Blackboard Asset**. The **KEYS** dropdown of **BB_EnemyBlackboard** will appear in the **Blackboard** panel at the bottom:

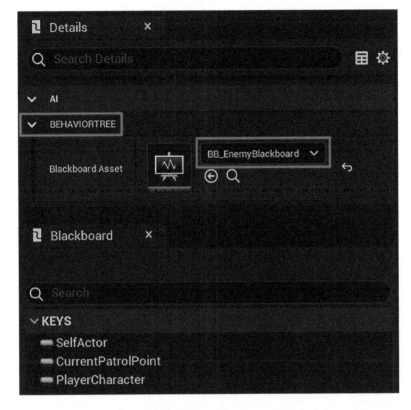

Figure 9.36 – Selecting the Blackboard asset used by the Behavior Tree

3. Look at the **Behavior Tree** graph. The top level of the logic tree will always be the **ROOT** node, which simply serves to indicate where the logic flow will start. The darker line at the bottom of the Behavior Tree nodes is the connection point between nodes:

Figure 9.37 – The logic flow starts in the ROOT node

4. Click and drag a wire from the dark area at the bottom of the **ROOT** node and drop it onto the empty graph space to open a selection menu popup. Select the **Sequence** option:

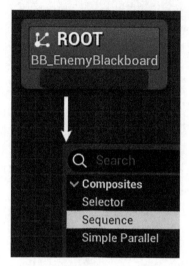

Figure 9.38 – Adding a Sequence node

5. In the **Details** panel, change **Node Name** to Move to Patrol.

6. Drag a wire down from the **Move to Patrol** node and add a **Move To** node. This type of node is a **task node**, has a purple color, and will always be the bottom-most node in a Behavior Tree. Therefore, you will notice that there is no attachment point for additional nodes at the bottom of a task node:

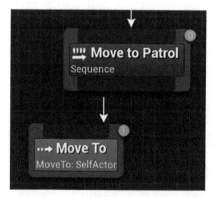

Figure 9.39 – The Move To node is a task node

7. In the **Details** panel of the **Move To** task node, change **Blackboard Key** to **CurrentPatrolPoint**. This Blackboard key determines the location that the actor will be moved to:

Figure 9.40 – This Blackboard key determines the destination

8. Drag a wire down from the **Move to Patrol** sequence node and add a **Wait** node.

9. In the **Details** panel of the **Wait** node, set **Wait Time** to 3.0 to add a 3-second pause between patrols. Set **Random Deviation** to 1.0 to add a 1-second variation. This will result in a pause of random length between 2 and 4 seconds:

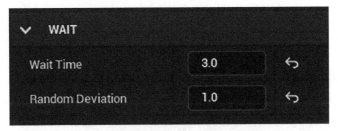

Figure 9.41 – Adjusting the wait time

10. Save the Behavior Tree. When running the game, the Behavior Tree will execute the **Move To** task node until the enemy reaches its destination. When this happens, the **Wait** task node will be executed:

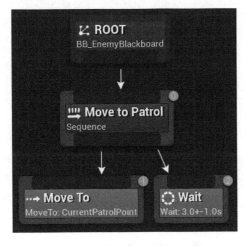

Figure 9.42 – Our first Behavior Tree

> **Note**
>
> Note the small gray circles with numbers inside of them that are positioned at the upper-right corner of the nodes. These indicate the execution order of the nodes, which are ordered according to their left-to-right and top-to-down positions. The first node to be evaluated will be labeled with a **0** badge.

Now, we have everything set up to test the enemy patrol.

Selecting the patrol points in the BP_EnemyCharacter instance

We created the **PatrolPoint1** and **PatrolPoint2** variables as **Instance Editable** in BP_EnemyCharacter to be able to set them in the Level Editor.

These are the steps to selecting the patrol points:

1. In the Level Editor, select the instance of BP_EnemyCharacter that we placed on the level.

2. In the **Details** panel, navigate down to the **Default** category and set **Patrol Point 1** to the **PatrolPoint1** instance and **Patrol Point 2** to the **PatrolPoint2** instance:

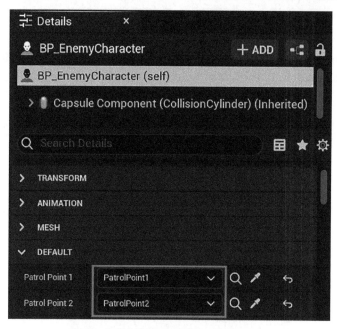

Figure 9.43 – Selecting the patrol points

3. Save the level and click the **Play** button to test.

You should see the red enemy character start navigating to the first of the two patrol points. When it reaches the first point, it will briefly pause and then start walking to the second patrol point. This pattern will continue back and forth while the game is running.

Now that we have a patrol behavior established, we will give the enemy the ability to see the player and pursue them.

Making the AI chase the player

There is a component named `PawnSensing` that can be used to add vision and hearing to the enemy. We will use this component and expand our Behavior Tree to make the enemy pose some threat to the player.

Giving the enemy sight with PawnSensing

To grant the enemy the ability to detect the player, we need to add the `PawnSensing` component to `BP_EnemyController` and store the `PlayerCharacter` reference in `BB_EnemyBlackboard` when the enemy sees the player.

These are the steps to use the `PawnSensing` component:

1. Open the `BP_EnemyController` Blueprint.

2. Create a variable in the **My Blueprint** panel. In the **Details** panel, name the variable `PlayerKeyName` and change **Variable Type** to **Name**. Compile the Blueprint and set **Default Value** to `PlayerCharacter`.

3. In the **Components** panel, click the **Add** button and search for `pawn`. Select the **Pawn Sensing** component:

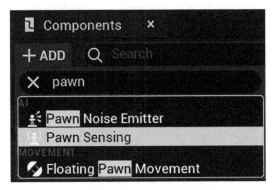

Figure 9.44 – Adding the Pawn Sensing component

4. In the **Details** panel of the **PawnSensing** component, look in the **Events** category and click the green button of the **On See Pawn** event to add it to the EventGraph:

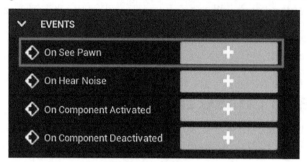

Figure 9.45 – Adding the On See Pawn event

5. The **On See Pawn** event triggers when the enemy sees an instance of the **Pawn** class (or its child class, **Character**) along its line of sight. We need to check whether the instance seen is the player (the **FirstPersonCharacter** class). If it is the player, then we store the instance reference in the Blackboard:

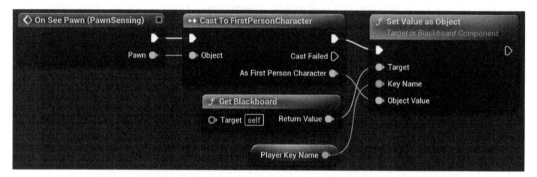

Figure 9.46 – Storing the PlayerCharacter reference in the Blackboard

6. Drag a wire from the **Pawn** output pin of the **On See Pawn** event and add a **Cast To FirstPersonCharacter** node.

7. Right-click on the graph and add a **Get Blackboard** node.

8. Drag a wire from the **Return Value** pin of **Get Blackboard** and add a **Set Value as Object** node.

9. Drag a wire from the **Key Name** pin of the **Set Value as Object** node and add a **GET Player Key Name** node.

10. Drag a wire from the **Object Value** pin of the **Set Value as Object** node and connect to the **As First Person Character** output pin.

11. Connect the white execution pins of the **Cast To FirstPersonCharacter** and **Set Value as Object** nodes. Compile the Blueprint.

These are the changes needed in the `BP_EnemyController` Blueprint to make the enemy see the player. Now, let's work on our Behavior Tree.

Creating a Behavior Tree Task

We can create new elements to use in our Behavior Tree, such as **Task**, **Decorator**, and **Service**. These elements are specialized types of Blueprints. We will create a simple Task to clear a Blackboard key.

Follow these steps to create a Task:

1. In the content browser, double-click the `BT_EnemyBehavior` asset to open the Behavior Tree Editor.

2. Click the **New Task** button on the toolbar:

Figure 9.47 – Creating a Behavior Tree Task

3. If you don't have Tasks in the project, the Blueprint Editor will open with a new Blueprint, using **BTTask_BlueprintBase** as the parent class. If you have Tasks, you need to select the **BTTask_BlueprintBase** class in the dropdown that appears.

4. The **Details** panel shows the class defaults. Change the **Node Name** field to `Clear BB Value`:

Figure 9.48 – Setting the node name

5. In the **Variables** category of the **My Blueprint** panel, click the + button to add a variable. In the **Details** panel, name the variable Key, change its type to **Blackboard KeySelector**, and check the **Instance Editable** attribute:

Figure 9.49 – Creating the Key variable

6. We will use the **Event Receive Execute** event that is called when the Task is activated within the Behavior Tree. We will add the event using the **My Blueprint** panel to see the other events available. Hover the mouse on the **FUNCTIONS** category of the **My Blueprint** panel, click the **Override** dropdown, and select **Receive Execute**:

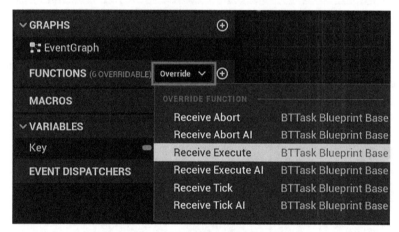

Figure 9.50 – Adding Event Receive Execute

7. We will clear the Blackboard value using the **Key** variable and use the **Finish Execute** function to finish the Task:

Figure 9.51 – The Event Receive Execute actions

8. Drag a wire from the white output pin of **Event Receive Execute** and add a **Clear Blackboard Value** node.

9. Drag a wire from the **Key** input pin of **Clear Blackboard Value** and add a **Get Key** node.

10. Drag a wire from the white output pin of **Clear Blackboard Value** and add a **Finish Execute** node. Check the **Success** parameter of the **Finish Execute** node.

11. Compile, save, and close the Blueprint Editor. In the content browser, rename **BTTask** BTTask_ClearBBValue.

We will use our new Task to clear the **PlayerCharacter** reference after an enemy attack to give the player a chance to run away.

Adding conditions to the Behavior Tree

We will need another **Sequence** node that will connect to tasks to get the enemy to chase the player and a **Selector** node that will run one of the two **Sequence** nodes. We need to ensure that the new Tasks only run when the enemy sees the player. To do this, we'll add a Decorator. A Decorator attaches to the top of a node and provides conditions that must be met before the Tasks can be performed.

The following screenshot shows the updated version of our Behavior Tree after the changes in this section. The Tasks of the **Attack Player** sequence will be added in the next section:

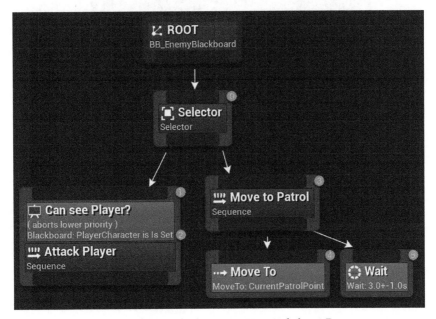

Figure 9.52 – The Attack Player sequence node has a Decorator

Follow these steps to modify the Behavior Tree:

1. In the content browser, double-click the `BT_EnemyBehavior` asset to open the Behavior Tree Editor.

2. Right-click on the middle of the **ROOT** node and select **Break Node Link(s)**.

3. Drag a wire from the dark area at the bottom of the **ROOT** node and drop it onto empty graph space to open a selection menu popup. Choose the **Selector** option.

4. Drag a wire down from the **Selector** node and connect it to the **Move To Patrol** node.

5. Drag another wire down from the **Selector** node and add a **Sequence** node. This new node must be on the left of the **Move To Patrol** node because it has priority over the patrol behavior.

6. In the **Details** panel, change **Node Name** to `Attack Player`.

7. Now, we will use a Decorator to verify whether the enemy sees the player. Right-click on the **Attack Player** node, hover over **Add Decorator** to expand the menu, and select **Blackboard** to add the Decorator.

8. Click the Decorator, and in the **Details** panel, set **Observer aborts** to **Lower Priority**, **Blackboard Key** to **PlayerCharacter**, and **Node Name** to **Can see Player?**:

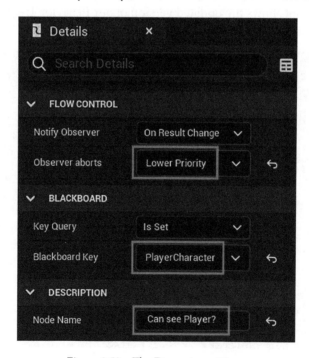

Figure 9.53 – The Decorator settings

9. Save the Behavior Tree. The Decorator will only allow the node to run when the `PlayerCharacter` key has a reference. It will also abort the **Move to Patrol** sequence to execute the **Attack Player** sequence.

The only parts missing to make the enemy chase the player are the Task nodes of the **Attack Player** sequence.

Creating a chasing behavior

To make the enemy chase the player, we will use the **Move To** Task node using the **PlayerCharacter** reference as the destination. We will create a pause between the attacks using the **Wait** node and use our **BTTask_ClearBBValue** Task to clear the **PlayerCharacter** reference:

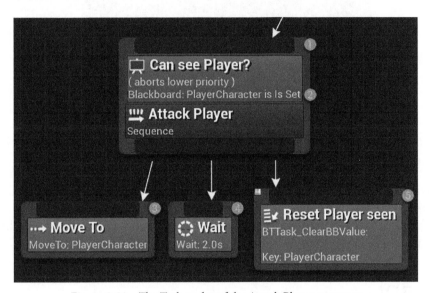

Figure 9.54 – The Task nodes of the Attack Player sequence

In the next chapter, we will make the enemy damage the player.

Follow these steps to add the Task nodes:

1. Drag a wire from the **Attack Player** sequence node and add a **Move To** Task node. In the **Details** panel, change **Blackboard Key** to **PlayerCharacter**.

2. Drag a wire from the **Attack Player** sequence node and add a **Wait** Task node. In the **Details** panel, set **Wait Time** to 2.0 seconds.

3. Drag another wire from the **Attack Player** sequence node and add a **BTTask_ClearBBValue** task node. In the **Details** panel, change **Key** to **PlayerCharacter** and change **Node Name** to Reset Player seen:

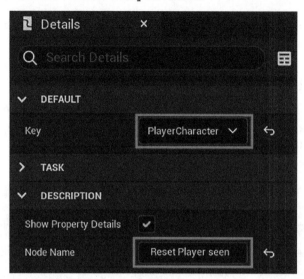

Figure 9.55 – Clearing the PlayerCharacter value in the Blackboard

4. Save the Behavior Tree and close the Behavior Tree Editor. Press the **Play** button in the Level Editor to test the enemy behavior.

As you navigate the player character in front of the patrolling enemy, the enemy will stop its patrol and chase the player. When the enemy reaches the player, it will stop for 2 seconds before returning to its patrol path. If it re-establishes a line of sight with the player, then it will interrupt its patrol and begin chasing the player again.

Summary

In this chapter, we began the process of changing our simple moving targets into fleshed-out game enemies that can challenge the player. In the process, you learned the basics of how AIControllers, Behavior Trees, and Blackboards can be leveraged together to create an enemy with the ability to sense the world around it and make decisions based on that information.

As we continue the process of developing our AI to pose a serious challenge to the player, you can use the skills you have learned to consider other kinds of behaviors you might be able to give an enemy. Continued exploration of AI mechanics will see you continually coming back to the core loop of sensing, decision-making, and acting that we began implementing here.

In the next chapter, we will extend our AI behavior to create an enemy that can truly challenge the player. We will add the ability for the enemy to listen for the player and investigate a sound, as well as giving the enemy an attack ability to damage the player when they get too close. To balance the game around this new threat, we will also give the player the ability to fight back against the enemies.

Quiz

1. The **Run Behavior Tree** function belongs to which class?

    a. `Actor`

    b. `Pawn`

    c. `AIController`

    d. `PlayerController`

2. A Blackboard is a specialized type of Blueprint that can have events and actions.

    a. True

    b. False

3. The Behavior Tree graph can have control flow nodes and Task nodes.

    a. True

    b. False

4. Which control flow node succeeds and stops running as soon as one child successfully runs?

    a. Selector

    b. Sequence

5. Which element can we add to a node to provide conditions that must be met to run it?

    a. Task

    b. Decorator

    c. Service

10

Upgrading the AI Enemies

In this chapter, we will add more functionality to our AI enemies to introduce the potential for a player to fail and to create greater gameplay diversity. At this point, we are going to begin settling on the kind of challenge we want to offer the player. We are going to create zombie-like enemies that will relentlessly pursue the player, creating an action-focused experience, where the player must try to survive against hordes of enemies. We will start by giving more capability to the AI, including the ability to deal damage and use wandering patterns to increase the difficulty of player survival. We will then turn our attention to the player, giving them the ability to fight back against these dangerous enemies. Finally, we will complete the balance of our increased difficulty by creating a system to gradually spawn new enemies in the game world.

In this process, we will cover the following objectives:

- Introducing an enemy melee attack that will damage the player's health
- Giving the AI the ability to hear the player's footsteps and shots
- Having the enemy investigate the last known location of the player based on sound
- Allowing the player to destroy enemies with their gun
- Spawning new enemies in the world
- Setting AI enemies to wander the level randomly

By the end of the chapter, we will have an enemy spawner that will be spawning AI enemies that attack the player, can hear the player's footsteps and shots, and wander the level randomly.

Creating an enemy attack

If the enemies we create are going to pose a genuine obstacle to the player achieving the goals we create for them, then we will first need to give the enemies the ability to damage the player. In *Chapter 9, Building Smart Enemies with Artificial Intelligence*, we set up the basic structure of an enemy attack pattern. It is triggered when the player enters the enemy's line of sight. We are now going to introduce a damage element to this attack, ensuring that there is some consequence of the enemy reaching the melee range of the player.

Making an attack task

We will create an attack task named BTTask_DoAttack that does damage, and we will extend the **Attack Player** sequence we created in the enemy Behavior Tree. The task will have two variables – one to store the target of the damage and one to store the amount of damage to be applied.

Follow these steps to create the attack task:

1. In the content browser, access the Content/FirstPersonBP/Enemy folder and double-click on the BT_EnemyBehavior asset to open the Behavior Tree Editor.

2. Click the **New Task** button on the Toolbar and select the **BTTask_BlueprintBase** option from the drop-down menu that appears. The task is created in the same folder as the Behavior Tree – Content/ FirstPersonBP/Enemy.

3. In the content browser, rename the newly created **BTTask_BlueprintBase_New** asset to BTTask_DoAttack. Double-click on **BTTask_DoAttack** to return to the Blueprint Editor.

4. The **Details** panel shows the class defaults. Change the **Node Name** field to DoAttack.

5. In the **My Blueprint** panel, click the + button of the **Variables** category. In the **Details** panel, name the variable TargetActorKey, change its type to **BlackboardKeySelector**, and check the **Instance Editable** attribute:

Figure 10.1 – Creating the TargetActorKey variable

6. Create another variable in **My Blueprint** panel. In the **Details** panel, name the variable Damage, change **Variable Type** to **Float**, and check the **Instance Editable** attribute. Compile the blueprint and set **DEFAULT VALUE** to 0.25, which means an attack will take 25% of the player's health:

Figure 10.2 – The Damage variable has a default value of 0.25

7. Hover the mouse on the **Functions** category of the **My Blueprint** panel, click the **Override** dropdown, and select **Receive Execute** to add the event.

8. In **Event Receive Execute**, we will ensure **Target Actor** is valid and then apply damage to it. The event gets the **Target Actor** reference from the blackboard and checks whether it is valid before calling the **Apply Damage** function:

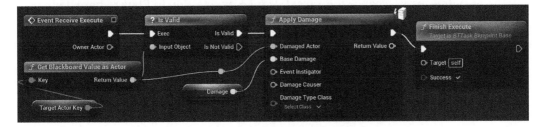

Figure 10.3 – The Event Receive Execute actions

9. The nodes of *steps 9–12* are to get the **Target Actor** reference from the blackboard and check whether it is valid. Drag a wire from the white pin of **Event Receive Execute** and add an **Is Valid** macro node.

10. Drag the **Target Actor Key** variable from the **My Blueprint** panel, drop in **EventGraph**, and select **Get Target Actor Key**.

11. Drag a wire from the **Target Actor Key** node and add **Get Blackboard Value as Actor**.

12. Drag a wire from **Return Value** of **Get Blackboard Value as Actor** and connect to the **Input Object** pin of the **Is Valid** node.

13. The nodes of *steps 13–15* are to call the **Apply Damage** function using the **Target Actor** reference. Drag another wire from **Return Value** of **Get Blackboard Value as Actor** and add an **Apply Damage** node. Connect the **Is Valid** output pin to the white input pin of the **Apply Damage** node.

14. Drag a wire from the **Base Damage** input pin of **Apply Damage** and add a **Get Damage** node.

15. Drag a wire from the white output pin of **Apply Damage** and add a **Finish Execute** node. Check the **Success** parameter of the **Finish Execute** node.

16. Compile, save, and close the Blueprint Editor.

Now, we need to add our attack task to the attack sequence in BT_EnemyBehavior.

Using the attack task in the Behavior Tree

The attack of the enemy is a melee attack, so the enemy will only perform the attack after reaching the player.

Follow these steps to use the DoAttack task:

1. In the Behavior Tree Editor, drag a wire down from the **Attack Player** sequence node and add a **BTTask_DoAttack** task node between the **Move To** and **Wait** task nodes.

2. In the **Details** panel, change the **Target Actor Key** selection to **PlayerCharacter**. Change **Node Name** to Damage Player to describe how we are using **BTTask_DoAttack**:

Figure 10.4 – The BTTask_DoAttack properties

3. Save the Behavior Tree. The **Attack Player** sequence should look like this:

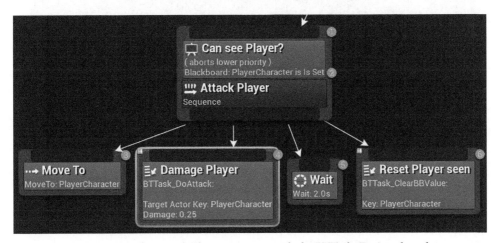

Figure 10.5 – The Attack Player sequence with the BTTask_DoAttack node

The **Attack Player** sequence is complete. Now, we need to update the
FirstPersonCharacter blueprint to decrease the health meter when damage is dealt
out.

Updating the health meter

The health meter bar is linked to the **Player Health** variable of the
FirstPersonCharacter blueprint. We will use **Event AnyDamage** to decrease the
value of the **Player Health** variable.

These are the steps to create **Event AnyDamage**:

1. In the content browser, access the `Content/FirstPersonBP/Blueprints` folder and double-click on the `FirstPersonCharacter` blueprint.

2. Right-click on the empty space of **Event Graph** and add the **Event AnyDamage** node. We will add these nodes to the Event:

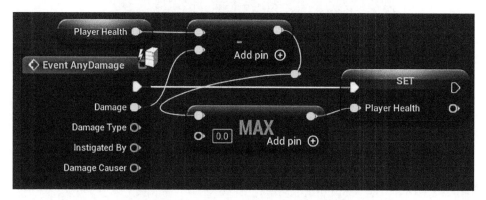

Figure 10.6 – The Event AnyDamage actions

3. Drag a wire from the white output pin of the **Event AnyDamage** node and add a **SET Player Health** node.

4. Drag a wire from the input pin of **SET Player Health** and add a **MAX** (float) node. We use this node to ensure that **Player Health** will never be less than 0.0.

5. Drag a wire from the top input pin of the **Max** (float) node and create a **Subtract** node.

6. Drag a wire from the top input pin of the **Subtract** node and add a **GET Player Health** node.

7. Drag a wire from the bottom input pin of the **Subtract** node and connect to the **Damage** output pin of **Event AnyDamage**.

8. Compile, save the blueprint, and press the **Play** button to test.

Note that the player's health meter depletes when an enemy gets within range of the player and attacks.

Now that our enemy is attacking the player, we want to give more options on how the enemy can detect the player.

Making enemies hear and investigate sounds

Enemies that can only pursue players who walk directly in front of them can easily be avoided. To address this, we will take advantage of the **PawnSensing** component to have the enemy detect nearby sounds that the player makes. If the player makes a sound within the detection range of an enemy, then the enemy will walk to the location of that sound to investigate. If they catch the player in their sight, they will try to attack; otherwise, they will wait at the location of the sound for a moment before returning to their patrol.

Adding hearing to the Behavior Tree

We will add a sequence of tasks that occur when the enemy hears a sound. We want the enemy to continue attacking the player once they see them, so investigating a sound has a lower priority on the Behavior Tree.

To have the enemy investigate the point where it heard a sound, we will need to create two keys within the blackboard. The `HasHeardSound` key is of the Boolean type and will be used to store whether a sound has been heard. The `LocationOfSound` key is of the `Vector` type and will be used to store the location that the sound came from – hence, the location that the enemy AI should investigate.

Follow these steps to create the blackboard keys and add the **Investigate Sound** sequence node to the Behavior Tree:

1. In the content browser, access the `Content/FirstPersonBP/Enemy` folder and double-click on the `BT_EnemyBehavior` asset to open the Behavior Tree Editor.

2. Click the **Blackboard** tab:

Figure 10.7 – Switching the Behavior Tree Editor to Blackboard mode

3. Click the **New Key** button and select **Bool** as the key type. Name this new key `HasHeardSound`:

Figure 10.8 – The HasHeardSound Bool key

4. Click the **New Key** button again and select **Vector** as key type. Name this new key `LocationOfSound`:

Figure 10.9 – The LocationOfSound Vector key

5. Save the blackboard and click the **Behavior Tree** tab.

6. Move the **Attack Player** sequence and all its task nodes further to the left in the Behavior Tree, leaving room between **Attack Player** and **Move to Patrol**. This is where we will add our hearing sequence.

7. Drag a wire down from the **Selector** node and add a **Sequence** node. Rename this node `Investigate Sound`.

8. Right-click on the **Investigate Sound** node, hover over **Add Decorator** to expand the menu, and select **Blackboard** to add a decorator.

9. Click on the decorator, and in the **Details** panel, set **Observer aborts** to **Lower Priority**, **Blackboard Key** to **HasHeardSound**, and **Node Name** to **Heard Sound?**:

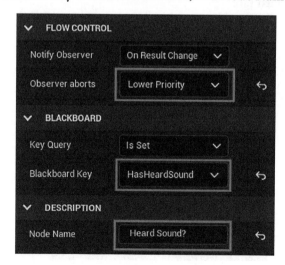

Figure 10.10 – The decorator settings

The following screenshot shows the **Investigate Sound** sequence node with the decorator. Note that the priority of nodes in a Behavior Tree is left to right:

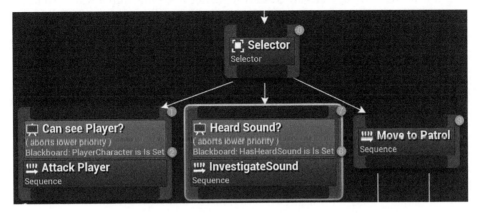

Figure 10.11 – The Investigate Sound sequence node

We have created the blackboard keys, the sequence node, and the decorator. Our next step is to create the task nodes of the **Investigate Sound** sequence.

Setting up the investigating tasks

The **Investigate Sound** sequence will be like the **Attack Player** sequence. If an enemy is patrolling and hears a sound, they will move to the location of the sound:

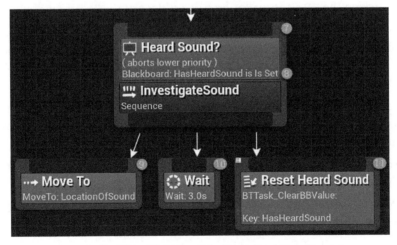

Figure 10.12 – The task nodes of the Investigate Sound sequence

Follow these steps to add the task nodes:

1. Drag a wire from the **Investigate Sound** sequence node and add a **Move To** task node. In the **Details** panel, change **Blackboard Key** to **LocationOfSound**.

2. Drag a wire from the **Investigate Sound** sequence node and add a **Wait** task node. In the **Details** panel, set **Wait Time** to 3.0 seconds.

3. Drag another wire from the **Investigate Sound** sequence node and add a **BTTask_ClearBBValue** task node. In the **Details** panel, change **Key** to **HasHeardSound** and change **Node Name** to **Reset Heard Sound**.

4. Save the Behavior Tree and close the Behavior Tree Editor.

Now, we need to return to the BP_EnemyController blueprint and add some actions that will instruct our AI how to react to sounds in the game.

Creating variables and a macro to update the blackboard

We will create variables and a macro in the BP_EnemyController blueprint to update the keys of the BB_EnemyBlackboard related to sound.

These are the steps:

1. In the content browser, access the Content | FirstPersonBP | Enemy folder and double-click on the BP_EnemyController blueprint.

2. In the **Variables** category of the **My Blueprint** panel, click the + button to add a variable. In the **Details** panel, name the variable HearingDistance and change **Variable Type** to **Float**. Compile the blueprint and set **DEFAULT VALUE** to 1600.0.

3. Create another variable in the **My Blueprint** panel. In the **Details** panel, name the variable HasHeardSoundKey and change **Variable Type** to **Name**. Compile the blueprint and set **DEFAULT VALUE** to HasHeardSound.

4. Create another **Name** variable called LocationOfSoundKey. Compile the blueprint and set **DEFAULT VALUE** to LocationOfSound.

5. In the **My Blueprint** panel, click the + button in the **Macros** category to create a macro. Change the name of the macro to UpdateSoundBB.

6. In the **Details** panel of the macro, create an input parameter named In of the **Exec** type, another input parameter named Location of the **Vector** type, and an output parameter named Out of the **Exec** type:

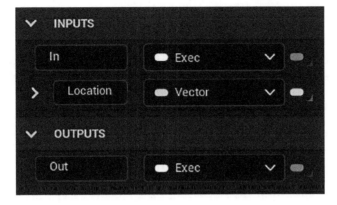

Figure 10.13 – Creating the macro parameters

7. The following screenshot shows the nodes we'll be creating in the following steps for the **UpdateSoundBB** macro:

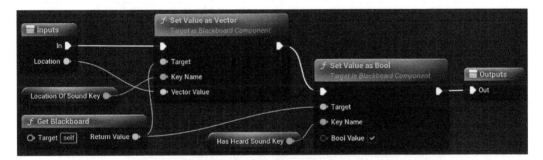

Figure 10.14 – The UpdateSoundBB macro

8. The nodes of *steps 8–11* are to store the location of sound in the blackboard using the **Location Of Sound Key** node. On the tab created for the **UpdateSoundBB** macro, right-click on the graph and add a **Get Blackboard** function node.

9. Drag a wire from the **Return Value** pin of **Get Blackboard** and add a **Set Value as Vector** node.

10. Drag a wire from the **Key Name** pin of **Set Value as Vector** node and add a **GET Location Of Sound Key** node.

11. Connect the **Location** pin of the **Inputs** node to the **Vector Value** pin of **Set Value as Vector**, and connect the white execution pins of the **Inputs** and **Set Value as Vector** nodes.

12. The nodes of *steps 12–14* are to set the **True** value in the **Has Heard Sound Key** of the blackboard. Drag another wire from the **Return Value** pin of **Get Blackboard** and add a **Set Value as Bool** node. Check the **Bool Value** parameter.

13. Drag a wire from the **Key Name** pin of the **Set Value as Bool** node and add a **GET Has Heard Sound Key** node.

14. Connect the white execution pins of the **Set Value as Vector**, **Set Value as Bool**, and **Outputs** nodes. Close the **UpdateSoundBB** macro tab and compile the blueprint.

With the **UpdateSoundBB** macro created, we will use another event of the **PawnSensing** component to detect sound.

Interpreting and storing the noise Event data

The **PawnSensing** component we added to `BP_EnemyController` gives us the foundation to build both visual and auditory sensing in our enemy AI. We will use the **On Hear Noise** event that activates any time the **PawnSensing** component detects a special type of sound broadcast by a pawn noise emitter.

We will have to set up the blueprint so that the enemies only detect noises that are made a short distance away; otherwise, it would feel unfair for the player to shoot their gun from the opposite corner of the map and let every enemy instantly know their location.

Follow these steps to create the **On Hear Noise** event:

1. In the **Components** panel, select the **PawnSensing** component. In the **Details** panel, look in the **Events** category and click the green button of the **On Hear Noise** event to add it to the Event Graph:

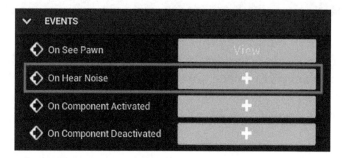

Figure 10.15 – Adding the On Hear Noise event

2. In the **On Hear Noise**, we call the **Update Sound BB** macro if the distance between the sound location and the enemy is less than the value of **HearingDistance**:

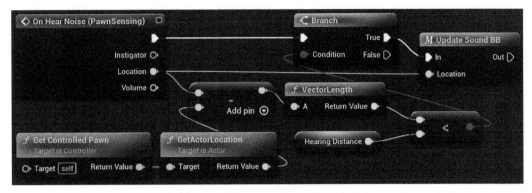

Figure 10.16 – The On Hear Noise actions

3. Drag a wire from the white pin of the **On Hear Noise (PawnSensing)** node and add a **Branch** node. The next steps will create an expression that uses the **VectorLength** function to calculate the distance between the sound location and the enemy location. If the result of this expression is less than the value of **Hearing Distance**, then the **True** output pin of the **Branch** node is executed.

4. Drag a wire from the **True** pin of the **Branch** node and add the **Update Sound BB** macro node. Connect the **Location** pin of the **On Hear Noise (PawnSensing)** node to the **Location** pin of the **Update Sound BB** macro.

5. Drag a wire from the **Condition** input pin of the **Branch** node and add a **Less** node.

6. Drag a wire from the bottom input pin of the **Less** node and add a **GET Hearing distance** node.

7. Right-click on the empty space of **Event Graph** and add a **Get Controlled Pawn** node to get the enemy instance that is being controlled by this `BP_EnemyController`.

8. Drag a wire from the **Return Value** pin of the **Get Controlled Pawn** node and add a **GetActorLocation** node to get the enemy location.

9. Drag a wire from the **Location** pin of the **On Hear Noise (PawnSensing)** node and add a **Subtract** node.

10. Connect the bottom input pin of the **Subtract** node to the **Return Value** pin of the **GetActorLocation** node.

11. Drag a wire from the output pin of the **Subtract** node and add a **VectorLength** node.

12. Connect **Return Value** of the **VectorLength** node to the top input pin of the **Less** node. **Return Value** of the **VectorLength** node is the distance between the location of the sound and the enemy location.

13. Compile and save the blueprint.

Now that we have modified our enemy AI to be able to detect sounds that are broadcast to the listener, we need to create the nodes in the `FirstPersonCharacter` blueprint that will trigger the hearing response and attach them to player actions.

Adding noise to the player's actions

The **Pawn Sensing** component of **EnemyController** is only able to detect noise if it is created from **Pawn Noise Emitter**. The existing sound effect that we play when the player fires their gun will not trigger the enemy's **Pawn Sensing** component. It is important to know that the nodes that produce noise for pawn sensing have no direct relationship with the sound a player hears. The noise exists only in terms of producing an event that the AI can hear and respond to.

The **Pawn Noise Emitter** component must be added to an actor for the noises it broadcasts to be detected by a pawn sensor. We will change two player abilities, namely sprinting and shooting, to produce detectable noise by utilizing this component.

These are the steps to use **Pawn Noise Emitter**:

1. In the content browser, access the `Content > FirstPersonBP > Blueprints` folder and double-click on the `FirstPersonCharacter` Blueprint.

2. In the **Components** panel, click the **Add** button and search for `pawn`. Select the **Pawn Noise Emitter** component:

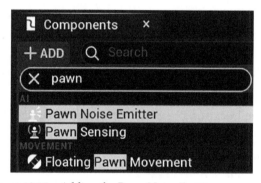

Figure 10.17 – Adding the Pawn Noise Emitter component

3. We will begin by adding noise to sprinting. In the **My Blueprint** panel, double-click the **ManageStaminaDrain** macro to open the macro tab. We will add the **Make Noise** node after the **SET Player Stamina** node:

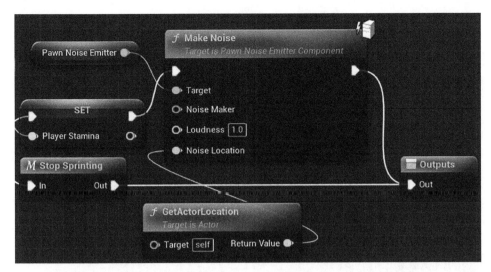

Figure 10.18 – Modifying the ManageStaminaDrain macro to make noise

4. Drag the **Outputs** node to the right to make room for another function node.

5. Drag a wire from the white output pin of the **SET Player Stamina** node, search for make noise, and add the **Make Noise (PawnNoiseEmitter)** function:

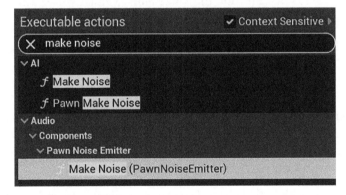

Figure 10.19 – Adding the Make Noise function of the PawnNoiseEmitter component

6. Change the **Loudness** input of the **Make Noise** node to 1.0.

7. Drag a wire from the **Noise Location** input of the **Make Noise** node and add a **GetActorLocation** node.

8. The next place we will add the **Make Noise** node is in the **InputAction Fire** event, after reducing the ammunition. You can find the **InputAction Fire** event in the **Graphs** category of the **My Blueprint** panel:

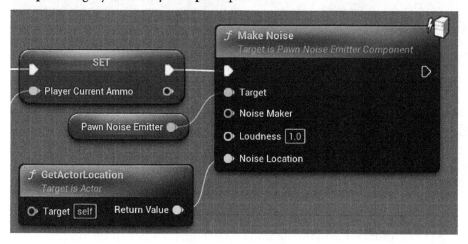

Figure 10.20 – Modifying the InputAction Fire event to make noise

9. Drag a wire from the white output pin of the **SET Player Current Ammo** node, search for `make noise`, and add the **Make Noise (PawnNoiseEmitter)** function.

10. Change the **Loudness** input of the **Make Noise** node to `1.0`.

11. Drag a wire from the **Noise Location** input of the **Make Noise** node and add a **GetActorLocation** node.

12. Compile, save, and then click on **Play** to test the game.

While behind an enemy, or otherwise outside their line of sight, sprinting or firing your gun should result in the enemy approaching the position you were at when you made the noise. If they establish a line of sight with you during their investigation, then they will begin heading directly toward you.

With detection possible with both sight and sound, you might now find it difficult to avoid being spotted by enemies. We will now turn our attention to the other side of gameplay balancing and equip the player with the means to combat their enemies.

Making the enemies destructible

Recall that in earlier chapters, we created enemy targets that the player could destroy after a couple of hits with a projectile. We want to give the player a similar ability to mitigate the threat provided by our new enemies. To do so, we will add blueprint nodes in `BP_EnemyCharacter` to handle damage-taking and destruction. The player needs to hit an enemy character three times to destroy them.

Follow these steps to deal with a hit:

1. In the content browser, access the Content > FirstPersonBP > Enemy folder and double-click on the BP_EnemyCharacter blueprint.

2. In the **Variables** category of the **My Blueprint** panel, click the + button to add a variable, and name the variable EnemyHealth.

3. In the **Details** panel, set **Variable Type** to **Integer**. Compile the blueprint and set **DEFAULT VALUE** to 3:

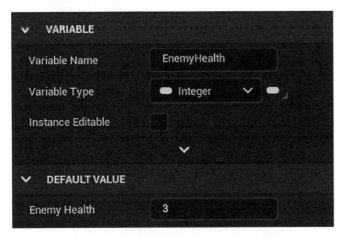

Figure 10.21 – EnemyHealth starts with 3 points

4. Right-click on the empty space of **Event Graph** and add an **Event Hit** node. The following screenshot shows the first part of the **Event Hit** actions:

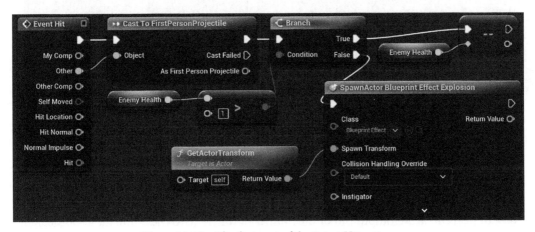

Figure 10.22 – The first part of the Event Hit actions

5. Drag a wire from the **Other** output pin of the **Event Hit** node and add a **Cast To FirstPersonProjectile** node. Connect the white pins of **Event Hit** and **Cast To FirstPersonProjectile**.

6. Drag a wire from the white output pin of the **Cast To FirstPersonProjectile** node and add a **Branch** node.

7. Drag a wire from the **Condition** pin of the **Branch** node and add a **Greater** node.

8. Drag a wire from the top input pin of **Greater** node and add a **Get Enemy Health** node. Set a value of 1 in the bottom input of the **Greater** node.

9. Drag a wire from the **True** output pin of the **Branch** node and add a **Decrement Int** node.

10. Drag a wire from the input pin of the **Decrement Int** node and add a **Get Enemy Health** node.

11. Drag a wire from the **False** output pin of the **Branch** node and add a **Spawn Actor from Class** node. In the **Class** parameter, select the **Blueprint_Effect_Explosion** class, which is a blueprint from the starter content.

12. Drag a wire from the **Spawn Transform** parameter and add a **GetActorTransform** node.

13. The nodes of the second part of **Event Hit** are the same used in the BP_CylinderTarget blueprint:

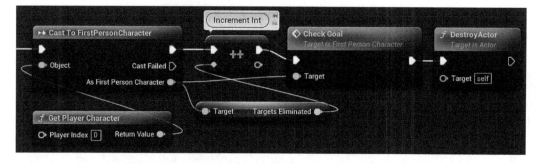

Figure 10.23 – The second part of the Event Hit actions

14. Open the BP_CylinderTarget blueprint located in the Content > FirstPersonBP > Blueprints folder.

15. Select and copy the nodes shown in *Figure 10.23*, and then paste the nodes into the BP_EnemyCharacter blueprint.

16. Connect the white output pin of the **Spawn Actor** node to the white input of the **Cast to FirstPersonCharacter** node.

17. Compile, save, and then press **Play** to test.

From now on, when the player shoots an enemy three times, the enemy will explode and be destroyed in a similar way to how the cylinder targets behaved.

Now that we can destroy enemies, we need to ramp up the difficulty for the player again by spawning more enemies.

Spawning more enemies during gameplay

We are going to spawn new enemies in the level periodically so that the game can continue if the player destroys the first few enemies, and if they are too slow to defeat enemies, then the difficulty will gradually increase.

Creating the BP_EnemySpawner blueprint

We will create a blueprint that will spawn enemies in random locations in the level. The time between spawns is determined by a variable called SpawnTime. There is another variable called MaxEnemies that limits the spawning of enemies.

Follow these steps to create the blueprint:

1. In the content browser, access the Content > FirstPersonBP > Enemy folder. Click the **Add** button and choose the **Blueprint Class** option.

2. On the next screen, choose **Actor** as the parent class. Name the blueprint BP_EnemySpawner and double-click it to open the Blueprint Editor.

3. In the **Variables** category of the **My Blueprint** panel, click the + button to add a variable, and name it SpawnTime. In the **Details** panel, change **Variable Type** to **Float**, and check the **Instance Editable** attribute. Compile the blueprint and set **DEFAULT VALUE** to 10.0:

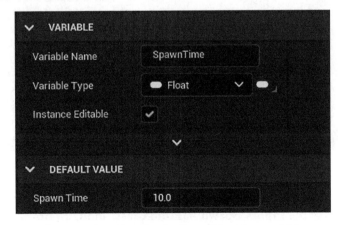

Figure 10.24 – Creating the SpawnTime float variable

4. Create another variable in the **My Blueprint** panel and name it `MaxEnemies`. In the **Details** panel, change **Variable Type** to **Integer**, and check the **Instance Editable** attribute. Compile the blueprint and set **DEFAULT VALUE** to 5:

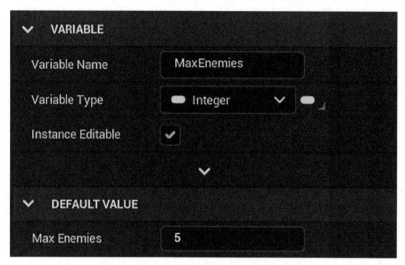

Figure 10.25 – Creating the MaxEnemies integer variable

5. In the **My Blueprint** panel, click the + button in the **Macros** category to create a macro. Change the name of the macro to `SpawnEnemy`.

6. In the **Details** panel of the macro, create an input parameter named `In` and an output parameter named `Out` both of the **Exec** type:

7. On the tab created for the **SpawnEnemy** macro, add these nodes to spawn a **BP_EnemyCharacter** instance in a random location in the level:

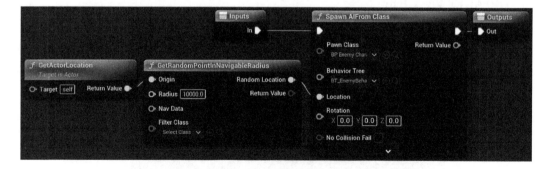

Figure 10.26 – The SpawnEnemy macro

8. Right-click on the graph and add a **Spawn AIFrom Class** node. Connect the white execution pins of the **Inputs**, **Spawn AIFrom Class**, and **Outputs** nodes.

9. In the **Pawn Class** parameter, select **BP_EnemyCharacter**. In the **Behavior Tree** parameter, select **BT_EnemyBehavior**.

10. Drag a wire from the **Location** parameter and add a **GetRandomPointIn NavigableRadius** node. Set **Radius** to 10000.0. This node returns a random location based on the navigation mesh.

11. Drag a wire from the **Origin** parameter and add a **GetActorLocation** node:

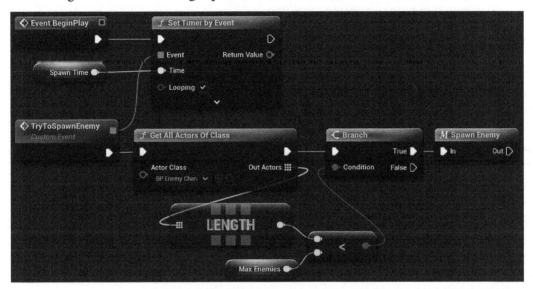

Figure 10.27 – Setting the timer to spawn enemies

12. In the Event Graph of BP_EnemySpawner, drag a wire from the white execution pin of **Event BeginPlay** and add a **Set Timer by Event** node.

13. Check the **Looping** parameter. Drag a wire from the **Time** parameter and add a **Get Spawn Time** node.

14. Drag a wire from the **Event** parameter and add a custom event. Name it TryToSpawnEnemy.

15. Drag a wire from the white pin of **TryToSpawnEnemy** and add a **Get All Actors Of Class** node. In the **Actor Class** parameter, select **BP_EnemyCharacter**.

16. Drag a wire from the white output pin of **Get All Actors Of Class** and add a **Branch** node.

17. Drag a wire from the **True** pin of the **Branch** node and add the **Spawn Enemy** macro node.

18. Drag a wire from the **Out Actors** pin of **Get All Actors Of Class** and add a **Length** node. The return value of the **Length** node will be the number of enemies in the level.

19. Drag a wire from the output pin of the **Length** node and add a **Less** node. Connect the output pin of the **Less** node to the **Condition** parameter of the **Branch** node.

20. Drag a wire from the bottom pin of the **Less** node and add a **Get Max Enemies** node.

21. Compile, save, and close the Blueprint Editor. Drag BP_EnemySpawner from the content browser and drop anywhere on the level to create an instance. Click the **Play** button to test your enemy spawning.

You will regularly see new enemies appear as you run the game. Note, however, that the enemies are not moving once spawned unless they hear or see the player. This is because they are not being created with an established patrol point to pursue. Rather than adding patrol points to our spawned enemies, we will add randomness to our enemy navigation behavior.

Creating enemy wandering behavior

In *Chapter 9, Building Smart Enemies with Artificial Intelligence*, we set the default behavior for enemies as a patrolling movement between two points. While this worked well as a testbed for our hearing and seeing components and would be appropriate for a stealth-oriented game, we are going to ramp up the challenge and action of this game's experience by replacing this behavior with random wandering. This will make avoiding enemies significantly harder, encouraging more direct confrontations. To do this, we are going to return to the BT_EnemyBehavior Behavior Tree.

Identifying a wander point with a custom task

We need to create a key in BB_EnemyBlackboard that will store the location of the next destination that the enemy should wander to. Unlike the **PatrolPoint** key, our destination won't be represented by an in-game actor but, rather, by vector coordinates. Then, we will create a task to determine where in the level the enemy should be wandering.

Follow these steps to create the key and the task:

1. In the content browser, double-click the BT_EnemyBehavior asset to open the Behavior Tree Editor.

2. Click the **Blackboard** tab to edit BB_EnemyBlackboard.

3. Click the **New Key** button and select **Vector** as the key type. Name this new key WanderPoint:

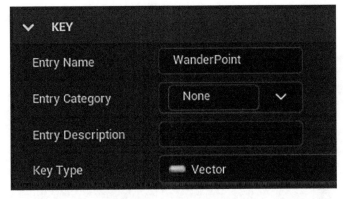

Figure 10.28 – Creating the WanderPoint key in the blackboard

4. Save the blackboard and click on the **Behavior Tree** tab to return to the Behavior Tree.

5. Click the **New Task** button on the Toolbar and select the **BTTask_BlueprintBase** option from the drop-down menu that appears.

6. In the content browser, rename the newly created **BTTask_BlueprintBase_ New** asset `BTTask_FindWanderPoint`. Double-click on `BTTask_ FindWanderPoint` to return to the Blueprint Editor.

7. The **Details** panel shows the class defaults. Change the **Node Name** field to `FindWanderPoint`.

8. In the **My Blueprint** panel, click the + button of the **Variables** category. In the **Details** panel, name the variable `WanderKey`, change its type to **Blackboard KeySelector**, and check the **Instance Editable** attribute:

Figure 10.29 – Creating the WanderKey variable

9. Hover the mouse on the **Functions** category of the **My Blueprint** panel, click the **Override** dropdown, and select **Receive Execute** to add the event.

10. In **Event Receive Execute**, we will get a random location of the level and store in the blackboard:

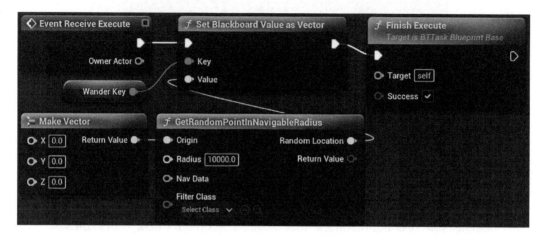

Figure 10.30 – The Event Receive Execute actions

11. Drag a wire from the white pin of **Event Receive Execute** and add a **Set Blackboard Value as Vector** node.

12. Drag a wire from the white output pin of **Set Blackboard Value as Vector** and add a **Finish Execute** node. Check the **Success** parameter of the **Finish Execute** node.

13. Drag a wire from the **Key** parameter of **Set Blackboard Value as Vector** and add a **Get Wander Key** node.

14. Drag a wire from the **Value** parameter of **Set Blackboard Value as Vector** and add a **GetRandomPointInNavigableRadius** node. Set **Radius** to 10000.0.

15. Drag a wire from the **Origin** parameter and add a **Make Vector** node.

16. Compile and save the blueprint.

Now that we have our custom task, we can modify BT_EnemyBehavior to make the enemy find and move to WanderPoint.

Adding wandering to the Behavior Tree

We will convert the **Move To Patrol** sequence to a **Wander** sequence. The new **Wander** sequence is represented in the Behavior Tree by these nodes:

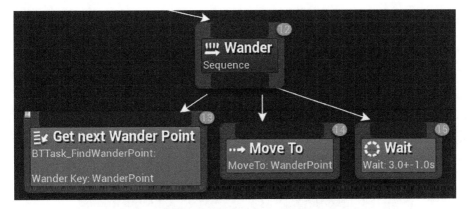

Figure 10.31 – The new Wander sequence

Follow these steps to modify the Behavior Tree:

1. In the content browser, double-click the BT_EnemyBehavior asset to open the Behavior Tree Editor.

2. Select the **Move To Patrol** sequence node. In the **Details** panel, change **Node Name** to Wander.

3. Select the **Move To** task node and change **Blackboard Key** to WanderPoint.

4. Drag a wire out from the **Wander** sequence node to the left of the other nodes and add the **BTTask_FindWanderPoint** node.

5. In the **Details** panel, set **Wander Key** to WanderPoint. Also, change **Node Name** to Get Next Wander Point.

6. Save and close the Behavior Tree Editor.

That is all we need to change in the Behavior Tree to include the enemy wandering behavior. There are some adjustments that we need to do in the two blueprints.

Last adjustments and test

We will remove **Event BeginPlay** of BP_EnemyCharacter that was used to set Patrol Point. We don't need it anymore because we are using the random WanderPoint.

The other change we need to do is modify the **Target Goal** value of FirstPersonCharacter to be higher so that the game can continue for longer. We will set this value to 20 so that the player must eliminate 20 enemies before winning the game.

These are the steps to adjust the blueprints:

1. Open the BP_EnemyCharacter blueprint.
2. In the Event Graph, delete **Event BeginPlay** and all the nodes connected.
3. Compile, save, and close the Blueprint Editor.
4. Open the FirstPersonCharacter blueprint.
5. In the **My Blueprint** panel, select the **TargetGoal** variable. In the **Details** panel, change **DEFAULT VALUE** to 20:

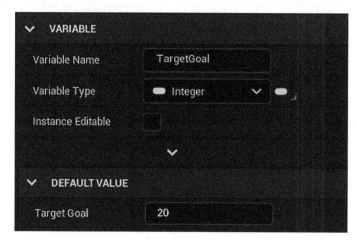

Figure 10.32 – Changing the default value of TargetGoal

6. Compile, save, and close the Blueprint Editor.
7. To test the enemy's wandering behavior, it is better to use the **Simulate** option that is in the menu, which can be accessed by clicking on the three dots next to the **Play** button:

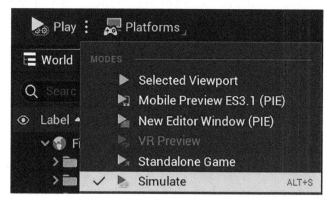

Figure 10.33 – Using Simulate to move freely in the level

Hold the right mouse button and use the *W*, *A*, *S*, and *D* keys and the mouse to move freely on the level. You will see the enemies spawning and moving to a random location in the level.

We created a custom task to find a random wander point and modified the Behavior Tree to use this new task. Now, the enemies spawned by `BP_EnemySpawner` know how to move in the level.

Summary

In this chapter, we started on the path of creating a challenging but balanced game experience by enhancing the capabilities of our AI-driven enemies. We gave our enemies zombie-like behavior by allowing them to wander aimlessly around the level until noticing the player by sight or sound. We also gave them the ability to charge forward when they notice the player and launch a melee attack, lowering the player's health. Then, we gave the player the chance to fight back by attacking the enemy, eventually destroying them once the enemy's health is depleted. Finally, we gave new flexibility to our game by setting up a system to create new enemies as the game is being played.

At this point, the core content of our game is nearly complete. You should feel proud of the significant progress you have made! You can take some time to tweak the many variables you have created to customize the gameplay to your liking, or you can continue reading if you are ready to move on to the final system.

In the next chapter, we will add the final elements necessary for a full game experience. We will end the game when the player runs out of health, create a round-based advancement system, and create a save system so that the player can return to a previously saved game state.

Quiz

1. What is the name of the event used in a Behavior Tree task?

   a. **Tick**

   b. **Event Receive Execute**

   c. **Event Begin Play**

2. What is the name of the component used to add sight and hearing to AI?

   a. **Pawn Sensing**

   b. **AI Sensing**

   c. **AI Perception**

3. A blackboard can have a key of the `Vector` type.

   a. True

   b. False

4. The **Set Timer by Event** node has a **Function Name** parameter.

   a. True

   b. False

5. The **GetRandomPointInNavigableRadius** node returns a random location based on the navigation mesh.

   a. True

   b. False

11

Game States and Applying the Finishing Touches

In this chapter, we will take the final steps to evolve our game into a complete and fun experience that challenges the player. First, we will introduce player death, which is activated when the player's health is fully drained. Then, we will introduce a round system that will elevate the challenge for the player by requiring increasingly numerous enemies to be defeated as they progress through the rounds. Finally, we will introduce a saving and loading system so that the player can leave the game and later return to the round that they were last playing. In this chapter, we will cover the following topics:

- Showing different menus based on player conditions
- Creating scaling difficulty with gameplay modifiers
- Supporting the game state being saved and reloaded later
- Branching level initialization based on the saved data
- Creating transition screens that display gameplay data

By the end of the chapter, we will have an arcade-style first-person shooter that a player can continually return to for an increasingly difficult challenge.

Making danger real with player death

In *Chapter 10, Upgrading the AI Enemies*, we made significant progress toward a balanced game in which enemies threaten the player but the player can use skill to overcome that challenge. One element remains glaringly missing. If the player runs out of health, then they should not be able to continue progressing through the game. So, we will take what we've learned about from the win screen we created in *Chapter 8, Creating Constraints and Gameplay Objectives*, and apply it to a lose screen. This screen will enable the player to restart the level with full ammo and a freshly filled health bar, but will also negate any progress they had made toward reaching their target goal.

Setting up a lose screen

The lose screen will be presented when the player runs out of health. We will present them with options to restart the last round or quit the game. You may remember the win screen we created; we presented similar options there. Rather than remaking the UI screen from scratch, we can save some time by using our **WinMenu** asset as a template.

Follow these steps to create **LoseMenu**:

1. In the **Content Browser**, access the Content|FirstPersonBP|UI folder. Right-click on **WinMenu** and select the **Duplicate** option.

2. Name this new Blueprint Widget LoseMenu:

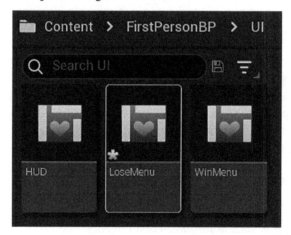

Figure 11.1 – Duplicating and renaming WinMenu

3. Double-click on the **LoseMenu** asset to open the UMG Editor. Select the text object showing **You Win!**. In the **Details** panel, rename the text element to Lose msg, change the **Text** field under **Content** to You Lose!, and change **Color and Opacity** to a dark red color:

Figure 11.2 – Setting the message of LoseMenu

4. Compile and save. The two buttons, **Restart** and **Quit**, can remain identical to their
    WinMenu counterparts in appearance and functionality for now.

Now we need to modify the FirstPersonCharacter Blueprint to show the lose screen.

Showing the lose screen

We will create a Custom Event named **LostGame** that will be called when the player runs
out of health.

These are the steps to create the Custom Event:

1. In the **Content Browser**, access the Content > FirstPersonBP >
    Blueprints folder and double-click on the FirstPersonCharacter Blueprint.

2. Right-click on the **Event Graph** and add a **Custom Event**. Rename it LostGame.
    These are the nodes we will add to the **LostGame** Event:

Figure 11.3 – LostGame actions

3. Drag a wire from the output execution pin of **LostGame**, add a **Set Game Paused**
    node, and check the **Paused** checkbox.

4. Right-click on the **Event Graph** and add a **Get Player Controller** node. Drag from
    the **Return Value** output pin and add a **SET Show Mouse Cursor** node. Check the
    checkbox next to **Show Mouse Cursor** and attach this node to the output execution
    pin of **Set Game Paused**.

5. Drag a wire from the output execution pin of the **SET Show Mouse Cursor** node and add a **Create Widget** node. In the **Class** parameter, select **LoseMenu**.

6. Drag the **Return Value** output pin of the **Create Widget** node and add an **Add to Viewport** node.

7. We will modify **Event AnyDamage** to call the **LostGame** Event if **Player Health** is **Nearly Equal** to 0 . 0:

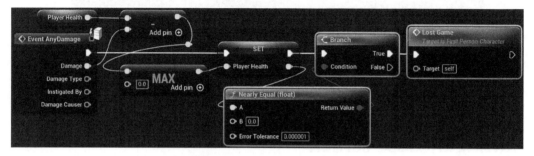

Figure 11.4 – Modifying Event AnyDamage

8. Drag a wire from the white output pin of the **SET Player Health** node and add a **Branch** node.

9. Drag a wire from the output pin of the **SET Player Health** node and add a **Nearly Equal (float)** node. Connect the **Return Value** pin to the **Condition** input pin of the **Branch** node.

10. Drag a wire from the **True** output pin of the **Branch** node and add the **LostGame** node.

11. Compile, save, and then click on **Play** to test your work. If you stand next to an enemy long enough for it to drain your health to zero, then you should see the **LoseMenu** we created.

Now, the player needs to be more careful with the enemies to not lose the game. The next step to make the game more interesting is to create a round-based experience.

Creating round-based scaling with saved games

We now have a game that supports a full play experience. However, the gameplay experience is limited by the number of enemies we have set as our target goal. This results in the game feeling shallow. To address this, we can adopt techniques used by arcade games, which increase the difficulty of the game as the player progresses through a series of rounds. This is a way to add depth and fun to your game using the existing assets, without requiring you to spend hours creating custom content.

The rounds we create will serve as the score of the player. The higher the round they reach, the more the player is thought to have achieved. To ensure that the maximum round the player reaches is limited only by their skill, rather than the amount of time for which they play the game in a single sitting, we will implement a save system so that the player can pick up from where they left off if they leave the game and come back to it later.

Storing game information using the SaveGame class

The first step we need to perform to create a save system is to create a Blueprint child of the SaveGame class that will store the game data that we want to save. We want to track which round the player was on before they quit the game. We do not need to store any data on how many enemies the player has killed because it would make more sense to the player for each game session to start at the beginning of a round.

Follow these steps to create a child of the SaveGame class:

1. In the **Content Browser**, access the Content|FirstPersonBP|Blueprints folder. Click the **Add** button and select **Blueprint Class**.

2. On the next screen, search for and select **SaveGame** as the parent class:

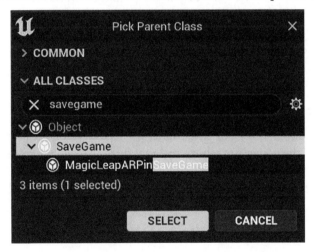

Figure 11.5 – Selecting SaveGame as the parent class

3. Name the Blueprint BP_SaveInfo and double-click it to open the Blueprint Editor.

4. In the **Variables** category of the **My Blueprint** panel, click on the + button to add a variable. In the **Details** panel, name it Round, and change **Variable Type** to **Integer**. Compile the Blueprint, and then set **Default Value** to 1:

Figure 11.6 – Creating the Round integer variable

5. Compile, save, and close the Blueprint editor.

That's all we need to do in the BP_SaveInfo Blueprint. The next step is to learn how to save and load using the BP_SaveInfo Blueprint.

Saving game information

Now that we have a container for our saved data, we need to ensure that the data is stored somewhere on the player's machine and that it is retrieved when the player returns to the game. Like the rest of our gameplay settings, we will add this process to the FirstPersonCharacter Blueprint. We will create some variables and a macro to save game information.

Follow these steps to create the variables and macro:

1. In the **Content Browser**, access the Content|FirstPersonBP|Blueprints folder and double-click on the FirstPersonCharacter Blueprint.

2. In the **Variables** category of the **My Blueprint** panel, click on the + button to add a variable. In the **Details** panel, name it CurrentRound, and change **Variable Type** to **Integer**. Compile the Blueprint, and then set **Default Value** to 1.

3. Create a variable in the **My Blueprint** panel and name the variable `SaveInfoRef`.

4. In the **Details** panel, click the **Variable Type** drop-down menu and search for `BP_SaveInfo`. Hover over **BP_SaveInfo** to display a submenu and then choose **Object Reference**:

Figure 11.7 – The SaveInfoRef variable references an instance of BP_SaveInfo

5. Create another variable in the **My Blueprint** panel. In the **Details** panel, name the variable `SaveSlotName` and change **Variable Type** to **String**. Compile the Blueprint and set **Default Value** to `SaveGameFile`. This variable stores the filename:

Figure 11.8 – SaveSlotName stores the filename

6. In the **My Blueprint** panel, click the + button in the **Macros** category to create a macro. Change the name of the macro to `SaveRound`. In the **Details** panel of the macro, create an input parameter named `In` of the **Exec** type and an output parameter named `Out` of the **Exec** type.

7. On the tab created for the macro **SaveRound**, add the nodes seen in the following screenshot. We check whether **SaveInfoRef** is valid. If it is not valid, we create an instance of BP_SaveInfo and store it in **SaveInfoRef**. We update the **Round** variable of **SaveInfoRef** and then save the contents of **SaveInfoRef**:

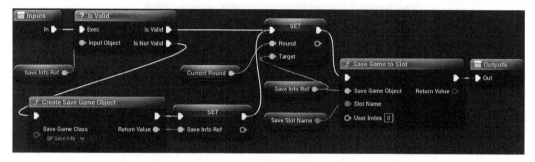

Figure 11.9 – The SaveRound macro

8. Drag a wire from the **In** pin of the **Inputs** node and add an **Is Valid** macro node.

9. Drag a wire from the **Input Object** parameter and add a **Get Save Info Ref** node.

10. Right-click on **Event Graph** and add another **Get Save Info Ref** node. Drag a wire from the **Get Save Info Ref** node and add a **SET Round** node.

11. Connect the **Is Valid** output pin to the white input pin of the **SET Round** node. Drag a wire from the **Round** input pin and add a **Get Current Round** node.

12. Drag a wire from the white output pin of the **SET Round** node and add a **Save Game to Slot** node. Connect the white output pin of **Save Game to Slot** to the **Out** pin of the **Outputs** node.

13. Connect the **Save Game Object** pin to the **Get Save Info Ref** node. Drag a wire from the **Slot Name** pin and add a **Get Save Slot Name** node.

14. Drag a wire from the **Is Not Valid** output pin and add a **Create Save Game Object** node. In **Save Game Class**, select **BP_SaveInfo**.

15. Drag a wire from the **Return Value** pin of **Create Save Game Object** and add a **SET Save Info Ref** node. Connect the white output pin of **SET Save Info Ref** to the white input pin of the **SET Round** node.

16. Compile and save the Blueprint.

Our next step is to create the macro to load the contents we save using the **SaveRound** macro.

Loading game information

We will create a macro named **LoadRound** that will retrieve the saved **Round** and store it in the **CurrentRound** variable.

These are the steps to create the macro:

1. In the **My Blueprint** panel of the `FirstPersonCharacter` Blueprint, click the + button in the **Macros** category to create a macro. Change the name of the macro to `LoadRound`. In the **Details** panel of the macro, create an input parameter named `In` of the **Exec** type and an output parameter named `Out` of the **Exec** type.

2. On the tab created for the **LoadRound** macro, add these nodes:

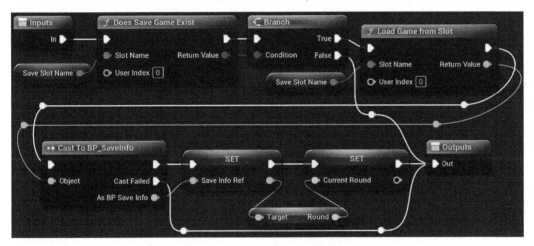

Figure 11.10 – The LoadRound macro

3. Drag a wire from the **In** pin of the **Inputs** node and add a **Does Save Game Exist** node. Drag a wire from the **Slot Name** pin and add a **Get Save Slot Name** node.

4. Drag a wire from the **Return Value** pin and add a **Branch** node. Connect the white output pin of **Does Save Game Exist** to the white input pin of the **Branch** node.

5. Connect the **False** pin of the **Branch** node to the **Out** pin of the **Outputs** node. You can double-click a wire to add a reroute node and modify the shape and position of a wire.

6. Drag a wire from the **True** pin of the **Branch** node and add a **Load Game from Slot** node. Drag a wire from the **Slot Name** pin and add a **Get Save Slot Name** node.

7. Drag a wire from the **Return Value** pin of **Load Game from Slot** and add a **Cast To BP_SaveInfo** node. Connect the white output pin of **Load Game from Slot** to the white input pin of the **Cast To BP_SaveInfo** node.

8. Connect the **Cast Failed** pin of the **Cast To BP_SaveInfo** node to the **Out** pin of the **Outputs** node. Add a reroute node if needed.

9. Drag a wire from **As BP Save Info** of **Cast To BP_SaveInfo** and add a **SET Save Info Ref** node. Connect the white pins of **Cast To BP_SaveInfo** and **SET Save Info Ref**.

10. Drag a wire from the output blue pin of **SET Save Info Ref** and add a **Get Round** node.

11. Drag a wire from the **Round** pin and add a **SET Current Round** node. We are getting the value of the **Round** variable that was saved and storing it in the **Current Round** variable of the `FirstPersonCharacter` Blueprint.

12. Connect the white pins of **SET Save Info Ref**, **SET Current Round**, and **Outputs** nodes.

13. Compile and save the Blueprint.

Using the **SaveRound** and **LoadRound** macros, we can make the player resume the game on the round they stopped. To increase the challenge, let's set the **TargetGoal** based on the round.

Increasing the TargetGoal

We will take advantage of the data we store in the save file to change the gameplay for the player as they progress. We will do this by creating a **RoundScaleMultiplier** variable that will multiply the **Current Round** to find the new **TargetGoal**.

Follow these steps to increase the **TargetGoal**:

1. In the **Variables** category of the **My Blueprint** panel, click on the + button to add a variable. In the **Details** panel, name it `RoundScaleMultiplier`, then change **Variable Type** to **Integer**. Compile the Blueprint, and then set **Default Value** to 2:

Figure 11.11 – The RoundScaleMultiplier variable

2. In the **My Blueprint** panel, click the + button in the **Macros** category to create a macro. Change the name of the macro to `SetRoundTargetGoal`. In the **Details** panel of the macro, create an input parameter named `In` of the **Exec** type and an output parameter named `Out` of the **Exec** type.

3. On the tab created for the **SetRoundTargetGoal** macro, add these nodes:

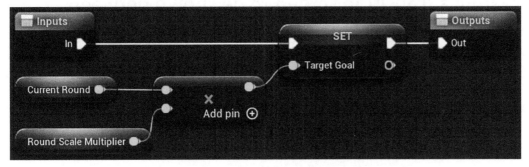

Figure 11.12 – The SetRoundTargetGoal macro

4. Drag a wire from the **In** pin of the **Inputs** node and add a **SET Target Goal** node. Connect the white output pin of **SET Target Goal** to the **Out** pin of the **Outputs** node.

5. Drag a wire from the **Target Goal** pin and add a **Multiply** node.

6. Drag a wire from the top input pin of the **Multiply** node and add a **Get Current Round** node.

7. Drag a wire from the bottom input pin of the **Multiply** node and add a **Get Round Scale Multiplier** node.

8. Compile, save the Blueprint, and return to the **Event Graph** tab.

9. Access **Event BeginPlay** in the **Graphs** category of the **My Blueprint** panel and add the **Load Round** and **Set Round Target Goal** macro nodes:

Figure 11.13 – Modifying Event BeginPlay

When a round starts, we use the **Load Round** macro to load a saved file if it exists. Then we use the **Set Round Target Goal** macro to set the **TargetGoal**.

When the player reaches the **TargetGoal**, we need to show a transition screen.

Creating a transition screen to be shown between rounds

Currently, when the player defeats enough enemies to meet the requirements displayed by **TargetGoal**, they are presented with **WinMenu**. It congratulates them and offers them the opportunity to restart the game or quit the application. Now that we are adopting round-based gameplay, we will adapt this **WinMenu** screen as a transition screen that will bring the player into the next round of gameplay.

Follow these steps to create the transition screen:

1. In the **Content Browser**, access the /Content/FirstPersonBP/UI folder and rename the WinMenu Widget Blueprint to RoundTransition so that it more accurately reflects its new purpose.

2. Double-click the **RoundTransition** Widget Blueprint to open the UMG Editor. The new **RoundTransition** screen will have these elements:

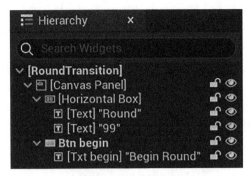

Figure 11.14 – RoundTransition hierarchy panel

3. In the **Hierarchy** panel, delete the **You Win!** text element and delete the **Btn quit** button as we will not need to present an option to quit during the round transitions.

4. Click the **Graph** tab. In the **Event Graph**, delete the **On Clicked (Btnquit)** Event. Click the **Designer** tab to return to UMG Editor.

5. Select the **Txt restart** element and rename it to `Txt begin`. In the **Details** panel, change the text from `Restart` to `Begin Round`. Rename the **Btn restart** to `Btn begin`. The functionality of reloading the level will remain the same.

6. Drag a **Horizontal Box** from the **Palette** panel onto the **Hierarchy** panel above the **Btn restart** button.

7. In the **Details** panel, click on the **Anchors** dropdown and select the top-center option. Set **Position X** to `-300.0`, and set **Position Y** to `200.0`. Check the **Size To Content** property, so we don't need to change the values of **Size X** and **Size Y**. The size of this horizontal box will automatically adjust based on the size of its child elements:

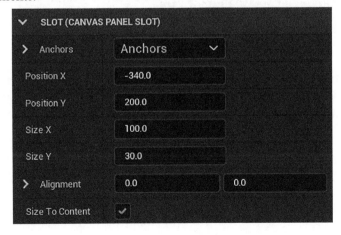

Figure 11.15 – Horizontal Box properties

8. Drag a **Text** object onto the **Horizontal Box**. In the **Details** panel, change the **Text** field under the **Content** category to Round. In the **Appearance** category, change the font **Size** to 120.

9. Drag another **Text** object onto the **Horizontal Box**. In the **Details** panel, set **Padding Left** to 20.0 and change the **Text** field under the **Content** category to 99 as a reference. In the **Appearance** category, change the font **Size** to 120. The **RoundTransition** layout should look like this:

Figure 11.16 – RoundTransition screen elements

10. In the **Details** panel, find the **Bind** button next to the **Text** field and create a new binding, as shown here:

Figure 11.17 – Creating a binding for a round

11. In the **Get Text 0** graph view that appears, add a **Get Player Character** node, cast it using the **Cast To FirstPersonCharacter** node, and then drag from the **As First Person Character** pin to add a **Get Current Round** node.

12. Attach the cast node and the **Current Round** node to **Return Node**. The editor will create a **ToText (integer)** node to convert the number into a text format:

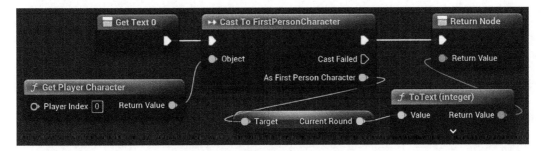

Figure 11.18 – We will show onscreen the value of the Current Round variable

13. Compile, save, and close the UMG Editor.

To complete the round-based system, we just need to modify the **End Game** Event.

Transitioning to a new round when the current round is won

The modifications of the **End Game** Event in the `FirstPersonCharacter` Blueprint will be simple because the **RoundTransition** screen will be displayed since it is a modified version of **WinMenu**.

When the player wins a round, we will increment the **Current Round** variable and save.

Follow these steps to modify the **End Game** Event:

1. In the **Content Browser**, access the `Content > FirstPersonBP > Blueprints` folder and double-click on the `FirstPersonCharacter` Blueprint.

2. In **Event Graph**, select the **End Game** Event. In the **Details** panel, change the Event name to `End Round`.

3. Change the comment box label to `End Round: Shows Transition Menu`:

Figure 11.19 – The new nodes of the End Round Event

4. Break the wire between the **End Round** and **Set Game Paused** nodes. Move the **End Round** node to the left to make room for some more nodes.

5. Right-click on **Event Graph** and add a **Get Current Round** node.

6. Drag a wire from the output pin of the **Get Current Round** node and add an **Increment Int** node. Connect the white pins of the **Increment Int** and **End Round** nodes.

7. Drag a wire from the output white pin of **Increment Int** and add the **Save Round** macro node.

8. Connect the **Out** pin of **Save Round** to the white input pin of the **Set Game Paused** node.

9. Compile, save, and click the **Play** button to test.

When you load the game, you should notice that the target goal counter at the top of the game has a low number of enemies as the goal. Defeat the number of enemies indicated by the goal and you should see the round transition screen appear, displaying **Round 2**. When you press the **Begin Round** button, you will reload the level with your health and ammo restored, but with a higher number of enemies as the target. If you quit the game and then click on the **Play** button again, you will see that the game loads the round that you were last on.

Now that we can track the player's progress, we should offer them the ability to reset their save file if they wish to begin the game from the start.

Pausing the game and resetting the save file

We will create **PauseMenu**, which will present the player with options to resume playing the game, reset the game to round one, or quit the application.

Creating a pause menu

PauseMenu is like our **LoseMenu**. So, we will use it as a template. The following screenshot shows the elements we want in **PauseMenu**:

Figure 11.20 – Pause menu elements

Follow these steps to create **PauseMenu**:

1. In the **Content Browser**, access the Content > FirstPersonBP > UI folder. Right-click on **LoseMenu** and select the **Duplicate** option.

2. Name this new Blueprint Widget **PauseMenu**.

3. Select the text displaying **You Lose!** and, in the **Details** panel, change the **Text** field to Paused and change the **Color and Opacity** to a blue color:

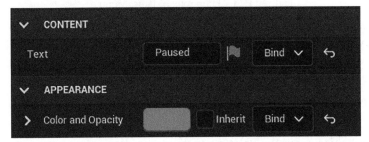

Figure 11.21 – Setting the message of PauseMenu

4. We will move the **Paused** text further up to make room for another button. In the **Slot** category, set **Position X** to -170.0, and set **Position Y** to -450.0:

Figure 11.22 – Setting the position of the Paused text

5. We will add a button to be the **Resume** option and will change the **Restart** button to be the **Reset All** option. The **Hierarchy** of **PauseMenu** will look like this:

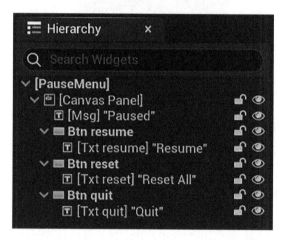

Figure 11.23 – Hierarchy of PauseMenu

6. Drag a **Button** element from the **Palette** panel onto the **CanvasPanel** object in the **Hierarchy** panel below the **Paused** message. In the **Details** panel, change the name to Btn resume, click on the **Anchors** dropdown, and select the option with the anchor in the center of the screen.

7. Set **Position X** to -180.0, **Position Y** to -250.0, **Size X** to 360.0, and **Size Y** to 100.0.

8. Drag a **Text** object from the **Palette** panel onto the **Btn resume** element in the **Hierarchy** panel. In the **Details** panel, set the name to Txt resume, change the **Text** field under the **Content** category to Resume, and set the font **Size** to 48.

9. Now, let's transform the **Restart** button into the **Reset All** button. Change the **Btn restart** button name to Btn reset, **Txt restart** to Txt reset, and then change the **Text** field to Reset All.

10. Compile and save.

We've already added the visual elements of **PauseMenu**; now let's work on the functionality.

Resuming the game

To resume the game, we need to remove **PauseMenu** from the viewport, hide the mouse cursor, and unpause the game.

These are the steps to add the functionality:

1. Click on the **Btn resume** element, scroll down to the bottom of the **Details** panel, and click on the + button next to the **On Clicked** Event.

2. On the **Graph** view, add these nodes to the **On Clicked (Btnresume)** Event:

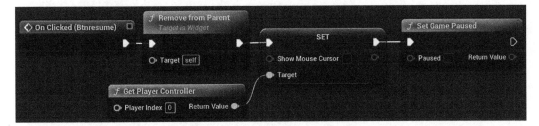

Figure 11.24 – Resume button actions

3. Drag a wire from the **On Clicked (Btnresume)** node and add a **Remove from Parent** node.

4. Right-click on **Event Graph** and add a **Get Player Controller** node.

5. Drag a wire from **Return Value** of **Get Player Controller** and add a **SET Show Mouse Cursor** node. Connect the white output pin of **Remove from Parent** to the white input pin of **SET Show Mouse Cursor**. Leave the **Show Mouse Cursor** parameter unchecked.

6. Drag a wire from the white output pin of **SET Show Mouse Cursor** and add a **Set Game Paused** node. Leave the **Paused** parameter unchecked.

These are the actions of the **Resume** button. Now, let's add the actions of the **Reset All** button.

Resetting the save file

The **Reset All** button will delete the save game if it exists and then reload the game level. We will create a macro with the actions to delete the save game.

Follow these steps to create the macro:

1. In the **My Blueprint** panel, click the + button in the **Macros** category to create a macro. Change the name of the macro to DeleteFile. In the **Details** panel of the macro, create an input parameter named In of the **Exec** type and an output parameter named Out of the **Exec** type.

2. On the tab created for the **DeleteFile** macro, add the nodes seen in the following screenshot. We get a reference to the **FirstPersonCharacter** instance to retrieve the value of the **Save Slot Name** variable.

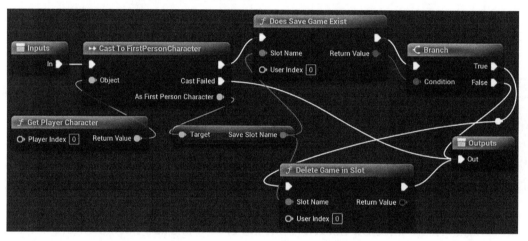

Figure 11.25 – DeleteFile macro actions

3. Add a **Get Player Character** node, cast it using the **Cast To FirstPersonCharacter** node, and then drag from the **As First Person Character** pin to add a **Get Save Slot Name** node.

4. Drag a wire from the white output pin of **Cast To FirstPersonCharacter** and add a **Does Save Game Exist** node. Connect the **Slot Name** pin to the **Get Save Slot Name** node.

5. Drag a wire from **Does Save Game Exist** and add a **Branch** node. Connect the **Return Value** pin to the **Condition** pin.

6. Drag a wire from the **True** output of the **Branch** node and add a **Delete Game in Slot** node. Connect the **Slot Name** pin to the **Get Save Slot Name** node. Connect the white output pin to the **Out** pin of the **Outputs** node.

7. Connect the **Cast Failed** pin of **Cast To FirstPersonCharacter** and the **False** pin of the **Branch** node to the **Out** pin of the **Outputs** node.

8. On **Event Graph**, add the **Delete File** macro node after the **On Clicked (Btnreset)** Event:

Figure 11.26 – Modifying the On Clicked (Btnreset) Event

9. Compile and save **PauseMenu**.

We created our **PauseMenu** screen. Now we need a way for the player to bring up **PauseMenu**.

Triggering the pause menu

We will use the *Enter* key to pause the game and open **PauseMenu**. We need to add a **Pause** action mapping in **Project Settings…** and add actions to the **InputAction** Event created for the **Pause** action mapping.

Follow these steps to trigger **PauseMenu**:

1. To change the input settings for your game, click on the **Settings** button on the far right of the toolbar, and select the **Project Settings…** option:

Figure 11.27 – Accessing Project Settings

2. On the left side of the window that appears, look for the **Engine** category and select the **Input** option. Click on the + sign next to **Action Mappings**. Name the new action **Pause** and select the **Enter** key from the drop-down menu to map that key to the **Pause** Event:

Figure 11.28 – Creating an Action Mapping

3. In the **Content Browser**, access the `Content > FirstPersonBP > Blueprints` folder and double-click on the `FirstPersonCharacter` Blueprint.

4. Right-click on **Event Graph**, search for `input action pause`, and add the **Pause** Event node. Copy all the nodes from the **LostGame** Custom Event and paste them near the **InputAction Pause** node:

Figure 11.29 – InputAction Pause Event actions

5. Connect the **Pressed** pin of the **InputAction Pause** node to the white input pin of the **Set Game Paused** node.

6. Change the **Class** parameter of the **Create Widget** node to **Pause Menu**.

7. Compile, save, and then click on **Play** to test.

Now, while playing, you should be able to press the *Enter* key you set up to bring up the pause menu. Clicking on the **Resume** button should close the pause menu and return you to the game. If you progress several rounds through the game and then press the **Reset All** button from the pause menu, then you should automatically reload the level, with your progress reset to the first round of the game. If this is what you see, then congratulations! You have accomplished a significant achievement in creating a save system that is able to store, load, and reset progress across multiple rounds of gameplay.

Summary

In this chapter, we have made significant strides toward making our game a complete experience that can be played and enjoyed by other people. You learned how to show different screens based on whether the player has won or lost. You also learned how to implement a save system that allows the player to return to their earlier game sessions with their progress intact. Then, we implemented a round system that modifies the gameplay goal each time the player progresses to a new round. Finally, we implemented additional menu systems that give the player information about which round they are on and give them the opportunity to pause the gameplay and even reset their own save file.

In the next chapter, we will explore making builds of the game we created so that we can share the experience with others.

Quiz

1. The **Create Widget** node creates an instance of the widget class selected in the parameter.

    a. True

    b. False

2. What is the name of the class that is used to store data that will be saved?

    a. `SaveData`

    b. `SaveInfo`

    c. `SaveGame`

3. The **Save Game to Slot** function receives a structure as an input parameter with the data that will be saved.

    a. True

    b. False

4. The **Load Game from Slot** function returns an instance of the SaveGame class. We need to use the **Cast To** node to access the variables that were saved.

    a. True

    b. False

5. An **Action Mapping** named **Shoot** triggers an Event named **InputAction Shoot**.

    a. True

    b. False

12

Building and Publishing

One of the best ways to grow as a game developer is to share your work with others so that you can get feedback on how to evolve your designs and content. An early priority should be to create shareable builds of your game so that other people can play it for themselves. Fortunately, Unreal Engine 5 makes it extremely simple to create builds of your game for multiple platforms. In this chapter, we will look at how to optimize the settings of our game and the process of building for your target desktop platform. In the process, we will cover the following topics:

- Optimizing your graphics settings
- Setting up our game to be played by others
- Packaging the game into a build

By the end of the chapter, you will have a packaged version of our game that you can share and install on other machines.

Optimizing your graphics settings

Prior to creating a build, or a version of our game that has been optimized to play on a particular platform, you should change the graphics settings of our game to ensure that they are suited to your target machines. The graphics settings in Unreal Engine 5 are identified as **Engine Scalability Settings**. This settings interface is composed of several graphics settings, each of which determines the final visual quality of one element of the game. With any game, there is a trade-off between high-quality effects and visuals, and the performance of that game in terms of frame rate.

Games that struggle with low frame rates feel bad from a gameplay perspective, even if the mechanics are otherwise solid. As such, it is important to balance the desire to make your game look as good as it can with the need to understand what the performance impact will be on the machines that your players will be running the game on.

Because of the varying hardware performance of PCs and macOS computers, many games targeting those platforms use custom menu settings to allow the player to tweak the graphics settings of the game themselves. However, the game we have created only uses very simple assets and a relatively constrained level size, so we are simply going to define some workable defaults before generating a build to distribute.

Follow these steps to modify **Engine Scalability Settings**:

1. Click the **Settings** button located on the right-hand side of the Level Editor toolbar.

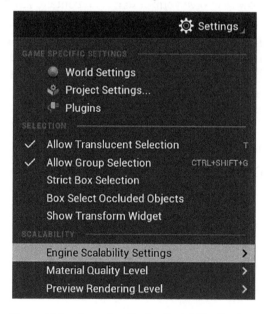

Figure 12.1 – Accessing Engine Scalability Settings

2. Hover over **Engine Scalability Settings** to see a pop-out display of the **Quality** settings that you can tweak, as seen in the following screenshot:

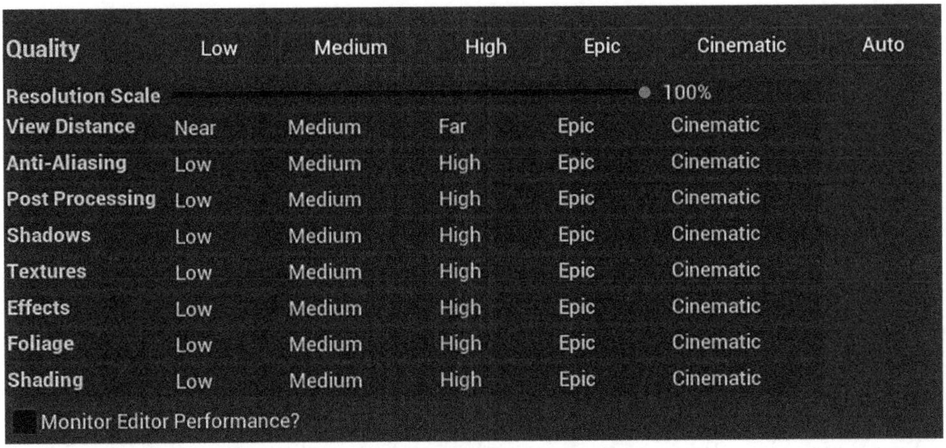

Quality	Low	Medium	High	Epic	Cinematic	Auto
Resolution Scale					100%	
View Distance	Near	Medium	Far	Epic	Cinematic	
Anti-Aliasing	Low	Medium	High	Epic	Cinematic	
Post Processing	Low	Medium	High	Epic	Cinematic	
Shadows	Low	Medium	High	Epic	Cinematic	
Textures	Low	Medium	High	Epic	Cinematic	
Effects	Low	Medium	High	Epic	Cinematic	
Foliage	Low	Medium	High	Epic	Cinematic	
Shading	Low	Medium	High	Epic	Cinematic	
Monitor Editor Performance?						

Figure 12.2 – Engine Scalability Settings elements

3. The buttons along the top of this menu, ranging from **Low** to **Epic**, serve as presets of the settings based on the broad level of performance versus quality that you want to target at runtime. Clicking on the **Low** button will set all the quality settings to the minimum, giving you the best possible performance, in exchange for the least visually attractive settings. **Epic** is the opposite end of the spectrum, raising all the engine quality settings to their maximum, at the expense of significant performance, depending on the assets you have chosen to use.

4. The **Cinematic** button will set all the quality settings to cinematic quality, which is used for rendering cinematics. This setting is not intended for use during gameplay or at runtime.

5. The **Auto** button will detect the hardware of the machine you are currently running the Editor on and adjust the graphics settings to a level that strikes a good balance between performance and a graphical quality that is suitable for your machine. If you are intending to target hardware that is roughly equivalent to the machine you are developing on, using the **Auto** setting can be a simple way to establish the graphics settings for your build.

6. If you wish to tweak the settings individually, you can use this brief description of their functions to help you:

-   **Resolution Scale**: This setting causes the engine to render the game in a lower resolution than the resolution that your player will be targeting and uses software to upscale the game to the targeted resolution. This improves the performance of the game, at the cost of perceived fuzziness at lower-resolution scales.

-   **View Distance**: This determines the distance from the location of the camera where objects will be rendered. Objects beyond this distance will not be rendered. Shorter view distances increase performance but can cause objects to pop into view suddenly as they cross the view distance boundary.

-   **Anti-Aliasing**: This setting softens the jagged edges of 3D objects in the world, which can dramatically improve the look of your game. At the higher settings, you will see fewer jagged edges, but this will decrease performance.

-   **Post Processing**: This setting changes the baseline quality settings of several filters that get applied to the screen after the scene is created, such as motion blur and light bloom effects.

-   **Shadows**: This changes the base quality of several bundled settings that combine to determine the look of shadows in the game. Highly detailed shadows often have a dramatic impact on performance.

-   **Textures**: This setting will affect the process by which the textures used in your game are managed by the engine. If you have many large textures in your game, reducing this setting can help avoid running out of graphics memory and thus increases performance.

-   **Effects**: This setting changes the baseline quality settings of several special effects applied to the game, such as material reflections and translucency effects.

-   **Foliage**: This setting will affect the quality of foliage used in the game.

-   **Shading**: This setting will affect the quality of the materials.

Ultimately, the best way of optimizing the performance of your game is to regularly test it on the machines you intend for people to play it on. If you notice sluggish performance, take note of where you see it occur. If the performance of your game is always low, you might need to reduce some of the postprocessing or anti-aliasing effects. If performance is low only in certain areas of your level, you might need to look at reducing the object density in that area or reducing the quality of a particular game model.

Now that we know how to adjust the graphics settings, let's customize some project settings before the build.

Setting up our game to be played by others

Unreal Engine 5 offers a wide variety of platforms that you can choose from to build your game, and this list will continue to expand as newer versions of the engine are released and new technologies emerge. You can deploy your game on Windows, macOS, iOS, Android, and Linux. The engine supports the creation of content for various virtual reality platforms, such as **Oculus Quest**. There is also support for 8th and 9th generation consoles, but you need to be a registered console developer with the appropriate development kit.

Each platform has its own unique requirements and best practices associated with it for game development. Mobile games have higher optimization requirements to get games to perform well.

We can customize some of the settings that will determine how our project appears on the target machine.

Follow these steps to customize the project settings:

1. Click on the **Settings** button in the Level Editor toolbar, and then click on **Project Settings...**, as shown here:

Figure 12.3 – Accessing Project Settings

2. Inside **Project Settings**, you will see a wide variety of options in the left panel for the customization of different aspects of the game, engine, and platform interactions. By default, the **Project - Description** page will open. Here, you can customize the project name, the thumbnail as it will appear in the Unreal Engine project selector, and a brief description of the project and its creator or publisher, as shown in this screenshot:

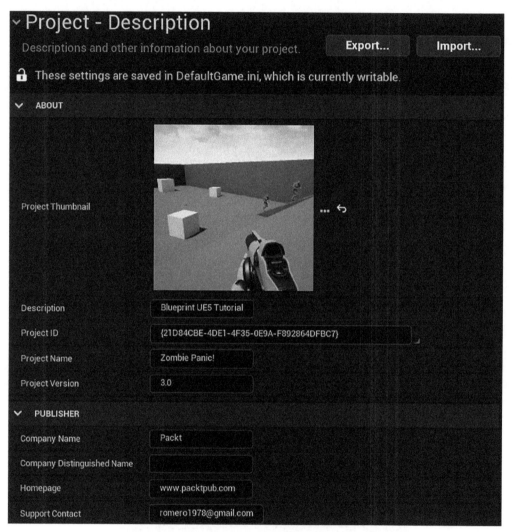

Figure 12.4 – Project - Description page

3. Clicking on **Maps & Modes** in the left panel will bring you to a page where you can determine which map the game will load by default. Our game has only one map, so that makes this choice easy, but you will often need to designate a map dedicated to your main menu screen to be the first map to load. When you create games with multiple maps, you will need to ensure that the first map loaded can manage which map is loaded next in the play experience.

Figure 12.5 – Project - Maps & Modes page

4. Finally, clicking on the platform you are targeting with this build will bring you to that platform's customization page.

5. In the **Windows** example shown in the following screenshot, the **Splash** screens and the game's **Icon** image are available for changing. Mobile and console platform targets will have more options to change, which will be specific to each of those platforms.

Figure 12.6 – Platforms - Windows page

6. Replace the default **SPLASH** and **ICON** settings with the images you would like to use for your game. This can be as simple as an edited screenshot from the game, or you can show off a custom piece of art made specifically for icons and splash screens.

Once you are satisfied with your project settings, close the **Project Settings** window so we can start packaging our project.

Packaging the game into a build

Creating a distributable form of your game for one of these platforms involves a process called **packaging**. Packaging takes all the code and assets of the game and sets them up in the proper format to be able to perform on the selected platform. We will be following the path to making a Windows or macOS release of your game.

> **Note**
>
> It is important to note that Unreal Engine 5 can only create Windows builds from a copy of the engine running on a Windows system, and OS X builds from copies installed on a macOS running OS X. Thus, the platforms that you can target with your game will be partially limited by the machine you are developing the game on. If you are developing on a Windows PC and wish to create an OS X build of the game, you can install Unreal Engine 5 on a macOS and copy your project files to this new machine. From there, you will be able to generate an OS X build, with no further changes required.

These are the steps to package your game to be played on a particular platform:

1. Click the **Platforms** button in the toolbar, hover over the desired platform, and then click on **Package Project**, as follows:

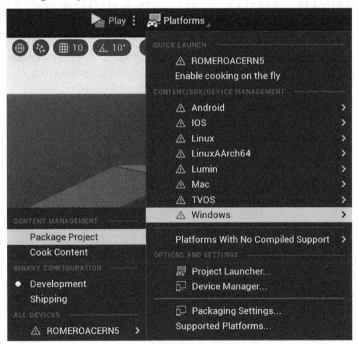

Figure 12.7 – Packaging the project for Windows

2. Once you click on a platform, you will be prompted to select a location on your computer to store the build you make. After selecting a location, you will see a popup that tells you that the engine is packaging the project. If something goes wrong in the packaging process, you will be shown the details of the error in the output log window that pops up. Packaging a project can take a bit of time, depending on how complex and large the project is, but if you don't encounter any errors, then you will eventually see a message saying that the packaging is complete. Congratulations – you have created a packaged copy of your game!

3. Navigate to the folder where you chose to store your build. On macOS, open the folder called **MacNoEditor** and double-click on the application to launch it. For Windows, open the **WindowsNoEditor** folder and double-click on the executable to run the game. Take a moment to go through the game you created in its final form and reflect on just how far you have come. You now have a functional game that other people can play and enjoy. Making even simple games is no easy feat, so you should feel proud of your accomplishment!

We packaged the project using the default settings, but there are a lot of options that you can modify in the packaging.

Build configurations and packaging settings

In this section, we will see some of the settings available for build and packaging.

The **Platforms** submenu has the **Packaging Settings** option, which displays the **Project - Packaging** page with configuration options that can be modified.

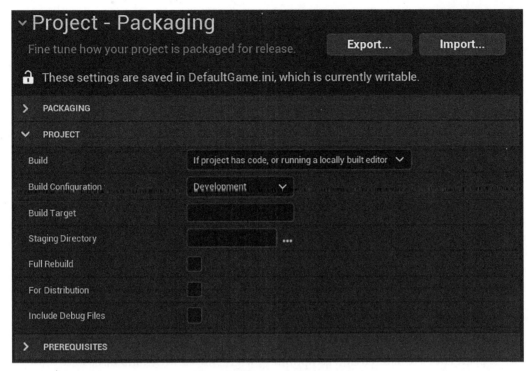

Figure 12.8 – Project - Packaging page

The **PACKAGING** category contains a lot of technical options that can be used to optimize the packaging. The **Build Configuration** option defines how the build will be done. In Blueprint-only projects, you have two options: **Development** and **Shipping**. Development builds contain information that is used in debugging to help you find errors. Shipping builds are cleaner as they do not have debug information and should be used to create the final version of the game that will be distributed.

The **Staging Directory** property is used to define the folder where the packaged build will be stored. The **For Distribution** option is required when submitting a game to the App Store or Google Play Store.

You can now close the **Project - Packaging** page.

When you want to move the project to another computer or to pass the project to someone else, you can use the **Zip Project** option available in the **File** menu of the Level Editor. The **Zip Project** option copies and compresses the essential project files.

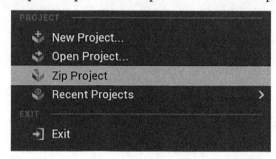

Figure 12.9 – Zip Project

There are many packaging options and some of them are platform-specific. Take the time to study the various packaging options for your game's target platform.

Summary

In this chapter, we discussed creating playable builds of the game we created across multiple platforms. We learned how to optimize the graphics settings and discussed how to set up the game to be played by others. Finally, we saw how to change the build configurations and packaging settings.

With what you've learned in this chapter, you will be able to better present your project and distribute it on different platforms so that others can enjoy it.

This chapter concludes *Part 3* and ends our implementation of the playable shooter game. *Part 4* will cover advanced Blueprints concepts. In the next chapter, we will learn about data structures and flow control.

Quiz

1. You can adjust the graphics settings of your game in the **Engine Scalability Settings** panel.

    a. True

    b. False

2. In Unreal Engine 5, you can package your game for consoles without being a registered console developer.

    a. True

    b. False

3. To package your game, you need to access a menu by clicking the **Platforms** button.

    a. True

    b. False

4. Which option is not a **Build Configuration** option in Blueprint-only projects?

    a. Development

    b. Shipping

    c. Test

5. The **Staging Directory** property is used to define the folder where the packaged build will be stored.

    a. True

    b. False

Part 4: Advanced Blueprints

This part will explore advanced Blueprints concepts that will help you when you are developing complex games. We will examine data structures, flow control, math nodes, trace nodes, and Blueprints tips to increase the quality of Blueprints. The final chapter explains some **Virtual Reality (VR)** concepts and explores the VR template.

This part comprises the following chapters:

- *Chapter 13, Data Structures and Flow Control*
- *Chapter 14, Math and Trace Nodes*
- *Chapter 15, Blueprints Tips*
- *Chapter 16, Introduction to VR Development*

13

Data Structures and Flow Control

In *Part 3*, we learned how to create a basic AI game using Behavior Trees, how to add game states, and how to package a game for distribution.

Part 4 will teach you about advanced Blueprint concepts that will help when developing complex games. We will learn about data structures, flow control, math nodes, and Blueprint tips, and gain an understanding of virtual reality development.

This chapter will explain what data structures are and how they can be used to organize data in Blueprints. We will learn about the concept of containers and how to use arrays, sets, and maps to group multiple elements, as well as other ways to organize data using enumerations, structures, and data tables. In this chapter, we will also see how to control a Blueprint's flow of execution by using various types of flow control nodes.

We will cover the following topics in this chapter:

- Exploring different types of containers
- Exploring other data structures
- Flow control nodes

By the end of the chapter, you will know about various data structures and flow control nodes that will increase your ability to solve problems in Blueprints.

Exploring different types of containers

A container is a type of data structure whose instances can store collections of values or instances. The values in a container must be of the same type. An element of a container can be retrieved later by using a label that the element is associated with.

The containers available in Blueprints are arrays, sets, and maps. To turn a variable into a container, click the icon next to **Variable Type** and choose one of the containers that appear, as shown in the following screenshot:

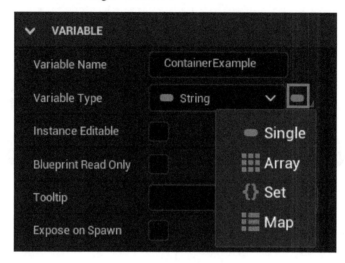

Figure 13.1 – Creating a container

We will start by learning about the most used container type – an array.

Array

An **array** is a container type that stores one or more values of a specific data type. Thus, a single variable can be used to store multiple values instead of using separate variables for each value.

Arrays provide indexed access to their elements, so the label used to retrieve an element is the element's sequential index in the container. Every element keeps its place in the array unless an element is inserted in the middle of it.

These are the steps to create an array:

1. In the **My Blueprint** panel, create a variable and define its type.

2. Click the icon next to the **Variable Type** drop-down menu and select the icon of an array, as shown in this screenshot:

Figure 13.2 – Creating an array of integers

3. Compile the Blueprint to be able to add the default values of the array. In the **DEFAULT VALUE** panel of the variable, click the + icon to add elements to the array.

    The following screenshot shows an example of an **Integer** array named **Ammo Slot** with four elements used to store the amount of ammunition the player has. Each element of the array stores the amount of ammunition of a type of weapon:

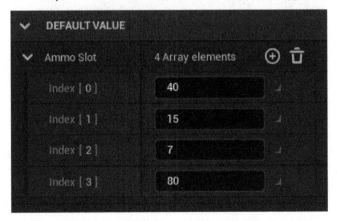

Figure 13.3 – Adding the default values of an array

> **Note**
>
> Arrays always start from index 0. So, in the previous example with four elements, the index of the first element is 0, and the index of the last element is 3.

To get a value from an array, use the **Get (a copy)** node. This node has two input parameters, which are a reference to an array and the index of the element, as shown in the following screenshot. The **Get (a copy)** node creates a temporary copy of the value stored in the array; therefore, any changes to the value retrieved will not affect the value stored in the array:

Figure 13.4 – Getting a value from an array

To modify an element of an array, use the **Set Array Elem** node. The example in the following screenshot sets the **Item** value to 10 of the element with **Index** set to 2:

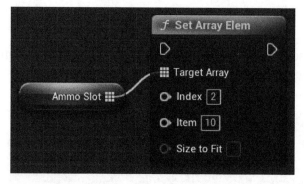

Figure 13.5 – Setting a value in an array element

Two nodes can be used to add elements to an array. The **ADD** node adds an element to the end of the array. The **INSERT** node adds an element at the index passed as an input parameter, and all the elements that used to be in this index onward will move to the next indexes. For example, if we insert an element at index 2, then the previous element that was at index 2 will be moved to index 3. The element that was at index 3 will be moved to index 4, and so on. The length of the array dynamically increases when using these nodes. Both nodes receive a reference as parameters to an array and a reference to the element that will be added to the array:

Figure 13.6 – Adding elements to an array

You can get the number of elements in an array by using the **LENGTH** node. Since the index of an array starts at zero, then the index of the last element will be **LENGTH** – 1. Alternatively, you can use the **LAST INDEX** node, which returns the index of the last element of the array. The following screenshot shows these two nodes:

Figure 13.7 – Getting the length and last index of an array

> **Note**
> Be careful not to access an index in an array greater than the last index. It may give unexpected results and, in turn, cause crashes that may be difficult to track down later.

You can use the **Random Array Item** node to get a random element of the array. The **IS EMPTY** or **IS NOT EMPTY** nodes are used to check whether the array has elements:

Figure 13.8 – Nodes to get a random array element and to check whether the array has elements

The **Make Array** node is used to create an array from variables in the EventGraph. Click on **Add pin +** to add input pins. The example in the screenshot is from a Level Blueprint. There are four instances of **PointLight** in the level, and the **Make Array** node is used to create **Point Lights Array**:

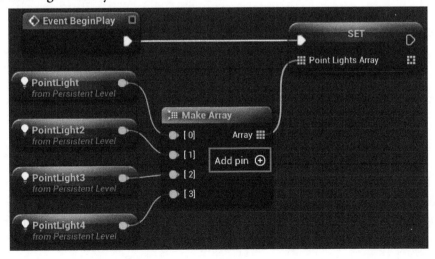

Figure 13.9 – Using the Make Array node

Let's create an example to examine the use of arrays that store object references.

Array example – creating BP_RandomSpawner

In this example, we'll create a Blueprint called BP_RandomSpawner, which will have an array of **Target Points**. The elements of the Target Points array can be set in the Level Editor. When the level starts, the BP_RandomSpawner Blueprint will randomly select one element of Target Points and spawn an instance of a specified Actor class in the same location of the Target Point selected.

These are the steps to create this example:

1. Create a project based on the Third Person template with the starter content.

2. In the Content Browser, access the Content folder. Right-click in the empty space next to the list of folders and select the **New Folder** option. Name the folder BookUE5. We will use this folder to store this chapter's assets.

3. Open the BookUE5 folder you just made, then click the **Add** button in the Content Browser, and choose the **Blueprint Class** option.

4. On the next screen, choose **Actor** as the parent class. Name the Blueprint BP_RandomSpawner and double-click it to open the Blueprint Editor.

5. In the **My Blueprint** panel, create a new variable named TargetPoints. In the **Details** panel, click the **Variable Type** drop-down menu and search for target point. Hover over **Target Point** to display a submenu and then choose **Object Reference**. Click the icon to the right of **Variable Type** and select the **Array** icon. Check the **Instance Editable** attribute, as shown in the following screenshot:

Figure 13.10 – Creating an array of Target Point

6. Create another variable and name it SpawnClass. Click the **Variable Type** drop-down menu and search for actor. Hover over **Actor** to display a submenu and then choose **Class Reference**:

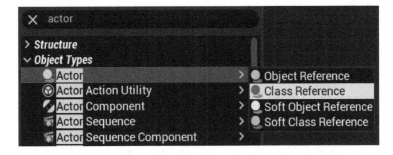

Figure 13.11 – Creating a variable that references an Actor class

7. Click the icon to the right of **Variable Type** and select the single variable icon. Check the **Instance Editable** attribute. We will use the class specified in the **SpawnClass** variable when spawning an Actor:

Figure 13.12 – SpawnClass can be specified in an instance on the level

In **Event BeginPlay**, we will use a **Branch** node to validate the **Spawn Class** and **Target Points** variables. Any variable storing a reference should be validated before use to avoid runtime errors. If the variables are valid, then we spawn an Actor using the class stored in the **Spawn Class** variable and the transform of a randomly selected Target Point stored in the array:

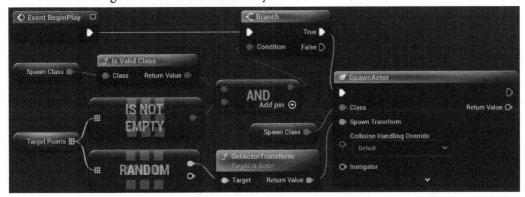

Figure 13.13 – The Event BeginPlay actions

8. The nodes of *steps 8–13* are to validate the **Spawn Class** and **Target Points** variables. Drag the **Spawn Class** variable from the **My Blueprint** panel, drop it into the EventGraph near **Event BeginPlay**, and select **Get Spawn Class**.

9. Drag a wire from the **Spawn Class** node and add an **Is Valid Class** node.

10. Drag a wire from the **Return Value** pin of **Is Valid Class** and add an **AND** node. We are using the **AND** node because we will only spawn the Actor if both variables are valid.

11. Drag the **Target Points** array variable from the **My Blueprint** panel, drop it into the EventGraph near the **Spawn Class** node, and select **GET Target Points**.

12. Drag a wire from the **TargetPoints** node and add an **IS NOT EMPTY** node. Connect the output pin of the **IS NOT EMPTY** node to the bottom input pin of the **AND** node. We need to check whether the array has elements.

13. Drag a wire from the output pin of the **AND** node and add a **Branch** node. Connect the white pin of **Event BeginPlay** to the white input pin of the **Branch** node.

14. The nodes of *steps 14–18* are to spawn an Actor using the class stored in **Spawn Class**. Drag a wire from the **True** output pin of the **Branch** node and add a **SpawnActor** from the **Class** node.

15. Drag a wire from the **Class** input pin of the **SpawnActor** node and add a **Get Spawn Class** node.

16. Drag a wire from the **Target Points** node and add a **Random Array Item** node.

17. Drag a wire from the top output pin of the **Random** node and add a **GetActorTransform** node.

18. Connect the **Return Value** pin of **GetActorTransform** to the **Spawn Transform** input pin of the **SpawnActor** node.

19. Compile and save the Blueprint.

Now, we need to prepare the level to be able to test **BP_RandomSpawner**.

Testing BP_RandomSpawner

We will add some instances of **Target Point** on the level. The **BP_RandomSpawner** instance will use the transform of one of these Target Points:

1. In the Level Editor, we will use **Place Actors Panel** to easily find the **Target Point** class. Click on the **Create** button on the toolbar to open a submenu, and then click on **Place Actors Panel**:

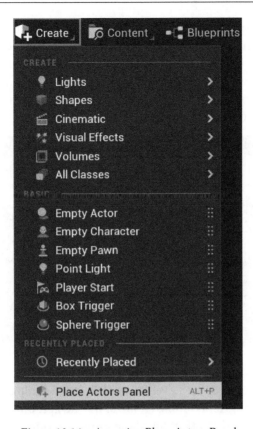

Figure 13.14 – Accessing Place Actors Panel

2. Search for `target` in the **Place Actors** panel, as shown in the following screenshot. Drag **Target Point** and drop some instances in different locations in the level:

Figure 13.15 – Finding the Target Point class

3. Drag **BP_RandomSpawner** from the Content Browser and drop it on the level. The **TargetPoints** and **Spawn Class** variables appear in the **Details** panel of the instance because we checked the **Instance Editable** attribute. Click on the + icon to add elements to the array. Expand the drop-down menu of each element and select one of the **TargetPoint** instances that are in the level. In **Spawn Class**, select **Blueprint_Effect_Smoke**:

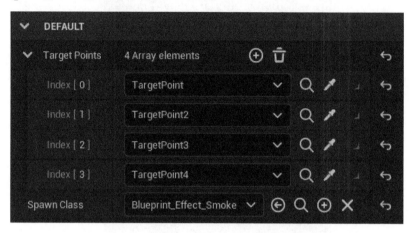

Figure 13.16 – Setting the variables of the BP_RandomSpawner instance

4. Click on the **Play** button of the Level Editor. **BP_RandomSpawner** will spawn an instance of **Blueprint Effect Smoke** at one of the **TargetPoint** instances. Exit and play again to see **Blueprint Effect Smoke** spawning in different locations:

Figure 13.17 – The instance of Blueprint Effect Smoke spawned on the level

Arrays are widely used in game development. Now, let's look at other types of containers.

Set

A **set** is another type of container. It is an unordered list of unique elements. The search for an element of a set is based on the value of the element itself. There is no index. The elements of a set must be of the same type, and repeated elements are not allowed.

Follow these steps to create a set:

1. In the **My Blueprint** panel, create a variable and define its type.
2. Click on the icon next to the **Variable Type** drop-down menu and select the icon of a set, as shown in this screenshot:

Figure 13.18 – Creating a set of strings

3. Compile the Blueprint so that you can add default values to the set. In the **DEFAULT VALUE** panel of the variable, click on the + icon to add elements to the set.
4. The following screenshot shows an example of a string set with four elements:

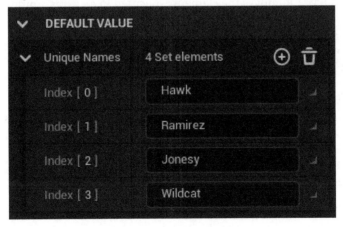

Figure 13.19 – Adding default values to a set

The next screenshot shows some of the nodes of the set container. Here is a brief description of each node:

- **ADD**: Adds an element to a set.
- **ADD ITEMS**: Adds elements from an array to a set. The array must be of the same type as the set.
- **CONTAINS**: Returns `true` if the set contains the element.
- **LENGTH**: Returns the number of elements in a set:

Figure 13.20 – Nodes of the set container

A set does not have a **GET** element node, so if you need to iterate through the elements of a set, then you can copy the elements of a set to an array. The next screenshot shows the **TO ARRAY** node and other nodes that are used to remove elements:

- **TO ARRAY**: Copies the elements of a set to an array. Note that copying a whole array of large objects can be a very costly operation.
- **CLEAR**: Removes all elements of a set.
- **REMOVE**: Removes an element of a set, or returns `True` if an element was removed and `False` if the element was not found.
- **REMOVE ITEMS**: Removes the elements specified in an array from a set:

Figure 13.21 – Nodes to remove items and convert a set to an array

Some nodes perform operations with two sets and return a different set. These nodes are shown in the next screenshot:

- **UNION**: The resulting set contains all the elements from the two sets. Since the result is a set, all duplicates will be removed.
- **DIFFERENCE**: The resulting set contains the elements of the first set that are not in the second set.
- **INTERSECTION**: The resulting set contains only the elements that exist in both sets:

Figure 13.22 – Operations with two sets

Use the **Make Set** node to create a set from variables in the EventGraph. Click on **Add pin** + to add input pins:

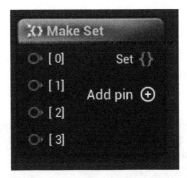

Figure 13.23 – The Make Set node

The following screenshot shows a simple example of the use of a set. There is a set named **Unique Names** that keeps the names of the players who have won a round. In this case, we want to know the players who have won at least one round; we do not need to know how many rounds a player has won:

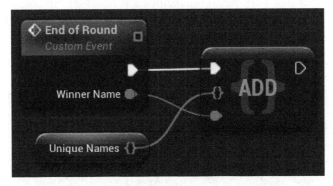

Figure 13.24 – A set container usage example

The set container is not used as much as the array. Now, let's look at the last container available in Blueprint – map.

Map

A **map** container uses a key-value pair to define each element. The key type can be different from the value type. A map is unordered and is searched by using the key value, so duplicate keys are not allowed. Duplicate values, however, are allowed.

These are the steps to create a map:

1. Create a variable, and in **Variable Type**, select the type that will be used as the key type.

2. Click on the icon next to the **Variable Type** drop-down menu, and select the icon of a map, as shown in the following screenshot.

3. After that, you need to choose the value type on the second dropdown that appeared. The example in the following screenshot uses **String** as the key type and **Float** as the value type:

Figure 13.25 – Creating a map container

4. Just like any other new variable in Blueprints, it is necessary to compile the Blueprint before adding the default values of the map. In the **DEFAULT VALUE** panel of the variable, click on the + icon to add elements to the map.

5. The following screenshot shows an example of a map with four elements. Each element has a string key and a float value:

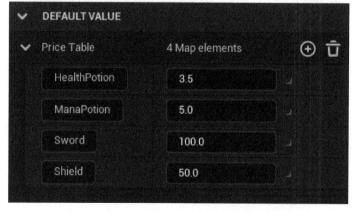

Figure 13.26 – Adding default values to a map

The following screenshot shows some map nodes to add an element, remove an element, and remove all elements of a map:

- **ADD**: Adds a key-value pair to a map. If the key already exists in the map, then the value associated with the key will be overwritten.

- **REMOVE**: Removes a key-value pair from a map. It returns `True` if the key-value pair was removed. If the key was not found, then the node returns `False`.

- **CLEAR**: Removes all elements of a map:

Figure 13.27 – Map nodes to add and remove elements

The following nodes are used to get the length of a map, check whether a key exists, and get the value associated with a key in the map:

- **LENGTH**: Returns the number of elements in a map.

- **CONTAINS**: Receives a key as an input parameter and returns `True` if the map contains an element that uses that key.

- **FIND**: The **FIND** node is like the **CONTAINS** node, but it also returns the value associated with the key used in the search:

Figure 13.28 – Map nodes to get the length and search for a key

The following nodes are used to copy the keys and values of a map to arrays:

- **KEYS**: This copies all the keys of a map to an array.

- **VALUES**: This copies all the values of a map to an array:

Figure 13.29 – Map nodes to copy the keys and values to arrays

Use the **Make Map** node to create a map from variables in the EventGraph. Click on **Add pin** + to add input pins:

Figure 13.30 – The Make Map node

The following screenshot shows an example usage of a map. **Price Table** is a map that uses **Product Name** as its key and the price of the product as its value. There is a function named **Calculate Total Price** that receives as input parameters **Product Name** and **Amount**, which counts the products being bought. **Product Name** is searched in the **Price Table** map to get the price of the product. The price of the product is multiplied by **Amount** to find **Total Price**:

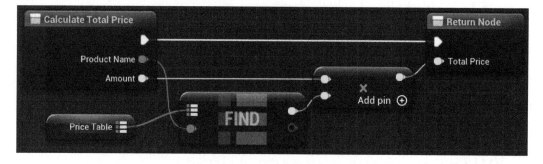

Figure 13.31 – Using a map to get the price of a product

We covered the containers available in Blueprints, which are arrays, sets, and maps, and learned when we should use each of them. The use of containers avoids the need to create several single variables to store information. In the next section, we will see other data structures that help to organize data within a game or application.

Exploring other data structures

There are data structures that are not created within a Blueprint class. They are independent auxiliary assets that can be used in a Blueprint. With these data structure assets, you are able to add your own data types to a project and can learn how to use tools that help you deal with a large volume of data in your project.

Let's learn how to create and use enumerations, structures, and data tables.

Enumerations

An **enumeration**, also known as an **enum**, is a data type that contains a fixed set of named constants and can be used to define the type of a variable. The value of a variable whose type is an enumeration is restricted to the set of constants defined in the enumeration.

Follow these steps to create an enumeration:

1. Click the **ADD** button in the Content Browser, and in the **Blueprints** submenu, select **Enumeration**, as shown in the following screenshot:

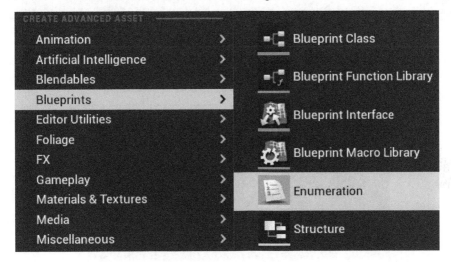

Figure 13.32 – Creating an enumeration

2. There is a naming convention of starting the name of an enumeration with an uppercase *E*. Give the name `EWeaponCategory` to the created enumeration and double-click it to edit its values.

3. In the Enumeration Editor, click on the **New** button to add a named constant to this enumeration. Add the five named constants shown in the following screenshot. You can add descriptions to the enumeration and for each constant:

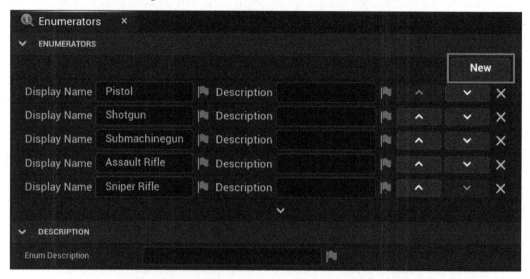

Figure 13.33 – Adding the elements of an enumeration

4. To use the enumeration data type, create a variable in the Blueprint Editor, expand the **Variable Type** drop-down menu, and search for the name of the enumeration, as shown in the following screenshot:

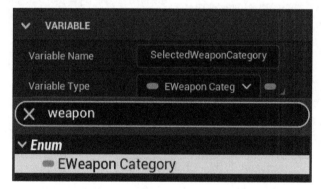

Figure 13.34 – Using the enumeration data type

The following screenshot shows that a variable defined with an enumeration type is restricted to the constants of the enumeration:

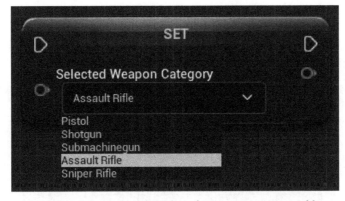

Figure 13.35 – Setting the value of an enumeration variable

For each enumeration type, there is a **Switch on** node that is used to change the execution flow based on the enumeration value, as shown in the following screenshot:

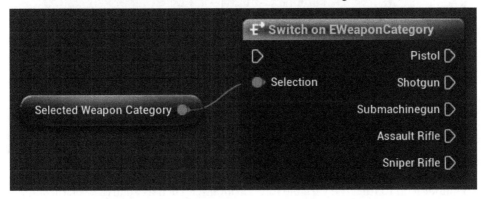

Figure 13.36 – Using the Switch on node on an enumeration

This is all we need to know about enumerations. The next data asset we will look at is the structure.

Structures

A **structure**, also known as a **struct**, is a composite data type that can group variables of different types into a single type. An element of a structure can be of a complex type, such as another structure, array, set, map, or object reference.

These are the steps to create a structure:

1. Click the **ADD** button in the Content Browser, and in the **Blueprints** submenu, select **Structure**, as shown in the following screenshot:

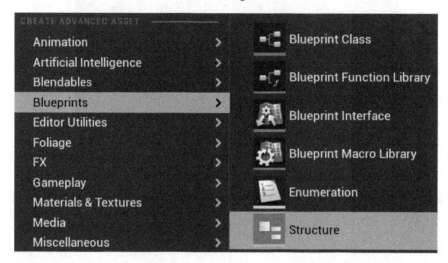

Figure 13.37 – Creating a structure

2. Rename the created structure as Weapon Type and double-click it to define its variables.

3. In the **STRUCTURE** Editor, click the **New Variable** button to add variables to the structure. Each variable can be of a different type, and you can click on the container icon to turn the variable into a container, such as an array, set, or map.

4. Add the variables shown in the following screenshot. Note that the **Category** variable is of the **EWeapon Category** enumeration type that was previously created:

Figure 13.38 – The variables of a Weapon Type structure

5. To use the **Structure** data type, create a variable in the Blueprint Editor, click the **Variable Type** drop-down menu, and search for the name of the structure, as shown in the following screenshot:

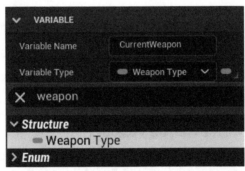

Figure 13.39 – Using a structure data type

6. Compile the Blueprint so that you can edit **DEFAULT VALUE**. The following screenshot shows the structure, filled with example values of weapons:

Figure 13.40 – Adding default values to a structure type variable

> **Note**
>
> The float variables in the previous screenshot use relative values that represent percentages – for example, *0.5* is *50%* and *1.0* is *100%*.

For each structure type, there are **Make** and **Break** nodes available for use in a Blueprint. The **Make** node receives the separate elements as input and creates a structure. The **Break** node receives a structure as input and separates its elements. The next screenshot shows the **Make** and **Break** nodes of the **Weapon Type** structure:

Figure 13.41 – Nodes to make a structure and get its elements

The structure is very useful in Blueprints for combining several variables into a new type. The last data structure we will look at is the data table.

Data tables

A **data table** is a table of values based on a structure. It can be used to represent a spreadsheet document. This is useful for data-driven gameplay where game data needs to be constantly modified and balanced. In these cases, the data can be modified in a spreadsheet editor and then imported into the game.

Follow these steps to create a data table:

1.   Click on the **ADD** button in the Content Browser, and in the **Miscellaneous** submenu, select **Data Table**, as shown in the following screenshot:

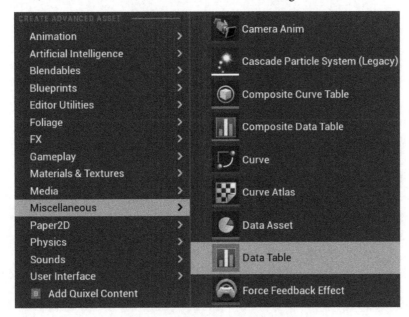

Figure 13.42 – Creating a data table

2.   After selecting **Data Table**, the Unreal Editor will ask you to choose a structure that represents the data type of the table. Select the **WeaponType** structure:

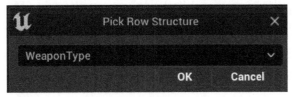

Figure 13.43 – Selecting the structure used by the data table

3. Rename the created data table `WeaponTable` and double-click on it to open the Data Table Editor.

4. Click on the **Add** button to add a row to the table. Each row has a row name that identifies the row, which must be unique. To change a row name, you need to right-click on a row and select **Rename**. In the example in the following screenshot, the row name is a simple index. Add some rows to the data table, as shown in the following screenshot:

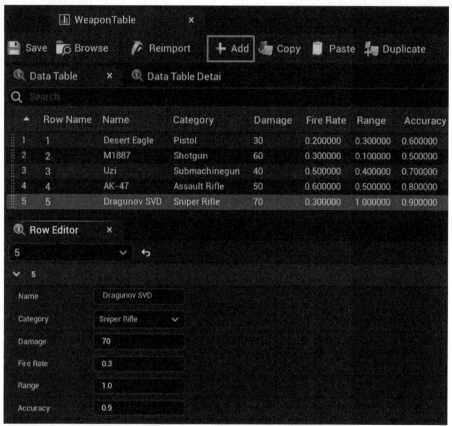

Figure 13.44 – Editing a data table

The data table can also be imported from a plain text **Comma-Separated Values** (**CSV**) file. The following screenshot shows an example of a CSV file. A spreadsheet editor can export a spreadsheet to the CSV format:

```
---,Name,Category,Damage,Fire Rate,Range,Accuracy
1,"Desert Eagle","Pistol","30","0.200000","0.300000","0.600000"
2,"M1887","Shotgun","60","0.300000","0.100000","0.500000"
3,"Uzi","Submachinegun","40","0.500000","0.400000","0.700000"
4,"AK-47","Assault Rifle","50","0.600000","0.500000","0.800000"
5,"Dragunov SVD","Sniper Rifle","70","0.300000","1.000000","0.900000"
```

Figure 13.45 – WeaponTable in the CSV format

5. To import a CSV file, click on the **Import** button in the Content Browser and select the CSV file. A dialog box will appear, asking you to select a structure in the **Choose DataTable Row Type** field, as shown in the following screenshot:

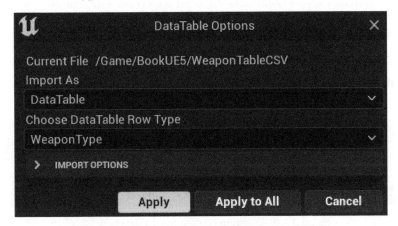

Figure 13.46 – Importing a data table from a CSV file

6. To use a data table in a Blueprint, create a variable in the Blueprint Editor and select **Data Table** > **Object Reference** as **Variable Type**:

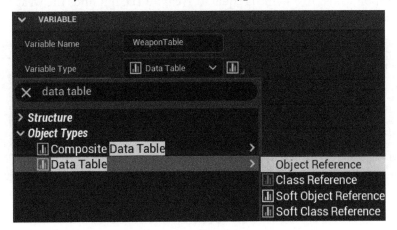

Figure 13.47 – Creating a data table reference

7. Compile the Blueprint, and in **DEFAULT VALUE**, select one data table, as shown in the following screenshot:

Figure 13.48 – Setting the default data table

The following screenshot shows some actions to get data from a data table:

- **Get Data Table Row**: Returns a structure with the data of a specific row

- **Get Data Table Row Names**: Copies all the row names of a data table to an array

- **Get Data Table Column as String**: Copies all the values of a column to an array of strings:

Figure 13.49 – Getting content from a data table

The following screenshot shows an example of how a data table is used. **Select Weapon** is a function that receives **Weapon ID** as an input parameter and searches in **Weapon Table** for a weapon whose row name is equal to **Weapon ID**. If it finds the weapon, then it copies the weapon data to the **Current Weapon** variable:

Figure 13.50 – Getting data from a row of a data table

We saw some data structure assets that we can create to organize data in a project. Now, we will learn about more Blueprint nodes that are useful to organize your script.

Flow control nodes

There are some nodes that control the flow of the execution of a Blueprint. These nodes determine the execution path based on conditions. We've already seen the **Branch** node, which is a commonly used flow control node. Let's learn about the other main types of flow control nodes.

Switch nodes

A **switch node** determines the flow of execution based on the value of an input variable. There are different types of switch nodes. The next screenshot shows an example of the **Switch on Int** node:

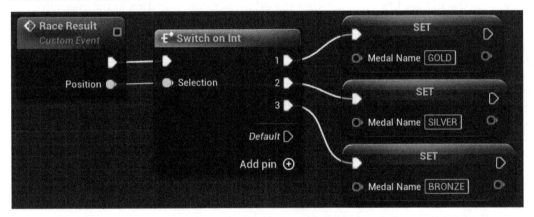

Figure 13.51 – An example of the Switch on Int node

The **Selection** input parameter receives an integer value that determines the output pin that will be executed. If the input value has no pin, then the **Default** pin will execute. You can change the start index in the **Details** panel of **Switch on Int**. The output pins are added by using the **Add pin +** option.

Another type of switch is the **Switch on String** node, which is shown in the following screenshot. The output values must be added in the **Details** panel of the **Switch on String** node, under **Pin Options | Pin Names**:

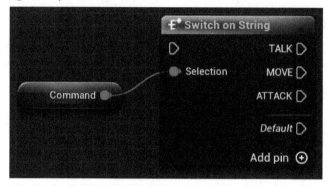

Figure 13.52 – An example of the Switch on String node

There is also **Switch on Enum**, which uses the values of an enumeration as the available output pins.

Flip Flop

Every time a **Flip Flop** node is executed, it toggles between two output pins – **A** and **B**. There is a Boolean output parameter named **Is A**. If the **Is A** parameter is `True`, then it indicates that pin **A** is running. If it is `False`, then pin **B** is running.

> **Note**
> The **Flip Flop** node does not work properly inside a function because **Flip Flop** has an internal variable that is deleted when the function ends. So, every time, the A pin will be executed inside a function.

The following screenshot shows an example of the **Flip Flop** node:

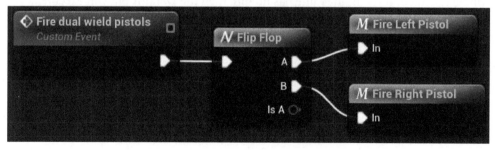

Figure 13.53 – An example of the Flip Flop node

If the player is using dual wield pistols, then when they fire, only one of the pistols fires. In the next shot, the other pistol fires. **Fire Left Pistol** and **Fire Right Pistol** are custom macros, used here to simplify this example.

Sequence

When a **Sequence** node is triggered, it executes all the Actions connected to the output pins in order. Thus, it executes all the Actions of a pin, then all the Actions of the next pin, and so on. It is useful to organize groups of Actions.

The next screenshot shows the **Sequence** node in use. The **Print String** functions are used to show the order of execution:

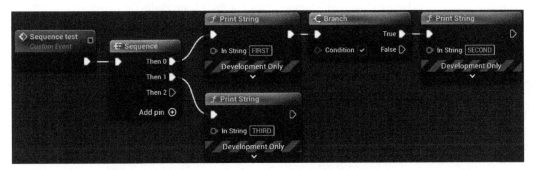

Figure 13.54 – An example of the Sequence node

The **Add pin** + option adds output pins. To remove a pin, right-click on the pin and choose the **Remove execution pin** option.

For Each Loop

A **For Each Loop** node receives an array as an input parameter and performs the Actions of the **Loop Body** output pin for each element of the array. The current **Array Element** and **Array Index** are available as output pins. The **Completed** output pin is executed when **For Each Loop** finishes its execution.

In the next screenshot, the **For Each Loop** node is used to iterate through an array of **Point Light** references that contain the lamps of a room:

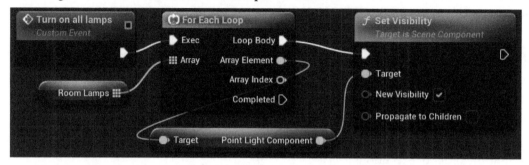

Figure 13.55 – An example of the For Each Loop node

The lamps are turned on by using the **Set Visibility** function of **Point Light Component**, which is inside the **Point Light** array element.

Do Once

The **Do Once** node executes the output pin only once. If it is triggered again, then its output pin will not be performed. The **Reset** input pin needs to be triggered to allow the **Do Once** node to run the output pin again.

The following screenshot shows an example of how it is used:

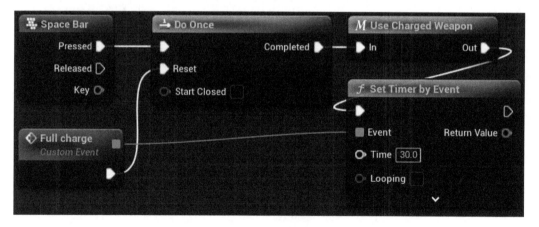

Figure 13.56 – An example of the Do Once node

When the player presses **Space Bar**, the **Do Once** node is triggered, and a charged weapon is used. After that, a timer is created to execute **Full charge Custom Event**, which resets the **Do Once** node after 30.0 seconds. If the player presses **Space Bar** again before 30 seconds have elapsed, then the **Do Once** node will not execute its output pin.

Do N

The **Do N** node allows you to specify how many times the output pin can execute. After the number of executions has completed, the Actions of the output pin will only be executed again if the **Reset** pin is triggered.

The following screenshot shows an example of how the **Do N** node is used:

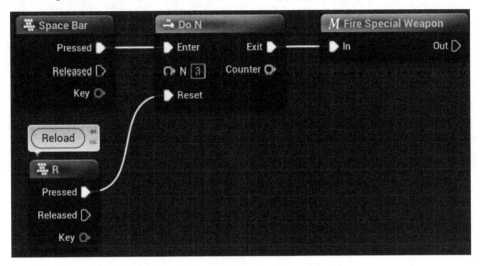

Figure 13.57 – An example of a Do N node

The player can press **Space Bar** to fire a special weapon. After the third shot, they need to press the *R* key to reset the **Do N** node to be able to fire three more times.

Gate

The **Gate** node has an internal state; it can be opened or closed. If it is open, then the output pin will execute when the **Gate** node is triggered. If it is closed, then the output pin will not execute.

These are the input pins of the **Gate** node:

- **Enter**: An execution pin that receives the flow of execution
- **Open**: An execution pin that sets the state of **Gate** to open
- **Close**: An execution pin that sets the state of **Gate** to closed
- **Toggle**: An execution pin that toggles the state of the **Gate** node
- **Start Closed**: A Boolean variable that determines whether the **Gate** node should start in the closed state

The example in the next screenshot is of a Blueprint that applies damage to actors that are overlapping it:

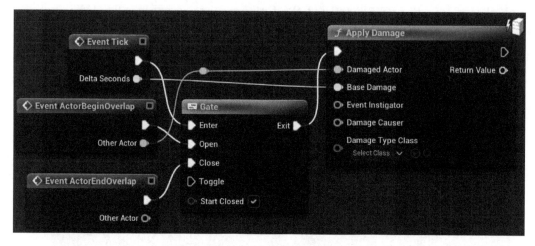

Figure 13.58 – An example of the Gate node

When an actor is overlapping, the **Gate** node stays open, and damage is applied to the actor on every tick. If the actor stops overlapping, then the **Gate** node will close, and the damage will no longer be applied.

MultiGate

When a **MultiGate** node is triggered, one of the output pins is executed. A **MultiGate** node can have multiple output pins. To add another output pin, use the **Add pin** + option.

These are the input pins of the **MultiGate** node:

- **Reset**: An execution pin used to reset the **MultiGate** node and allow new executions of the output pins.

- **Is Random**: A Boolean variable. If the value is True, then the order of execution of the output pins is random.

- **Loop**: This is a Boolean variable that indicates how the **MultiGate** node will behave after the last output pin is executed. If the value is **True**, then the **MultiGate** node continues to execute the output pins. If False, then the **MultiGate** node will stop executing the output pins.

- **Start Index**: An integer value indicating the first output pin to be executed.

The following screenshot shows an example of the **MultiGate** node:

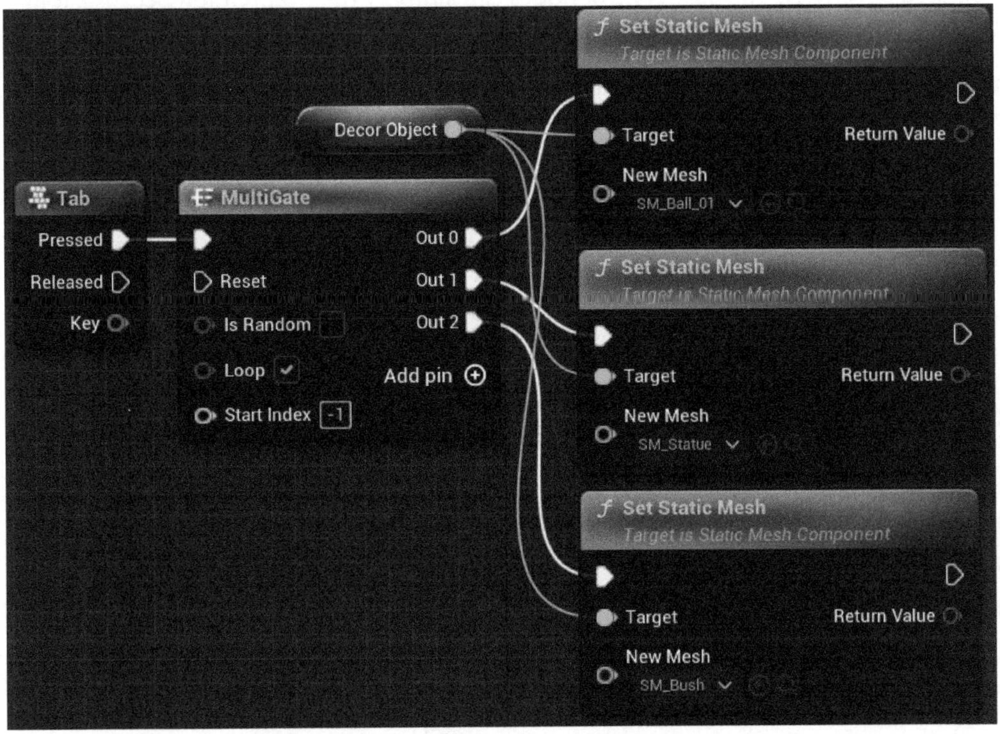

Figure 13.59 – An example of the MultiGate node

When the *Tab* key is pressed, a **MultiGate** node is used to set a different Static Mesh at each execution. The **Loop** parameter is checked, so **MultiGate** will continue executing from the first output pin after the last output pin is executed.

These are the flow control nodes available in Blueprints. It's good to know about their existence because we can find problems that can be easily solved using one of them.

Summary

In this chapter, we learned how to use data structures to organize data in Blueprints. We learned how to store various elements in an array and how to retrieve any of those elements. We learned how to use other types of containers, such as sets and maps, to store data.

After that, we learned how to create and use enumerations, structures, and data tables, and we saw examples of how they can be related. It was presented to us as several flow control nodes, such as **Switch**, **Gate**, and **For Each Loop**.

This chapter showed various Blueprint features that will help us to organize data so that it can be used effectively. The flow control nodes can simplify the EventGraph because, for each situation, there may be a more suitable node.

In the next chapter, we will learn about world and local coordinates, vector operations, and the use of traces to test collisions.

Quiz

1. Arrays do not allow repeated elements.

    a. True

    b. False

2. For each enumeration type, there is a **Switch On** node available in Blueprints.

    a. True

    b. False

3. All variables in a structure must be of the same type.

    a. True

    b. False

4. A data table uses a structure to define the data type of the table.

    a. True

    b. False

5. Which node is not a flow control node?

    a. `For Each Loop`

    b. `Spawn Actor from Class`

    c. `Do Once`

    d. `Gate`

14
Math and Trace Nodes

The representation of a 3D world is based on mathematical concepts. If you do not understand these concepts, then it will be more difficult to understand certain operations performed in a 3D game. This chapter explains some math concepts that are needed for 3D games. We will learn about the difference between world and relative transforms and how to use them when working with components. We will learn how to use vectors to represent the position, direction, velocity, and distance. The concept of traces is explained and various types of traces are presented. This chapter also shows how to use traces to test collisions in a game.

These are the topics covered in this chapter:

- World and relative transforms
- Points and vectors
- Introduction to traces and trace functions

By the end of the chapter, you will know how to use vectors and traces to make the player interact with other actors in the level.

World and relative transforms

The `Actor` class has a **Transform** structure. This structure has three variables, which are used to represent **Location**, **Rotation**, and **Scale**. The **Transform** structure of an actor that is on the Level can be modified by using the **Details** panel.

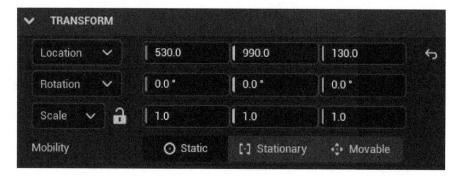

Figure 14.1 – Modifying the transform in the Details panel

In the Level Editor, you can use the transformation widget that appears when you select an actor. There are buttons to select the type of transformation the widget will apply to an actor, as we can see in the following screenshot:

Figure 14.2 – Using the widget to modify the transform

The 3D space is represented by three axes: *x*, *y*, and *z*. These axes are represented by colors: red is the *x* axis, green is the *y* axis, and blue is the *z* axis.

The **Location** variable of the **Transform** structure has a set of values for **X**, **Y**, and **Z**, which determines the position on each axis. These values are also known as the world location of the actor. The following screenshot shows some actions that we can use to get and set an actor's location:

- **GetActorLocation**: Returns the current location of the actor
- **SetActorLocation**: Sets **New Location** for the actor
- **AddActorWorldOffset**: Uses the **Delta Location** input parameter to modify the current location of the actor.

Figure 14.3 – Getting and setting the actor location

The **Rotation** variable of the **Transform** structure has a set of values for **X**, **Y**, and **Z** in degrees, which determines the rotation on each axis. The following screenshot shows the following rotation nodes:

- **GetActorRotation**: Returns the current rotation of the actor
- **SetActorRotation**: Sets **New Rotation** for the actor
- **AddActorWorldRotation**: Adds the **Delta Rotation** input parameter to the current rotation of the actor.

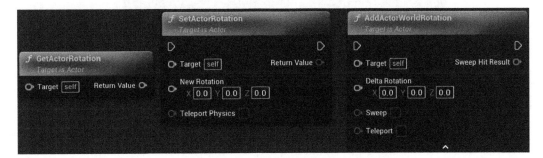

Figure 14.4 – Getting and setting the actor rotation

The **Scale** variable of the **Transform** structure has a set of values for **X**, **Y**, and **Z**, which determines the scale on each axis. The following screenshot shows the nodes that are used to get and set an actor's scale:

Figure 14.5 – Getting and setting the actor scale

When a Blueprint has Actor components, the transforms of those components are known as **relative transforms** because they are relative to the component's parent. The following screenshot shows an example of components. **DefaultSceneRoot** is a small white sphere that is hidden in the game and used to store the actor's position in the world. It can be replaced with another Scene component.

Below it, in the component's hierarchy shown in the screenshot, there is a **Static Mesh** component named **Table**, and below the **Table** component in the hierarchy, there is another **Static Mesh** component named **Statue**. The transform of **Table** is relative to the **DefaultSceneRoot** transform, and the transform of the **Statue** component is relative to the **Table** transform. So, if you move the **Table** component in the Viewport, then the **Statue** component will move too, but if you change the relative transform of the **Statue** component instead, then the **Table** component will remain where it is.

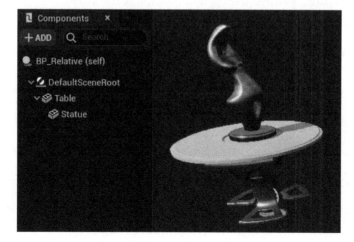

Figure 14.6 – Component's hierarchy

There are nodes to get and set a component's relative location. You can also get a component's world location, as you can see in the following screenshot:

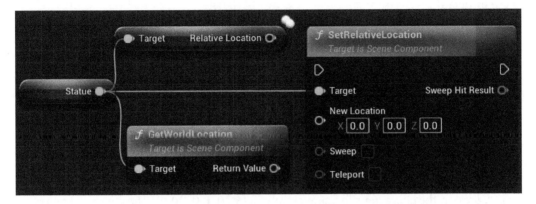

Figure 14.7 – Getting and setting the component's relative location

The **Location** and **Scale** variables are represented by **Vector** structures, which is our next topic.

Points and vectors

There is a structure in Unreal Engine named **Vector**, which has three variables of the float type: **X**, **Y**, and **Z**. Same as the concept of a vector in mathematics, this **Vector** can be used to represent a point (location) in 3D space or velocity (speed in a specified direction).

Let's first look at an example of using **Vector** as a point in 3D space. The following screenshot has two actors. One actor represents a character and the other represents a couch.

Figure 14.8 – Two actors on the level

The following screenshot shows the character's location. The **Location** variable of the **Transform** structure is of the **Vector** type (**X**, **Y**, and **Z**), and one Unreal unit equals 1.0 cm by default.

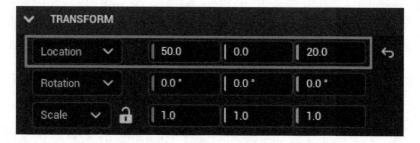

Figure 14.9 – The character's location

We can represent the character's location simply as (**50.0, 0.0, 20.0**). The couch's location is (**450.0, 0.0, 20.0**), which can be seen in the following screenshot:

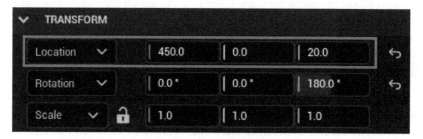

Figure 14.10 – The couch's location

Now, let's see how to use a vector to represent movement. We are going to instruct our character on how to get to the couch. They need to know the direction and distance in which they must move. The following screenshot shows that we are instructing the character to move **400 cm** on the *x* axis:

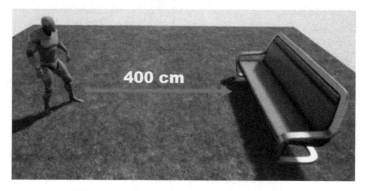

Figure 14.11 – Moving 400 cm on the *x* axis

Both the direction and distance are represented by a single vector, using **X**, **Y**, and **Z** values. In the previous screenshot, the value of the vector that describes the movement is (400, 0, 0).

If we take the character location vector and add it to the vector that represents this movement, then the result is the couch location vector. To add two vectors, add each of their elements:

```
couch_location = character_location + vector_movement
couch_location = (50, 0, 20) + (400, 0, 0)
couch_location = (50 + 400, 0 + 0, 20 + 0)
couch_location = (450, 0, 20)
```

If we have a start point and a destination point, and we want to find out the movement vector, then we just need to get the destination point and subtract the start point.

For example, if we want to know the vector that leads from the start point of (25, 40, 55) to the destination point of (75, 95, 130), then we need to solve this expression:

```
vector_movement = destination_point - start_point
vector_movement = (75, 95, 130) - (25, 40, 55)
vector_movement = (75 - 25, 95 - 40, 130 - 55)
vector_movement = (50, 55, 75)
```

Now, let's see how we can represent a vector.

Representation of a vector

A vector is a directed line segment and can be represented by an arrow.

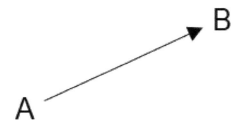

Figure 14.12 – Arrow representing a vector

Point **A** is the initial point of the vector and point **B** is the terminal point. The initial point of all world locations is always (0, 0, 0), whereas the initial point of all relative locations is always the terminal point of the parent of the component.

A vector has a magnitude (or length) and a direction. Two vectors are equivalent if they have the same magnitude and direction.

Vector operations

Several mathematical operations can be done with vectors. Understanding these operations is fundamental to manipulating objects in 3D space:

- **Vector addition**: The sum of two vectors is determined by adding each of their elements. The following example shows the sum of vectors (3, 5, 0) and (5, 2, 0):

```
V1 = (3, 5, 0)
V2 = (5, 2, 0)
V1 + V2 = (3 + 5, 5 + 2, 0 + 0)
V1 + V2 = (8, 7, 0)
```

The following is a graphical representation of the previous example of vector addition. To simplify the graph, we are only drawing the *x* and *y* axes. The initial point of V1 is the world origin (*x*=0, *y*=0, *z*=0). The terminal point of V1 is (*x*=3, *y*=5, *z*=0). The initial point of V2 is the terminal point of V1 and the terminal point of V2 is the result of the sum (*x*=8, *y*=7, *z*=0).

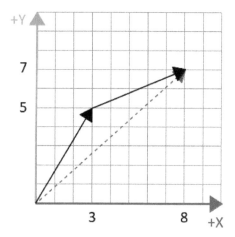

Figure 14.13 – Adding vectors

For example, if V1 is the character's world location and V2 is the relative location of the character's weapon, then V1 + V2 will be the weapon's world location.

The following screenshot shows the vector addition node:

Figure 14.14 – Node to add vectors

- **Vector subtraction**: The subtraction of one vector from another is determined by subtracting each of its elements. This is an example of vector subtraction using the vectors (6, 8, 0) and (1, 4, 0):

```
V1 = (6, 8, 0)
V2 = (1, 4, 0)
V1 - V2 = (6 - 1, 8 - 4, 0 - 0)
V1 - V2 = (5, 4, 0)
```

The following is a graphical representation of the previous example of vector subtraction. Since this is subtraction, the V2 vector is represented by its opposite vector:

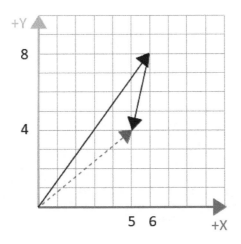

Figure 14.15 – Subtracting vectors

For example, if V1 is the character weapon's world location and V2 is the relative location of the character's weapon, then V1 - V2 will be the character's world location.

The vector subtraction node is shown in the following screenshot:

Figure 14.16 – Node to subtract vectors

- **Length of a vector**: The length (or magnitude) of a vector is the distance between its initial and terminal points. If you have two world locations, the length of the difference between the two will be the distance between those world locations. The length of a vector is calculated using the Blueprint node shown in the following screenshot:

Figure 14.17 – VectorLength node

- **Normalizing vectors**: We use vector normalization to find a unit vector. The unit vector has a length equal to one. It is often used when direction needs to be indicated. There is a node named **Normalize** that receives a vector as input and returns the normalized vector:

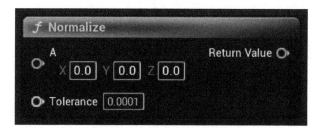

Figure 14.18 – Normalize vector node

- **Scalar vector multiplication**: An integer or float number is also known as a **scalar value**. The multiplication of a vector by a scalar value is done by multiplying each of its elements by the scalar value. This operation changes the length of the vector, but the direction remains the same unless the scalar is negative, in which case the vector will point in the opposite direction following multiplication.

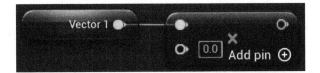

Figure 14.19 – Multiplying a vector by a float

> **Note**
>
> The multiply node is a wildcard node. This means that when you connect
> a vector variable to the node, it will be converted into a **Vector x Vector** node.
> You need to right click on the second input pin, hover over **Convert Pin**,
> and select **Float**.

- **Dot product**: The dot product is a projection of one vector onto another vector. The
  dot product of two normalized vectors is equal to the cosine of the angle formed
  between the vectors and can range from -1.0 to 1.0:

Figure 14.20 – Dot product node

The dot product can be used to verify the relationship between two vectors, such
as whether they are perpendicular or parallel. The following diagram shows some
examples of a dot product between two vectors, **A** and **B**:

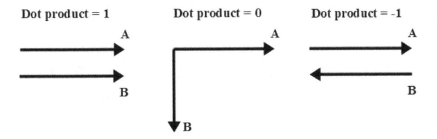

Figure 14.21 – Examples of the dot product

- **Actor vectors**: There are functions that return the forward, right, and up vectors of an actor. The returned vectors are normalized (*length = 1*). The following screenshot shows these functions, which are often used to direct movement:

Figure 14.22 – Getting actor vectors

To find the opposite vector, just multiply the vector by -1. By doing this, you can find the backward, left, and down vectors of an actor. The following screenshot shows how to find the backward vector:

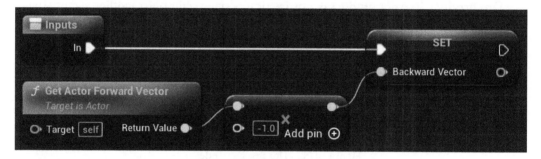

Figure 14.23 – Finding the opposite vector

Vectors are widely used in game programming; they can be used to indicate directions and to represent speed, acceleration, and a force acting on an object.

In the next section, we will see another important concept used to interact with a 3D world, which is traces.

Introduction to traces and trace functions

Traces are used to test whether there are collisions along a defined line segment. A trace can be done by channel or object type and can return the single or multiple objects that have been hit.

The trace channels available are **Visibility** and **Camera**. The object type can be **WorldStatic**, **WorldDynamic**, **Pawn**, **PhysicsBody**, **Vehicle**, **Destructible**, or **Projectile**. You can create more channels and object types in **Project Settings | Engine | Collision**.

Actors and components need to define how they react to each trace channel and object type. The response can be **Ignore**, **Overlap**, or **Block**.

The following screenshot shows the collision responses of a **Static Mesh** actor. There are collision presets that can be selected, such as **BlockAll**, **OverlapAllDynamic**, and **Pawn**. Alternatively, you can choose **Custom…** for **Collision Presets** and define the **Collision Responses** properties individually. The object type is set via the **Object Type** property dropdown, while the **Visibility** and **Camera** channels are defined in the **Trace Responses** section of the **Collision Responses** table.

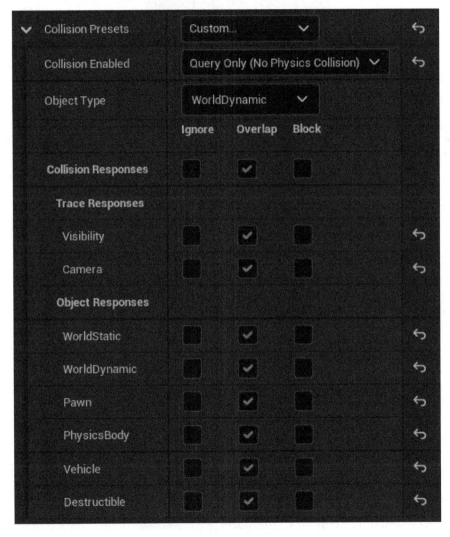

Figure 14.24 – Collision Responses table

When a trace function collides with something, it returns one or more **Hit Result** structures. The **Break Hit Result** node can be used to access the **Hit Result** variables, as shown in the following screenshot:

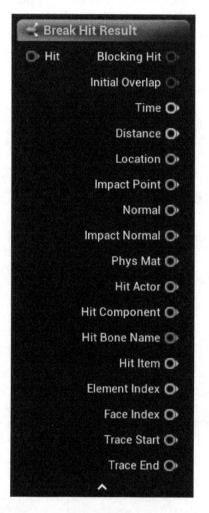

Figure 14.25 – Hit result structure variables

These are some of the variables of the **Hit Result** structure:

- **Blocking Hit**: A Boolean value that indicates whether the trace hit something
- **Location**: The location of the hit
- **Impact Normal**: The normal vector that is perpendicular to the surface that was hit
- **Hit Actor**: The reference to the actor hit by the trace

In the next sections, we will see the trace functions available in Blueprint.

Traces for objects

The **LineTraceForObjects** function tests for collisions along a defined line and returns a **Hit Result** structure with data for the first actor hit that matches one of the **Object Types** values specified in the input parameter.

The **MultiLineTraceForObjects** function has the same input parameters as the **LineTraceForObjects** function. The difference between the functions is that the **MultiLineTraceForObjects** function returns an array of **Hit Result** structures describing all actors hit by the trace, rather than a single result, making it more expensive to perform. The following screenshot shows the two **TraceForObjects** functions:

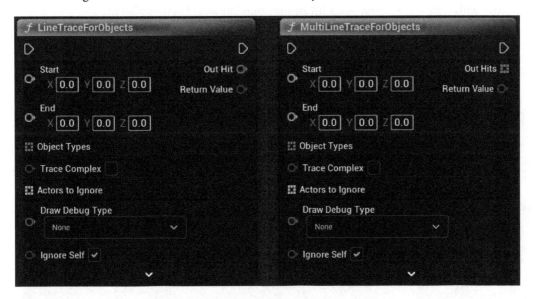

Figure 14.26 – TraceForObjects functions

These are the input parameters of the two **TraceForObjects** functions:

- **Start**: The location vector that defines the start of the line to be used for the collision test.

- **End**: The location vector that defines the end of the collision test line.

- **Object Types**: An array that contains object types that will be searched with the trace. The trace will ignore all objects of any other types.

- **Trace Complex**: A Boolean value. If it is **True**, then the trace will test against the actual Mesh. If it is **False**, then the trace will test against simplified collision shapes.

- **Actors to Ignore**: An array with actors that should be ignored in the collision tests.

- **Draw Debug Type**: This allows the drawing of a 3D line that represents the trace.

- **Ignore Self**: A Boolean value that indicates whether the Blueprint instance that is calling the function should be ignored in the collision test.

There are other line trace functions that use **Trace Channel** instead of **Object Types**, as we will see in the next section.

Traces by channel

The **LineTraceByChannel** function tests for collisions along a defined line using **Trace Channel**, which can be set to **Visibility** or **Camera**, and returns a **Hit Result** structure with data for the first actor hit in the collision test. There is also the **MultiLineTraceByChannel** function, which returns an array of **Hit Result** structures describing all actors hit by the trace.

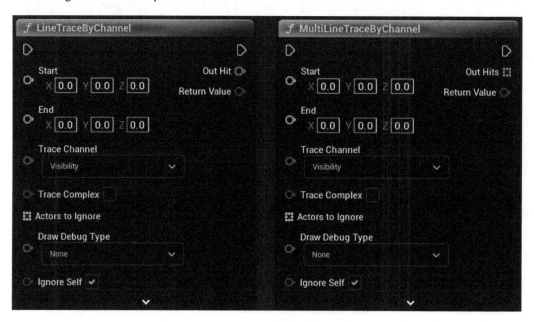

Figure 14.27 – TraceByChannel functions

The input parameters of these functions are as follows:

- **Start**: The location vector that defines the start of the line to be used for the collision test.

- **End**: The location vector that defines the end of the collision test line.

- **Trace Channel**: A channel used for the collision test. It can be **Visibility** or **Camera**. The trace will search for objects that overlap or block the trace channel selected.

- **Trace Complex**: A Boolean value. If it is **True**, then the trace will test against the actual Mesh. If it is **False**, then the trace will test against simplified collision shapes.

- **Actors to Ignore**: An array with actors that should be ignored in the collision tests.

- **Draw Debug Type**: This allows the drawing of a 3D line that represents the trace.

- **Ignore Self**: A Boolean value that indicates whether the Blueprint instance that is calling the function should be ignored in the collision test.

A line trace is not the only type of trace function. You can also use shapes to do traces.

Shape traces

There are trace functions for the sphere, capsule, and box shapes, but these functions are more expensive to perform than line traces.

The following screenshot shows the **SphereTraceForObjects**, **CapsuleTraceForObjects**, and **BoxTraceForObjects** functions:

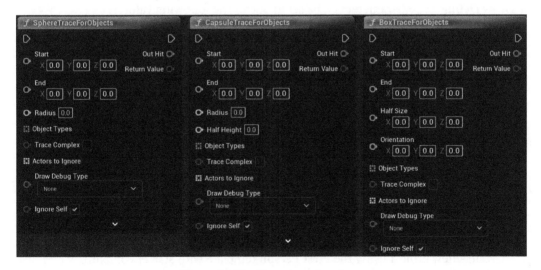

Figure 14.28 – Shape trace functions

For all these shapes, there are functions to trace by channel and object type. There are also functions that return a single hit or multiple hits.

Debug lines

The trace functions have an option to draw debug lines that help when testing traces. Click on the small arrow at the bottom of the trace functions to display the **Trace Color**, **Trace Hit Color**, and **Draw Time** parameters, as shown in the following screenshot:

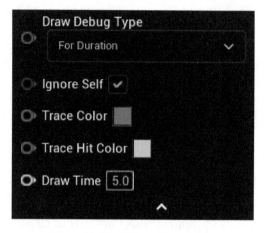

Figure 14.29 – Debug line options

The **Draw Debug Type** parameter can be set to one of the following values:

- **None**: Don't draw the line.
- **For One Frame**: The line only appears for one frame.
- **For Duration**: The line stays for the time specified in the **Draw Time** parameter.
- **Persistent**: The line does not disappear.

Debug lines are useful to find the problem when the traces are not acting as expected.

Example of vectors and trace nodes

Let's do an example to see the use of vectors and trace nodes. We will modify the Player Character to use a line trace to find and toggle the light of another Blueprint:

1. Create a new project using the **First Person** template with starter content.
2. Open the FirstPersonCharacter Blueprint, which is in the Content | FirstPersonBP | Blueprints folder.

3. In the **My Blueprint** panel, create a Macro and name it `Trace Locations`. In the **Details** panel, add two output parameters of the **Vector** type. Name the parameters `Start Location` and `End Location`, as shown in the following screenshot. We do not need input parameters.

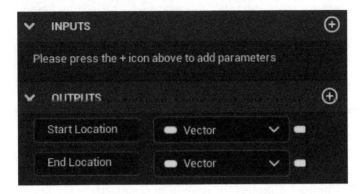

Figure 14.30 – Macro output parameters

4. In the graph of the `Trace Locations` macro, add the nodes shown in the following screenshot. This macro calculates the **Start** and **End** locations that will be used by **Line Trace**. Since this is a first-person game, we are using the camera as **Start Location**, and **End Location** is 300 cm ahead of **Camera**.

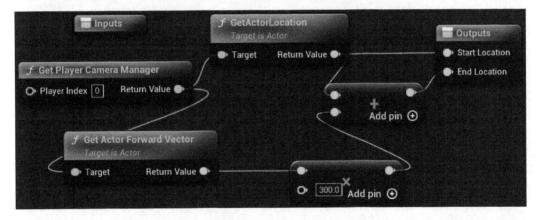

Figure 14.31 – The nodes of the Trace Locations macro

5. Click the **Event Graph** tab, right-click on **Event Graph**, and add an input event for the *Enter* key.

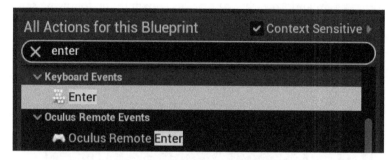

Figure 14.32 – Adding the Enter keyboard event

6. Add a **LineTraceByChannel** node and add the **Trace Locations** macro to **Event Graph**. Connect the **Pressed** pin of the **Enter** event to the white pin of **LineTraceByChannel**. Connect the outputs of the macro to the **Start** and **End** inputs of **Line Trace**, as shown in the following screenshot:

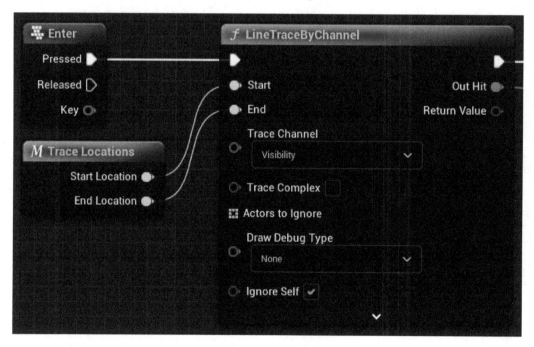

Figure 14.33 – Using the LineTraceByChannel node

7. Connect the nodes shown in the following screenshot to the output of the **LineTraceByChannel** node. These nodes test whether **Hit Actor** is of the **Blueprint_WallSconce** type. If it is, then the light of **Blueprint_WallSconce** is toggled. Compile the Blueprint to apply the changes.

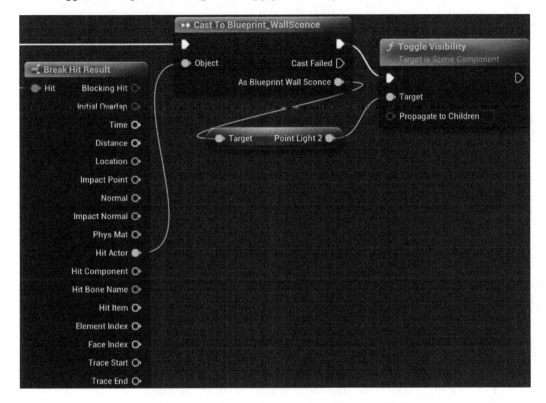

Figure 14.34 – Testing whether Hit Actor is of the Blueprint_WallSconce type

8. Add an instance of Blueprint_WallSconce (which is in the Content | StarterContent | Blueprints folder) to the Level, and then play the Level.

9.   Move your character close to the instance of `Blueprint_WallSconce`, look at it, and press the *Enter* key to toggle the light. The following screenshot shows the Player Character and `Blueprint_WallSconce`:

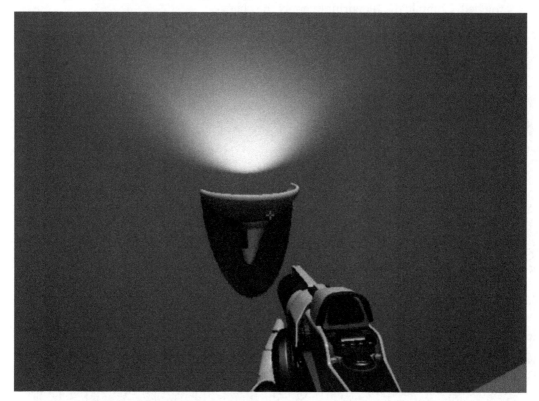

Figure 14.35 – Interacting with Blueprint_WallSconce

This example showed a practical use of vectors and trace nodes. It is important to understand these concepts because they will help to solve many problems in 3D game development.

Summary

This chapter presented some math concepts and showed you how to use world and relative transforms. We saw how several Blueprint nodes are used to modify an element of a transform, such as **Location**, **Rotation**, and **Scale**.

This chapter has shown that a vector structure can be used to represent a point in 3D space or a mathematical vector. We learned how to do several vector operations using Blueprint nodes.

Finally, we saw how to test collisions using trace nodes. There are many trace nodes, which are based on the type of collision response, the shapes used, and whether the trace nodes return single or multiple hits.

In the next chapter, we will learn several tips for dealing with the complexity of Blueprints and increasing the quality of Blueprints.

Quiz

1. In Unreal Engine, **Transform** is a structure that contains the **Location, Rotation,** and **Scale** variables.

   a. True

   b. False

2. The **Location** and **Scale** variables of the **Transform** structure are of the **Vector** type.

   a. True

   b. False

3. A normalized vector can be any length.

   a. True

   b. False

4. **Visibility** and **Camera** are examples of object types.

   a. True

   b. False

5. The **MultiLineTraceByChannel** function returns an array of **Hit Result** structures.

   a. True

   b. False

15
Blueprints Tips

This chapter contains several tips on how to improve the quality of Blueprints. We will learn how to use various editor shortcuts that speed up our work. We will also learn about some Blueprint best practices that will help you to decide what type of implementation should be done and where. Finally, we'll learn about more useful miscellaneous Blueprint nodes.

These are the topics covered in this chapter:

- Blueprint Editor shortcuts
- Blueprint best practices
- Using miscellaneous Blueprint nodes

By the end of the chapter, you will be familiar with shortcuts, best practices, and Blueprint nodes that will help you when developing more complex games.

Blueprint Editor shortcuts

In the Blueprint Editor, we are going to work with variables a lot, so let's start with the shortcuts related to variables.

When you drag a variable from the **My Blueprint** panel and drop it in **EventGraph**, a submenu appears for you to choose either the **GET** or **SET** nodes. However, there are shortcuts to create **GET** and **SET** nodes. If you hold the *Ctrl* key and drag a variable to the graph, then the editor will create a **GET** node. To create a **SET** node, hold the *Alt* key and drag a variable to the graph. The following screenshot shows the **GET** and **SET** nodes:

Figure 15.1 – Shortcuts to create GET and SET nodes

There is another way to create **GET** and **SET** nodes. If you drag a variable and drop it on a compatible pin of another node, then the editor will create a **GET** or **SET** node depending on the parameter type.

The following screenshot shows an example of the **Score** variable being dropped on an input parameter pin. If the pin is compatible, then the editor will show a tooltip with a check icon and a label such as **Make B = Score**. This expression means that the **B** pin of the node will get the value of the **Score** variable. So, the editor will create a **GET Score** node:

Figure 15.2 – Dragging a variable and dropping it on an input pin to create a GET node

If you drop the **Score** variable on an output parameter pin, as shown in the following screenshot, then the editor will show the **Make Score = ReturnValue** label, and it will create a **SET Score** node using the **ReturnValue** label of the other node as the input parameter:

Figure 15.3 – Dragging a variable and dropping it on an output pin to create a SET node

The Blueprint Editor has an automatic type conversion system. To use it, drag a wire from the pin of one variable type and drop it on a pin of another variable type. The following screenshot shows that a tooltip appears to confirm that the conversion is possible:

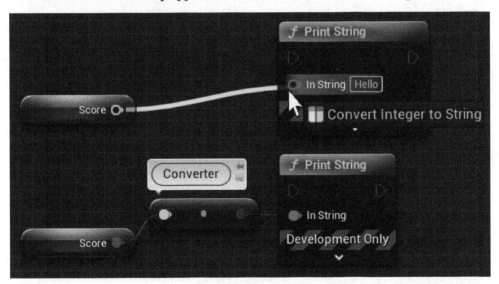

Figure 15.4 – Creating a converter node

Another useful feature of the Blueprint Editor is that it is possible to change an existing node for another node that uses the same variable type without breaking the connections.

There is an example of this in the following screenshot. **Player Health** and **PlayerStamina** are float variables. If you drag the **PlayerStamina** variable and drop it on the **SET Player Health** node, then the node will change to a **SET PlayerStamina** node and keep all the connections.

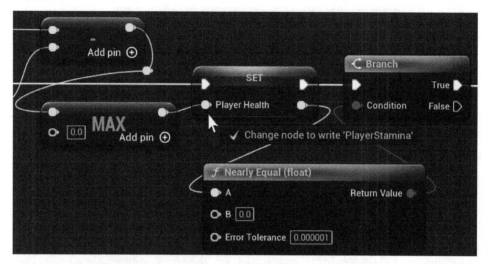

Figure 15.5 – Changing a node and keeping all connections

There is a shortcut to create variables based on the type of an input or output pin of a node. To do this, right-click on a data pin and select the **Promote to Variable** option, as shown in the following screenshot. This option creates a variable and connects it to the pin.

Figure 15.6 – Promoting the return value to a variable

If you need to break all the connections of a pin, hold the *Alt* key and click on the pin. You can move all the connections of a pin to another compatible pin by holding the *Ctrl* key, dragging the connections, and dropping them on another pin. This is very useful because you don't need to redo the connections one by one. In the following screenshot, all the connections of the **As First Person Character** pin will be moved to the **As BP Player Character**.

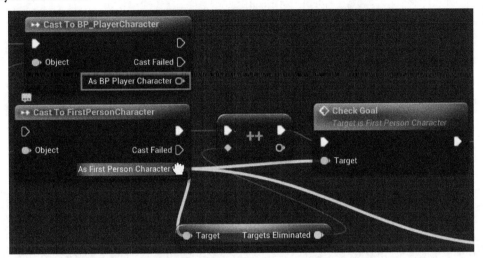

Figure 15.7 – Dragging all connections to another pin

The Blueprint Editor offers several options for node alignment. To use them, select some Blueprint nodes and right-click on one of them to open a menu. **Alignment** is one of the options on this menu. The following screenshot shows the **Alignment** options available:

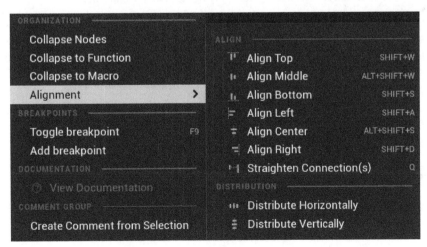

Figure 15.8 – The Alignment options

Most of the **Alignment** options are self-explanatory, but let's look at an example: **Straighten Connection(s)**. The following screenshot shows three nodes selected:

Figure 15.9 – These nodes will be aligned

After applying **Straighten Connection(s)**, the nodes will be aligned, as shown in the following screenshot:

Figure 15.10 – The nodes after applying Straighten Connection(s)

There are shortcut keys to create some common nodes in Blueprints. If you want to create a **Branch** node, then hold the *B* key and left-click on the graph. To create a **Sequence** node, hold the *S* key and left-click on the graph, as shown in the following screenshot:

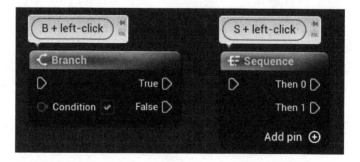

Figure 15.11 – Shortcuts for Branch and Sequence nodes

Other shortcut keys are *F + left-click*, which creates a **For Each Loop** node, and *D + left-click*, which creates a **Delay** node. These can be seen in the following screenshot:

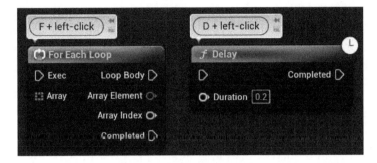

Figure 15.12 – Shortcuts for the For Each Loop and Delay nodes

To create a comment box around some nodes, first select the nodes, then right-click on one of the selected nodes and select the **Create Comment** option from **Selection**, or you can just press the *C* key. The following screenshot shows a comment box that is labeled **More shortcut keys**. Inside the comment box, there are more examples of shortcut keys used to create flow control nodes.

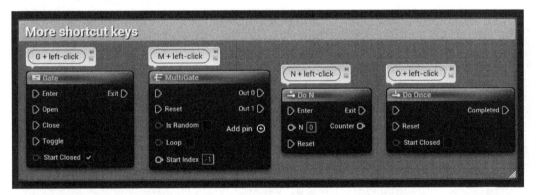

Figure 15.13 – Shortcuts for some flow control nodes

When you get used to some shortcuts, you will see how they speed up your work. Now, let's look at tips to help you build better Blueprints.

Blueprint best practices

In a project, you will deal with several Blueprint classes, and some of these Blueprint classes will be complex, with many nodes. The tips in this section will help you analyze your project and carry out some practices that will make your Blueprint classes more manageable. I separated these tips into two categories: Blueprint responsibilities and Blueprint complexities.

Blueprint responsibilities

When creating a Blueprint, you need to decide what its responsibilities will be. This refers to what it will do and what it will not do. You need to make the Blueprint as independent as possible. A Blueprint must be responsible for its internal state.

To illustrate the concept of Blueprint responsibilities, let's work with a simple example created for teaching purposes. In a game, the player is represented by the **FirstPersonCharacter** Blueprint. If the player collides with an enemy Blueprint, then the player will die, and an explosion effect will be spawned. The following screenshot shows the event hit that was implemented in the enemy Blueprint:

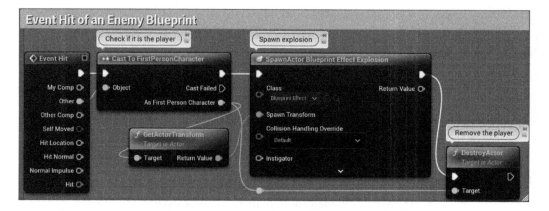

Figure 15.14 – Event hit of an enemy Blueprint

After that, you'll create another Blueprint that can also kill the player. So, you copy **Event Hit** and the nodes of the previous screenshot and paste them into the new Blueprint. Then, you create another different type of enemy Blueprint and copy and paste **Event Hit** again. But you decide to change the way the player dies. The player does not explode anymore; instead, a death animation is executed. However, to make this change in your game, you will have to search for all Blueprints that can kill the player and modify the script of all of them. This is a problem because you might forget one of the Blueprints, and the script may have frequent changes.

There is a way to avoid this type of problem. The script that defines how player death works must be implemented in the player Blueprint, which, in this example, is the **FirstPersonCharacter** Blueprint. The point is that the player Blueprint is responsible for the way the player dies. Let's redo our example, but now, we will create a custom event named **Death** in the **FirstPersonCharacter** Blueprint, as shown in this screenshot:

Figure 15.15 – Creating the Death event in the FirstPersonCharacter Blueprint

This way, if there are changes in the way the player dies, then these changes will need to be done only in the **Death** event of the **FirstPersonCharacter** Blueprint.

When a collision occurs, the other Blueprints that can kill the player will just have to trigger the **Death** event of the **FirstPersonCharacter** Blueprint. The following screenshot shows the new version of **Event Hit** of the **Enemy** Blueprint:

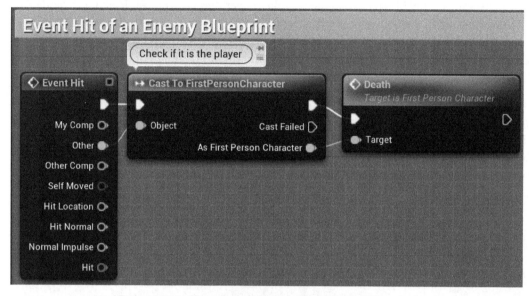

Figure 15.16 – New version of Event Hit of Enemy Blueprint

So, you can use events and functions to define how a Blueprint can communicate with other Blueprints. If you need to send data between Blueprints, then it can be sent through input or output parameters.

Another topic related to Blueprint responsibilities is Level Blueprint. Each Level has a Level Blueprint, so if you create your game rules logic inside a Level Blueprint, then when you add another Level, you will need to copy and paste all Blueprint nodes to the Level Blueprint of the new Level. If your game rules logic changes, then you will need to modify all the Level Blueprints, and this can become a maintenance nightmare.

A Level Blueprint must be used only for logic and situations specific to one Level. A typical example is to put a hidden trigger on a Level. When the player overlaps it, an enemy is spawned in another room.

A better place to implement game rules logic is in a GameMode Blueprint class. The logic for other actors should be implemented in Blueprint classes rather than being implemented in the Level Blueprint because instances of a Blueprint class can be added to any Level, so you do not need to copy and paste Blueprint nodes to use the same functionality in another Level.

Managing Blueprint complexities

A Blueprint **EventGraph** can become very complex and scary. When you open a Blueprint of this kind that was done by someone else, you might wonder, *what's going on?*

Some practices and Blueprint tools will help you to manage the complexities of a Blueprint and keep it readable.

The most important concept that will help you deal with complex Blueprints is **abstraction**. Abstraction is used to handle complexities by hiding low-level details, allowing the developer to focus on a problem at a high abstraction level without worrying about unnecessary details of other parts of the script.

In an **EventGraph**, there is a simple way to apply abstraction. You can select a group of nodes and convert them into a collapsed graph, Function, or Macro. To convert the nodes, right-click on the selected nodes. In the submenu that appears, within the **ORGANIZATION** category, you will see the options shown in the following screenshot:

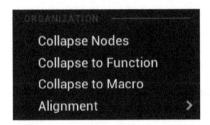

Figure 15.17 – Collapse options

Let's look at an example. The following screenshot shows some nodes connected to the InputAction Pause event. These nodes are responsible for showing the Pause Menu:

Figure 15.18 – Nodes used to show the Pause Menu

If we select the nodes, right-click on one of the selected nodes and use the **Collapse Nodes** option, then the editor will create **Collapsed Graph**, which is represented by a single node. You can give a meaningful name to this node. The following screenshot shows the node named **Show Pause Menu**, which represents **Collapsed Graph**. If you want to see or edit the nodes of **Collapsed Graph**, then double-click on the collapsed node:

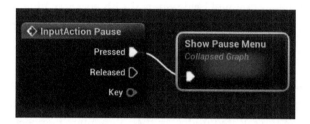

Figure 15.19 – The nodes were converted into a collapsed graph

Only use collapsed nodes if the group of nodes is not going to be used in another place. If the same group of nodes is used in other places of the **EventGraph**, then you can use **Collapse to Macro**. If you think that a group of nodes could be called from another Blueprint, then use **Collapse to Function**.

Now, let's imagine that you are opening a very complex Blueprint. But instead of seeing a giant graph of nodes, you see collapse graphs, macros, and functions with meaningful names. At least you will get an overview of what the Blueprint does. The complexities are there, but they are hidden, and you can look at the low-level details of a specific part when needed.

Another handy tool that can increase the readability of a complex **EventGraph** is a comment box. A comment box helps to identify a logic block. Its label stays visible when you zoom out of the **EventGraph**, and you can even change the color of comment boxes. The following screenshot shows an **EventGraph** zoomed out with three comment boxes:

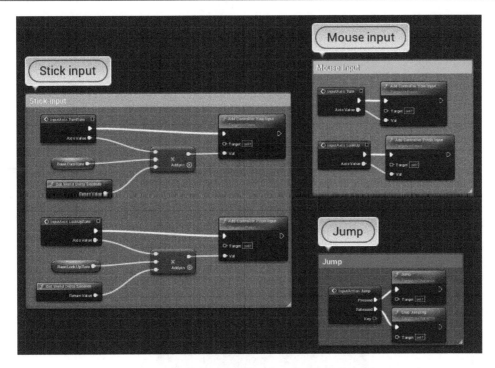

Figure 15.20 – The comments are visible when the EventGraph is zoomed out

You can see a list of the comment boxes of a graph in the **Bookmarks** window, which can be accessed from the top menu by going to **Window | Bookmarks**. The following screenshot shows the **Bookmarks** window:

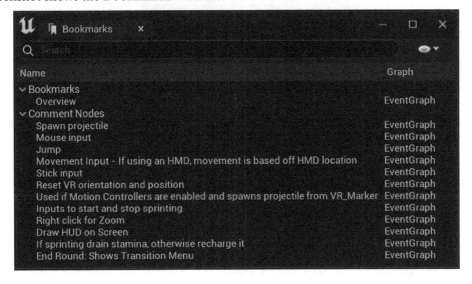

Figure 15.21 – Bookmarks window

If you double-click on an item in the **Bookmarks** window, then the **EventGraph** will be positioned in the associated location. You can create bookmarks to reference a location of the **EventGraph** by clicking on the icon located in the top left of the **EventGraph** and giving a name to the bookmark, as shown in the following screenshot:

Figure 15.22 – Creating a bookmark

In the **My Blueprint** panel, you can see a list of the events being used in the **EventGraph**, as can be seen in the following screenshot. Double-click on an event name to move the **EventGraph** to the position of the event:

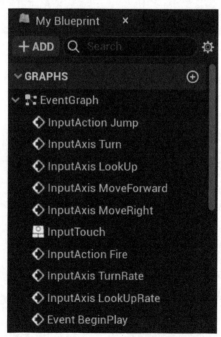

Figure 15.23 – List of events in the EventGraph

A complex Blueprint can have many variables. There are two variable properties, named **Tooltip** and **Category**, which help you identify and organize variables. These properties are found in the **Details** panel of a variable, as shown in the following screenshot:

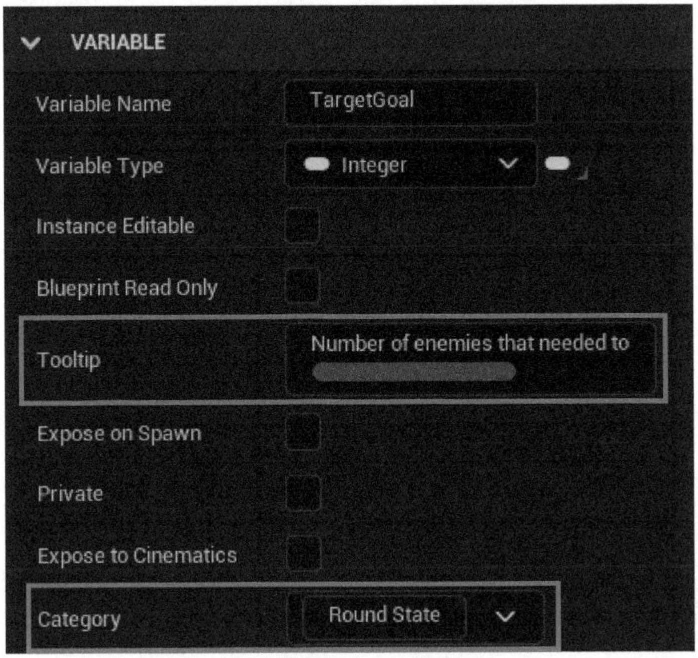

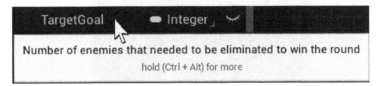

Figure 15.24 – Tooltip and Category properties

You can describe the purpose of the variable in the **Tooltip** property. The tooltip is shown when the mouse cursor is over the variable, as shown in the following screenshot. If the variable is set to **Instance Editable**, then it should have a tooltip so that the purpose of the variable is clear to the designer who is using an instance of the Blueprint in the Level.

Figure 15.25 – The tooltip appears when hovering over a variable

The **Category** property is used to group related variables. You can create categories or select an existing category in the drop-down menu. Variables are separated by categories in the **My Blueprint** tab, which you can open and close when you need it. This separation makes it easier to understand the variables of a Blueprint. The following screenshot shows a category named **Round State**, which has three variables:

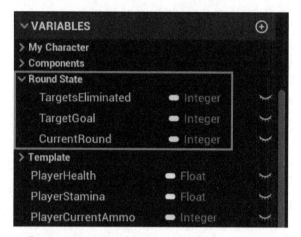

Figure 15.26 – Variables are grouped by categories

If you need to create variables that hold temporary values to help with more complex logic, then consider creating a function. A function allows the creation of local variables, which are only visible within the function. When you are editing a function, there is one more category for local variables in the **My Blueprint** panel, as shown in the following screenshot. Just a note; the values of local variables are discarded at the end of the function execution.

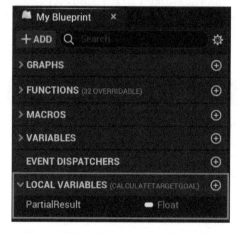

Figure 15.27 – Creating a local variable

This section covers some best practices to deal with Blueprint responsibilities and complexities. We will now see how to use some interesting miscellaneous Blueprint nodes.

Using miscellaneous Blueprint nodes

In this section, we will learn about some Blueprint nodes that can be very useful in certain situations.

These are the nodes covered in this section:

- **Select**
- **Teleport**
- **Format Text**
- **Math Expression**
- **Set View Target with Blend**
- **AttachActorToComponent**
- **Enable Input** and **Disable Input**
- The **Set Input Mode** nodes

Select

The **Select** node is very flexible. It can work with several types of variables for the index and the values of options. The node returns a value associated with the option that corresponds to the index that is passed as input. The following screenshot shows the **Select** node:

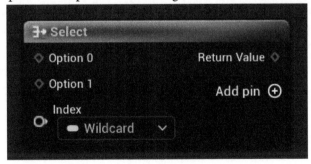

Figure 15.28 – The Select node

To add more input option pins, click on **Add pin +**. You can set a pin type of **Option 0**, **Option 1**, or **Index** by dragging a variable reference or wire onto the pins. **Option 0** and **Option 1** can be of any type, but the **Index** type must be **Integer**, **Enum**, **Boolean**, or **Byte**.

The following screenshot shows the **Select** node in use:

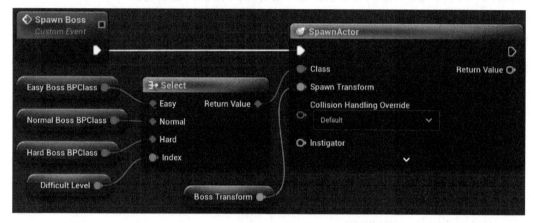

Figure 15.29 – Example of a Select node

There is an enumeration named **Difficult Level** that has the values of **Easy**, **Normal**, and **Hard**. The **Spawn Boss** custom event will spawn a different class of the **Boss** Blueprint, depending on the value of the **Difficult Level** enumeration variable. The option type in this example is `Actor Class Reference`.

Teleport

The **Teleport** node moves an actor to the specified location. The advantage of using **Teleport** rather than setting the actor's location is that if there is an obstacle at the location, then the actor is moved to a nearby place where there will be no collision.

The following screenshot shows an example of using the **Teleport** node:

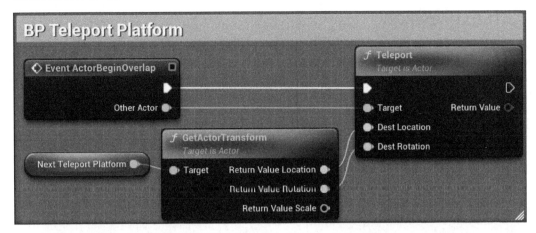

Figure 15.30 – Example of a Teleport node

There is a **BP Teleport Platform** Blueprint that has a reference to **Next Teleport Platform**. When the player overlaps **BP Teleport Platform**, they are teleported to **Next Teleport Platform**.

Format Text

The **Format Text** node builds text based on a template text and parameters specified in the **Format** input parameter. To add new parameters in **Text**, use the { } delimiters with the name of the new parameter inside the delimiters. An input parameter is created for each { } delimiter found in the **Format** parameter.

The following screenshot shows the **Format Text** node being used to print the result of a round, along with the template text {Name} wins the round with {Score} points:

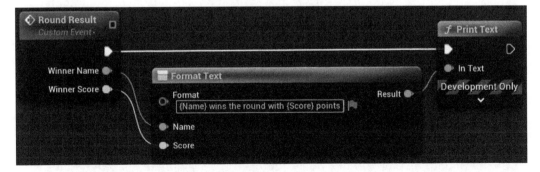

Figure 15.31 – Example of a Format Text node

An example output is Sarena wins the round with 17 points.

Math Expression

The **Math Expression** node is a collapsed graph created by the editor and is based on the expression typed in the name of the node. An input parameter pin is created for each variable name found in the expression. The **Return Value** output parameter is the result of the expression.

The following screenshot shows an example of using the **Math Expression** node:

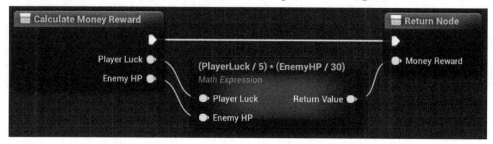

Figure 15.32 – Example of a Math Expression node

There is a function named **Calculate Money Reward**, which uses a **Math Expression** node. The expression of the node is (PlayerLuck/5) * (EnemyHP/30).

Set View Target with Blend

The **Set View Target with Blend** node is a function from the **Player Controller** class. It is used for switching the game view between different cameras. The **New View Target** input parameter is the actor to set as a view target, usually a camera.

The following screenshot shows an example of using the **Set View Target with Blend** node:

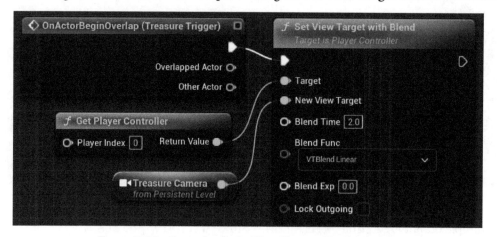

Figure 15.33 – Example of a Set View Target with Blend node

There is an event of the Level Blueprint that is triggered when the player enters the treasure room. The **Set View Target with Blend** function is used to change the game view to the camera that is in the treasure room.

AttachActorToComponent

The **AttachActorToComponent** node attaches an actor to the component referenced in the **Parent** input parameter. The transformations of the **Parent** component affect the actor attached. Optionally, **Socket Name** can be used to identify the place where the actor will be attached.

The following screenshot shows an example of using the **AttachActorToComponent** node:

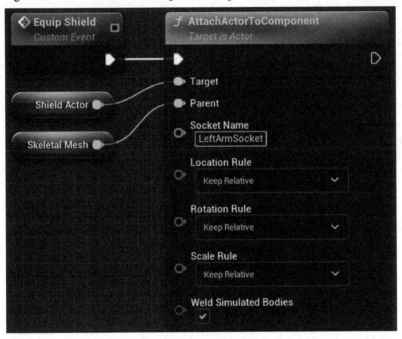

Figure 15.34 – Example of an AttachActorToComponent node

The **Equip Shield** custom event uses the **AttachActorToComponent** node to equip a **Shield Actor** component on a **Skeletal Mesh** component. The **Skeletal Mesh** component has a socket named **LeftArmSocket**, which is used to position the shield on the arm.

Enable Input and Disable Input

The **Enable Input** and **Disable Input** nodes are functions used to define whether an actor should respond to inputs events such as from a keyboard, mouse, or gamepad. The nodes need a reference to the **Player Controller** class in use.

A common use of these nodes is to allow an actor to only receive input events when the player is near the actor, as shown in the following screenshot:

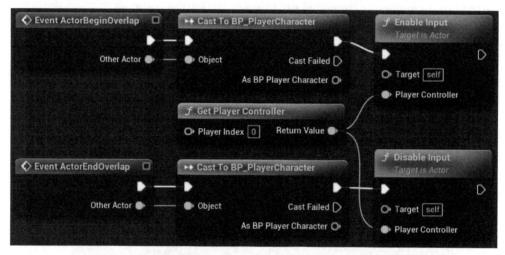

Figure 15.35 – Example of Enable Input and Disable Input nodes

The **Enable Input** node is called when the player begins to overlap the Blueprint. When the player finishes overlapping the Blueprint, the **Disable Input** node is called.

The Set Input Mode nodes

There are three **Set Input Mode** nodes that are used to define whether the priority in handling user input events is with the UI or with the player input. These are the nodes:

- **Set Input Mode Game Only**: Only **Player Controller** receives input events.

- **Set Input Mode UI Only**: Only the UI receives input events.

- **Set Input Mode Game and UI**: The UI has priority in handling an input event, but if the UI does not handle it, then **Player Controller** receives the input event. For example, when the player overlaps a Blueprint representing a shop, a UI is displayed with options for the player to choose to use the mouse, but the player can still use the arrow keys to move away from the shop.

Figure 15.36 – The Set Input Mode nodes

I recommend you get used to these miscellaneous Blueprint nodes. When working on a project, you will have to deal with some problems that can easily be solved with some specific Blueprint nodes.

Summary

In this chapter, we saw how to use editor shortcuts to create variables in various ways and how to organize Blueprint nodes using alignment tools. We also learned about some shortcut keys that are used to create specific Blueprint nodes.

Then, we looked at some Blueprint best practices to define Blueprint responsibilities and manage the complexities of Blueprints.

Finally, we learned about some more useful Blueprint nodes. All of these tips will help you to improve your scripts and build quality projects.

In the next chapter, we will explore the virtual reality template that is available in the Unreal Engine Editor.

Quiz

1. To create a **GET** node, hold the *Alt* key and drag a variable to the graph.

   a. True

   b. False

2. A Blueprint must be responsible for its internal state and be as independent as possible.

   a. True

   b. False

3. You can select a group of nodes and convert them into a collapsed graph, Function, or Macro.

   a. True

   b. False

4. The **Index** parameter of the **Select** node can be of any type.

   a. True

   b. False

5. The **Math Expression** node creates an input parameter pin for each variable name found in the expression.

   a. True

   b. False

16
Introduction to VR Development

This chapter explains several **Virtual Reality** (**VR**) concepts and explores the VR template. As VR headsets are becoming more affordable, the number of users is increasing fast. Therefore, the demand for VR games and business applications is rising as well. We will focus on the Blueprints of the VR template. This will be another opportunity to see Blueprint nodes being used in practice. You will be able to use some Blueprint concepts from this chapter in several other types of projects, so this is a useful chapter even if you do not have a VR headset.

In this chapter, we will analyze the functionality of the **VRPawn** Blueprint of the VR template. We will explain how to create objects that can be grabbed by the player using motion controllers, and we will learn about the Blueprint functions used to implement teleportation and how to use interfaces for Blueprint Communication. We will also see how the menu works in the VR template.

These are the topics we will cover in this chapter:

- Exploring the VR template
- The **VRPawn** Blueprint
- Teleportation

- Object grabbing
- Blueprint Communication using interfaces
- Interacting with the menu

By the end of the chapter, you will understand how the VR template works and will know how to create interfaces to allow different Blueprints to share data with each other.

Exploring the VR template

The Unreal Engine Editor has a Blueprint VR template that makes it easy to start experimenting with VR development. The VR template uses the **OpenXR** framework, which is an open standard for VR and augmented reality development. Because of OpenXR, the VR template works on multiple devices without any platform-specific modification.

The VR template is in the **GAMES** category. The following screenshot shows the creation of a project using the VR template:

Figure 16.1 – Selecting the VR template

The next screenshot shows the VR template map with a ball, weapons, and cubes that can be grabbed by the user:

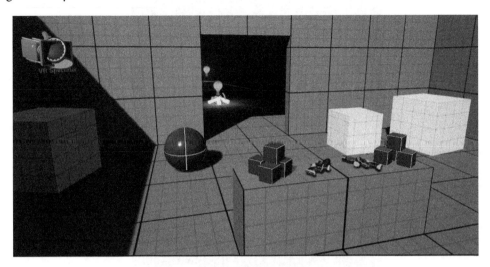

Figure 16.2 – The VR template map

If there is a VR display device installed on your computer and set up for development, then you can launch the Level in VR by clicking on the dropdown of the **Play** button and selecting **VR Preview**. If you don't have a VR display device, you can launch the Level by using the **New Editor Window** option of the **Play** button and pressing the *Tab* key to toggle Spectator Mode. You will be able to move around the Level using the *W*, *A*, *S*, and *D* keys and the mouse.

In VR Mode, you can teleport to different locations in the Level by pressing up on the right motion controller's thumbstick to mark a location and releasing the thumbstick to execute the teleport. Some objects in the Level can be grabbed. To grab an object, bring the motion controller closer to the object and hold the grip button. To drop the object, release the grip button.

The Blueprints used in the template are in the **Content > VRTemplate > Blueprints** folder. Let's learn about how they work to make it easier to adapt them to our projects. Also, this will be an excellent opportunity to see practical examples of Blueprints.

The VRPawn Blueprint

The **VRPawn** Blueprint represents the user in the Level. This Blueprint contains the logic for input events from the motion controllers, which are the physical devices that the user holds to interact in VR.

The following screenshot shows the **Components** panel of the **VRPawn** Blueprint:

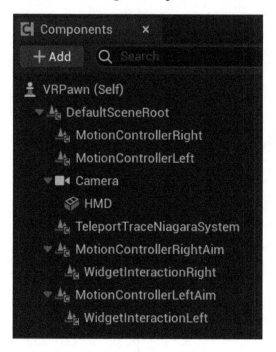

Figure 16.3 – The VRPawn components

MotionControllerRight and **MotionControllerLeft** are Motion Controller components that track motion controller devices. When you move the motion controller device, the data of this movement is sent to the Motion Controller component.

The **Camera** component is the user view. There is a Static Mesh component named **HMD** to visually represent the head-mounted display in the Level. When using the spectator camera, we can see a representation of the user because of the **HMD** and Motion Controller components:

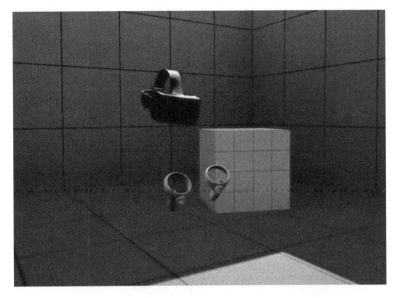

Figure 16.4 – A user representation in the VR template

Another component in **VRPawn** is **TeleportTraceNiagaraSystem**, which is a Niagara particle system component used to represent the teleport trace.

Then, we have another pair of Motion Controller components. The VR template uses these extra components as a simple way to get the aim locations. By default, the Motion Controller component uses the grip location, but you can change **Motion Source** in the **Details** panel. The next screenshot shows the properties of **MotionControllerRightAim**. The **Display Device Model** property is unchecked so that this Motion Controller component is not displayed in the Level:

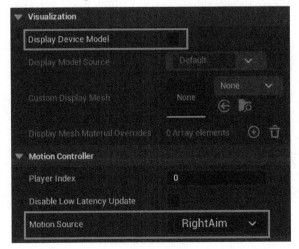

Figure 16.5 – The properties of MotionControllerRightAim

The last component left to mention is the `Widget Interaction` component. It works like a laser pointer and is used to interact with the Widget menu, which is activated by pressing the **Menu** button on the motion controller:

Figure 16.6 – Interacting with the Widget menu

In the EventGraph of **VRPawn**, there are several input events from motion controllers, which we will see in detail in the *Teleportation* and *Object grabbing* sections.

Teleportation

In this section, we'll see the event and functions used in teleportation.

To start the teleport, press up on the right motion controller's thumbstick to mark a location. When you release the thumbstick, you will teleport to the marked location. The teleport destination is represented by the **VRTeleportVisualizer** Blueprint:

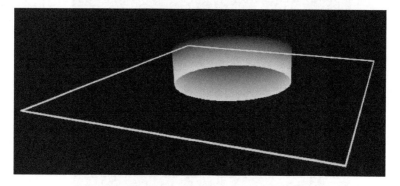

Figure 16.7 – The VRTeleportVisualizer Blueprint

The input event used for teleportation is **InputAxis MovementAxisRight_Y**. The first nodes of the event check whether **Axis Value** is positive, which means the thumbstick was pressed up, and check whether **Axis Value** is greater than the deadzone, which is a minimum **Axis Value** to start the teleport:

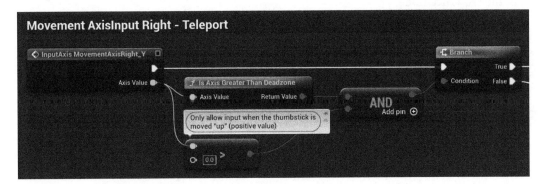

Figure 16.8 – The first nodes of InputAxis MovementAxisRight_Y

The next screenshot shows the nodes connected to the **True** output of the **Branch** node of *Figure 16.8*. The **Do Once** node is used to ensure that the **Start Teleport Trace** function will not run again while the teleport trace is active. The **Teleport Trace** function keeps updating the destination while the user presses up on the thumbstick:

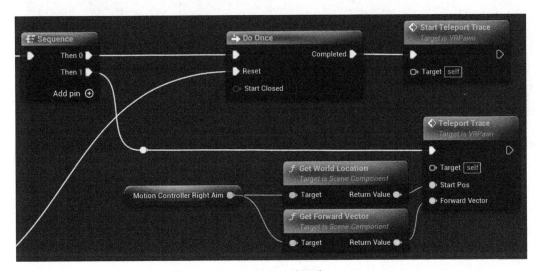

Figure 16.9 – Activating the teleport trace

The following screenshot shows the nodes connected to the **False** output of the **Branch** node of *Figure 16.8*, which means that the user is not pressing up on the right motion controller's thumbstick. If the teleport trace was active, then the event ends the teleport trace and tries to teleport to the destination. The **Try Teleport** node connects to the **Reset** pin of the **Do Once** node:

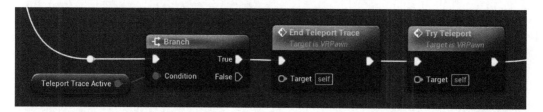

Figure 16.10 – Ending the teleport trace and teleporting

Let's analyze the **Start Teleport Trace**, **TeleportTrace**, **End Teleport Trace**, and **Try Teleport** functions used in teleportation.

The **Start Teleport Trace** function sets True in the **Teleport Trace Active** Boolean variable, sets visibility as True in the **Teleport Trace Niagara System** component, and spawns an instance of **VRTeleportVisualizer**:

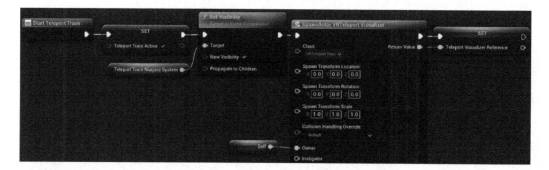

Figure 16.11 – The Start Teleport Trace function

The **TeleportTrace** function uses a function named **Predict Projectile Path By Object Type** to calculate **Projected Teleport Location** and **Teleport Trace Path Positions**. The following screenshot shows the last nodes of the **TeleportTrace** function, which update the **TeleportVisualizer** location and set the vector array used by the Niagara particle system component for teleport trace visual effects:

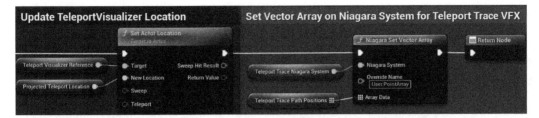

Figure 16.12 – The last nodes of the Teleport Trace function

The **End Teleport Trace** function is the opposite of the **Start Teleport Trace** function. It sets the **Teleport Trace Active** Boolean variable as `False`, destroys the **Teleport Visualizer** instance, and hides the **Teleport Trace Niagara System** component:

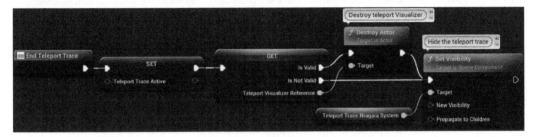

Figure 16.13 – The End Teleport Trace function

The **End Teleport Trace** function uses a **Validated Get** node. When you have an **Object Reference Get** node, you can right-click it and select **Convert to Validated Get**:

Figure 16.14 – Converting a Get node to a Validated Get node

The original node is converted to a **GET** node with execution pins that can be used to check whether the object reference is valid:

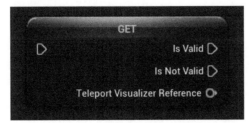

Figure 16.15 – A GET node with branching execution pins

The **Try Teleport** function checks whether **Valid Teleport Location** is **True** and then uses the **Teleport** function to teleport the user to the destination location:

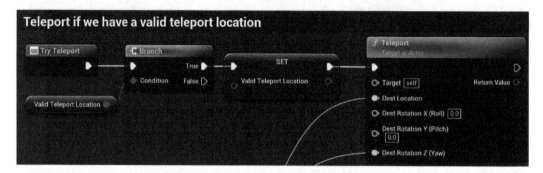

Figure 16.16 – The Try Teleport function

There is another type of movement in the VR template named **Snap Turn**. In this movement, you can rotate your virtual character by pressing left or right on the left motion controller's thumbstick. The input event used for Snap Turn is **InputAxis MovementAxisLeft_X**.

We saw the events and functions used for teleportation. In the next section, we will see how object grabbing works in the VR template.

Object grabbing

The object grabbing system is based on a **GrabComponent** Blueprint that was created for the VR template, which can be found in the Content > VRTemplate > Blueprints folder.

GrabComponent is a child class of **SceneComponent**. For more information about Blueprint components, see *Chapter 18, Creating Blueprint Libraries and Components*.

To make any Actor of the Level grabbable, add **GrabComponent** to the Actor and set **Mobility** to **Movable**:

Figure 16.17 – Making an Actor grabbable

There is an enumeration named **Grab Type** that defines how the object attaches to the motion controller. For more information about enumeration, see *Chapter 13, Data Structures and Flow Control*.

You can set **Grab Type** in the **Details** panel of **GrabComponent**:

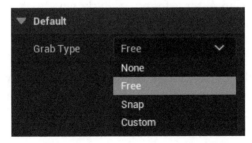

Figure 16.18 – Grab Type enumeration

These are the grab types available:

- **None**: Use this option when you want to disable grabbing without removing the Grab component of an Actor.

- **Free**: The object attaches to the motion controller while maintaining its relative location and orientation to it. This type is best used for objects that don't need to be held in a certain way to be used, such as the cubes in the VR template.

- **Snap**: When picked up, the object snaps to a specific predefined location and rotation relative to the motion controller that grabbed it. This grab type is usually used for objects with a clear grip location, such as the weapons in the VR template.

- **Custom**: This option allows the developers to create their own grab type. The Grab component has the `bIsHeld` Boolean variable and the `OnGrabbed` and `OnDropped` event dispatchers, which can be used to create custom logic.

The events of **VRPawn** that deal with grabbing are **InputAction GrabLeft** and **InputAction GrabRight**, which are triggered by the grip button of the motion controllers. To grab an Actor on the Level, bring the motion controller closer to the Actor and hold the grip button. To drop the Actor, release the grip button.

Let's analyze the **InputAction GrabLeft** event. The following screenshot shows the first nodes of the event:

Figure 16.19 – The first nodes of InputAction GrabLeft

The **Get Grab Component Near Motion Controller** function uses a sphere trace to search for a nearby Actor. If an Actor is found, it checks whether it has **GrabComponent**. If it does, a reference to **GrabComponent** is returned.

For more information about traces, see *Chapter 14, Math and Trace Nodes*.

If no Actor was found or if the Actor found had no component of **GrabComponent** type, the **Nearest Component** output pin would return an invalid component (since there wasn't any). Hence, the **Is Valid** node checks for the validity of the output. If the output is valid, the **Try Grab** function of **GrabComponent** is executed. This function disables the Actor physics if enabled and attaches the Actor to the motion controller. The **GrabComponent** reference is stored in the **Held Component Left** variable:

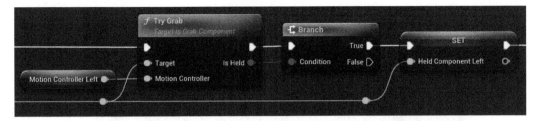

Figure 16.20 – Executing the Try Grab function of GrabComponent

If the object grabbed was being held by the other hand, then the other hand needs to release the object. This is done by clearing the reference in the **Held Component** variable of the other hand:

Figure 16.21 – Clearing the Held Component Right variable

The next screenshot shows the nodes connected to the **Release** pin of the **InputAction GrabLeft** event. The **Try Release** function detaches the Actor from the motion controller. After that, the **Held Component Left** variable is cleared:

Figure 16.22 – Nodes executed when the user drops the Actor

The user can interact with some grabbed Actors, such as the pistols, through Blueprint Interfaces.

Blueprint Communication using interfaces

A Blueprint Interface is a special type of Blueprint that only contains function names and parameters. It is used to allow communication between different types of Blueprints.

To create a Blueprint Interface, follow these steps:

1. Click the **Add** button in the content browser, and in the **Blueprints** submenu, select **Blueprint Interface**:

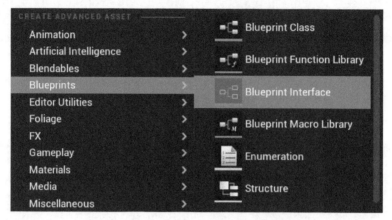

Figure 16.23 – Creating a Blueprint Interface

2. The VR template has a Blueprint Interface named **VRInteraction BPI** in the `Content > VRTemplate > Blueprints` folder. Double-click it to open the Blueprint Interface Editor. The following screenshot shows the functions of the **VRInteraction BPI** interface:

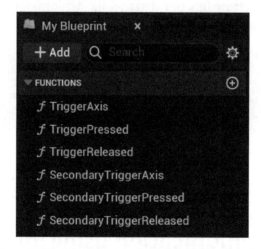

Figure 16.24 – The VRInteractionBPI interface functions

3. Open the **Pistol** Blueprint to see an example of an interface implementation. Click the **Class Settings** button of the Blueprint Editor. In the **Details** panel, go to the **Interfaces** category to see that the **VRInteraction BPI** interface was added to the **Pistol** Blueprint:

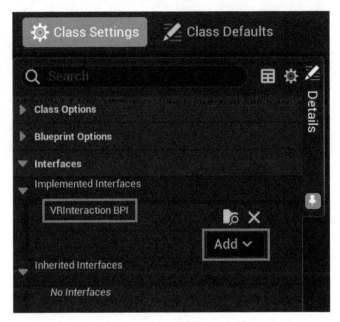

Figure 16.25 – Adding an interface

The **Pistol** Blueprint implemented the **Trigger Pressed** function of the **VRInteraction BPI** interface. Since the **Trigger Pressed** function does not have output parameters, it is implemented as an event:

Figure 16.26: Implementing a function of the interface

4. In this event, the **Pistol** Blueprint spawns an instance of the **Projectile** Blueprint. The **Trigger Pressed** function is called by the **VRPawn** Blueprint in the **InputAction TriggerLeft** and **InputAction TriggerRight** events:

Figure 16.27 – The VRPawn Blueprint calls the Trigger Pressed function of the interface

The **VRPawn** Blueprint gets the Actor owner of **GrabComponent** and calls the **Trigger Pressed** function using the Actor owner reference. If the Actor has an implemented **VRInteraction BPI** interface, then **Trigger Pressed** is executed. Nothing happens if the Actor did not implement the **VRInteraction BPI** interface.

In the next section, we will see how the user interacts with the menu in the virtual world.

Interacting with the menu

The VR template has a menu system that is activated by pressing the **Menu** button on the motion controller. The menu system is implemented by the **Menu** Blueprint and the **WidgetMenu** Blueprint. Both Blueprints are in the Content > VRTemplate > Blueprints folder.

The events of **VRPawn** that deal with the menu are **InputAction MenuToggleLeft** and **InputAction MenuToggleRight**, which are triggered by the **Menu** button of the motion controllers. The **Menu** button is used to show and hide the menu.

The next screenshot shows the **InputAction MenuToggleRight** event that executes the **Toggle Menu** function of **VRPawn**:

Figure 16.28 – The InputAction MenuToggleRight event

The **Toggle Menu** function checks whether the menu is active. In this case, it calls the **Close Menu** function of the **Menu** Blueprint. If the menu is not active, it spawns an instance of the **Menu** Blueprint:

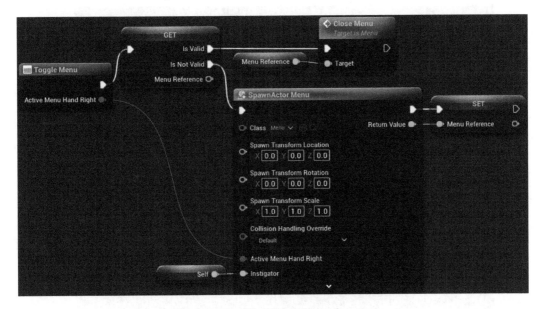

Figure 16.29 – The Toggle Menu function

The **Menu** Blueprint is responsible for showing **WidgetMenu** attached to the motion controller and defining the interaction between them.

Double-click **WidgetMenu** to open the UMG Editor:

Figure 16.30 – The WidgetMenu in the UMG editor

In the **Graph** tab of the UMG Editor, we can see the **On Clicked** events of the buttons. The **On Clicked (RestartButton)** event uses the **Open Level** function to reload the Level:

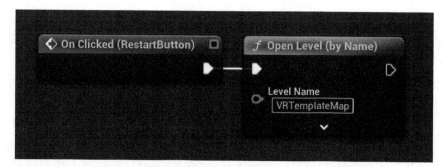

Figure 16.31 – The On Clicked (RestartButton) event

The **ExitButton** button has the **Real Life** label. The **On Clicked (ExitButton)** event uses the **Quit Game** function to exit the application:

Figure 16.32 – The On Clicked (ExitButton) event

If you want to add command buttons to the menu, you only need to modify the **WidgetMenu** Blueprints. For more information about UMG, see *Chapter 7, Creating Screen UI Elements*.

We have analyzed the main elements used in the VR template, so it will now be easier to understand more complex parts of the VR template.

Summary

In this chapter, we explored the VR template, which is a simple way to start experimenting with VR development. We saw that the main functionalities of the VR template are in the **VRPawn** Blueprint.

We analyzed the Blueprint functions used to implement teleportation and saw how **GrabComponent** is used to make grabbable objects.

We learned about the concept of **Blueprint Interfaces** and saw how they can be used to allow the user to shoot using the **Pistol** Blueprint. We also saw how to modify the UMG menu used by the VR template.

This chapter concludes *Part 4, Advanced Blueprints*, about advanced Blueprint concepts. *Part 5, Extra Tools*, will cover some extra tools available in Unreal Engine. In the next chapter, we will learn about Animation Blueprints.

Quiz

1. The VR template does not use the OpenXR framework.

    a. True

    b. False

2. The **VRPawn** Blueprint has `Motion Controller` components to track the motion controller devices.

    a. True

    b. False

3. You can right-click an **Object Reference Get** node and convert it to a **Validated Get** node with execution pins that can be used to check whether a reference is valid.

    a. True

    b. False

4. To create a grabbable Actor, you need to create a Blueprint class child of the **GrabComponent** Blueprint.

    a. True

    b. False

5. When an interface function does not have output parameters, it is implemented as an event.

    a. True

    b. False

Part 5: Extra Tools

This part will cover several tools that are very useful for solving specific problems. We are going to learn how to script an animation blueprint as well as how to create Blueprint macro/function libraries and components. We will also look at procedural generation and see how to create a product configurator using the variant manager.

This part comprises the following chapters:

17
Animation Blueprints

Part 4 presented data structures, flow control, math nodes, Blueprints tips, and an introduction to virtual reality development.

In *Part 5*, we will look at Animation Blueprints, Blueprint libraries and components, procedural generation, and the Product Configurator template.

This chapter presents the main elements of the Unreal Engine animation system, such as Skeleton, Skeletal Mesh, Animation Sequences, and Blend Spaces. It shows how to script an Animation Blueprint using **EventGraph** and **AnimGraph**. It also explains how State Machines are used in an animation and how to create new states for an animation.

These are the topics covered in this chapter:

- Animation overview
- Creating Animation Blueprints
- Exploring State Machines
- Importing the Animation Starter Pack
- Adding Animation States

By the end of the chapter, you will know how to use Animation Blueprints and how to add Animation States.

Animation overview

The animation system in Unreal Engine is very flexible and powerful. It consists of numerous tools and editors that work together. In this chapter, we will look at the main concepts of animation in Unreal Engine with a focus on Animation Blueprints.

We will start with a project using the Third Person template to see animation concepts and explore the Animation Editor.

Follow these steps to create the project:

1. Create a project using the **Third Person** template with starter content:

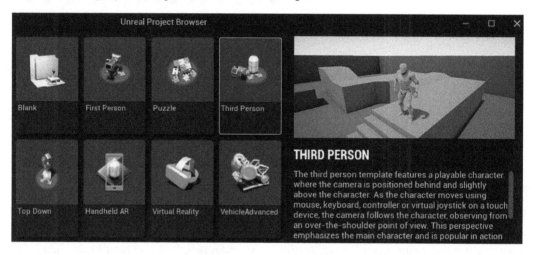

Figure 17.1 – Creating a project using the Third Person template

2. Press the **Play** button to try the default gameplay that is built into the Third Person template. You can move the player Character using the *WASD* keys and look around by moving the mouse. Press the *spacebar* to make the Character jump.

Now that we have an example project, let's explore the Animation Editor.

Animation Editor

There are five Animation Tools for working with Skeleton animation. These tools can be accessed by opening an associated asset. There are five buttons at the top right of each of the Animation Tools, as shown in the following screenshot, which are used to switch between the different tools:

Figure 17.2 – Using the buttons to switch between the Animation Tools

The Animation Tools accessed by the buttons are from left to right:

- **Skeleton Editor**: Used to manage Skeleton bones
- **Skeletal Mesh Editor**: Used to modify the Skeletal Mesh that is linked to the Skeleton and represents the Character visually
- **Animation Editor**: Allows the creation and modification of animation assets
- **Animation Blueprint Editor**: Allows the creation of scripts and State Machines to control the animations that the Character must use according to its current state
- **Physics Asset Editor**: Used to create physics bodies that will be used in simulations

Let's see the relationship between Skeleton and Skeletal Mesh.

Skeleton and Skeletal Mesh

A Skeletal Mesh is linked to a Skeleton. A Skeleton is a hierarchy of interconnected bones used to animate the polygon vertices of a Skeletal Mesh.

In Unreal Engine, Skeleton is a separate asset from Skeletal Mesh. As the animation is done in Skeleton, the animation can be shared by several other Skeletal Meshes that use the same Skeleton.

Let's visualize the Skeleton used by the Third Person template. Access the **Content >
Mannequin > Character > Mesh** folder and double-click on the **UE4_Mannequin_
Skeleton** asset to open the Skeleton Editor, as shown in the following screenshot:

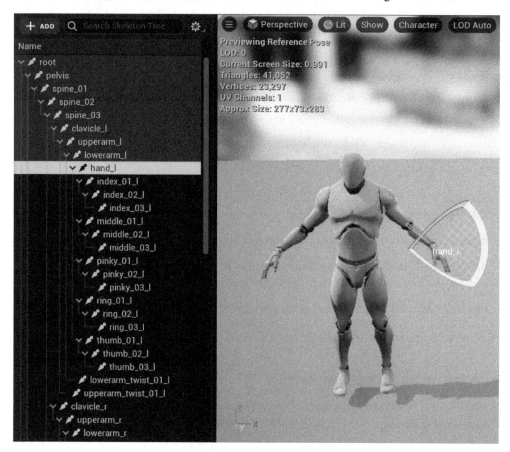

Figure 17.3 – The Skeleton Editor

The left-side panel has the Skeleton Tree with the hierarchy of bones that are part of this
Skeleton. You can select a bone and adjust its position and rotation relative to the Skeleton.

Animation Sequence

An Animation Sequence asset contains keyframes that specify bone transformations at
specific times. It is used to play a single animation on a Skeletal Mesh.

The Animation Sequences available to a Skeleton can be viewed in the **Asset Browser** of
the Animation Editor. The following screenshot shows the Animation Sequences of the
Third Person template:

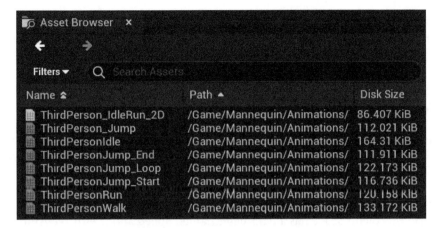

Figure 17.4 – The Animation Sequences

Double-click on an Animation Sequence to play it in the Viewport. The **ThirdPersonRun**
Animation Sequence is playing in the following screenshot:

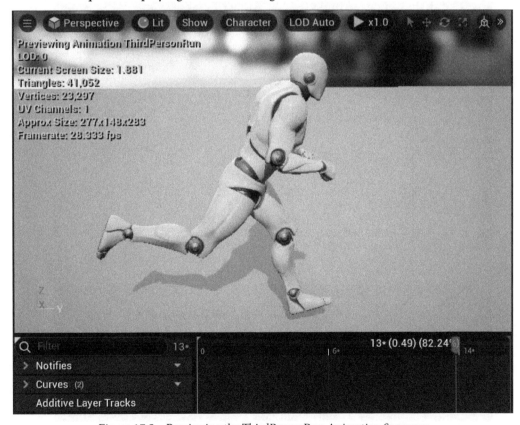

Figure 17.5 – Previewing the ThirdPersonRun Animation Sequence

The **Asset Browser** of the Animation Editor lists other types of animation assets besides Animation Sequences. For example, in *Figure 17.4*, the **ThirdPerson_IdleRun_2D** asset has a different-colored icon because it is a **Blend Space**, which we will see in the next section.

Blend Space

Blend Space is an asset type that allows the blending of animations based on one or two parameter values. To facilitate understanding, let's analyze the **ThirdPerson_IdleRun_2D** asset, which is a Blend Space based on one parameter.

Double-click on the **ThirdPerson_IdleRun_2D** asset in the **Asset Browser** to open it in the Viewport. This Blend Space has a parameter named **Speed** and uses three Animation Sequences, which are **ThirdPersonIdle**, **ThirdPersonWalk**, and **ThirdPersonRun**. Hold the *Shift* key to move the preview value of the **Speed** parameter, which is represented by the green plus icon:

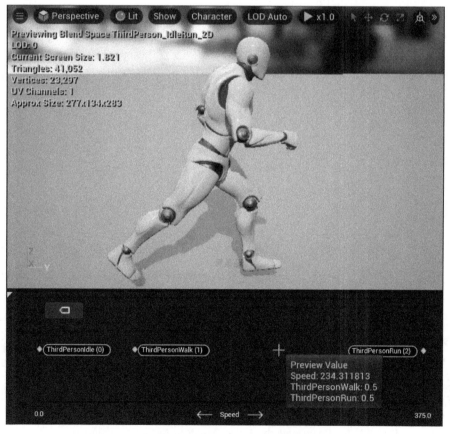

Figure 17.6 – Blending the walking and running Animation Sequences

The **ThirdPerson_IdleRun_2D** Blend Space mapped the following **Speed** values for each Animation Sequence:

- **ThirdPersonIdle**: 0.0

- **ThirdPersonWalk**: 93.75

- **ThirdPersonRun**: 375.0

In the example of *Figure 17.6*, the value used for **Speed** is approximately 234.3, then the resulting animation is using 50% of **ThirdPersonWalk** and 50% of **ThirdPersonRun**.

Animation in Unreal Engine is an extensive topic that requires the study of specific documentation aimed at animators. The purpose of this animation overview section was to introduce the main animation concepts so that you can work with **Animation Blueprints**, which we will introduce in the following section.

Creating Animation Blueprints

An Animation Blueprint is a specialized Blueprint with tools geared toward Character animation scripting. The Animation Blueprint Editor is like the Blueprint Editor, but it has some specific panels for animation.

Follow these steps to create an Animation Blueprint:

1. Click the **ADD** button in the **Content Browser**, and in the **Animation** submenu, select **Animation Blueprint**, as shown in the following screenshot:

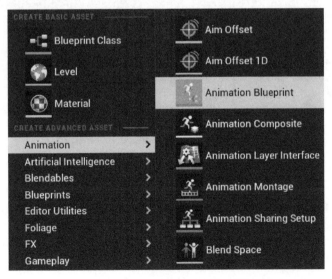

Figure 17.7 – Creating an Animation Blueprint

2. In the next window, you need to select the target Skeleton. The animation assets and the Animation Blueprint are linked to a specific Skeleton. Optionally, you can select a different parent class instead of the default class. For this example, do not select a parent class and select **UE4_Mannequin_Skeleton**, which is in the /Game/Mannequin/Character/ path:

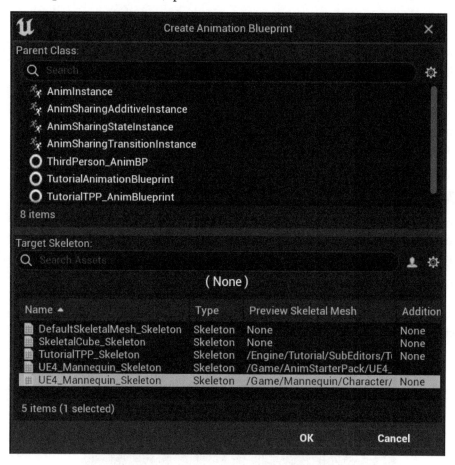

Figure 17.8 – Selecting the target Skeleton

3. Give a name to the Animation Blueprint created in the **Content Browser** and double-click it to open the Animation Blueprint Editor.

The Animation Blueprint Editor has two types of graphs that work together to create the animation. The **EventGraph** is the same as the one from the Blueprint Editor, but with some specific nodes for animation. In the **AnimGraph**, we can create State Machines and use nodes to play Animation Sequences and Blend Spaces.

Let's start by analyzing the **EventGraph**.

EventGraph

We use the **EventGraph** of an Animation Blueprint to get data from the Pawn/Character that is using the Animation Blueprint instance and update the variables of the Animation Blueprint. The **EventGraph** has two nodes already added to the graph:

Figure 17.9 – Animation Blueprint Editor EventGraph

These are descriptions of the nodes:

- **Event Blueprint Update Animation**: This event is executed at every frame, allowing for the updating of variables used by the animation. The **Delta Time X** parameter is the amount of time elapsed since the last frame.

- **Try Get Pawn Owner**: This function tries to get the reference of the Pawn or Character that is using the Animation Blueprint instance. We need this function so we can get Character data to use in the animation.

If you need to do some initialization on the animation, you can use **Event Blueprint Initialize Animation**:

Figure 17.10 – Event used to initialize animation

As an example of using the **EventGraph**, let's create the Speed variable and update its value using data from the Pawn/Character that is using the Animation Blueprint instance.

These are the steps to create the example:

1. In the **My Blueprint** panel of the Animation Blueprint Editor, create a variable named Speed and set **Variable Type** to **Float**:

Figure 17.11 – Creating the Speed variable

2. In the **EventGraph**, we will add the nodes shown in the following screenshot. If the **Pawn Owner** reference is valid, then we get the velocity vector of the Pawn and calculate its length to find the scalar value of **Speed**:

Figure 17.12 – Updating the Speed variable

3. Drag a wire from the white output pin of **Event Blueprint Update Animation** and add an **Is Valid** macro node. Connect the **Input Object** pin to the **Return Value** pin of the **Try Get Pawn Owner** node.

4. Drag a wire from the **Is Valid** output pin and add a **SET Speed** node.

5. Drag a wire from the **Return Value** pin of the **Try Get Pawn Owner** node and add a **Get Velocity** node.

6. Drag a wire from the **Return Value** pin of the **Get Velocity** node and add a **VectorLength** node.

7. Connect the **Return Value** pin of the **VectorLength** node to the **Speed** input pin.

8. Compile and save the Animation Blueprint.

Now that the **Speed** variable is updated, we can use it in the **AnimGraph**.

AnimGraph

In the **AnimGraph**, we use nodes to play Animation Sequences and Blend Spaces. We can also create State Machines to organize the animation into states.

The **AnimGraph** can only access variables from the Animation Blueprint, so we use the **EventGraph** to get the updated values from the Pawn.

The final node of an Animation Graph is the **Output Pose** node, which will receive the resulting pose of each frame to apply to the Skeletal Mesh:

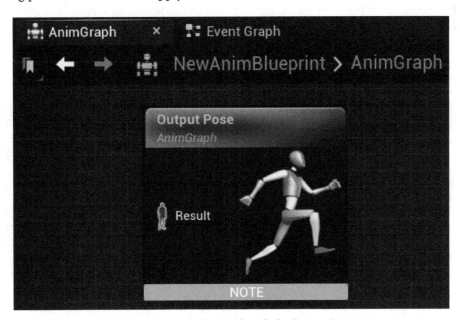

Figure 17.13 – AnimGraph with the Output Pose

There is an **Asset Browser** available in the bottom right of the Animation Blueprint Editor:

Name ⇕	Path ▲	Disk Size
ThirdPerson_IdleRun_2D	/Game/Mann	86.407 KiB
ThirdPerson_Jump	/Game/Mann	112.021 KiB
ThirdPersonIdle	/Game/Mann	164.31 KiB
ThirdPersonJump_End	/Game/Mann	111.911 KiB
ThirdPersonJump_Loop	/Game/Mann	122.173 KiB
ThirdPersonJump_Start	/Game/Mann	116.736 KiB
ThirdPersonRun	/Game/Mann	120.158 KiB
ThirdPersonWalk	/Game/Mann	133.172 KiB

Figure 17.14 – Asset Browser in the Animation Blueprint Editor

You can drag an animation asset from the **Asset Browser** and drop it in the **AnimGraph** to create the equivalent node. In the example shown in the following screenshot, the **ThirdPersonRun** Animation Sequence was dropped in the **AnimGraph** to create the **Play ThirdPersonRun** node. You need to connect the white character icon of the **Play ThirdPersonRun** node to the white character icon of the **Output Pose** node and compile the Animation Blueprint to preview the animation in the Viewport:

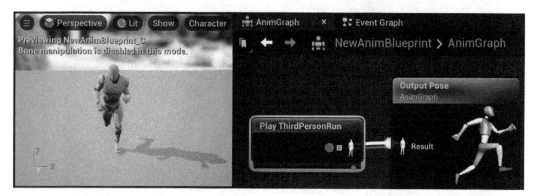

Figure 17.15 – Playing the ThirdPersonRun animation in the Animation Blueprint Editor

To create a **Blendspace Player** node, just drag a Blend Space asset, such as **ThirdPerson_IdleRun_2D**, and drop it in the **AnimGraph**. In the following screenshot, the value of the **Speed** variable is being used as the parameter of the Blend Space:

Figure 17.16 – Playing a Blend Space in the Animation Blueprint Editor

After compiling the Animation Blueprint, you can modify the value of the **Speed** variable in the **Anim Preview Editor**, located at the bottom right of the Animation Blueprint Editor:

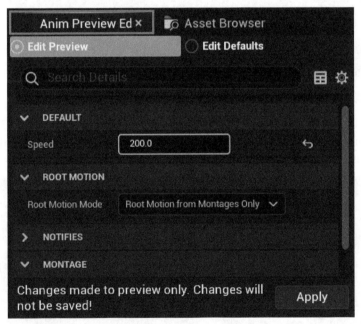

Figure 17.17 – Anim Preview Editor

Assign different values to the **Speed** variable between 0 and 375 and see the resulting animation in the Viewport.

We saw how to connect the animation nodes directly to the **Output Pose** node, but the **AnimGraph** was created with a State Machine in mind. We will discuss State Machines in the following section.

Exploring State Machines

A State Machine in the **AnimGraph** allows you to organize the animation into a series of states. To exemplify this, we will create a State Machine with two states: idle and moving.

We need to define **Transition Rules** to control the transition from one state to another.

Follow these steps to create the State Machine:

1. Remove the other animation nodes and leave only the **Output Pose** node in the **AnimGraph**.

2. Right-click on the **AnimGraph**, search for state machine, and select **Add New State Machine…**:

Figure 17.18 – Adding a State Machine

3. Rename the State Machine to Char States. You can rename it in the **Details** panel. Connect the white icon of the State Machine to the white icon of the **Output Pose** node:

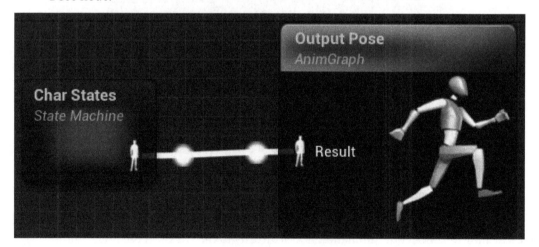

Figure 17.19 – Connecting the State Machine to the Output Pose node

4. Double-click on the **Char States** node to edit the State Machine. Then, right-click on the graph and select **Add State…**. Rename the state to `Idle` and drag a wire from the **Entry** to **Idle** state node:

Figure 17.20 – Adding states

5. Add another state and rename it to `Moving`. Drag a wire from the outer border of the **Idle** state node and connect it to the outer border of the **Moving** state node. Drag another wire from the **Moving** state node to the **Idle** state node. The arrow indicates that a transition is possible between the states:

Figure 17.21 – The states and their transitions

6. Double-click on the **Idle** state node to edit the state. Drag the **ThirdPersonIdle** Animation Sequence from the **Asset Browser** and drop it in the **AnimGraph**. Connect the white icons of the **Play ThirdPersonIdle** and **Output Animation Pose** nodes:

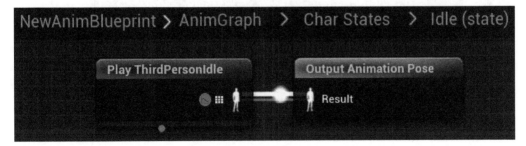

Figure 17.22 – The Idle state

7. You can alternate between the **AnimGraph** state screens by clicking the name of the screen in the path located at the top of the graph. This path is known as a **breadcrumb**. Click **Char States** in the breadcrumb and double-click on the **Moving** state.

8. Drag the **ThirdPerson_IdleRun_2D** Blend Space from the **Asset Browser** and drop it in the **AnimGraph**. Drag a wire from the **Speed** input pin and add a **Get Speed** node. Connect the white icons of the **ThirdPerson_IdleRun_2D** and **Output Animation Pose** nodes:

Figure 17.23 – The Moving state

9. Our next step is to specify the Transition Rules. Return to the **Char States** graph. The Transition Rules icons are created together with the transition arrows:

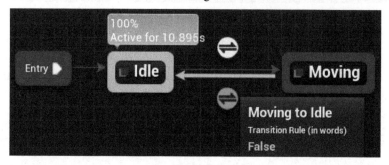

Figure 17.24 – The Transition Rules icons

10. Double-click on the **Idle to Moving** transition rule, which is the one at the top. The transition happens when the **Result** node receives the **True** value. In our example, if **Speed** is greater than 5 . 0, then the animation will change from the **Idle** to the **Moving** state. Add these nodes to the graph:

Figure 17.25 – Idle to Moving rule

11. Return to the **Char States** graph and double-click on the **Moving to Idle** transition rule. Add the nodes to check whether **Speed** is less than 5 . 0. If it is **True**, then the animation will change from the **Moving** to the **Idle** state:

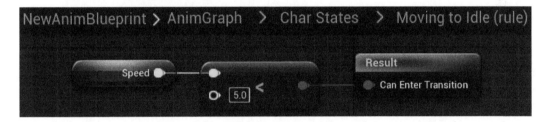

Figure 17.26 – Moving to Idle rule

12. Compile the Animation Blueprint and return to the **Char States** graph. You can modify the value of the **Speed** variable in **Anim Preview Editor** to see the transition between the states.

13. Save and close the Animation Blueprint Editor.

After this introduction to State Machines, we can now work with a more complex State Machine.

Importing the Animation Starter Pack

In the next sections, we will use the Animation Starter Pack because it has more animations available.

Follow these steps to import the Animation Starter Pack:

1. Access the Epic Games Launcher and go to **Unreal Engine | Library | Vault**. Search for **Animation Starter Pack** and click the **Add To Project** button:

Figure 17.27 – Adding the Animation Starter Pack to a project

> **Note**
>
> If you don't have the Animation Starter Pack installed, follow the instructions in *Chapter 9, Building Smart Enemies with Artificial Intelligence*, to install it.

2. Select the project you created for this chapter. A folder called `AnimStarterPack` will be added to the `Content` folder of your project.

3. Look in the Viewport of the Level Editor and delete the **ThirdPersonCharacter** instance that is in the Level. We will use the Character of the Animation Starter Pack.

4. Open the `ThirdPersonGameMode` Blueprint located in the `Content > ThirdPersonBP > Blueprints` folder. The Blueprint will open as a data-only Blueprint.

5. In the **CLASSES** category, change **Default Pawn Class** to Ue4ASP_Character, which is the Character Blueprint of the Animation Starter Pack:

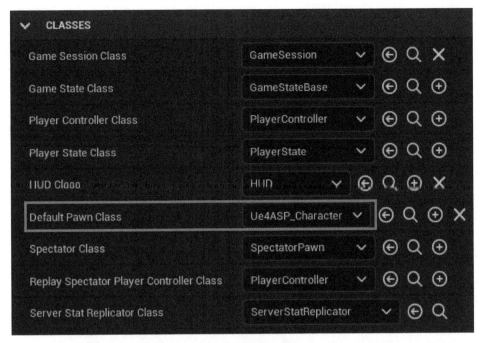

Figure 17.28 – Changing Default Pawn Class in the Game Mode Blueprint

6. Compile, save, and close the `ThirdPersonGameMode` Blueprint.

7. Open the `Ue4ASP_Character` Blueprint located in the **Content >**
    AnimStarterPack folder.

8. We need to hide the Capsule component in the game. In the **Components** panel,
    click on **CapsuleComponent (CollisionCylinder) (Inherited)**. In the **Details**
    panel, in the **RENDERING** category, check the **Hidden in Game** property:

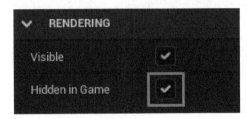

Figure 17.29 – Hiding CapsuleComponent

9. Compile, save, and close the `Ue4ASP_Character` Blueprint.

Now, our project is using the Character of the Animation Starter Pack and we are going to
start modifying the animations it uses.

Adding Animation States

In this section, we will modify the Character Blueprint and Animation Blueprint that come in the Animation Starter Pack. We will add the following states to the State Machine:

- **Prone**

- **ProneToStand**

- **StandToProne**

We will use the project created at the start of the chapter, which is using the Character from the Animation Starter Pack.

First, let's create the input mappings that we are going to use in our example. We will create two input actions: **Crouch** and **Prone**.

> **Note**
>
> The actions and states for the **Crouch** input action are already present in the Animation Starter Pack. To make **Crouch** work, we just need to add, in **Project Settings**, an action mapping named **Crouch**.

Follow these steps to create the input mappings:

1. Click the **Settings** button on the far right of the toolbar, and then select the **Project Settings...** option:

Figure 17.30 – Accessing Project Settings

2. On the left side of the window that appears, look for the **Engine** category and select the **Input** option.

3. Inside the **Engine** category, in the **Input Settings** menu, you will see two sections under the **Bindings** category called **Action Mappings** and **Axis Mappings**. Click on the > symbol in the **Action Mappings** section to show the existing mappings.

4. Click on the + sign next to **Action Mappings** twice to add two action mappings:

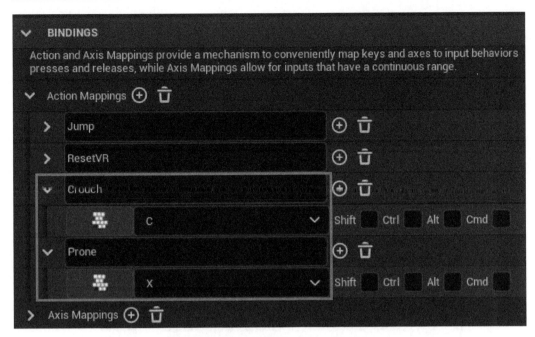

Figure 17.31 – Adding action mappings

5. Name the first action `Crouch`. Click the keyboard icon and press the *C* key to map that key to your **Crouch** event.

6. Name the second action `Prone`. Click the keyboard icon and press the *X* key to map that key to your **Prone** event.

The changes are saved when you close the window. We can now implement the **Prone** event in the Character Blueprint.

Modifying the Character Blueprint

We will add a Boolean variable named **Proning** to the Character Blueprint of the Animation Starter Pack. This variable will indicate whether the Character is prone. The **Prone** event will toggle the value of the **Proning** variable.

We will also disable the Character's movement when it is prone.

Follow these steps to modify the Character Blueprint:

1. Open the `Ue4ASP_Character` Blueprint located in the `Content > AnimStarterPack` folder.

2. In the **My Blueprint** panel, create a variable named `Proning` of the **Boolean** type:

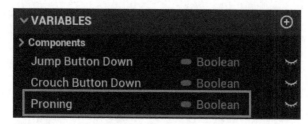

Figure 17.32 – Creating the Proning Boolean variable

3. Right-click on some empty space in the **EventGraph** and search for `prone`. Select the **Prone** event to place the node:

Figure 17.33 – Adding the input action Prone event

4. Add a **Set Proning** node and a **Get Proning** node near the **Prone** event. Also, add the **Not Boolean** node and connect them, as shown in the following screenshot. The **Not Boolean** node will toggle the Boolean value (true/false) of the **Proning** variable every time the **Prone** event is executed:

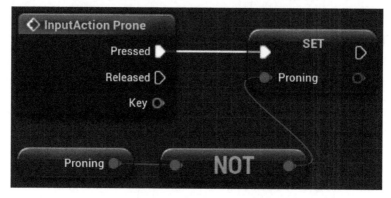

Figure 17.34 – The nodes of the input action Prone event

5. Now, we will disable the Character movement when it is prone. Find the **InputAxis MoveForward** event in the **EventGraph**. Hold the *Alt* key and click the white execution pin of **InputAxis MoveForward** to break the connection.

6. Add a **Branch** node and a **Get Proning** node and connect them, as shown in the following screenshot. The **Add Movement Input** node will only be executed if the value of the **Proning** variable is **False**:

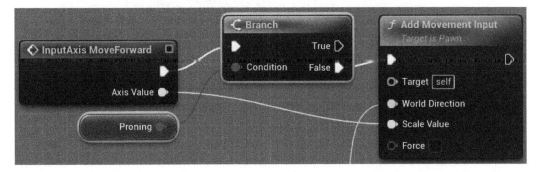

Figure 17.35 – Disabling the forward and backward movement when prone

7. Repeat *step 5* and *step 6* in the **InputAxis MoveRight** event:

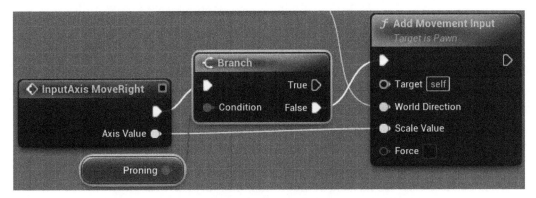

Figure 17.36 – Disabling the right and left movement when prone

8. Before closing the Blueprint, let's look at where we associate the Character Blueprint with the Animation Blueprint. In the **Components** panel, select **Mesh (CharacterMesh0) (Inherited)**. In the **Details** panel, in the **ANIMATION** category, **Animation Mode** must be set to **Use Animation Blueprint** and **Anim Class** must specify the Animation Blueprint being used:

Figure 17.37 – Specifying the Animation Blueprint used by the Character

9. Compile, save, and close the Blueprint.

We have completed the Character Blueprint adjustments. Now, we can add the prone Animation States to the Animation Blueprint.

Modifying the Animation Blueprint

We will also add the **Proning** Boolean variable to the Animation Blueprint to be able to use it in the Transition Rules. Then, we will add three states to the State Machine.

Follow these steps to modify the Animation Blueprint:

1. Double-click on the **UE4ASP_HeroTPP_AnimBlueprint** asset located in the Content > AnimStarterPack folder to open the Animation Blueprint Editor.

2. In the **My Blueprint** panel, create a variable named Proning of the **Boolean** type. We need to create this variable in the Animation Blueprint because it will be used in the state Transition Rules:

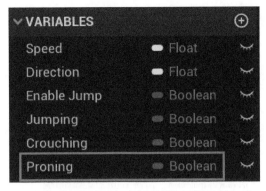

Figure 17.38 – Creating the Proning variable in the Animation Blueprint

3. Find **Event Blueprint Update Animation** in the **EventGraph**. At the end of the event, drag a wire from the white output pin of the **SET Crouching** node and add a **SET Proning** node.

4. Drag a wire from the blue output pin of the **Cast To Ue4ASP_Character** node and add a **Get Proning** node. Connect the output pin of **Get Proning** to the input pin of **SET Proning**:

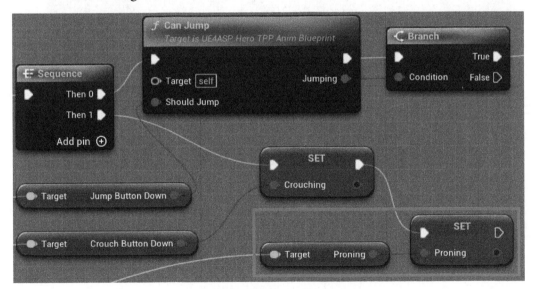

Figure 17.39 – Updating the Proning variable of the Animation Blueprint

5. In the **My Blueprint** panel, double-click on **Locomotion** to open the State Machine:

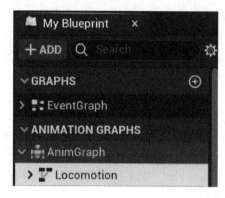

Figure 17.40 – Opening the Locomotion State Machine

6. The following screenshot shows the current **Locomotion** states:

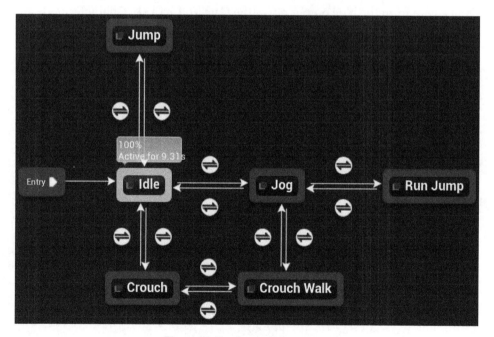

Figure 17.41 – Locomotion states

7. We will add three states related to the prone action:

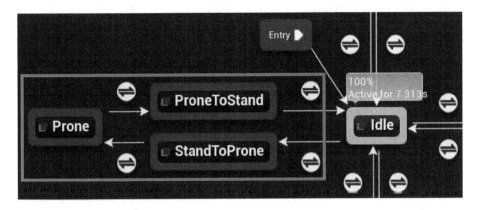

Figure 17.42 – The new states

8. We will start creating the three states. Right-click on the graph and select **Add State**. Rename the state to StandToProne. Create two more states, named Prone and ProneToStand.

9. Drag a wire from the outer border of the **Idle** state node and connect it to the outer border of the **StandToProne** state node. Drag another wire from the outer border of **StandToProne** and connect it to the outer border of the **Prone** state node.

10. Drag a wire from the outer border of the **Prone** state node and connect it to the outer border of the **ProneToStand** state node. Drag another wire from the outer border of **ProneToStand** and connect it to the outer border of the **Idle** state node.

11. Double-click on the **Prone** state node to edit the state. Drag the **Prone_Idle** Animation Sequence from the **Asset Browser** and drop it in the **AnimGraph**:

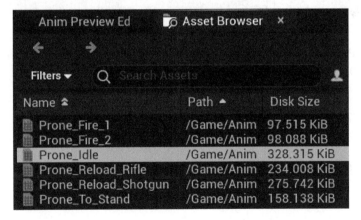

Figure 17.43 – Using the Prone_Idle Animation Sequence

12. Connect the white icons of the **Play Prone_Idle** and **Output Animation Pose** nodes:

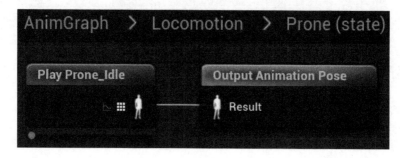

Figure 17.44 – The Prone state

13. Click on **Locomotion** in the breadcrumb to return to the previous graph and double-click on the **ProneToStand** state.

14. Drag the **Prone_To_Stand** Animation Sequence from the **Asset Browser** and drop it in the **AnimGraph**. Connect the white icons of the **Play Prone_To_Stand** and **Output Animation Pose** nodes:

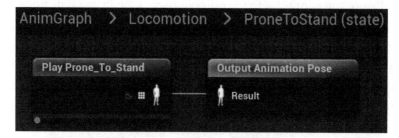

Figure 17.45 – The ProneToStand state

15. Select the **Play Prone_To_Stand** node. In the **Details** panel, uncheck the **Loop Animation** property, because this animation should run only once:

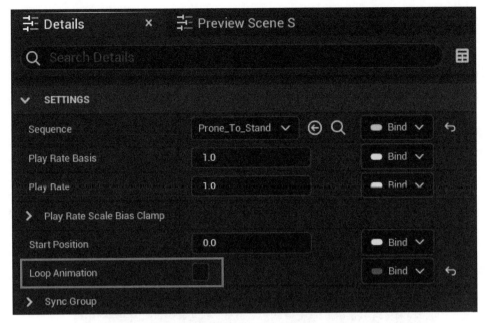

Figure 17.46 – Unchecking the Loop Animation property

16. Click on **Locomotion** in the breadcrumb to return to the previous graph and double-click on the **StandToProne** state.

17. Drag the **Stand_To_Prone** Animation Sequence from the **Asset Browser** and drop it in the **AnimGraph**. Connect the white icons of the **Play Stand_To_Prone** and **Output Animation Pose** nodes:

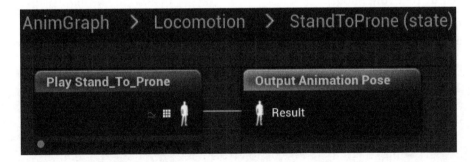

Figure 17.47 – The StandToProne state

18. Select the **Play Stand_To_Prone** node. In the **Details** panel, uncheck the **Loop Animation** property.

19. Click on **Locomotion** in the breadcrumb to return to the **Locomotion** graph.

We have finished defining the content of each state. Now, we just need to define the Transition Rules of the states.

Defining the Transition Rules

In our new states, we will use two types of Transition Rules. In the Transition Rules from the **Idle** and **Prone** states, we will check the value of the **Proning** variable. In the Transition Rules from **StandToProne** and **ProneToStand**, the transition happens when the animation ends.

These are the steps to define the Transition Rules:

1. Double-click on the **Idle to StandToProne** transition rule icon. Add a **Get Proning** node and connect to the **Result** node:

Figure 17.48 – Idle to StandToProne rule

2. Return to the **Locomotion** graph and double-click on the **StandToProne to Prone** transition rule icon. Right-click on the graph and add a **Time Remaining (ratio) (Stand_To_Prone)** node.

3. Drag a wire from **Return Value** and add a **Less** node. Type 0.1 in the bottom parameter of the **Less** node. Connect the output of the **Less** node to the **Result** node:

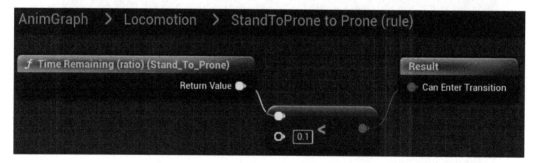

Figure 17.49 – StandToProne to Prone rule

4. Return to the **Locomotion** graph and double-click on the **Prone to ProneToStand** transition rule icon. Add a **Get Proning** node and a **NOT Boolean** node. Connect the nodes, as shown in the following screenshot:

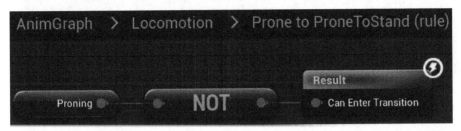

Figure 17.50 – Prone to ProneToStand rule

5. Return to the **Locomotion** graph and double-click on the **ProneToStand to Idle** transition rule icon. Right-click on the graph and add a **Time Remaining (ratio) (Prone_To_Stand)** node.

6. Drag a wire from **Return Value** and add a **Less** node. Type 0.1 in the bottom parameter of the **Less** node. Connect the output of the **Less** node to the **Result** node:

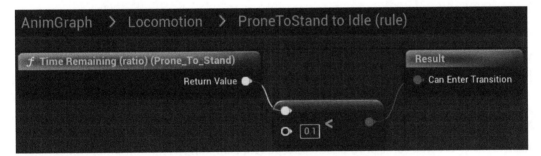

Figure 17.51 – ProneToStand to Idle rule

7. Compile, save, and close the Animation Blueprint.

8. Click the **Play** button of the Level Editor. Use the *C* key to crouch and the *X* key to prone:

Figure 17.52 – Press the X key to prone

The Animation Blueprint has specific tools that allow you to control complex animations by breaking them into states. A great advantage of Animation Blueprints is the separation of animation logic and game logic in a project.

Summary

This chapter presented some animation concepts, focusing on Animation Blueprints. We looked at Animation Editor, Skeleton, Skeletal Mesh, Animation Sequence, and Blend Space.

This chapter showed how to use the **EventGraph** and **AnimGraph** of an Animation Blueprint. We also learned how to create State Machines in the **AnimGraph**.

We also saw a practical example of how to add states to the Character of the Animation Starter Pack.

In the next chapter, we will learn how to create Blueprint libraries and components that can be used throughout a project.

Quiz

1. A Blend Space allows the blending of animations based on parameters.

    a. True

    b. False

2. An Animation Blueprint has **AnimGraph** but doesn't have an **EventGraph**.

    a. True

    b. False

3. The **Output Pose** node needs to be the final node of an Animation Graph.

    a. True

    b. False

4. A State Machine is an independent auxiliary asset that contains a fixed set of named constants.

    a. True

    b. False

5. The transition from one state to another is controlled by a Transition Rule.

    a. True

    b. False

18

Creating Blueprint Libraries and Components

In this chapter, you will learn how to create Blueprint Macro and Function libraries with common functionalities that can be used throughout a project. It will explain in more detail the concept of components. We will also learn how to create Actor Components with encapsulated behavior and Scene Components with location-based behaviors.

These are the topics covered in this chapter:

- Blueprint Macro and Function libraries
- Creating Actor Components
- Creating Scene Components

By the end of this chapter, you will have created a Blueprint Function Library to simulate dice rolls, an Actor Component to manage experience points and leveling up, and a Scene Component that rotates around the Actor.

Blueprint Macro and Function libraries

Sometimes, in a project, you identify a macro or function that can be used in several Blueprints. The Unreal Editor allows you to create a Blueprint Macro Library to gather the macros that you want to share between all Blueprints. In the same way, you can create a Blueprint Function Library to share utility functions between all Blueprints.

The menu options to create **Blueprint Function Library** and **Blueprint Macro Library** are in the **Blueprints** submenu that appears when creating an asset:

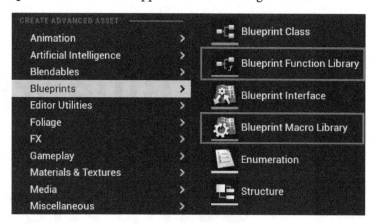

Figure 18.1 – The menu options to create Blueprint Macro and Function Libraries

When creating a Blueprint Macro Library, you need to choose a Parent class. The macros of the library will have access to variables and functions of the Parent class selected, but the Macro Library can only be used by subclasses of the chosen Parent class. Selecting the Actor class will be the best option in most cases.

Let's create a Blueprint Function Library to see in practice how we can share functions between all Blueprints.

A Blueprint Function Library example

We will create a Blueprint Function Library for a dice roll named `BP_DiceLibrary` with three functions – `RollOneDie`, `RollTwoDice`, and `RollThreeDice`. All functions have the same input parameter named `NumberOfFaces` and return the result of each dice and the sum.

This Blueprint Function Library can be used when creating digital board games or in **RPGs (Role-Playing Games)** based on a dice roll.

Follow these steps to create a Blueprint Function Library:

1. Create a project based on the **Third Person** template with the starter content.

2. In the content browser, access the Content folder. Right-click in the empty space next to the list of folders and select the **New Folder** option. Name the folder Chapter18. We will use this folder to store this chapter's assets.

3. Open the **Chapter18** folder you just made, then click the **Add** button in the content browser, hover over **Blueprints**, and choose the **Blueprint Function Library** option:

Figure 18.2 – Creating a Blueprint Function Library

4. Name the Blueprint BP_DiceLibrary and double-click it to open the Blueprint Editor.

5. The Blueprint Editor opens with a default function. Rename the function RollOneDie.

6. In the **Details** panel, add an input parameter named NumberOfFaces of the **Integer** type. Click the > symbol to expand the options and set **Default Value** to 6:

Figure 18.3 – Creating an input parameter and setting the default value

7. In the **Details** panel, add an output parameter named `Result` of the **Integer** type:

Figure 18.4 – Creating an output parameter

8. In the EventGraph, add the nodes of the following screenshot. These nodes check whether **Number Of Faces** is greater than 1. It is good practice to validate input parameters to avoid unexpected and hard-to-find errors:

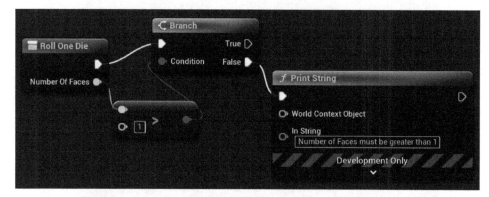

Figure 18.5 – Checking whether Number Of Faces is greater than 1

> **Note**
> You can simulate coin flipping using a number of faces equal to two.

9. Right-click the EventGraph and add a **Random Integer in Range** node. This node returns a random integer value greater than or equal to **Min** and less than or equal to **Max**. Type 1 in the **Min** input parameter:

Figure 18.6 – Using the Random Integer in Range node

10. Drag a wire from the **Number Of Faces** parameter and connect to the **Max** input pin. Connect the **Return Value** output pin to the **Result** pin. Connect the **True** pin of the **Branch** node to the white pin of **Return Node**.

11. Let's create the second function of our Blueprint Function Library. In the **My Blueprint** panel, click the + icon at the right of **FUNCTIONS**:

Figure 18.7 – Creating another function

12. Name the function RollTwoDice. Create an input parameter named NumberOfFaces of the **Integer** type. Click the > symbol to expand the options and set **Default Value** to 6.

13. Create output parameters named Sum, Die1, and Die2, all of the **Integer** type:

Figure 18.8 – Creating the output parameters

14. In the EventGraph, we will do the same validation of the **RollOneDie** function to check whether **Number Of Faces** is greater than 1. Add the nodes of *Figure 18.5*. You can also access the **RollOneDie** function, and select and copy the validation nodes to paste into the **RollTwoDice** function.

Creating Blueprint Libraries and Components

15. Add two **Random Integer in Range** nodes to the EventGraph. Type 1 in the **Min** input parameter of the two nodes:

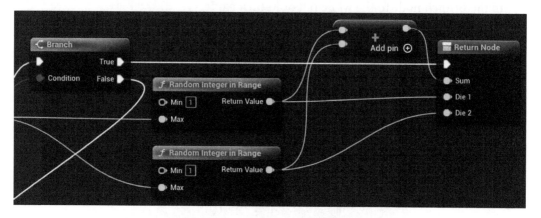

Figure 18.9 – Generating two random integer numbers

16. Drag wires from the **Number Of Faces** parameter and connect to the **Max** input pin of the two nodes.

17. Connect the **Return Value** output pin of the first **Random Integer in Range** node to the **Die 1** pin. Connect the **Return Value** output pin of the second **Random Integer in Range** node to the **Die 2** pin.

18. Right-click the EventGraph and create an **Add** node. Connect the **Return Value** output pin of the first **Random Integer in Range** node to the top input pin of **Add** node. Connect the **Return Value** output pin of the second **Random Integer in Range** node to the bottom input pin of the **Add** node.

19. Connect the output pin of the **Add** node to the **Sum** pin of **Return Node**. Connect the **True** pin of the **Branch** node to the white pin of **Return Node**.

20. Compile and save the Blueprint.

With these steps, we have concluded creating the second function of the library. In the next section, we will create the third function, which will be done differently from the second function to show an alternative example. Then, we will test our Blueprint Function Library.

Creating the third function and testing

In the third function, we will use **local variables** to store temporary values. Local variables are only visible within the function where they are defined. The values of local variables are discarded at the end of the function execution.

Another important point to note is that we will use only one **Random Integer in Range** node to generate the values of the three dice.

These are the steps to create the third function and test:

1. In the **My Blueprint** panel, click the + icon at the right of **FUNCTIONS**. Name the function RollThreeDice:

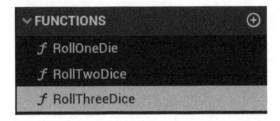

Figure 18.10 – Creating the third function of the library

2. Create an input parameter named NumberOfFaces of the **Integer** type. Click the > symbol to expand the options and set **Default Value** to 6.

3. Create output parameters named Sum, Die1, Die2, and Die3, all of the **Integer** type:

Figure 18.11 – Creating the output parameters

4. The **My Blueprint** panel shows the local variables of the function being edited.
    Click the + icon at the right of **Local Variables** to create the Die1Var, Die2Var,
    and Die3Var local variables of the **Integer** type. The name of a local variable must
    be different from the names of the input and output parameters of the function:

Figure 18.12 – Creating the local variables

5. In the EventGraph, we will do the same validation of the **RollOneDie** function to
    check whether **Number Of Faces** is greater than 1. Add the nodes of *Figure 18.5*.

6. Add one **Random Integer in Range** node to the EventGraph. Type 1 in the **Min**
    input parameter. Add the **SET Die1Var**, **SET Die2Var**, and **SET Die3Var** nodes and
    connect them as shown in the following screenshot:

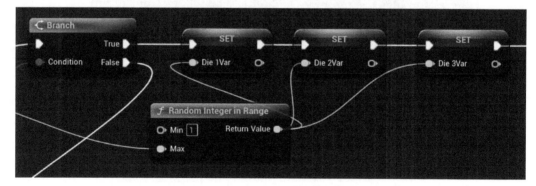

Figure 18.13 – Generating three random integer numbers

> **Note**
>
> When each **SET** node is executed, the **Random Integer in Range** node is executed again to generate a new random number.

7. Connect the white output pin of the **SET Die3Var** node to the white pin of **Return Node**. Add the **GET Die1Var**, **GET Die2Var**, **GET Die3Var**, and **Add** nodes. Click **Add pin** + to add the third pin of the **Add** node. Connect the nodes as shown in the following screenshot:

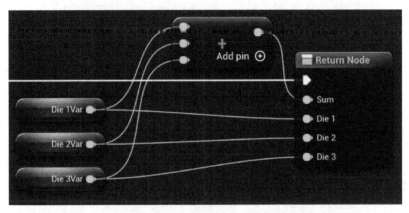

Figure 18.14 – Returning the values of the local variables

8. Compile and save the Blueprint. Close the Blueprint Editor.

9. We will use the Level Blueprint to test our **BP_DiceLibrary** Function Library. Click the **Blueprints** button on the toolbar and select **Open Level Blueprint**:

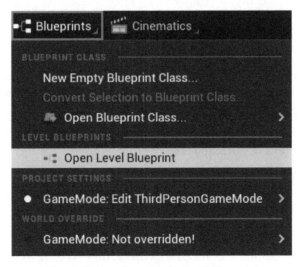

Figure 18.15 – Opening the Level Blueprint

10. Right-click the EventGraph near the **Event BeginPlay** node. Search for `roll`. The functions of our Blueprint Library will be available in the **BP Dice Library** category:

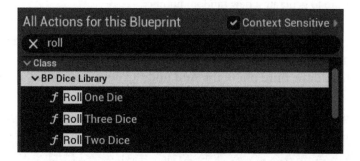

Figure 18.16 – The BP Dice Library functions are available for all Blueprints of the project

11. Select the **Roll Three Dice** function and connect the white pin of **Event BeginPlay** to the white input pin of the **Roll Three Dice** node. Right-click the EventGraph and add the **Format Text** and **Print Text** nodes:

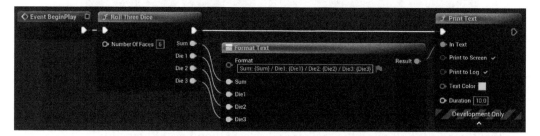

Figure 18.17 – Testing the Roll Three Dice function

12. Add the following expression in the **Format** parameter of the **Format Text** node:

```
Sum: {Sum} / Die1: {Die1} / Die2: {Die2} / Die3: {Die3}
```

13. The names between { } will be converted to input parameters in the **Format Text** node. For more information about this node, see *Chapter 15, Blueprints Tips*.

14. Connect the output white pin of the **Roll Three Dice** node to the input white pin of **Print Text**. Connect the other output pins input of **Roll Three Dice** to the equivalent input pins of **Format Text**.

15. Connect the **Result** pin of **Format Text** to the **In Text** pin of **Print Text**. Click the small arrow on the bottom of the **Print Text** node to expand the optional parameters. Set **Duration** to `10.0` seconds.

16. Compile, save, and close the Level Blueprint Editor.

17. Click the **Play** button of the Level Editor. The result of rolling three dice will be printed on screen:

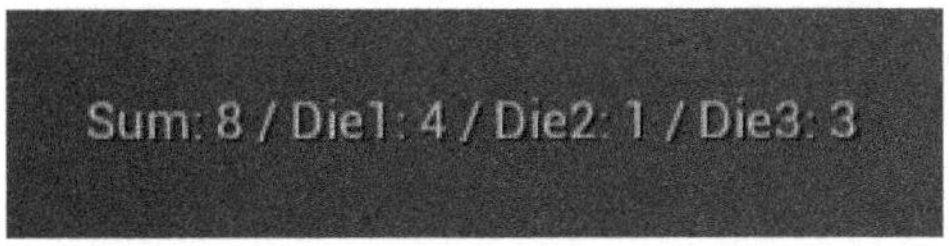

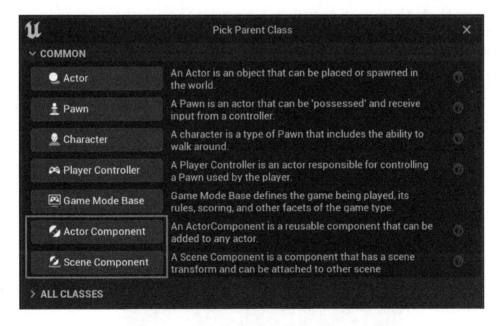

Figure 18.18 – The result of rolling three dice

The functions of `BP_DiceLibrary` can be used in any Blueprint. The same idea applies to a Blueprint Macro Library, but instead of functions, we create macros. For more information on the differences between macros and functions, see *Chapter 2, Programming with Blueprints*.

In the next section, we will see another way to share common functionalities by creating Actor Components.

Creating Actor Components

When creating an Actor Blueprint, we often add components with encapsulated functionality ready to use, such as Projectile Movement, Static Mesh, and Collision components. We can also create our own Actor Components using Blueprints.

When creating a Blueprint, in the **Pick Parent Class** panel, there are two **COMMON** classes that can be used to create components, namely **Actor Component** and **Scene Component**:

Figure 18.19 – Creating Actor and Scene Components

The Scene Component is a Child class of the Actor Component that has the Transform structure (location, rotation, and scale). Because of the Transform, a Scene Component can be attached to another Scene Component. We will explore the Scene Component in the next section.

When scripting a component in the EventGraph, you can get a reference of the Actor that is using the component with the **Get Owner** node:

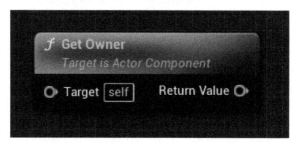

Figure 18.20 – Getting the reference of the Actor that is using the component

We will create an Actor Component named BP_ExpLevelComp that has an array of integers to store the experience points of each level needed to level up. The component will have a function named IncreaseExperience to increase the experience points and to check whether the Actor should level up.

If you want to add a level-up manager to an Actor, you can just add the BP_ExpLevelComp component to the Actor, adjust the array with the experience points needed to level up, and use the functions of the component.

These are the steps to create our Actor Component:

1. Click the **Add** button in the content browser and choose the **Blueprint Class** option.

2. On the next screen, choose **Actor Component** as the Parent class. Name the Blueprint BP_ExpLevelComp and double-click it to open the Blueprint Editor. Note that the **Components** tab is not shown because we cannot add components inside another component.

3. In the **My Blueprint** panel, create **CurrentLevel** and **CurrentXP** variables of the **Integer** type:

Figure 18.21 – Creating the variables of the component

> **Note**
> The acronym **XP** means **Experience Points**.

4. Create another variable of the **Integer** type named `ExpLevel`. In the **Details** panel, click the icon at the right of **Variable Type** and select **Array**:

Figure 18.22 – Creating an array to store the experience points needed for each level

5. Compile the Blueprint. In **Default Value**, add `10` elements in the **ExpLevel** array. In `BP_ExpLevelComp`, the **CurrentLevel** variable will be used as the index of the **ExpLevel** array. Type the values of the following screenshot for each element:

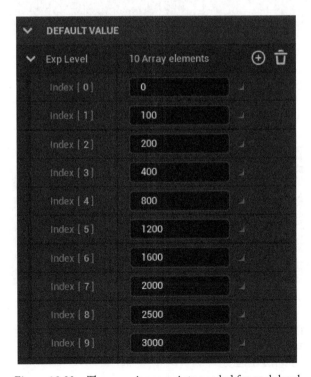

Figure 18.23 – The experience points needed for each level

6. We will create a function named **IncreaseExperience** to increase the experience and level up. But first, we will create two macros to simplify the function graph.

7. In the **My Blueprint** panel, create a macro named `CanLevelUp`:

Figure 18.24 – Creating the CanLevelUp macro

8. In the **Details** panel, create the input and output parameters of the macro:

Figure 18.25 – Creating the input and output parameters of the CanLevelUp macro

9. Add the nodes of the following screenshot in the **CanLevelUp** macro. This macro checks whether the Actor is at the maximum level by comparing the **Current Level** variable with **LAST INDEX** of the **Exp Level** array:

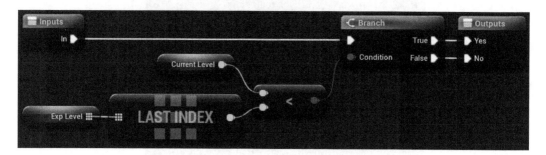

Figure 18.26 – The nodes of the CanLevelUp macro

10. In the **My Blueprint** panel, create another macro named **XpReachesNewLevel**. In the **Details** panel, create the same input and output parameters of the **CanLevelUp** macro shown in *Figure 18.25*.

11. Add the nodes of the following screenshot to the **XpReachesNewLevel** macro. We need to use the **Get (a copy)** node of the **Exp Level** array because we just need to read the value stored in the array. This macro checks whether **Current XP** is equal to or greater than the experience points stored in the next index of the **Exp Level** array:

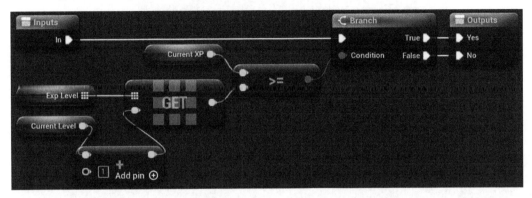

Figure 18.27 – The nodes of the XpReachesNewLevel macro

12. Compile the Blueprint. In the **My Blueprint** panel, create a function named `IncreaseExperience`:

Figure 18.28 – Creating the IncreaseExperience function

13. In the **Details** panel, create the input and output parameters of the function:

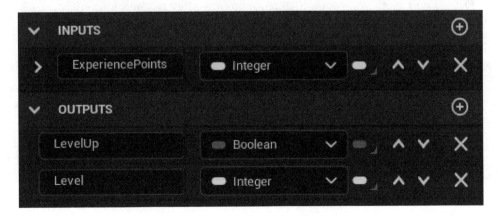

Figure 18.29 – Creating the input and output parameters

14. In the **My Blueprint** panel, create a local variable named `LevelUpVar` of **Boolean** type. This local variable will store the value that will be returned by the function, indicating whether the Actor has leveled up. The default value of a Boolean variable is `False`:

Figure 18.30 – Creating a local variable

15. The next screenshot shows the first part of the **Increase Experience** function. The function is using the two macros that we created. Add the nodes of the screenshot and connect the **No** output pin of **Can Level Up** to the white input pin of **Return Node**:

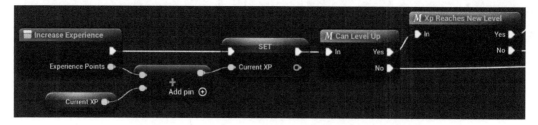

Figure 18.31 – The first part of the IncreaseExperience function

16. The next screenshot shows the second part of the **IncreaseExperience** function. If the **Yes** pin of the **Xp Reaches New Level** macro is executed, then we increment the **Current Level** variable by one and set the **Level Up Var** variable to `True`. Add the nodes of the screenshot and compile the Blueprint:

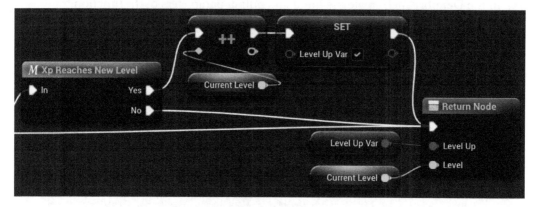

Figure 18.32 – The second part of the IncreaseExperience function

17. Compile the Blueprint and close the Blueprint Editor.

We have finished the BP_ExpLevelComp component. To test it, we need to add the component to an Actor.

Testing the Actor Component

We will add the BP_ExpLevelComp component to ThirdPersonCharacter and use a timer to increase the experience points every second. We will print a message on screen every time ThirdPersonCharacter levels up.

Follow these steps to test the BP_ExpLevelComp component:

1. Open the ThirdPersonCharacter Blueprint located in the Content > ThirdPersonBP > Blueprints folder.

2. In the **Components** panel, click the **ADD** button and search for level. Select **BP Exp Level Comp**:

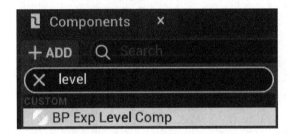

Figure 18.33 – Adding BP Exp Level Comp

3. In the **Details** panel, you can modify the default values of the **Exp Level** array or add more array elements:

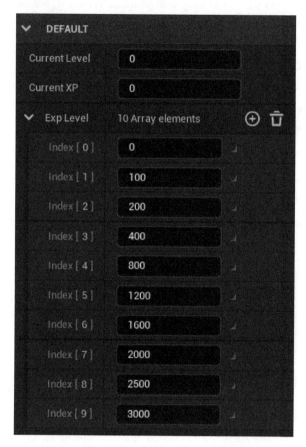

Figure 18.34 – The Exp Level array is editable

4. In the EventGraph, add the **Event BeginPlay** node and the **Set Timer by Event** node. We will use the timer to call an event once a second, which will increase the experience points. Set the **Time** parameter to 1.0 and check the **Looping** parameter:

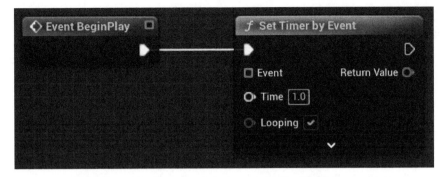

Figure 18.35 – Creating a timer to run an event once a second

5. Drag a wire from the **Event** pin of the **Set Timer by Event** node and select **Add Custom Event** in the Context Menu. Rename the custom event `GainXP`. This event will run the **Increase Experience** function of the **BP Exp Level Comp** component, passing a value of `100` as the input parameter. These are the nodes we will add to the **GainXP** event:

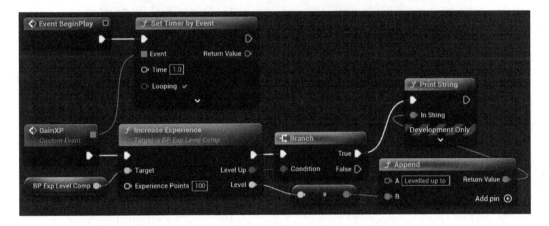

Figure 18.36 – The nodes of the GainXP custom event

6. Drag **BP Exp Level Comp** from the **Components** panel and drop it in the EventGraph to create a **Get** node.

7. Drag a wire from the **Get BP Exp Level Comp** node and add the **Increase Experience** function node. Type `100` in the **Experience Points** parameter.

8. Add a **Branch** node to check whether the Actor has leveled up. Add the **Print String** and **Append** nodes to the EventGraph and connect them as shown in *Figure 18.36*. The conversion node is created automatically when you connect pins of different types.

9. In the **A** pin of the **Append** node, type `Levelled up to` with a space at the end. This node will create a `String` using the values of the **A** and **B** pins.

10. Compile the Blueprint and click the **Play** button of the Level Editor. A message will be printed on screen every time `ThirdPersonCharacter` levels up:

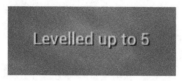

Figure 18.37 – Printing a message on screen when the character levels up

If you need to display the experience points and the level of the character on screen, you can get the values by using the **Get Current XP** and **Get Current Level** nodes of the **BP Exp Level Comp** component:

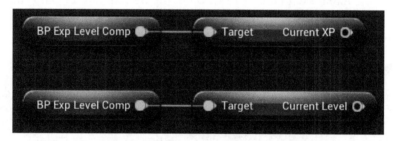

Figure 18.38 – Getting the Current XP and Current Level variables

We've learned how to create an Actor Component. Our next step is to create a Scene Component to attach other components to it.

Creating Scene Components

We will create a Scene Component named `BP_CircularMovComp` that rotates around the Actor. Then, we will attach a Static Mesh Component to the `BP_CircularMovComp` component to simulate a rotating shield.

Follow these steps to create our Scene Component:

1. Access the `Chapter18` folder that we created in the first example of this chapter.

2. Click the **Add** button in the content browser and choose the **Blueprint Class** option.

3. On the next screen, choose **Scene Component** as the parent class. Name the Blueprint `BP_CircularMovComp` and double-click it to open the Blueprint Editor.

4. In the **My Blueprint** panel, create the `RotationPerSecond` and `DeltaAngle` variables of the **Float** type:

Figure 18.39 – Creating the variables of the component

5. Compile the Blueprint and select the **RotationPerSecond** variable. In the **Details** panel, set **DEFAULT VALUE** to `180.0`. This value is in degrees, so the component will complete a rotation around the Actor in 2 seconds:

Figure 18.40 – Setting the default value of the Rotation Per Second variable

6. We will use **Event Tick** to create a smooth movement for the component. **Event Tick** is executed every frame. It has the **Delta Seconds** parameter, which stores the time elapsed since the last execution of **Event Tick**. We will multiply **Delta Seconds** by **Rotation Per Second** to find **DeltaAngle**, which is the value of the angle that we will rotate in the current frame. Add the nodes of the screenshot in the EventGraph:

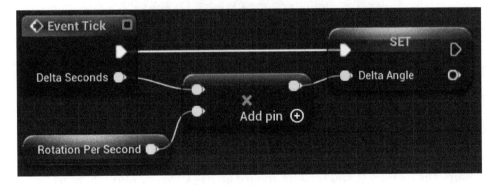

Figure 18.41 – Calculating the value of Delta Angle

7. The next screenshot shows the other nodes that we will add to **Event Tick**. These nodes are used to calculate and set the new relative location of the Scene Component and to modify the local rotation to make the Scene Component always point toward the center of rotation. You need to right-click the **Delta Rotation** parameter of **AddLocalRotation** and select **Split Struct Pin** to access the **Delta Rotation Z (Yaw)** pin:

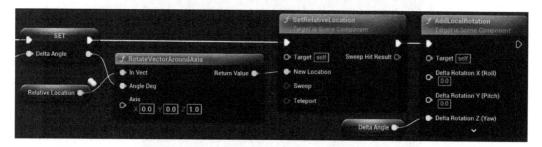

Figure 18.42 – The other nodes of Event Tick

8. Compile the Blueprint. This is all `BP_CircularMovComp` does. Our next step is to add this component to an Actor and then attach a Static Mesh Component to it.

9. Open the `ThirdPersonCharacter` Blueprint located in the `Content >  ThirdPersonBP > Blueprints` folder.

10. In the **Components** panel, select **Capsule Component** to make sure that our Scene Component will be attached to the Root Component. Click the **ADD** button and search for `circular`. Select **BP Circular Mov Comp**:

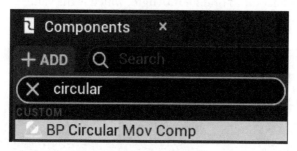

Figure 18.43 – Adding BP Circular Mov Comp

11. In the **Components** panel, select **BP_Circular Mov Comp** that was added and click the **ADD** button. Select the **StaticMesh** component to attach it to **BP_Circular Mov Comp**. The movement and rotation applied on **BP_Circular Mov Comp** will affect **StaticMesh**:

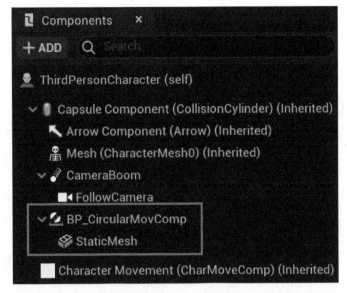

Figure 18.44 – Attaching a StaticMesh component to our Scene Component

12. Now, we need to configure the components. Access the **Viewport** tab so we can see the result of the next change. Select **BP_Circular Mov Comp** in the **Components** panel. In the **Details** panel, set the *x* (red) value of **Location** to 70.0. You can modify the value of **Rotation Per Second** in the **DEFAULT** category:

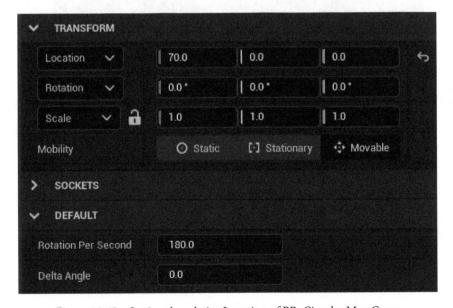

Figure 18.45 – Setting the relative Location of BP_Circular Mov Comp

13. Select the **StaticMesh** component in the **Components** panel. In the **Details** panel, select **Shape_Cube** as the Static Mesh and **M_Tech_Hex_Tile_Pulse** as the Material. You can view the components in the **Viewport** tab. Set the z (blue) value of **Location** to -80.0 and **Scale** to $x = 0.1$, $y = 1.0$, and $z = 1.5$:

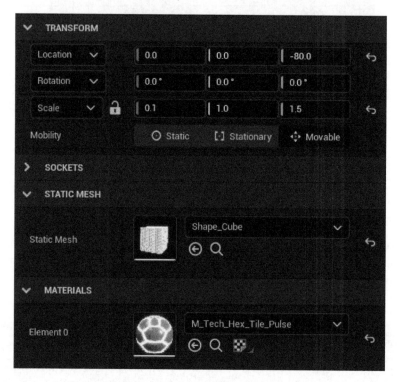

Figure 18.46 – Setting up the Static Mesh Component

14. Compile the Blueprint and click the **Play** button of the Level Editor. **BP_Circular Mov Comp** will make the shield rotate around the character:

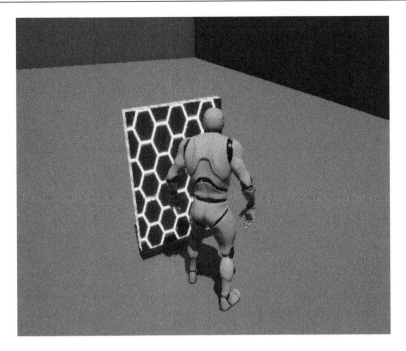

Figure 18.47 – The character has a rotating shield

The Scene Component is used as a reference location for other components. You can create a hierarchy by attaching Scene Components to each other. Actors need to have a Scene Component that is designated as the **root** component. The Actor's transform is obtained from the root component.

Summary

In this chapter, we learned how to create Blueprint Macro and Function Libraries to be used throughout the project. We created a Blueprint Function Library to simulate dice rolls.

This chapter explained the difference between Actor Components and Scene Components. We learned how to create an Actor Component to manage experience points and leveling up.

We also created a Scene Component that rotates around the Actor and attached a Static Mesh Component to it to simulate a rotating shield.

In the next chapter, we will learn how to use the Construction Script of a Blueprint to script procedural generation. We will also learn how to use the Spline tool and how to create an Editor Utility Blueprint.

Quiz

1. The macros of a Blueprint Macro Library have access to variables and functions of the Parent class.

   a. True

   b. False

2. A Blueprint Function Library can have functions and macros.

   a. True

   b. False

3. An Actor Component is a Child class of a Scene Component.

   a. True

   b. False

4. In an Actor Component, you can use the **Get Owner** node to get a reference of the Actor that is using the component.

   a. True

   b. False

5. A Scene Component can be placed directly in a Level.

   a. True

   b. False

19
Procedural Generation

In this chapter, we will look at several ways to generate level content automatically. You can use the Construction Script of a Blueprint to script procedural generation and use the Spline tool to define a path that will be used as a reference to position the instances. Also, you can create an Editor Utility Blueprint to manipulate Assets and Actors in edit mode.

In this chapter, we will cover the following topics:

- Procedural generation with the Construction Script
- Creating Blueprint Splines
- Editor Utility Blueprints

By the end of this chapter, you will know how to generate Level contents using the Construction Script and how to create a Blueprint Spline to place Actors on a predefined path. You will also be able to create Blueprint functions that run in the Editor.

Procedural generation with the Construction Script

Procedural generation is a method of creating level content using scripts instead of manually. It can be used to avoid repetitive tasks in level editing. Our main tool to make procedural generation in Blueprints is the **Construction Script**.

We saw how to use the Construction Script in *Chapter 3, Object-Oriented Programming and the Gameplay Framework*, to allow a Level Designer to change the Static Mesh of a Blueprint in the Level Editor.

A useful component for procedural generation is the **Instanced Static Mesh** component. This component is optimized to render multiple copies of the same mesh in the level.

> **Note**
>
> There is also the **Hierarchical Instanced Static Mesh** component, which is similar to **Instanced Static Mesh** but is useful when the mesh has a **Level of Detail (LOD)**.

We set the Static Mesh in the component and use the **Add Instance** function to add an instance on the level using **Instance Transform**:

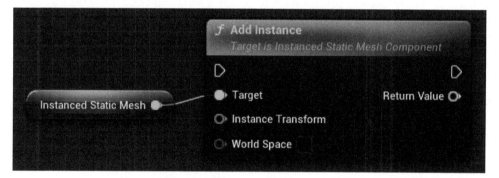

Figure 19.1 – The Add Instance function

We will create a Blueprint named `BP_ProceduralMeshes` to see the procedural generation in action. This Blueprint will add rows of static mesh instances on the level. The Level Designer will be able to specify the Static Mesh used, the number of rows, and how many instances per row.

We will use a **Blank** project because we will be able to see the result in the Level Editor of the Blueprints of this chapter.

Follow these steps to create the Procedural Generation Blueprint:

1. Create a **Blank** project with the starter content:

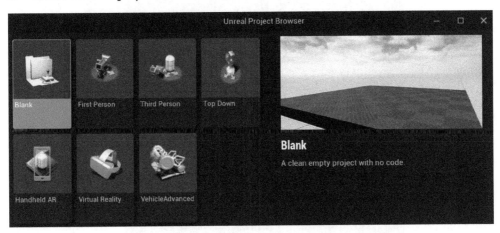

Figure 19.2 – Creating a Blank project

2. In the content browser, access the Content folder. Right-click in the empty space next to the list of folders and select the **New Folder** option. Name the folder Chapter19. We will use this folder to store this chapter's assets.

3. Open the **Chapter19** folder you just made, then click the **Add** button in the content browser, and choose the **Blueprint Class** option.

4. On the next screen, choose **Actor** as the parent class. Name the Blueprint BP_ProceduralMeshes and double-click it to open the Blueprint Editor.

5. In the **My Blueprint** panel, create a variable named StaticMeshVar. Click on **Variable Type** and search for static mesh. Hover over **Static Mesh** and select **Object Reference**:

Figure 19.3 – Creating a variable to reference a Static Mesh

6.   In the **Details** panel, check the **Instance Editable** property so that we can change in the Level Editor the static mesh used by the instance:

Figure 19.4 – The StaticMeshVar variable

7.   Compile the Blueprint. In the **Static Mesh Var** default value, select the **SM_Chair** Static Mesh:

Figure 19.5 – Selecting the default Static Mesh used in the generation

8.   In the **My Blueprint** panel, create the variables shown in the following screenshot. All of them must be set to **Instance Editable**. You can click on the eye icon to make a variable instance editable:

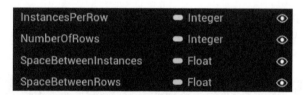

Figure 19.6 – The variables used in the generation script

9.   Compile the Blueprint and set the following default values for the variables:

- **InstancesPerRow**: 1
- **NumberOfRows**: 1
- **SpaceBetweenInstances**: 100.0
- **SpaceBetweenRows**: 150.0

10. In the **Components** panel, click the + **Add** button and search for `instance`. Select **Instanced Static Mesh**:

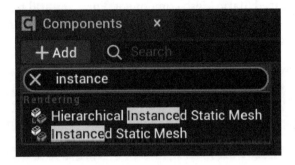

Figure 19.7 – Adding the Instanced Static Mesh component

We have the variables and the component we need for this Blueprint. Now, let's work on the script.

Creating the script to add the instances on the level

The scripting of this Blueprint will all be done in the Construction Script. Follow these steps to create the procedural generation script:

1. Click the **Construction Script** tab:

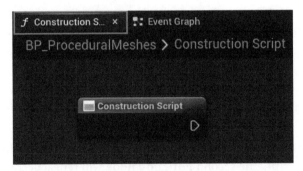

Figure 19.8 – Accessing the Construction Script

2. In the **My Blueprint** panel, create a local variable named `InstanceLocationX` of the **Float** type:

Figure 19.9 – Creating a local variable

3. The next screenshot shows the first part of the nodes we will add to **Construction Script**. We get the Static Mesh stored in the **Static Mesh Var** variable and set it to be used by the **Instanced Static Mesh** component. **For Loop** will repeat according to **Number Of Rows**. We calculate **Instance Location X** for each row by multiplying the current **Index** of **For Loop** by **Space Between Rows**:

Figure 19.10 – The first part of the Construction Script

4. Add the **Get Instanced Static Mesh** and **Get Static Mesh Var** nodes near the **Construction Script** node.

5. Drag a wire from the **Get Instanced Static Mesh** node and add the **Set Static Mesh** node. Drag a wire from the **Get Static Mesh Var** node and connect it to the **New Mesh** parameter.

6. Drag a wire from the white output pin of **Set Static Mesh** and add a **For Loop** node. Type 1 in the **First Index** parameter. Drag a wire from the **Last Index** parameter and add a **Get Number Of Rows** node.

7. Add the **Get Space Between Rows** node. Drag a wire from the **Index** output node and add a **Multiply** node. Drag a wire from **Get Space Between Rows** and connect it to the bottom pin of the **Multiply** node. The pin will be converted from integer to float.

8. Drag a wire from the **Loop Body** output pin and add a **Set Instance Location X** node. Connect the output pin of the **Multiply** node to the input pin of **Instance Location X**.

9. The next screenshot shows the second part of the nodes we will add to **Construction Script**. The second **For Loop** node will repeat according to **Instances Per Row**. The **Add Instance** node will add a Static Mesh instance on the level. The relative **Location X** will be the same for all instances of the current row. The relative **Location Y** is calculated by multiplying the current index of the second **For Loop** node by **Space Between Instances**:

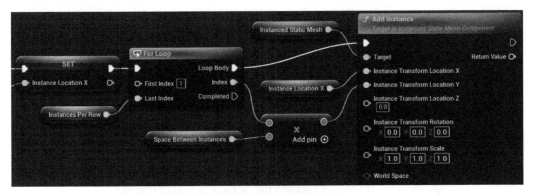

Figure 19.11 – The second part of the Construction Script

10. Drag a wire from the white output pin of **Set Instance Location X** and add a **For Loop** node. Type 1 in the **First Index** parameter. Drag a wire from the **Last Index** parameter and add a **Get Instances Per Row** node.

11. Add the **Get Space Between Instances** node. Drag a wire from the **Index** output node and add a **Multiply** node. Drag a wire from **Get Space Between Instances** and connect it to the bottom pin of the **Multiply** node. The pin will be converted from integer to float.

12. Add the **Get Instanced Static Mesh** node. Drag a wire from its output pin and add the **Add Instance** node. Connect the **Loop Body** output pin to the white input pin of the **Add Instance** node.

13. Right-click on the **Instance Transform** parameter and select **Split Struct Pin**. Right-click on the **Instance Transform Location** parameter and select **Split Struct Pin** again.

14. Drag a wire from **Instance Transform Location X** and add the **Get Instance Location X** node.

15. Connect the output pin of the **Multiply** node to the input pin of **Instance Transform Location Y**.

16. Compile the Blueprint and close the Blueprint Editor. Drag **BP_ProceduralMeshes** from the content browser and drop it in the level.

17. In the **Details** panel of Level Editor, set **Instances Per Row** to `10` and **Number Of Rows** to `10`:

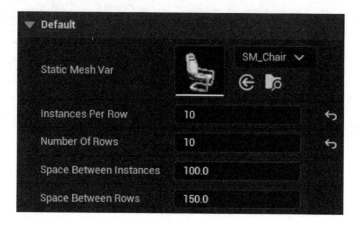

Figure 19.12 – Setting up the BP_ProceduralMeshes properties on the level

18. The result of the procedural generation can be seen in the next screenshot:

Figure 19.13 – Generating 10 rows of 10 chairs

19. We can generate a plantation using the same **BP_ProceduralMeshes** instance. In the **Details** panel of the Level Editor, change **Static Mesh Var** to `SM_Bush`, and set **Space Between Instances** to `300.0` and **Space Between Rows** to `300.0`:

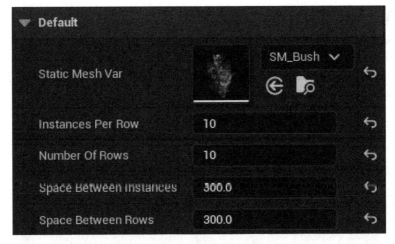

▼ Default		
Static Mesh Var	[SM_Bush ∨]	↰
Instances Per Row	10	↰
Number Of Rows	10	↰
Space Between Instances	300.0	↰
Space Between Rows	300.0	↰

Figure 19.14 – Modifying the BP_ProceduralMeshes properties on the level

20. This is the result of the procedural generation with the new parameters:

Figure 19.15 – Generating a plantation

As we can see, small changes in the parameters produce very different results. This example is just the tip of the iceberg of what can be done with procedural generation.

In the next section, we will learn how to spawn instances along a path.

Creating Blueprint Splines

A **Spline** is a special mathematical function used to define curves. A Blueprint **Spline** component can be used to define a path to move Actors in the level. We can also get locations along the path to place instances. We can edit the spline in the Level Editor by adding, translating, and rotating spline points.

The next screenshot shows three common functions of the **Spline** component:

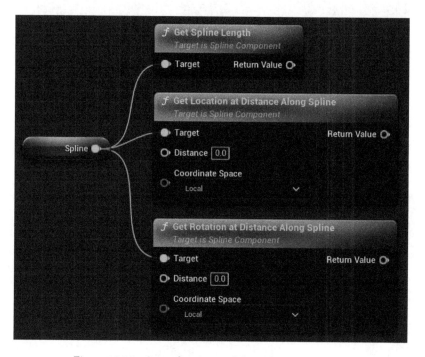

Figure 19.16 – Some functions of the Spline component

Here is a description of the functions:

- **Get Spline Length**: This function returns a **Float** value with the length of the **Spline**.
- **Get Location at Distance Along Spline**: This function receives **Distance** as an input parameter and returns the location found in the **Spline**. **Coordinate Space** can be **Local** (relative) or **World**.
- **Get Rotation at Distance Along Spline**: The same idea as the previous function, but it returns the rotation.

We will create a Blueprint named BP_SplinePlacement that adds Static Mesh instances along the spline. The Level Designer can edit the spline in the Level Editor and specify the space between the instances.

These are the steps to create the Blueprint:

1. Click the **Add** button in **Content Browser** and choose the **Blueprint Class** option. On the next screen, choose **Actor** as the parent class. Name the Blueprint BP_ SplinePlacement and double-click it to open the Blueprint Editor.

2. In the **My Blueprint** panel, create a variable named StaticMeshVar. Click on **Variable Type** and search for static mesh. Hover over **Static Mesh** and select **Object Reference**. Click the eye icon to make the **variable instance editable**.

3. Compile the Blueprint. In the **Static Mesh Var** default value, select the **SM_ FieldArrow** Static Mesh:

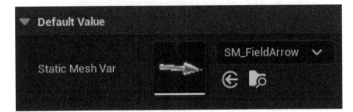

Figure 19.17 – Selecting the default Static Mesh used in the generation

> **Note**
> If the SM_FieldArrow Static Mesh does not appear, click the settings icon of the content browser and select **Show Engine Content**.

4. In the **My Blueprint** panel, create a variable named SpaceBetweenInstances of the **Float** type. Click the eye icon to make the **Instance Editable** variable.

5. Compile the Blueprint and set **Default Value** of SpaceBetweenInstances to 100.0.

6. In the **Components** panel, click the **+ Add** button and search for spline. Select the **Spline** component:

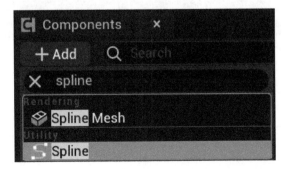

Figure 19.18 – Adding the Spline component

7. Select **DefaultSceneRoot** in the **Components** panel and add an **InstancedStaticMesh** component:

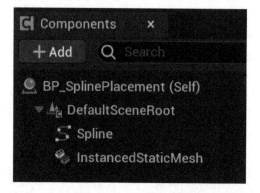

Figure 19.19 – The components used by BP_SplinePlacement

8. We will create a macro to simplify the Construction Script graph. In the **My Blueprint** panel, create a macro named `CalculateNumberOfInstances`:

Figure 19.20 – Creating the macro

9. In the **Details** panel, create an **Outputs** parameter named `Number Of Instances` of the **Integer** type:

Figure 19.21 – Creating the output parameter

10. Add the nodes shown in the following screenshot in the **CalculateNumberOfInstances** macro. This macro gets the spline length and divides it by **Space Between Instances** to find the number of instances that will be created along the spline. The **Floor** node is used to round down the result of the division:

Figure 19.22 – The nodes of the CalculateNumberOfInstances macro

> **Note**
> If the denominator of a division is zero, it generates a divide by a zero runtime error. Blueprint has a node named **Safe Divide** that returns zero if the denominator is zero, but it does not generate an error.

11. Click the **Construction Script** tab. The next screenshot shows the first part of the nodes to add to **Construction Script**. We get the Static Mesh stored in the **Static Mesh Var** variable and set it as the Static Mesh that will be used by the **Instanced Static Mesh** component. **For Loop** will repeat according to **Number Of Instances**. We calculate the distance along the spline by multiplying the current **Index** of **For Loop** by **Space Between Instances**:

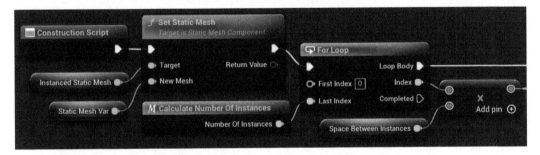

Figure 19.23 – The first part of the Construction Script

12. The following screenshot shows the second part of the nodes to add to **Construction Script**. The **Add Instance** node will add a static mesh instance on the level using the location and rotation received from the spline. Note that **Coordinate Space** must be **Local**, and you need to right-click on the **Instance Transform** parameter and select **Split Struct Pin**:

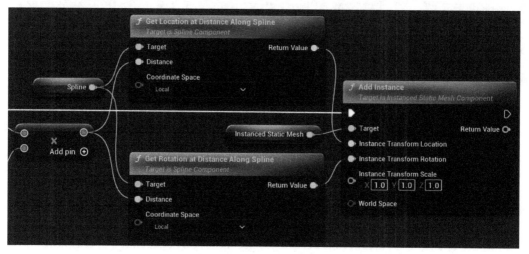

Figure 19.24 – The second part of the Construction Script

13. Compile the Blueprint and close the Blueprint Editor. Drag **BP_SplinePlacement** from the content browser and drop it in the level.

14. A spline has spline points represented by white points in the Level Editor. You can select one spline point to translate and rotate it. To add spline points, right-click the spline and select **Add Spline Point Here**:

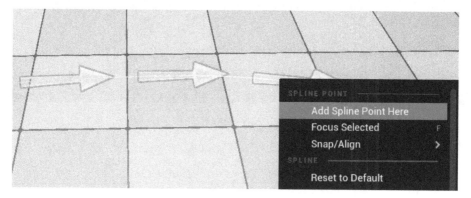

Figure 19.25 – Adding spline points

15. You can make a path by adding, translating, and rotating spline points. The Static Mesh instances will be added along the spline:

Figure 19.26 – The Static Mesh instances follow the spline

The Level Designer will have the flexibility to define the spline path around the level content.

A spline can also be used to deform a Static Mesh, as we will see in the next section.

A Spline Mesh component

There is another component that uses splines named the **Spline Mesh** component. This component is used to deform a Static Mesh along a two-point spline. We can edit the points of the spline in the Level Editor or set them using Blueprint functions.

The **Set Start and End** function can be used in the Construction Script to define the Spline Mesh:

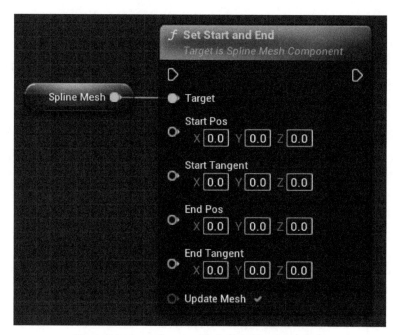

Figure 19.27 – A function to define the spline mesh

The next screenshot shows an example of a Static Mesh deformed by a spline:

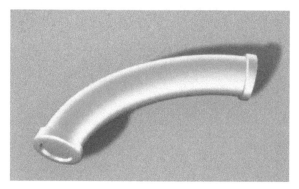

Figure 19.28 – A Static Mesh deformed by a spline

We could modify the example of the previous section to add Spline Mesh components instead of Static Mesh instances to create curved pipes on the level. Unfortunately, the calculation of the tangents for the spline instances would require mathematical concepts that are beyond the scope of this book.

In the next section, we will learn some ways to expand the Unreal Editor.

Editor Utility Blueprint

Editor Utility Blueprint is a type of Blueprint that is executed only in the Unreal Editor. You can use them to manipulate Assets in the content browser and Actors in the level.

There is also **Editor Utility Widget**, which is a UMG widget that we can use to create panels for the Unreal Editor with new functionalities.

We can create **Editor Utility Blueprint** and **Editor Utility Widget** by accessing the **Editor Utilities** submenu in the Asset creation menu:

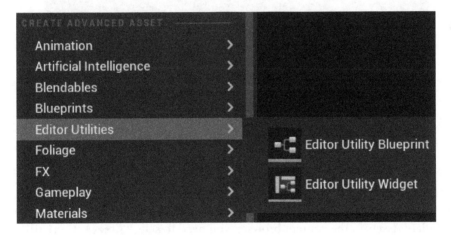

Figure 19.29 – Menu options to create Editor Utility Blueprints

Right-click on the EventGraph of an Editor Utility Blueprint and look in the **Editor Scripting** category to get an idea of the functions available to script the Editor:

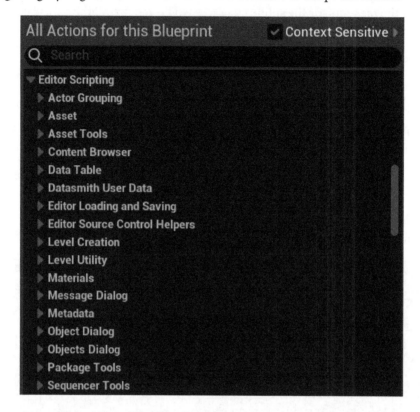

Figure 19.30 – The Editor Scripting category and subcategories

The functions created in an Editor Utility Blueprint will appear in the **Script Actions** submenu when you right-click an Asset or an Actor in the level. To create functions that will manipulate Assets in the content browser, you need to select **AssetActionUtility** as the parent class. To manipulate Actors in the level, use **ActorActionUtility** as the parent class.

Creating an Actor Action Utility

We will create an Editor Utility Blueprint named `BPU_ActorAction` using **ActorActionUtility** as the parent class. This Blueprint will have a function named `AlignOnXAxis` that will get the Location X of the first Actor selected and set the same value in the other selected Actors.

These are the steps to create the Blueprint:

1. Click the **Add** button in the content browser, hover over **Editor Utilities**, and select the **Editor Utility Blueprint** option:

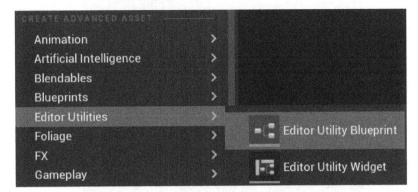

Figure 19.31 – Creating an Editor Utility Blueprint

2. On the next screen, choose **ActorActionUtility** as the parent class:

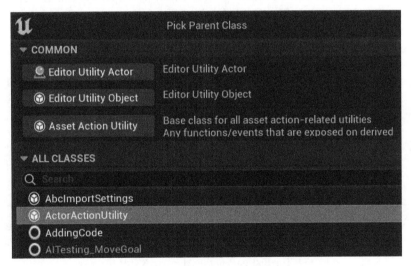

Figure 19.32 – Selecting the parent class

3. Name the Blueprint BPU_ActorAction and double-click it to open the Blueprint Editor.

4. In the **My Blueprint** panel, create a function named `AlignOnXAxis`:

Figure 19.33 – Creating the function that will be called in the Editor

5. In the **LOCAL VARIABLES** category of the **My Blueprint** panel, create a local variable named `LocationX` of the **Float** type. This variable will store **Location X** of the first selected Actor to set in the other selected Actors:

Figure 19.34 – Creating a local variable

6. Add the nodes shown in the following screenshot, which shows the first part of the **Align on XAxis** function. The **Get Selection Set** node returns an array of the Actors selected in the Level Editor. We get the first Actor of the array (index 0) and store its **Location X**:

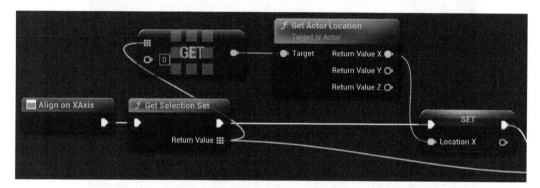

Figure 19.35 – The first part of the Align on XAxis function

7. Add the nodes of the second part of the **Align on XAxis** function. **For Each Loop** iterates on the array returned by **Get Selection Set**. For each Actor, we update **Location X**. We need to right-click the **Location** parameters and use **Split Struct Pin** to see the **X**, **Y**, and **Z** pins:

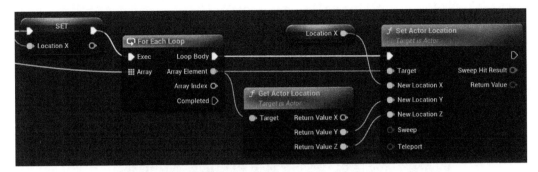

Figure 19.36 – The second part of the Align on XAxis function

8. Compile the Blueprint and close the Blueprint Editor. Drag and drop in the level three times the **SM_TableRound** asset, located in the `Content >
StarterContent > Props` folder:

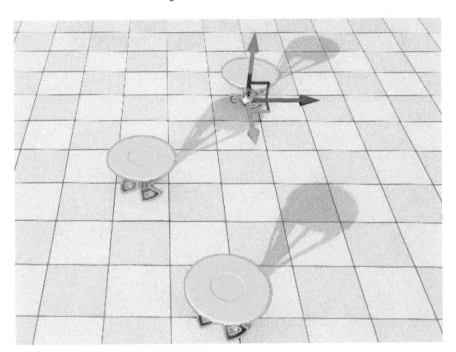

Figure 19.37 – Adding three instances of SM_TableRound

9. Hold down the *Ctrl* key and click the **SM_TableRound** instances to add them to the selection. After selecting the three instances, right-click one of them, hover over **Scripted Actor Actions**, and select the **Align on XAxis** function:

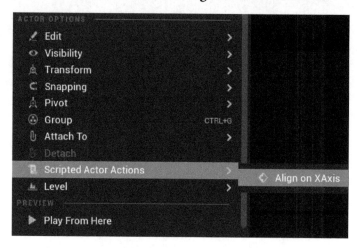

Figure 19.38 – Running the utility function in the Editor

10. After the execution of the function, all instances selected will have the same **Location X**:

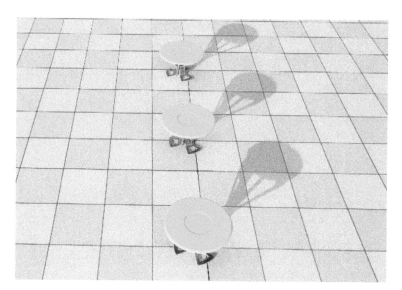

Figure 19.39 – All instances with the same Location X

By using Editor Utility Blueprints and Editor Utility Widgets, we can expand the Unreal Editor with new functionalities that can speed up the development of a project with specific characteristics.

Summary

This chapter showed how to do procedural generation using the Construction Script. We created a Blueprint that adds rows of static mesh instances in the level. The Static Mesh, the number of rows, and how many instances per row can be changed in the level.

We also learned how to create Blueprint Splines to spawn instances along a path and saw that there is a Spline Mesh Component that can be used to deform a Static Mesh.

We also looked at the Editor Utility Blueprint, which is useful to create functions that run in the Editor and can manipulate Assets and Actors in edit mode. We created an Editor Utility Blueprint with a function that aligns the selected Actors.

The next chapter will explain what a Product Configurator is. We will learn how to use the Variant Manager panel and Level Variant Sets to define a Product Configurator.

Quiz

1. The best place to write a procedural generation script is in **Event Begin Play**.

   a. True

   b. False

2. We can only edit a spline in the Viewport of the Blueprint Editor.

   a. True

   b. False

3. We can use a **Spline Mesh** component to deform a Static Mesh.

   a. True

   b. False

4. The functions of an Editor Utility Blueprint can only manipulate Assets in the content browser.

   a. True

   b. False

5. We can create panels for the Unreal Editor using Editor Utility Widgets.

   a. True

   b. False

20
Creating a Product Configurator Using the Variant Manager

This chapter explains how to create a Product Configurator, which is a type of application used in industry to attract consumers to a specific product. You will learn how to use the Variant Manager panel and Variant Sets to define a Product Configurator. The Product Configurator template is an excellent resource for studying various Blueprint concepts in practice. We will analyze the `BP_Configurator` Blueprint that dynamically creates the user interface using UMG Widget Blueprints with the Variant Sets.

These are the topics covered in this chapter:

- The Product Configurator template
- The Variant Manager panel and Variant Sets
- The `BP_Configurator` Blueprint
- UMG Widget Blueprints

By the end of the chapter, you will know how to create a Product Configurator using the Product Configurator template, the Variant Manager panel, and Variant Sets. You will know how the `BP_Configurator` Blueprint and the UMG Widget Blueprints work to be able to adapt them to your applications.

The Product Configurator template

The main idea behind the Product Configurator application is to let users switch between different options for a product and visualize them in real-time 3D experiences. This type of application is becoming common in the industry.

Unreal Engine has a Product Configurator template that can be used as a starting point to make your own Product Configurator. Follow these steps to use the Product Configurator template:

1. In the **New Project** panel, select the **AUTOMOTIVE PRODUCT DESIGN & MANUFACTURING** category, and then select the **Product Configurator** template:

Figure 20.1 – Selecting the Product Configurator template

2. Choose a folder and a name for the project, and then click on the **Create** button.

3. After the Unreal Editor loads the project, click the **Play** button to run the template. The next screenshot shows the main interface of the guitar example that comes with the Product Configurator template:

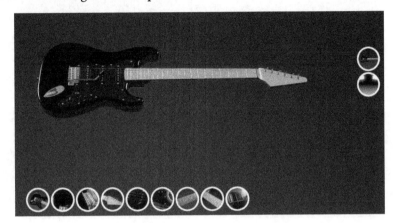

Figure 20.2 – The guitar example of the Product Configurator template

4. The two buttons on the right allow you to change the camera and environment lighting. When you click on a button, other buttons are displayed to choose the current option of the group. Click the **Camera** button and select another camera:

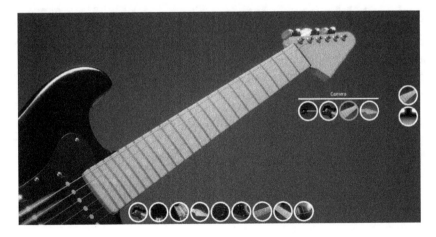

Figure 20.3 – Selecting another camera

5. The buttons at the bottom allow you to change various parts of the guitar. Try each one to see the potential of a Product Configurator:

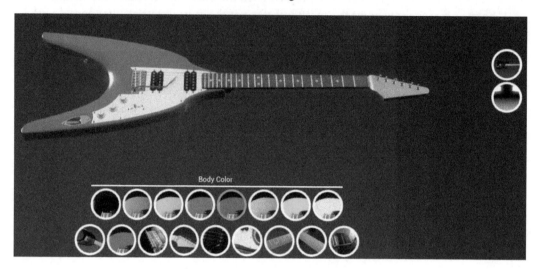

Figure 20.4 – Selecting the body color

Now that we have seen how to use the Product Configurator template, we can analyze the tools used in a Product Configurator.

The Variant Manager panel and Variant Sets

The main tool behind a Product Configurator is the **Variant Manager**. We use the Variant Manager panel to edit the **Level Variant Sets** Asset, which allows us to modify the properties of Actors in the level. Each configuration of a part of the product is a **Variant**, and we can group Variants into **Variant Sets**.

In the Product Configurator template, each button that appears on the screen when you start the application represents a Variant Set. When you click on one of these Variant Set buttons, other buttons are displayed that represent the **Variants** that belong to the current Variant Set.

These are the steps to use the Variant Manager panel:

1. Double-click the `VariantSet` asset located in the `Content >
    ProductAssets` folder to open the Variant Manager panel:

Figure 20.5 – The Level Variant Sets of the template

2. The Variant Sets and the Variants are listed on the left. In the next screenshot,
    we can see that **Body Shape** is a Variant Set with three Variants: **Strat Type**, **I Type**,
    and **V Type**. Click on **I Type** to see its properties:

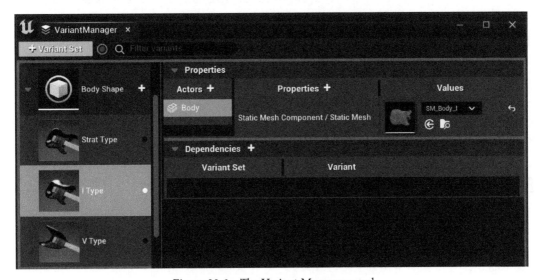

Figure 20.6 – The Variant Manager panel

3. For each Variant, we can add Actors from the level that will be modified by the
    Variant. In the previous screenshot, **Body** is a `StaticMeshActor` that has its
    Static Mesh modified by the Variant.

4. Use the +**Variant Set** button to add Variant Sets, and use the + button at the right of the Variant Set name to add the Variants in the Variant Set.

5. Double-click a Variant to activate it. The change is applied immediately in the level.

6. The Static Mesh Actors representing guitar parts are grouped by an Actor named **GuitarRoot** in the level, so you can move them together. The following screenshot is from the **Outliner** panel in the Level Editor:

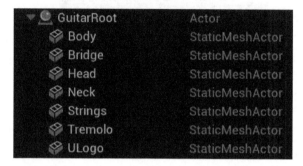

Figure 20.7 – The Static Mesh Actors of the guitar

To be able to change the Variants during runtime, the `VariantSet` asset was dropped in the level to create `Level Variant Sets Actor`.

The Product Configurator template is very flexible. You just need to learn to use the Variant Manager panel and import your Static Meshes to create your own Product Configurator.

In the next section, we will analyze the `BP_Configurator` Blueprint. You do not need to know how it works to use the Product Configurator, but it is a great opportunity to see advanced Blueprint techniques in practice.

The BP_Configurator Blueprint

The Product Configurator template has a Blueprint named `BP_Configurator` that uses the data of a Level Variant Set to create an interface using UMG Widget Blueprints. This is a very interesting Blueprint to study because we will see several Blueprint concepts being used together.

There is an instance of `BP_Configurator` on the level that you can select in the **Outliner** panel. In the **Details** panel, under the **Default** category, there are two instance-editable variables. The **LVSActor** variable is a reference to the **Level Variant Sets Actor**, and **Camera Actor** is a reference to the camera used to visualize the Product:

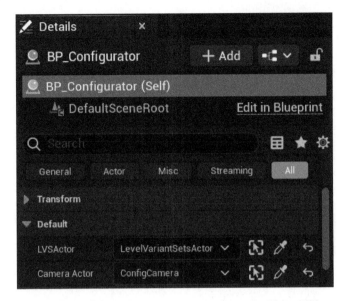

Figure 20.8 – The BP_Configurator instance-editable variables

Before we open the BP_Configurator Blueprint, let's look at **STRUCT_VarSet**, located in the Content > ProductConfig > Blueprints folder:

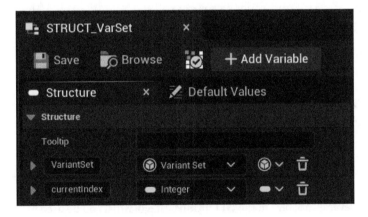

Figure 20.9 – The STRUCT_VarSet variables

The structure has two variables. **VariantSet** is a reference to a **Variant Set** and **currentIndex** is an integer variable used to store the index of the selected Variant in a Variant Set.

Open the BP_Configurator Blueprint, located in the Content > ProductConfig > Blueprints folder. Let's start by looking at the variables in the **My Blueprint** panel:

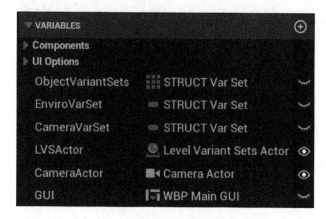

Figure 20.10 – The BP_Configurator variables

This is what each variable does:

- **ObjectVariantSets**: An array of **STRUCT Var Set** that stores all Variant Sets of the product

- **EnviroVarSet**: A Variable of the **STRUCT Var Set** type that stores the Variant Set of environment lighting

- **CameraVarSet**: A Variable of the **STRUCT Var Set** type that stores the camera Variant Set

- **LVSActor**: A reference to **Level Variant Sets Actor**

- **CameraActor**: A reference to the camera used to visualize the product

- **GUI**: A reference to the main UMG Widget Blueprint

> **Note**
>
> There are several variables in the **UI Options** category that can be used to modify the appearance of the Product Configurator. These variables are instance-editable, so you can modify them in the instance that is in the level.

Now, let's look at the functions:

Figure 20.11 – The BP_Configurator functions

This is what each function does:

- **initConfigVarSets**: It gets the Variant Sets of the Level Variant Sets Actor and stores them in the `ObjectVariantSets` array, the `EnviroVarSet` variable, and the `CameraVarSet` variable.

- **resetAllVariants**: Calls the **resetVariant** function for `EnviroVarSet`, `CameraVarSet`, and each element of the `ObjectVariantSets` array.

- **resetVariant**: Resets a Variant Set by activating the first element of the Variant Set.

- **callVariantActorAction**: Calls the `Variant Switched On` function for all Actors and components used by the current Variant that implements the `BPI_RuntimeAction` interface. This allows Actors to run script when the Variant is activated.

- **callVariantActorInit**: Calls the `Variant Initialize` function for all Actors and components used by the current Variant that implements the `BPI_RuntimeAction` interface.

- **activateVariant**: Activates a Variant of a given Variant Set.

- **initCamera**: Initializes the camera.

Event BeginPlay has a **Sequence** node with three outputs. The first output wire connects to the nodes that store the **BP_Configurator** reference in **BP_ConfigGameMode** so that other Blueprints can get the **BP_Configurator** reference by accessing the game mode:

Figure 20.12 – Storing the BP_Configurator reference in the game mode

The second output wire connects to initialization functions that store the Variant Sets, initialize the camera, and reset all Variant Sets to the first (default) Variant:

Figure 20.13 – Initialization functions

On the second output wire, there are also nodes that create an instance of the **WBP Main GUI** widget and store the reference in the **GUI** variable. The widget is added to the Viewport, and the input mode is set to **Game and UI**:

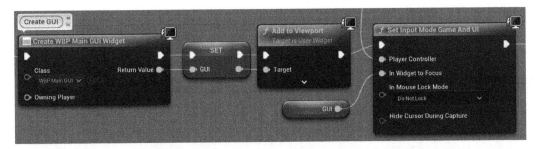

Figure 20.14 – Configuring the user interface

The third output wire connects to nodes that perform the GUI event bindings. This is where the magic happens. We will see in the next section that the **WBP Main GUI** Widget Blueprint has an event dispatcher named **Variant Selected**. The nodes on the next screenshot bind a Custom Event named **GUIVariantSelected** to the **Variant Selected** event dispatcher:

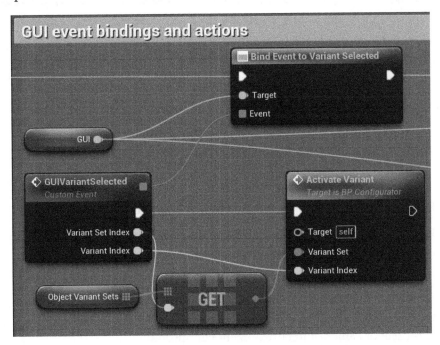

Figure 20.15 – GUI event binding

When the user clicks on a button to activate a Variant, **WBP Main GUI** calls the **Variant Selected** event dispatcher. The **GUIVariantSelected** Custom Event will execute because it is bound to the **Variant Selected** event dispatcher.

For more information about event dispatchers and bindings, see *Chapter 4, Understanding Blueprint Communication.*

The **GUIVariantSelected** Custom Event calls the **Activate Variant** function, using the selected **Variant Set** and **Variant Index** parameters. The **Switch On** function of the Variant is used to activate the Variant:

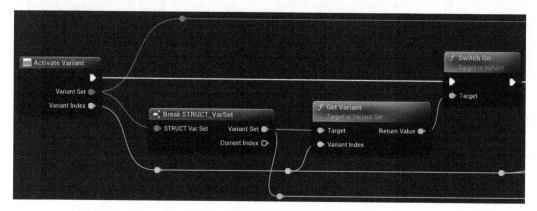

Figure 20.16 – The Activate Variant function

The dynamic interface is created by some UMG Widget Blueprints that work together and use the variables from **BP_Configurator**.

UMG Widget Blueprints

There are five UMG Widget Blueprints used in the Product Configurator interface. For more information about UMG, see *Chapter 7, Creating Screen UI Elements*.

These are the UMG Widget Blueprints:

- **WBP_MainGUI**: The main Widget Blueprint that contains the other widgets.

- **WBP_MainSelector**: This is the Widget responsible for reading the Level Variant Sets and creating the corresponding buttons.

- **WBP_VariantRibbonSelector**: This Widget is used to show the Variant options of the selected Variant Set.

- **WBP_PopupSelector**: This Widget is similar to **WBP_VariantRibbonSelector**, but it is used for camera and environment lighting.

- **WBP_Button**: This Widget represents the button used to select a Variant or a Variant Set.

The next screenshot shows the relationship between some of the Widgets:

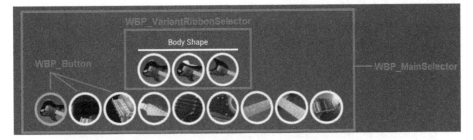

Figure 20.17 – The relationship of the Widgets

The Widget Blueprints are located in the `Content > ProductConfig > UMG` folder. Let's start by looking at **WBP_MainGUI**. The following screenshot is from its **Hierarchy** panel:

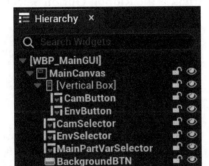

Figure 20.18 – The WBP_MainGUI Hierarchy panel

WBP_MainGUI uses two **WBP_Button** Widgets and two **WBP_PopupSelector** Widgets to manage the camera and environment lighting options. **MainPartVarSelector** is a **WBP_MainSelector** Widget that manages the Variants of the product.

The buttons of the Variant Sets and each Variant are created in **Event Construct** of the **WBP_MainSelector** Widget. The **Populate Options** function creates the buttons using the thumbnails from the Level Variant Sets:

Figure 20.19 – Event Construct of WBP_MainSelector

All five Widget Blueprints have event dispatchers. The first event dispatcher is triggered when the user clicks on **WBP_Button**:

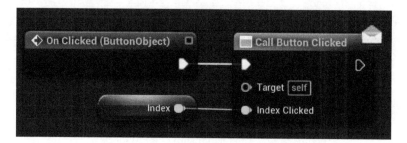

Figure 20.20 – The WBP_Button On Clicked event

WBP_VariantRibbonSelector binds an event to the **Button Clicked** event dispatcher of **WBP_Button**. The new event triggers the **Ribbon Option Selected** event dispatcher:

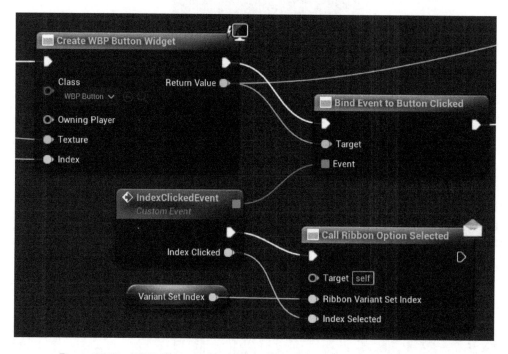

Figure 20.21 – WBP_VariantRibbonSelector binding an event to Button Clicked

WBP_MainSelector has the **PartSelectedEvent** Custom Event to trigger the **Part Selected** event dispatcher:

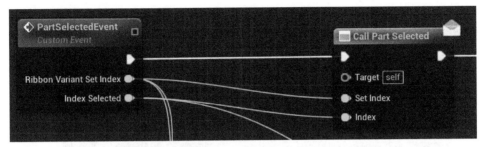

Figure 20.22 – WBP_VariantRibbonSelector binding an event to Button Clicked

The binding of **PartSelectedEvent** to the **Ribbon Option Selected** event dispatcher is done in the **Create Event Bindings** function using the **Create Event** node:

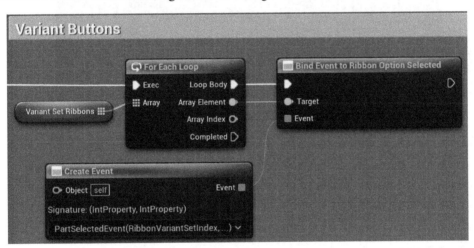

Figure 20.23 – Using the Create Event node to bind an event

To use the **Create Event** node, drag a wire from the **Event** input pin of a **Bind Event** node and select **Create Event**:

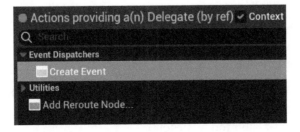

Figure 20.24 – Using the Create Event node to bind an event

In the **Create Event** node, you will be able to select an event that has the same type of input parameters as the event dispatcher.

The last event dispatcher is from **WBP_MainGUI**, which binds a Custom Event to the **Part Selected** event dispatcher of **WBP_MainSelector**:

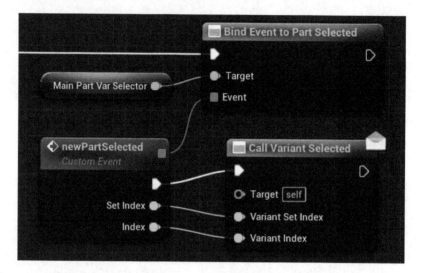

Figure 20.25 – WBP_MainGUI binding an event to Part Selected

The **Variant Selected** event dispatcher is the one that is bound in the **BP_Configurator** Blueprint.

In this section, we saw how UMG Widget Blueprints can be used together to create a dynamic and configurable interface.

Summary

In this chapter, we explained what a Product Configurator is, and we showed how to use the Product Configurator template. We learned how to use the Variant Manager panel to create Variants and Variant Sets.

We also learned how the **BP_Configurator** Blueprint stores all the information of the Level Variant Sets Actor needed to create a dynamic interface. We had an overview of the **BP_Configurator** functions and saw how to activate a Variant in a Blueprint.

Then, we saw how the **WBP_MainGUI** Widget uses the other UMG Widget Blueprints to create a user interface and saw how several event dispatchers were used to make the **BP_Configurator** act when a button was clicked.

Epilogue

I can't believe we have reached the end of the book. This was an extensive project, and I consider this book as my definitive work on Blueprints. It's been a long journey since I started programming games in the C language in 1993, when I was 14 years old. My first games were in text mode, and they looked like the game *ZZT* by Tim Sweeney, founder of Epic Games.

In 1999, I started the first game development company in the state of Pará, northern Brazil. The company name was *RH Games*. In 2001, I developed the *MRDX*, which is a framework for 2D game programming using the C/C++ languages. In 2002, I presented the *MRDX* at the first Brazilian Games Workshop. In 2003, I founded a local group called *Beljogos*, with the goal of encouraging the development of games in northern Brazil.

In 2011, I started a blog named *Romero UnrealScript*, with the goal of teaching game programming with UnrealScript. Because of this blog, in June 2013, Epic Games invited me to be part of the Unreal Engine 4 closed beta program so I could have early access to Unreal Engine 4. I started the blog *Romero Blueprints* in March 2014, when Unreal Engine 4 was launched.

In August 2015, Epic Games awarded me an *Unreal Engine Educational Dev Grant* for the work that I had done in the *Romero Blueprints* blog to help people learn Unreal Engine 4 scripting. In 2016, I wrote the *Blueprints Compendium* for Epic Games, which was distributed to the public at the **Game Developer Conference** (**GDC**). In June 2017, I finished writing the third volume of the *Blueprints Compendium*.

In 2018, Epic Games hired me to write the official *Blueprint Instructor Guide*. In 2019, I wrote the book *Blueprints Visual Scripting for Unreal Engine – Second Edition*, published by Packt. In 2020, my project to teach C++ programming in Unreal Engine was selected for the *Epic MegaGrants* program. In August 2020, Epic Games invited me to a live stream named *Teaching & Learning Blueprints with Marcos Romero*, which is available on Unreal Engine's YouTube channel.

I am grateful for the opportunity to write this book, and I hope it will help the journey of the next generation of Unreal Engine developers.

Quiz

1. The Product Configurator template allows the user to modify parts of the product, camera, and environment lighting.

   a. True

   b. False

2. The changes made in the **Variant Manager** panel will only be visible in the level at runtime.

   a. True

   b. False

3. Variants are organized into Variant Sets, and each set can only have one active Variant.

   a. True

   b. False

4. `BP_Configurator` stores the product Variant Sets in an array.

   a. True

   b. False

5. The user interface of the Product Configurator template is defined in only one UMG Widget Blueprint.

   a. True

   b. False

Appendix

Quiz answers

The following are the answers to all the quiz questions, chapter-wise:

- *Chapter 1, Exploring the Blueprint Editor*: 1-a; 2-b; 3-b; 4-b; 5-c.
- *Chapter 2, Programming with Blueprints*: 1-c; 2-b; 3-a; 4-c; 5-a.
- *Chapter 3, Object-Oriented Programming and the Gameplay Framework*: 1-b; 2-b; 3-a; 4-b; 5-c.
- *Chapter 4, Understanding Blueprint Communication*: 1-a; 2-b; 3-a; 4-b; 5-a.
- *Chapter 5, Object Interaction with Blueprints* 1-b; 2-a; 3-a; 4-b; 5-a.
- *Chapter 6, Enhancing Player Abilities*: 1-a; 2-b; 3-a; 4-a; 5-b.
- *Chapter 7, Creating Screen UI Elements*: 1-b; 2-a; 3-b; 4-a; 5-a.
- *Chapter 8, Creating Constraints and Gameplay Objectives*: 1-b; 2-a; 3-a; 4-b; 5-a.
- *Chapter 9, Building Smart Enemies with Artificial Intelligence*: 1-c; 2-b; 3-a; 4-a; 5-b.
- *Chapter 10, Upgrading the AI Enemies*: 1-b; 2-a; 3-a; 4-b; 5-a.
- *Chapter 11, Game States and Applying the Finishing Touches* : 1-a; 2-c; 3-b; 4-a; 5-a.
- *Chapter 12, Building and Publishing*: 1-a; 2-b; 3-a; 4-c; 5-a.
- *Chapter 13, Data Structures and Flow Control*: 1-b; 2-a; 3-b; 4-a; 5-b.
- *Chapter 14, Math and Trace Nodes*: 1-a; 2-a; 3-b; 4-b; 5-a.
- *Chapter 15, Blueprints Tips*: 1-b; 2-a; 3-a; 4-b; 5-a.
- *Chapter 16, Introduction to VR Development*: 1-b; 2-a; 3-a; 4-b; 5-a.
- *Chapter 17, Animation Blueprints*: 1-a; 2-b; 3-a; 4-b; 5-a.
- *Chapter 18, Creating Blueprint Libraries and Components*: 1-a; 2-b; 3-b; 4-a; 5-b.
- *Chapter 19, Procedural Generation*: 1-b; 2-b; 3-a; 4-b; 5-a.
- *Chapter 20, Creating a Product Configurator Using the Variant Manager*: 1-a; 2-b; 3-a; 4-a; 5-b.

Index

B

Behavior Tree
attack task, using 260-262
hearing, adding 263-265
binding 170
Blend Space 434, 435
Blueprint
actions that connect to events,
creating 27, 28
best practices 390
casting 76-82
Components, adding 17-19
events, adding 26, 27
execution path 28
Blueprint, best practices
complexities, managing 393-399
responsibilities 390-392
Blueprint Class Editor interface
about 11
Event Graph panel 16, 17
panels 11
Blueprint Class Editor interface, panels
Components panel 13, 14
Details panel 15
My Blueprint panel 14
Toolbar panel 12, 13
Viewport panel 16
Blueprint Communication
interfaces, using for 419-422
Blueprint Editor
about 11
shortcuts 384-389
Blueprint Function Library
about 464
example 464-468
third function, creating 469-473
third function, testing 469-473

Blueprint Macro Library 464
Blueprint Splines
about 498
creating 499-503
functions 498
Blueprints Visual Scripting
about 8
Blueprint Class, creating 10, 11
Level Blueprint Editor, opening 8-10
BP_Configurator Blueprint
about 518-524
functions 521
variables 520
BP_EnemySpawner blueprint
creating 275-278
BP_RandomSpawner
creating 330-332
testing 332-334
branches
target states, changing with 146, 148
breadcrumb 444
Build configurations 318-320

C

canvas 159
casting
in Blueprints 76-82
Character Blueprint
modifying 449-452
Character class 61
character movement
breaking down 130-134
children 242
classes 44
collectible objects
creating 196-201
Comma-Separated Values (CSV) 348

T

Packt.com

Subscribe to our online digital library for full access to over 7,000 books and videos, as well as industry leading tools to help you plan your personal development and advance your career. For more information, please visit our website.

Why subscribe?

- Spend less time learning and more time coding with practical eBooks and Videos from over 4,000 industry professionals
- Improve your learning with Skill Plans built especially for you
- Get a free eBook or video every month
- Fully searchable for easy access to vital information
- Copy and paste, print, and bookmark content

Did you know that Packt offers eBook versions of every book published, with PDF and ePub files available? You can upgrade to the eBook version at packt.com and as a print book customer, you are entitled to a discount on the eBook copy. Get in touch with us at customercare@packtpub.com for more details.

At www.packt.com, you can also read a collection of free technical articles, sign up for a range of free newsletters, and receive exclusive discounts and offers on Packt books and eBooks.

Other Books You May Enjoy

If you enjoyed this book, you may be interested in these other books by Packt:

Game Development Projects with Unreal Engine

Hammad Fozi , Gonçalo Marques , David Pereira and Devin Sherry

ISBN: 978-1-80020-922-0

- Create a fully-functional third-person character and enemies
- Build navigation with keyboard, mouse, gamepad, and touch controls
- Program logic and game mechanics with collision and particle effects
- Explore AI for games with Blackboards and Behavior Trees
- Build character animations with Animation Blueprints and Montages

Unreal Engine 4 Game Development Quick Start Guide

Rachel Cordone

ISBN: 978-1-78995-068-7

- Use project templates to give your game a head start
- Create custom Blueprints and C++ classes and extend from Epic's base classes
- Use UMG to create menus and HUDs for your game
- Create more dynamic characters using Animation Blueprints
- Learn how to create complex AI with Behavior Trees

Packt is searching for authors like you

If you're interested in becoming an author for Packt, please visit `authors.packtpub.com` and apply today. We have worked with thousands of developers and tech professionals, just like you, to help them share their insight with the global tech community. You can make a general application, apply for a specific hot topic that we are recruiting an author for, or submit your own idea.

Hi!

I am Marcos Romero, author of *Blueprints Visual Scripting for Unreal Engine 5*. I really hope you enjoyed reading this book and found it useful for increasing your productivity and efficiency in Blueprints.

It would really help me (and other potential readers!) if you could leave a review on Amazon sharing your thoughts on this book.

Go to the link below or scan the QR code to leave your review:

```
https://packt.link/r/180181158X
```

Your review will help us to understand what's worked well in this book, and what could be improved upon for future editions, so it really is appreciated.

Best wishes,